# GOSPEL
# ACCORDING TO
# THE KLAN

CultureAmerica

Erika Doss
Philip J. Deloria
*Series Editors*

Karal Ann Marling
*Editor Emerita*

# GOSPEL ACCORDING TO THE KLAN

## The KKK's Appeal to Protestant America, 1915–1930

### KELLY J. BAKER

UNIVERSITY PRESS OF KANSAS

Published by the University Press of Kansas (Lawrence, Kansas 66045), which was organized by the Kansas Board of Regents and is operated and funded by Emporia State University, Fort Hays State University, Kansas State University, Pittsburg State University, the University of Kansas, and Wichita State University

Library of Congress Cataloging-in-Publication Data

Baker, Kelly.

Gospel according to the Klan : the KKK's appeal to Protestant America, 1915–1930 / Kelly J. Baker.

    p. cm.

Includes bibliographical references and index.

ISBN 978-0-7006-1792-0 (cloth : alk. paper)

1. Ku Klux Klan (1915– )—History—20th century.

2. Protestantism—United States—History—20th century.

I. Title.

HS2330.K63B337   2011

322.4′2097309042—dc22

2011014243

British Library Cataloguing-in-Publication Data is available.

Printed in the United States of America

10  9  8  7  6  5  4  3  2  1

The paper used in this publication is recycled and contains 30 percent postconsumer waste. It is acid free and meets the minimum requirements of the American National Standard for Permanence of Paper for Printed Library Materials Z39.48-1992.

TO DOTTIE

# Contents

# Acknowledgments

History is an inherently collaborative yet often solitary enterprise, and during this endeavor from manuscript to book, many people, knowing and unknowing, enriched my scholarship with their kind thoughts, words, and actions. During the years of reading Klan print culture, I have been fortunate enough to discuss my tentative hypotheses, wild speculations, and historiography with people who supported my project yet had no desire to have Klan voices echoing in their heads as they do in mine. The many discussions, arguments, and conversations have made this work deeper and more nuanced than it might have been on its own.

Since this project is rooted in textual communities and print culture, I have come to appreciate the impact of reading, text, and words on my historical actors, as well as on myself as a scholar. Reading is never just a one-way transmission of knowledge but, rather, can open up the worldview of another. Reading conveyed the hopes and trepidations of my historical subjects, and I wish that my writing conveyed their printed experiences in terms that they might have recognized. Some might find that desire distasteful because of the subject matter, but my commitment, throughout this process, has been to read with my sources and to let their voices, if you will, guide my research. Not surprisingly, the Klan and I did not agree, but reading, hearing, and engaging their words are as important as engaging the words and thoughts of those we admire. Reading Klansmen's speeches, letters, and news magazines does not make me supportive of their cause but, rather, allows me to see how they are human in spite of their intolerance. This project has altered my vision of the world in which we live now, and I appreciate the support and candor of friends, relatives, and colleagues throughout various stages of my project.

Archivists and librarians plunged deep into Klan materials to help me uncover pages upon pages of printed sources. I owe many thanks to Sharon Sumpter, Kevin Cawley, and Elizabeth Hogan at the University of Notre Dame Archives, especially Sharon, who kept finding more and more materials that she thought were essential. She was right. I also appreciate the skill and expertise of Christa Hosmer, Florida State Archives; Susan Sutton and Eric Mundell, Indiana Historical Society; and Mary Linneman and Mary Ellen Brooks, the University of Georgia Archives. I cannot express enough gratitude for Bethany Fiechter and John Straw at Ball State University Archives, who not only rounded up archival materials but also gave me permission to use most of the stunning images of Klansmen and Klanswomen in this book. Additionally, I am not sure who is responsible, but the forward-thinking library staff at Florida State University purchased the microfilm of the *Imperial Night-Hawk, The Kourier,* and *The Dawn.* What started as a small project became a much larger one because of the microfilmed print.

Through grants from Florida State University and the Cushwa Center for the Study of American Catholicism at Notre Dame, I was able to spend more time in the archives. The staff in Graduate Studies at Florida State University and Tim Matovina and Paula Brach at Cushwa all provided financial and bureaucratic help.

The work of Michael Barkun, Kathleen Blee, and David Chidester deeply influenced this book from its earliest moments, and though I have not discussed this work with them personally, I find their scholarship influential in my approach to unloved groups. Without their respective works on Christian identity and the conspiratorial mind, the Klan, and Jonestown, this work would not be as sensitive to the ethics of historical and ethnographic practice, the importance of empathy, and the problem of studying those we find bizarre or unsettling.

At conferences and seminars, particularly the Southeast Commission for the Study of Religion (SECSOR), the American Academy of Religion, and the American Studies Association, others commented on my work or gave it direction, including David Morgan, Edward Ingebretsen, Kathy Peiss, and Tim Matovina. At Winterthur's Material Culture Symposium for Emerging Scholars (2005), the feedback of participants and respondents enhanced my approach to Klan artifacts. I am particularly thankful to Kathy Cummings and the Cushwa Center for the Study of American Catholicism. In 2009, Cushwa sponsored me in the American Catholic Studies seminar. The discussions from the seminar participants were quite helpful as I revised. In addition to the seminar, Mark Noll and Scott Appleby assigned a working copy of my manuscript to their graduate seminar. Mark, Scott, and their students helped me rethink not only why the Klan–Notre Dame Riot of 1924 was so important but also what is at stake in the official portrait of the Klan.

My work on *Gospel According to the Klan* spanned four institutions: Florida State University, the University of New Mexico, Central New Mexico Community College, and the University of Tennessee. Faculty and students at each institution improved my thinking and my work. The Department of Religion at Florida State University provided a warm, encouraging environment for my studies, especially David Kangas, Bryan Cuevas, John Kelsay, and Martin Kavka, who monitored the research and progress of this wayward Americanist. The colloquium in American Religious History provided a venue to present, discuss, and critique my project in its earliest stages. Amanda Porterfield, Amy Koehlinger, Robin Simon, and Neil Jumonville have all made this project possible with their thoughtful reflections. Amanda once asked me what American religious history would "look" like from the Klan's perspective, and I hope this book answers her question. In particular, Amy challenged me to think about what it really means to apply ethnographic methods to historical case studies. My book would not be the same without her continual insistence that I think about my position as a scholar to my sources/conversants. John Corrigan poked, prodded, and occasionally pushed me to explore larger themes and tackle historiographical themes that I would have rather avoided. His mentoring has made this book bolder than it might have been otherwise.

At the University of New Mexico, I am especially grateful to Richard Wood, Sharon Nepstad, Lisa Gerber, and Nancy Rice in the Department of Religion. At Central New Mexico, my colleagues Haava Houshmand, Jerry Sherman, and Zac Shank offered support. I have found a more permanent home at the University of Tennessee in Knoxville, and our faculty from many different disciplines welcomed my research, teaching, and writing. Rosalind Hackett is a wonderful department head and resource; Karen Windham is an office manager extraordinaire; and our faculty, Ayman Shabana, Gilya Schmiedt, Rachelle Scott, Tina Shepardson, Robert Goodding, Randal Hepner, John Hodges, and Mark Hulsether critiqued and bettered my work in our department seminar. Mark deserves special thanks for helping me with historiographies of religion and politics, the Religious Right, and American conservatism. My students at all of these institutions graciously read early drafts of chapters, and I am especially thankful to students in my Religious Intolerance classes (Spring 2009 and Spring 2010) at both the University of New Mexico and the University of Tennessee, especially Sarah Nezzer, Lisa Wham, David Williams, Katie Shires, Greg Zinneman, Victoria Coates, and Liz Cantrell.

Paul Harvey shares the distinction with Amy Koehlinger of making me a better historian. His comments on my manuscript made my book stronger historiographically, and he encouraged me to practice what I preach in methods. His insights make this a better book, and I am forever grateful. Sylvester Johnson also deserves accolade because he made me think more clearly about what is at stake in my work. He pushed me to be bolder in my analysis, and this book is bolder and more meaningful because of him. Lynn Neal, Katie Lofton, and Phil Sinitiere have all commented on pieces of my manuscript, and they have helped me make it better. In addition, the readers and contributors of the *Religion in the U.S.* blog tolerated and supported my interest in the Klan.

My anonymous reviewers at Kansas also made me consider how best to present my argument and strengthen my claims. Thank you. Working with the University Press of Kansas has been better than I could have imagined. My initial editor, Kalyanni Fernado, believed in this project when I did not, and for that I am forever grateful. My new editor, Ranjit Arab, has continued the enthusiastic support, as have the CultureAmerica series editors, Phil Deloria and Erika Doss, and the editorial board. In addition, the tireless efforts of Susan Schott, Jennifer Dropkin, and Kelly Chrisman Jacques produced a much better book.

Mike Pasquier, Howell Williams, Michael Gueno, Art Remillard, and Joseph Williams are excellent friends as well as thoughtful critics. Mike deserves special accolade as my go-to conversation partner, and our conversations improved this project from its inception to its publication. I thank them for their conversations, humor, and concern. Other friends, including Kristen Pasquier, Hope Nelson, Mike Pope, Heidi Thornquist, Denis Rizdal, Bryan and Susan Adams, Kate and

Tom Evans, Peg Doherty, Bill Phelan, Gail Dixon, Beth Golding, and Kay Casey, monitored my progress and offered kind words. Finally, my family supported me from the beginning, including Dot Taylor, the Harrisons, the Smiths, the Taylors, Marie Raines, many other Raines families, and the Basfords. Eddie Taylor and Robert Raines, both loving grandfathers, did not get to see the finished book, but their love made all of this possible. The Baker, Gerzina, and Williams families tolerated my dinner table discussions of research, which makes for lively conversation. Frank and Lynn Baker are excellent in-laws. In particular, Debbie Cook, Cary Barfield, Ashley Raines, and Stephanie and Jerry Basford have all endured my research with good grace and helpful encouragement. Ashley and Stephanie are enduring sisters who listen, support, and provide much-needed humor and balance. Hannah, Belle, and Zan, my furry distractions, provided comfort, solace, and occasional breaks. Writing would not be the same without all three at my feet or draped on my lap. My daughter, Kara, born during the transition from manuscript to book, has not proved particularly helpful to the writing, but I find myself more grounded in my approaches because of her. Her "distractions" are precious and useful, and I cannot wait for her to understand that she makes me not only a better person but also a better scholar.

My partner and favorite critic, Chris Baker, has shouldered this all. His humor, his copyediting, our discussions, and his unfailing belief in my ability assisted me in becoming a better scholar. Without him, this project would lack not only depth, finesse, and polish but also humor. He refuses to allow me to take my work or myself too seriously, and he continually prods with questions about why I research what I do and how that is significant. Our partnership sustained and improved this book because of his love, kindness, and wit. Chris, I thank you for never allowing me to doubt myself or quit.

My parents, Steve and Dottie Raines, encouraged me to pursue my dreams, but I do not think they ever imagined a published book. But their commitment stands. My father's pride is palpable and genuine, and my mother molded my approach to scholarship more than she might imagine. Because of her, I am satisfied not with just writing history but with re-creating the world and visions of others with empathy and compassion. Her ceaseless drive to make me a better person has made me a better scholar. To understand another—her most important lesson—has become possibly the most important way I understand myself as a person and a scholar. Mom, I can never say thank you enough.

I dedicate this book to my mom because without her support, it would not have been possible. Any faults remaining are all my own.

# GOSPEL
# ACCORDING TO
# THE KLAN

*"Let's Get behind Old Glory and the Church of Jesus Christ"*: Religion, American Narratives, and the 1920s Klan

*Forget the idea of the Knights of the Ku Klux Klan being an organization that flogs and tars and feathers people. Nor is it an organization that sneaks around into people's back yards trying to get something on somebody. We do, however, bring the transgressor to justice through the duly constituted officers of the law. Let us look beyond the horizon and see this thing from a national standpoint. Let us see to the influx of unfit foreign immigration. . . . Let's get behind Old Glory and the church of Jesus Christ.*
—IMPERIAL NIGHT-HAWK (1924)[1]

*In the long course of bigotry and violence, the Klan has evoked the rebelliousness of the Boston Tea Party, the vigilantism of American pioneers and cowboys, and the haughty religion of the New England Puritans. In its corruption of American ideals, it has capitalized on some of the best-loved aspects of the American tradition.*
—WYN CRAIG WADE (1987)[2]

In the hot Georgia summer of 1913, Mary Phagan, an employee of the National Pencil Company in Atlanta, Georgia, traveled to the factory to get her check. The day was Confederate Memorial Day, and "little Mary Phagan," as the Georgia press dubbed her, missed the parade held in honor of the Confederacy and the newer South. The next morning, Newt Lee, the night watchman, found her brutalized, dead body in the basement of the factory. The case of who murdered Phagan played out in the Georgia press, and her death proved to be apt fodder for the newspapers and their editors, who focused upon her youth, her innocence, and her job as a factory worker. Her image graced the front pages alongside lengthy descriptions of her unfortunate death. The iconic image of little Mary Phagan emphasized her youthful appearance, vulnerability, and her whiteness. Her faint smile and blonde hair tied in bows were incongruent with the horror of her murder and the possibility of rape. For the newspapers and Georgia's male citizenry, the death of little Mary Phagan required not only justice but also swift vengeance for the murderer of one so young and supposedly innocent. She became a warning to other girls, women, and their parents of the danger lurking for defenseless white women. Phagan's murder emerged as the tragic tale of a young white woman in the South as an unprotected member of the labor force, as well as of the obvious failure of white men to protect their families, especially their young daughters, from such a gruesome fate. The sensational murder gained coverage not only in the local Georgia press but also in the surrounding states and the larger nation. The *Columbus (Georgia) Ledger* editorialized that "whatever the investigations may disclose, this we know at once, that the victim was a brave little working girl, striving to take up her burden in life and to win her daily bread. This is an appeal to public conscience in this one fact which should not be disregarded. That she was in some way a victim to her own youth and beauty makes this tragedy complete."

The tragedy of Mary Phagan showcased the growing presence of teenagers and children in Southern factories and the dire and uncertain working conditions under which many young women labored. Phagan's symbolic import outweighed her individual life. The *Ledger* continued that "these defenseless little women" needed much protection and care.[3] Speculation ran wild in the Georgia press about whether the murderer would even be brought to justice. The decree for her murderer's death reverberated in the newspapers because of this loss of "one pure and innocent life."[4]

The Atlanta police detained several male suspects for Phagan's murder, but they finally settled upon Leo Frank, a Northern Jew who was the manager of the National Pencil Company, as the culprit behind Phagan's gruesome murder. Frank's nervousness, his outsider status, and the testimony of another employee, Jim Conley, an African American janitor, made him the prime suspect. Conley's testimony during the subsequent trial cinched the general solicitor Hugh Dorsey's case. Conley testified about Frank's supposed lewd sexual relationships with other young female factory workers as well as his own role in moving Phagan's dead body to the basement at Frank's insistence. His testimony revolving around Frank's supposed sexual encounters shocked and fascinated the press, who provided the sordid details to the general public.

In August of 1913, a jury convicted and sentenced Frank to death for the murder of Phagan, and Frank's lawyers appealed the conviction. By June of 1915, Governor William Slaton commuted Frank's sentence to life in prison because of his own doubt about various inconsistencies in evidence and the questionable witness testimony.[5] The threat of mob violence appeared real during Frank's trial, and the governor feared the impact of potential violence on the climate of the trial and the subsequent ruling. By and large, the citizens of Georgia, however, were not persuaded by Slaton's doubt and ruling on the trial, and some Georgians believed that the governor allowed a miscarriage of justice by changing the death sentence to life imprisonment. At demonstrations supporting the execution of Leo Frank, supporters sang "The Ballad of Mary Phagan" (1915), in which Phagan's murder was perpetrated by Frank, who was judged for his crime in the afterlife. The ballad proclaims, "Come, all you jolly people, / Wherever you may be, / Suppose little Mary Phagan / Belonged to you or me."[6] The ballad expressed the opinion of many Georgians, who wanted justice for Phagan's death. Those who sang the verses of the ballad assured little Mary Phagan's place in heaven with the angels and Frank's future residence in hell.[7] It is not surprising with the previous threats of violence, then, that some men decided to take Frank's life into their own hands and guarantee his punishment.

The Knights of Mary Phagan, a group of local men ranging from politicians to members of the Phagan family, organized, planned, and subsequently lynched Leo Frank. In August of 1915, a group of twenty-five men broke into the state prison in Milledgeville, Georgia, where Frank was serving a life term, and kidnapped Frank, delivering him to Phagan's hometown of Marietta, Georgia, to be lynched. The Knights hanged Frank in front of a gathering crowd as retribution for Phagan's death. Georgian newspapers were quick to report the details of Frank's "mashed and disfigured body" and the "clamoring mob." The *Columbus Sun-Enquirer* described with relish the mob's attempts at mutilating the body: "The crunching of flesh could be heard above the shouts to stop."[8] National news outlets did not report with the same glee the lynching of Frank. The *New Republic* ran a poem channeling little Mary Phagan's position on her alleged murderer's death: "You care a lot about me, you men of Georgia, not that I am dead. . . . You have broken into a prison and murdered a man that I might be avenged. . . . It is like what the preacher told me about Christ: People hated Him when He was alive. But when He was dead they killed man after man for His sake."[9]

While many white Georgians celebrated the death of Frank as fitting retribution for the murder of a young white girl, others in the nation decried the travesty of Frank's fate. One rabbi proclaimed, "The lynching of Leo Frank is an atrocious horror. . . . The whole Nation is humiliated by this sickening tragedy. The whole nation expresses its horror."[10] Yet the nation read and consumed newspaper accounts of Frank's lynching at the hands of vengeful white men. While some reports lamented Frank's fate and others celebrated his righteous death, the gruesome details appeared in both. Frank was a lingering lesson, which centered upon white men taking justice and, of course, punishment into their own hands. Frank's lynching metamorphosed from a grisly lynching into a moral stand for local communities, national culture, and the protection of the vulnerable white women. The death of little Mary Phagan and the lynching of Leo Frank primed Atlanta, the larger state of Georgia, and more largely the nation for the rebirth of a white men's movement from the recent past, the Ku Klux Klan. A reactionary populist and Georgia newspaper editor, Tom Watson even suggested that a newer version of the order could restore "HOME RULE."[11] The Knights of Mary Phagan paved the way for the Knights of the Ku Klux Klan.

An ex-minister, William Simmons, answered the call for rebirth and created the second incarnation of the Klan. His inspiration appeared in the form of D. W. Griffith's film *Birth of a Nation* (1915), based on Thomas Dixon's *The Clansman* (1905), a romanticized rendition of the Reconstruction Klan. Dixon, a Southerner and a minister, preached a "gospel of white supremacy."[12] *The Clansmen* showcased the Klan's role as the savior of the South. Griffith created a three-hour film on twelve reels at a record cost of $110,000 and renamed the film *Birth of a Nation*.[13] Like the novel, the film portrayed the Klan as the heroes of the South, who triumphed over the "animalistic" blacks that threatened to annihilate their culture. The film generated as much controversy as admiration, and for many white Americans, it confirmed their fears about African Americans. The romantic view of the Klan appealed to white America and affirmed a past that had not occurred. The KKK emerged from both film and novel as the "savior of the white race against the criminality of the black race."[14] In early 1915, Simmons, a fraternalist and former Methodist minister, was in a car accident that kept him bedridden for three months.[15] Simmons drew figures of Klansmen, created a new organizational structure based on the previous 1867 order, and developed new terminology for the fraternity.[16] When he regained his health, Simmons constructed a new Ku Klux Klan in an Atlanta atmosphere charged by anti-Semitism in the aftermath of the lynching of Leo Frank.[17] In October 1915, Simmons recruited thirty-four members to become his Knights of the Ku Klux Klan, which he later incorporated. On Thanksgiving Day, Simmons and nineteen of his Knights marched up Stone Mountain and lit a cross on fire.[18] The burning cross marked the beginning of the second order of the Klan. However, a dentist, Hiram Welsey Evans, eventually wrested control of the beloved order from Simmons. Evans, the newly appointed Imperial Wizard, continued Simmons's vision of an advanced fraternity.

Such is the standard story from Frank's demise to Simmons's creation to Evans's control. This narrative binds the lynching of Frank to the stellar rise and fall of the second Klan. But what is missing is not the 1920s Klan's dedication to nation, the rights of white men, and the vulnerability of white women but the prominent place of religion, specifically Protestant Christianity, in the Klan's print culture, fraternal ritual, and theatrical displays. When the Klan's vision of Protestantism is placed at the front and center of an analysis, a different presentation of the order emerges that illuminates the dominance of the Klan's racial, religious, and intolerant views in America from the 1910s through the 1930s. In the many tellings and retellings of the Klan story, narrators mention Simmons's religious involvement, but it is not essential to the story. Simmons was formerly a minister who created a new Klan firmly enshrouded in the language of Protestantism. For the first Imperial Wizard, God had smiled upon America. It was momentous that he founded the Klan on Thanksgiving Day, a day of celebration of the Pilgrims, who came to the New World in search of religious tolerance. As the angels had smiled upon the Pilgrims, so they did upon the new order.

Faith was an integral part of that incarnation of the order. Simmons articulated the religious vision, which Evans and many Klan lecturers (often ministers) continued. The Klan, for Simmons and Evans, was not just an order to defend America but also a campaign to protect and celebrate Protestantism. It was a *religious* order. The popular story, however, neglected the place of everyday religion within the ranks of Klansmen and Klanswomen and instead focused on the Klan's vitriol toward Catholics, Jews, and African Americans. The focus on Old Glory, the flag, and patriotism resonated in various tellings, yet the emphasis upon the dedication to the "church of Jesus Christ" remained underplayed and underanalyzed. Protestantism became secondary in descriptions of the Klan because of the order's apparent nativism, racism, and violence. The Klan gained a following because of its twin messages of nation and faith, and the fraternity progressed because of members' commitment to its religious vision of America and her foundations.

Moreover, those twin messages resounded because of social change in the United States. Immigration, urbanization, and the internal migrations of African Americans made the Klan's white, patriotic, and Protestant message appealing. From 1890 to 1914, over 16 million immigrants arrived in the United States, and 10 percent of those immigrants were Jewish. As historian Jay Dolan reported, a vast majority of those immigrants were Catholics from Ireland, Germany, Italy, and Poland. In reaction to immigration and World War I, nativism emerged as a popular response to "hyphenated" Americans. Immigrant groups who did not support the war were even more suspect.[19] As sociologist Kathleen Blee noted, "The Klan's underlying ideas of racial separation and white Protestant supremacy . . . echoed throughout the white society of the 1920s, as religious and racial hatreds determined the political dialogue in many communities."[20] White supremacy was a common belief in the early twentieth century, but the Klan's political action, public relations campaigns, and the production of material artifacts identified it as a distinct movement.[21] By 1918 there were fifteen chapters of the new Klan. With rising popularity, Simmons, and later Evans, sought to eliminate the violent image of the Reconstruction Klan without much success.

*Paramilitary movement to defend the hallowed Southern Way of Life.*

The Reconstruction Ku Klux Klan emerged in 1866 in Pulaski, Tennessee. Six Confederate veterans claimed they organized a club to play "pranks" on the residents of Pulaski to uplift the spirits of the war-torn region. The first Klan was primarily motivated by concerns about Reconstruction's effect on Southern social structure. As such, it particularly targeted African Americans, "carpetbaggers," and other Northern whites for the unsettling of Southern life. The "club" created their name from the Greek word *kuklos,* meaning circle, and they added the word "klan" to represent their Scotch-Irish ancestors.[22] The first Ku Klux Klan was a supposed social organization for white men. Immediately, they adopted a white uniform with "tall conical witches' hats of white cloth over cardboard [that] completely concealed their heads," which "exaggerated the height of the wearer, adding anywhere from eighteen inches to two feet to his stature."[23] The costumes mimicked the ghosts of the Confederate dead. However, the Klan's pranks were not innocent because members targeted freed blacks. The pranks were reminiscent of the decades-old actions performed by planters and overseers to frighten slaves into submission.[24] The popularity of the Klan grew in Tennessee, and by the end of 1866, the jokes had turned violent and occasionally deadly. In 1867 the ever-growing group needed structure and a popular leader that would spread the "social club" throughout the South. At a Nashville convention, the Klan reorganized and specified its aims of chivalry, humanity, mercy, and patriotism.

The early Klan saw Southern whites as victimized by Reconstruction, and members opposed any who destabilized their worldview, including blacks and supporters of blacks. A historian of the Klan, Michael Newton, has argued that in April 1867 the Klan shifted from a club to a "paramilitary movement to defend the hallowed Southern Way of Life."[25] The "Invisible Empire" divided into sections by region, and Lieutenant General Nathan Bedford Forrest, a lauded Confederate veteran, became the official leader of the first Klan.[26] By 1868 the Klan began raiding the homes of African Americans and supporters of black enfranchisement, interfering with elections and crafting a public image through parades as well as cryptic warnings. The Reconstruction Klan targeted African Americans because of the passage of the Fourteenth Amendment, which granted African American men the right to vote. Many of the black victims of the Klan were voting Republicans.[27] The Klan confronted the "violent and brutal" officials who upheld black civil rights while victimizing white men and women.[28] Whites saw themselves as victims of Reconstruction and a shifting political climate, and the Klan reacted to any threat to white dominance.

Also in 1868 the Klan had spread into Kentucky, Missouri, West Virginia, Maryland, North Carolina, Southern Carolina, Georgia, and Alabama. The Freedmen's Bureau and eventually the federal government became concerned with their raids and violent actions.[29] In 1871 Congress passed the Ku Klux Klan Act to protect voters and the Fourteenth Amendment, and with the federal crackdown on their actions the Klan declined. The Invisible Empire dissipated. However, the presence of the Klan had forever marked the Southern imagination, and William Simmons adopted the larger heritage of the Klan for his newer version, but he attempted to avoid the violent legacy. By June of 1920 Simmons approached the Southern Publicity Association to advertise his organization in order to modify its image. The association's owners, Elizabeth Tyler and Edward Clarke, presented the Klan as a fraternal Protestant organization that championed white supremacy as opposed to marauders of the night. Their efforts proved effective. Membership increased, and the Klan claimed chapters in all forty-eight continental states.[30]

By 1924 membership peaked at four million members as Americans pledged their support to the order, wore robes, lit crosses, and marched in parades.[31] Despite the large membership of the order, scholars, the media, and the general public relied on stereotypes of Klansmen as backward, rural people who lacked education, refinement, and tolerance. That portrayal claimed that Klansmen loathed societal changes, lamented their class status, and embraced their anger as a motivating tool for their activism. Anger and frustration motivated the second Klan's theatrics and political campaigning. Writing in the 1920s, John Moffatt Mecklin popularized that particular portrayal of Klansmen, which has remained the most common characterization of the order throughout the twentieth and twenty-first centuries. Mecklin's Klansmen embraced their supposed rural roots as well as fundamentalist Christianity to right the social wrongs; fundamentalism, then, became the backbone of the order and motivated Klansmen in their quest to restore the nation.

Parade at Anderson, Indiana, 1922. The photographer claimed that this was the largest crowd ever gathered in Anderson. The 1920s Klan often participated in parades and other public events to bring attention to the order's twin commitments of Americanism and Protestantism. Photograph by W. A. Swift. Courtesy of Ball State University Archives, Muncie, Indiana.

More recent studies of the order contradict this particular presentation of Klansmen, and occasionally Klanswomen, as backward, rural, uneducated, and fundamentalist.[32] These studies demonstrate that Klansmen were bankers, lawyers, dentists, doctors, ministers, businessmen, and teachers. Most of the membership was firmly of the middle class and had access to education. Klan members were Quakers, Baptists, Methodists, Church of Christ, Disciples of Christ, and United Brethren, to name only a few.[33] They were highly critical of liberal Protestant theologians who used historical criticism and science in biblical interpretation. Klansmen were more evangelical than fundamentalist. The order was more rooted in mainline Protestantism than the stereotype recognizes. Moreover, the 1920s Klan was a populist movement that attempted to reform so-called societal ills with religion and politics.[34] Geographically, the Klan emerged in the rural South, the urban North, the Midwest, and the Pacific Northwest. There were klaverns in Georgia, Alabama, and Florida, as well as in Indiana, New Jersey, Colorado, and Oregon. Rural and urban, educated and working class, the order proved more diverse and mainstream than those early popular stereotypes allow. Klansmen and Klanswomen were very similar to their neighbors, but they chose to join the order to communicate their distaste and poignant concern with the path of the nation.

In its heyday, the second incarnation of the KKK produced multiple newspapers and engendered flashy displays of membership ranging from outdoor naturalization ceremonies to marches and parades. The organization built membership from "ordinary, white Protestants," who embraced Klan events, like picnics and pageants, and read Klan pamphlets, newspapers, novels, and flyers. In that way, the portrait of Klansmen as white-robed terrorists who haunt the dreams of all of their enemies ignored the full rendering of Klan experience. That portrait sidelined the Klan to the margins of American history despite its large membership and cultural influence. By labeling the order as a fringe movement of terrorists, the nefarious elements of the movement appear in historical narratives without explorations of its broader appeal to white Protestants. Yet its numerical strength and popularity require a reevaluation of the order and its place in our narratives to see how such a movement fits within our tellings and retellings of American history, especially American religious history.

*To examine the Klan is to examine ourselves.*

Klan historian Kenneth Jackson claimed that "to examine the Klan is to examine ourselves."[35] For Jackson, the second revival of the Klan (1915–1930) was representative of American culture rather than a peripheral movement of extremism. To understand the 1920s Klan as central to narratives of American history and American religious history calls into question narratives of Protestant progress, the origins of nationalism, relationships between religion and race, and the often hidden presence of intolerance. Jackson's provocative statement demonstrates the need for a critical study of the 1920s Klan to under-

Indiana's First Public Initiation, 1922. Indiana Klansmen in full regalia observe
a public initiation into the Invisible Empire. Photograph by W. A. Swift.
Courtesy of Ball State University Archives, Muncie, Indiana.

stand how Klansmen and Klanswomen were part of the religious
mainstream. The Ku Klux Klan is the center of this study because it is
a hate movement with the longest history in the United States, a remarkable amount of print culture, and the most organizational revivals in multiple historical periods and places. Various movements of
men and women have reenvisioned the order to meet their pressing
social concerns. The second wave of the Klan lasted from the 1910s
through the 1930s, but most activity occurred in the 1920s.[36] That revival lamented the presence not only of African Americans but also
of Catholics and Jews, and its leaders openly presented the order's
principles to members through Klan newspapers and magazines as
well as the national press. Members embraced Protestant Christianity
and a crusade to save America from domestic as well as foreign
threats.

The Klan of the 1920s would be the last unified order.[37] Because of unity and popularity, the second order has generated the most scholarly ink and sometimes ire. As mentioned earlier, the second Klan was distinctly different from its predecessor, the Reconstruction Klan, as well as the successive waves of twentieth- and twenty-first-century Klan revivals. One explanation for that distinction is that the second revival was the most integrated into American society. The membership was composed of white men and women dedicated to nation, the superiority of their race, and Protestantism. Most histories briefly note the religious lives of Klansmen and Klanswomen in order to focus on the racism, anti-Catholicism, anti-Semitism, and violence of the order. While it is clear that the 1920s Klan was racist, anti-Catholic, and anti-Semitic, the order's members were indicative of mainstream prejudice of the time period. Their prejudices were not uncommon, but their methods were. In his *White Protestant Nation,* Allan Lichtman argues convincingly that the Klan was one of several conservative movements in the 1920s that "shared a common ethnic identity: they were white and Protestant and they had to fight to retain a once uncontested domination of American life."[38] He sees the Klan as a part of the trajectory of American conservatism, which also included the American Legion, the Daughters of the American Revolution, various proponents of scientific racism, business associations, and other Protestant organizations. He further notes that "the prohibition of vice, anticommunism, conservative maternalism, evangelical Protestantism, business conservatism, racial science and containment, and the grassroots organizing of the Ku Klux Klan" created a "stout defense of America's white Protestant, free enterprise civilization."[39] The Klan was just one component of a larger antipluralist campaign in America that sought compulsory moral reform. For Lichtman, the Klan and these other movements were the foundation of the American Right. The order's religion and politics were similar to its contemporaries. If the Klan is a part of the conservative trajectory, then it makes no sense to sideline the order's significance and historical presence in the 1920s. Instead of focusing on the order's difference, perhaps the focus should be on the order's similarities to other members in their local, regional, and national communities.

What made Klansmen and Klanswomen unique was their dedication and their adoption of print and material methods to further white su-

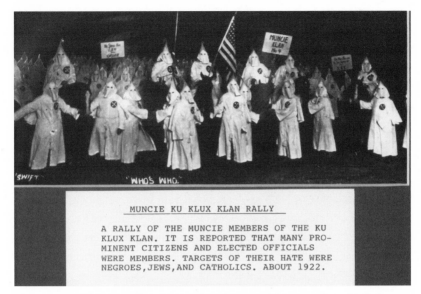

MUNCIE KU KLUX KLAN RALLY

A RALLY OF THE MUNCIE MEMBERS OF THE KU
KLUX KLAN. IT IS REPORTED THAT MANY PRO-
MINENT CITIZENS AND ELECTED OFFICIALS
WERE MEMBERS. TARGETS OF THEIR HATE WERE
NEGROES,JEWS,AND CATHOLICS. ABOUT 1922.

Muncie Ku Klux Klan Rally, c. 1922. The photograph's caption was "Who's who," in reference to the large number of prominent Indiana Klansmen who belonged to the order. Photograph by W. A. Swift. Courtesy of Ball State University Archives, Muncie, Indiana.

premacy and Protestantism. Their methods, not their beliefs, make this incarnation of the order different from their neighbors. The religious nature of their methods and print needs much more exploration. Klan print culture is often discarded as propaganda, rather than considered a resource for Klan beliefs, ideologies, and theologies. This disconnect between Klan print and actual Klan beliefs happens for a variety of reasons. Most important, the neglect of the 1920s Klan's print occurs because this instantiation of the order is viewed through the lens of its predecessor and the Klans of the mid- to late twentieth century and twenty-first century. The Reconstruction Klan and its modern brethren were and are blatantly violent and racist. They both spewed vitriol and committed acts of terrorism and mayhem—as did the 1920s Klan.

The close connection of these Klans to racist rhetoric and violence means that all Klans are interpreted in a similar vein. It is hard to look at the 1920s Klan and not connect it to the bombing of the Sixteenth Street Baptist Church in Birmingham, Alabama (1963), in which three

African American girls lost their lives, or the Klan initiation murder in the recent past (2008). The Klan in the American imagination is bound to crosses, robes, violence, and terror, and I am not seeking to rehabilitate that image. The image stands rightly so, but reliance upon this popular interpretation alone overshadows the complicated place of religion, specifically Protestantism, in the Klan's long history.[40] Understanding the central role of religion helps scholars understand better the motivation and appeal of these movements beyond simplistic presentations of frustration and anger, which remain popular excuses for membership in such movements. Moreover, examining movements like the Klan also suggests the ways that religion can inform ideologies of intolerance, violence, and terror, as well as bolster the commitment of members by relying on a more ultimate cause for such insidious agendas.

> *In its corruption of American ideals, [the Klan] has capitalized on some of the best-loved aspects of the American tradition.*

It is not surprising, then, that the scholarship on the Klan, as well as other hate movements, often emphasized violence, racism, gender ideology, and nationalism with religion as a secondary or tertiary concern. Often interpretations sought to define why Klansmen, and occasionally Klanswomen, embraced the order, but sometimes such analyses neglect what members of the order actually say about their experiences and hesitate to present the Klan in its own language.[41] There are, of course, dangers in presenting the order at face value, in that the scholar might become just a mouthpiece for a particular hate movement. There is also the issue of how to use the Klan's words and artifacts without heavy skepticism.[42] Building on John Moffatt Mecklin's *Ku Klux Klan: The Study of an American Mind* (1924), much scholarship described Klansmen as frustrated and resentful because of the poor conditions of their rural lives. Mecklin argued that Klansmen barely maintained control over their own lives, feared anything foreign, especially immigrants, and voiced paranoid concern about the influence of foreign ideas and peoples to transform local as well as national cultures.[43] Mecklin analyzed the psychology of Klansmen and claimed that their pathology could be essentialized to a fear of difference. Klan scholar Leonard Moore noted, "Like Mecklin . . . and other writers of the 1920s . . . all agreed that Klan radicalism could be traced to the benighted culture of rural, small-town America."[44]

Agrarian, white men faced disenfranchisement because of modernity, new social norms, and increasing racial and religious diversity of the nation. Mecklin's model of the Klansman's pathological anger and frustration still remains popular even in contemporary discussions of the Klan, though analysis of more generalized frustration becomes increasingly particular and nuanced in a contemporary context. The role of class emerged as central to the motivations of Klansmen, reiterating the frustration model by claiming that Klansmen encountered disadvantages because of socioeconomic status and societal change. Abrupt changes in gender norms added to the Klan's frustration because Klansmen reacted vehemently to flappers, women's suffrage, and men's dwindling status in larger society. All of those factors led white men to form an order to protect white women from African American men and women's supposed inherent weaknesses.[45]

Yet explanations of Klan frustration prove inadequate as an approach for elucidating why the Klan rose in popularity at such stellar speed. To link rampant frustration to the order's intolerance and hatred does not account for why those men (and women) expressed their anxiety and concern in extraordinary ways (the burning of crosses, dressing in robes, etc.) while their contemporaries did not. Members might have been, and likely were, resentful of societal changes, but that likelihood alone does not predict the complexity of their reactions. Moreover, the emphasis on frustration and anger bolstered analyses and commentary about Klan violence and brutality. Much Klan scholarship has overestimated KKK violence by assuming that brutality was endemic in the order.[46] The second order's rhetoric did not employ a terminology of violence; rather, leaders and editors carefully crafted their public opinions to avoid obviously violent content. Studies of the Klan highlighted the cruelty and white supremacy of the order by providing excruciating details of the violence against African Americans, race traitors, and others in the various and distinct Klan revivals. These actions clearly made the order appear reprehensible, dangerous, and menacing. For instance, a history of the Klan in Florida characterized the order by its use of lynching. This regional examination of the Klan demonstrated that Florida Klans were the most violent permutations of the organization. Yet the attempt to bind the order to various lynch mobs revealed that violence, at least in Florida, could not be directly attributed to Klansmen. The history of violence that began with the Reconstruction Klan and continued to current manifestations of the order was actually more suggestive of the regional character of the Florida Klans than the national traits of the order.[47] The legacy of Klan violence is very real, but the tendency to solely focus on such violence should not hide other motivations for continued membership and participation in the order.

Some social historians in newer studies of the Klan, particularly Leonard Moore and Shawn Lay, attempt to broach their subjects both compassionately and nonjudgmentally: Klansmen and Klanswomen become ordinary citizens primarily, and their affiliations with the order are secondary. The second order of the Klan emerges as an anomaly compared to the other orders. This Klan was more representative of 1920s culture because its actions and ideology reflected the white supremacy of American society. Klansmen, above all, were average folks who belonged to a fraternity, not a villainous organization. In examinations of Klan activity in different states and regions of the West, it becomes clear that the KKK was not as aggressive in the West as the instantiations in the South. Moore, in particular, challenges previous presentations of the Indiana Klan by arguing that the klaverns of the Hoosier State were just populist gatherings of white men. Furthermore, the Indiana Klan relied upon "ethnic scapegoats," particularly Catholics and Jews, as symbols of more complex fears.[48] For Moore, the Indiana Klansmen participated in figurative prejudice to assuage anxiety about foreign neighbors. The fraternal order operated much like a support group for white Protestant men who believed that their values were under assault.

Unfortunately, these case studies might also be more indicative of regional character than the national order. There is no doubt that populism characterized the 1920s Klan, but symbolic intolerance does not seem to accurately characterize the order's vehement rhetoric attacking Catholics, Jews, and African Americans. The sole focus on populism obscures the order's role in violent action and terror. While examining only the Klan's violent outpourings hides its religious and political endeavors, the examination of just populism obscures the reality of the order's ethnic and religious intolerance. The members of the order were white supremacists in a culture of white supremacy, but they acted quite differently from their neighbors.[49] Populism and local differences do not quite explain why the Klan gained membership so quickly or why they relied on theatrical means to express their ideologies. This empathetic approach remains a minority voice in the field of KKK history because other scholars continue to foreground the Klan's nativism, nationalism, and racial supremacy rather than the similarities of the order to the mainstream.[50]

It is clear that scholars deployed myriad factors to explain the motivation for the 1920s Klan and the order's contemporary manifestations, but among those religion served in a secondary and more often rhetorical role. Some scholars recognized the order's historical engagement with Christianity, yet this did not guarantee analysis of religion as a motivating factor for Klan actions. Generally, these studies cataloged religious affiliations. No matter what the cause for the order's rise and fall, most monographs on the Klan at least cite that the order was a nominally Protestant movement. Scholars document the denominational affiliations of members, purport the ties between the Klan and fundamentalism, highlight the recruitment of ministers and the popularity of church visits, and note the particular relationship of the women of the KKK and Protestantism.[51] Yet the use of the term "Protestant" to classify the Klan does not guarantee an exploration of the devotions, rituals, practices, scriptures, or theologies of the 1920s Klan. Scholars adopted the term "Protestant" as comprehensible to all readers, but in most works the term was neither defined nor examined critically. The Klan was Protestant, but discussion of what that exactly means is missing. Other scholarship argues that the religion of the Klan and other hate movements was patently "false" religion.[52] This tiresome declaration of false religion obscured the commitment of members to the religious vision of the order and marginalized the centrality of that vision to the Klan's appeal. The order relied on religious systems ranging from a white supremacist version of Protestantism in the 1920s to today's Christian Identity movement.[53]

This desire to set up boundaries between true and false religion does nothing to further the scholarly enterprise. More important, this distinction marks the religion of the hate movement as somehow not religion, which proves problematic for several reasons. First, this allows for the lack of attention to Klansmen and Klanswomen's religious leanings. If they are not authentically religious, then their motivations are not impacted by religion at all. Second and more important, presenting the religion of the Klan as false religion allows an assumption that religion is somehow not associated with movements and people who might be unsavory, disreputable, or dangerous. Religion is at best ambiguous, which means that it can be associated with movements we label "good" or "bad," but limiting the place of religion does not mean that religion, specifically Christianity, cannot be associated with the Klan or white supremacist movements more generally. A proper examination would explore how the religion of the Klan impacted its members, practices, and politics without engaging the so-called falsity of the order's religion. This association with false religion means that what Klansmen and Klanswomen wrote and said about their religious backgrounds becomes disingenuous and less credible than other people's writings and declarations.

Klansmen and Klanswomen avidly promoted their affiliations within Protestantism. The second revival of the order continually articulated its allegiance to Protestantism, nationalism, and white supremacy. Christianity played an essential part in the collective identity of the order, and neglecting religious commitment ignores a crucial self-identification. Religious faith washed over the pages of the Klan newspapers, fictional books, pamphlets, and speeches. Dedication to Protestantism emerged as a crucial part of membership and as the foundation for the order's ideals, principles, and even intolerance. To understand how religion influenced the order, it is necessary to appreciate how faith was foundational to characterizations of nation, race, and gender in that moment in American history. To examine the Klan forces us to take a hard look at the development of American nationalism and competing visions of nation. The assumption that religion was a rhetorical tool rather than a legitimate system of belief and practice means that the Klan's racial and gendered agendas often obscured religious motivation for actions and rhetoric. The hesitance about the relationship between religion and racial and/or religious hatred suggests that a religious studies approach is sorely needed in the literature. True or false, legitimate or illegitimate, the Klan still upheld its Protestantism. Identifying the Klan as white and Protestant does not further scholarship unless we can unearth how members employed and comprehended those terms. This book highlights how the Klan crafted its religion, nation, and race, and the varying interrelationships between those components, while taking the order's worldview quite seriously.

In addition, references to the Ku Klux Klan in larger narratives of American religious history are few and far between. Generally, religious historians presented the common narrative of nativism and intolerance of the Klan. In Sydney Ahlstrom's magnum opus, *A Religious History of the American People,* the Klan appears in its opposition to immigration.[54] In his grand narrative of American religious history, Martin Marty argued, "The revival of the Ku Klux Klan in the 1920s included an anti-Catholic note which attracted only the extreme reactionaries in some southern and midwestern white Protestantism."[55] In both works, the Klan proved to be a marginal movement of reactionaries rather than an authentic interpretation of Protestantism. The narratives ignored the Klan's requirement of church membership in a Protestant denomination, the centrality of churchgoing in print, and the Klan's creative theological endeavors. Moreover, the order launched campaigns to unify Protestants across denominational lines in its effort to save America from immigration and other "evils." The Klan was a part of the religious story of the nation, whether its members were likable or not.

Perhaps it is easier to relegate the order to subcultural status rather than to attempt to integrate the Klan into American religious history. The religious history of America would appear different to us if we viewed it through the eyes of a Klansman or Klanswoman. How might narratives of American religious history be told if the Klan was integrated rather than segregated? If a white supremacist movement proves pivotal rather than fringe, then what might happen to our narratives of nation? Would American religious history appear differently or would it stay shockingly similar? By inserting the Klan into narratives of American religious history, the relationship between faith and nationalism comes to the foreground. In crafting its vision of the nation, the order understood "true" America in religious, racial, and gendered terms. To move the Klan from subculture to a legitimate component of the white Protestant mainstream illuminates the complicated, fractious, and contradictory process of creating and claiming national identity. American nationalism materializes in its particular relationship to Protestant identities, and the exclusivist discourse of nation emerges in a study of the Klan.

By interpreting the 1920s Klan in light of its Protestantism, one must rethink the decision to relegate distasteful movements to the sidelines of history. For Klan historian Kenneth Jackson, such was remarkably problematic because the Klan was "typically American." He wrote that the Klan gained power because it capitalized "on forces already existent in American society: our readiness to ascribe all good or all evil to those religions, races, or economic philosophies with which we agree or disagree" and our ability to "profess the highest ideals while actually exhibiting the basest of all prejudices."[56] To assess the Klan as a religious movement shows how the order, like many other movements, struggled with conceptions of nation, race, gender, and even its professed Protestantism. By showcasing the similarity of Klan members to their contemporaries, who perhaps did not possess the white robe or light a fiery cross but found resonance in the order's white supremacy, it becomes clear that the 1920s Klan resonated with the larger American public.

[The Imperial Night-Hawk] *will continue to speak . . . as the courier of the Imperial Palace to the various Klans of the nation.*[57]

Sociologist James Aho argues quite convincingly that the hate movement is a reading culture: the members of white supremacist movements learn and embody the rhetoric and ideology from their encounters with print.[58] Klan print journals, speeches, fictional works, newspapers, pamphlets, position papers, and broadsides document the religious worldview of the Klan. These are the official sources of the order as opposed to diaries, journals, or letters from individual Klan members. Words helped create Klansmen, and the order's print is my primary route of study. This narrative, however, is an official one that primarily focuses on the words of Klan leaders, lecturers, klavern members, and anonymous editors of Klan newspapers. The official and ideal worldview of the Klan demonstrates how the leadership, and often members, attempted to supply a unified, structured vision of the order. The sources do not invite a thick ethnographic description of what it *actually* meant to be a Klansman or Klanswoman in the second incarnation. But using print culture deciphers how leaders constructed those roles as well as documented the occasional opposition of members to the order's dictates and demands. The print provides the KKK's portrayal of the faith and the nation, which shows the order's relentless dedication to its twin messages in ways that have not been achieved before. As mentioned previously, the Klan print often engenders suspicion from researchers and general audiences alike. Yet this suspicion underplays one of our most valuable primary sources from the Klan: its own newspapers. By taking the order's texts seriously through close and careful readings, one can see how the members, readers, and leaders were an avid part of creating the order through reading. The words signaled truth; print became the order's reality. By relying on print reflections, my approach offers more of a snapshot of what was expected of a Klansman (or a Klanswoman) in the 1920s instead of standard historical progression. Using Klan newspapers showcases how text functioned in the order's defense of nation and Protestantism, as well as the active interplay between members and leaders in the creation and maintenance of order. The printed word served to illustrate the order's hopes, and fears, to its members and eventually a larger public.

In January 1923 the Imperial Kloncilium, the governing body, ordered the creation of an official publication, and so the *Imperial Night-Hawk* was born. Whether or not it was created because of the aforementioned public relations campaign is not clear.[59] The weekly ran during the peak of Klan membership, from 1923 to 1924. The circulation of the paper in 1923 is unknown. However, by the end of 1924 the editors of the *Night-Hawk* claimed that 36,591 copies were printed each week, with subscriptions in all forty-eight continental states.[60] Each Klansman gained access to a subscription when he became a member. The editor described the weekly:

> It goes to our army camps and to many of our battleships. It goes to numerous newspapers, to hundreds of ministers, and untold numbers of school

teachers. It has told the truth in times when the Klan was not allowed to state its case through the public press. *It has explained the beliefs of the Klan in a most wonderful fashion.* It has performed its duty well. Without one cent of cost to those receiving it, the *Imperial Night-Hawk* has freely and gladly been sent, with the compliments of the Ku Klux Klan, Inc., to all those who desired its weekly visit.[61]

The *Kourier Magazine* (1924–1936) replaced the *Night-Hawk* in December 1924, and the weekly became a monthly in the transition. Another popular Klan weekly, *The Dawn: The Herald of a New and Better Day* (1922–1924), boasted a circulation of 50,000 in 1923 and even charged ten cents a copy on the newsstand.[62] There were other news magazines, including the *Fiery Cross,* an Indiana newspaper, and the *Official Bulletins of the Grand Dragons,* a series of regional bulletins that reported on local and national events.

The print culture, then, is an invaluable entrée into the Klan's worldview because it allows for a glimpse of public persona and sometimes the private communications to members. Klansmen made the newspapers for other Klansmen. They were not supposed to be publicly available, which meant the publications served to remind Klansmen of their duties, the expectations of the order, and the order's positions on various issues ranging from evolution to Catholics to the public schools. Studying Klan print gives access to the inner workings of the order, which highlights how leaders and editors constructed religion, nationalism, gender, and race for their community. Examining those texts demonstrates how the Klan wanted to *make* Klansmen into white, manly, Protestant Americans who both selflessly served and defended the ideals of the organization. Reading the publications embedded Klan ideology and identity into the bodies of Klansmen as well as their minds.[63] The order's hope was to create Klansmen who longed to be the chivalrous Knights the order desired. That, however, was a tenuous process—to convince readers of the *Night-Hawk* and other print to live up to the ideals the pages described. Editors and leaders sought to shape the membership, but the members often had different ideas, which led to strident denunciations, warnings, and sometimes threats from the Klan leadership regarding their behavior. Klan print

Cover, *The Imperial Night-Hawk* (1923–1924). The national newsweekly of the Knights of the Ku Klux Klan. It later became the *Kourier Magazine,* a monthly. Author's collection.

served as a method of communication between the national organization and each individual Klansman.

Both print culture and the act of reading are methods of communication—either transmission or ritual communication.[64] Communication as transmission means that a variety of media passed new ideas to readers, viewers, and listeners. The ritual communication, however, proposed that no new information was actually presented to readers; rather, media reaffirmed a particular worldview. The ritual process maintained, reproduced, or transformed the reality of the reader rather than furnishing new ideas. Print, then, functioned to inculcate a sense of community among readers, who already shared similar ideas, beliefs, or practices. The *Night-Hawk, Kourier,* and *Dawn* all served as a means to instantiate the Klan's worldview and to verse readers in the order's goals. By reading a Klan newspaper, members embraced its politics, ethics, and actions, and they assented to its portrayal of faith and nation.

American religious historians explore the function of print culture as a method of community building for various religious groups, from reading in early America to evangelical Christian attempts to craft ideal religious readers. Certain books, particularly the Bible, provided cultural scripts and themes for how reality was constructed. Reading always occurred in "cultural fields," which ensured that reading was never a purely individual act; rather, reading functioned as a common activity that bound together religious peoples and confirmed their faith worlds.[65] Communities could be created, maintained, and destroyed in print. The printed page furnished tools for readers to create their own communities in novel ways. In religious publishing, nineteenth-century evangelical publishers believed, and hoped, that meaning passed directly from text to reader with no interference or interpretation. Unfortunately for those publishers, cultural contexts heavily influenced how readers experienced texts. Despite the publishers' hope for ideal readers who would embrace the religious grace of the Bible or John Bunyan's *Pilgrim's Progress* (1678), readers haphazardly followed the publisher's goals. Despite the tension between religious publishers and their audiences, some people did "properly" read the spiritual works and embrace religious community.[66]

Evangelicals, in particular, embraced the power of the word. The print culture of evangelicals was their method to define the boundaries of their religious worlds, to circumscribe the members of the faithful, and to unify the church.[67] Nineteenth-century evangelicals constituted a "textual community," in which publishers, authors, and readers defined the practices. These religious readers gained a sense of collective identity by participating in textual communities that provided clear boundaries for the faithful. Print clearly functioned as ritual communication for religious movements, and the *Night-Hawk* (and later *Kourier*) operated in comparable ways for Klansmen because it reinstated a familiar worldview. It served as a textual community that supplemented meetings, rallies, and parades. Reading was a method to become a better member and engage more fully with the ideals of the order. However, the *Night-Hawk's* anxiety about members' activities signaled that readers defined their own Klan communities despite what editors and leaders articulated upon the printed page.

The editors claimed the centrality of the *Night-Hawk* and the *Kourier* in Klan culture. The *Night-Hawk,* in its own words, was the "only recognized national organ of the Knights of the Ku Klux Klan," and it was the "sole and only official publication," which meant that "statements to the contrary or claims of this official recognition on the parts of others" were without basis.[68] More important, the editors of the *Night-Hawk,* representatives of the Klan press, affirmed their positions as the "shock troops of the Klan armies." They protested against "utterly ruthless forces, who had attempted to hush the voice of the Protestant press." Those editors threw "their own money and personalities into the cause." They wrote that the newspaper had fought the first half of the battle, and it was "up to the Klansmen of the nation to help them make good." The weekly urged that "these newspapers are fighting your fight Klansmen, and you wade in and aid them."[69]

These newspapers bolstered the Klan. It was the responsibility of members to read, ascertain, and embody the ethics of the order. The practice of reading solidified notions that Klansmen were Christian Knights who upheld the law of the land and protected the faith. Both the *Night-Hawk* and the *Kourier* illuminated what mattered the most to the second Klan. They permit entry into a worldview that has been mischaracterized and misunderstood to condemn the Klan for its actions. Using Klan print documents the experiences of editors, leaders, and ordinary Klan members in the fraternity and the larger world. The print culture showcases the close alignment of the order to its contemporaries. It also demonstrates not only the religious foundations of the Klan but also the complicated relationships between religion, nation, gender, and race in the early twentieth century. To see the Klan members as citizens rather than villains narrates a more complex American story, and to imagine Klansmen in such a way requires a deliberate method to place their words in juxtaposition with their more insidious actions.

> If I wanted to know what Masonry stands for I would not go to its enemies, but to the Masons themselves. . . . The best way to find out just what the K.K.K. stands for is to go to their own published platform. If anyone can contradict their statement let him come forward with evidence.[70]

In his *Invisible Empire in the West* (1992), Shawn Lay argued that Klan studies must align with the dominant trends in social history so that Klansmen and Klanswomen can be studied compassionately and objectively like their contemporaries.[71] The Invisible Empire, like other organizations, political movements, and fraternities, deserved a sensitive, thoughtful study similar to those of more benevolent historical subjects. Sociologist Kathleen Blee, however, notes that more empathetic approaches to the Ku Klux Klan, and the hate movement generally, verge on the dangerous because such approaches could ignore the devastating effects of such movements on members as well as our larger society.[72] Blee warns that describing the normativity of Klansmen and Klanswomen downplays the Klan's violence and hatefulness. Such scholarship, then, presents a "false" sense of those groups and their respective missions. Yet the enterprise becomes even more complicated when we consider the religious faith of the Klan as an addition to the study. The Klan's claim of Protestantism begs the question of whether its religion should be portrayed as Protestantism simply because they assert Protestantism or whether the order's religion should be treated differently. The Klan is clearly a movement that gives even casual readers of history pause. It is clear that the Klan historically could be judged as bad or harmful, but studying this movement differently from more approachable and benign movements seems to suggest a particular historical standard that assumes deception on behalf of its members. The lingering question is whether scholars should treat insidious and hateful groups as unique from other historical subject matter. Much literature on the hate movements declares the unsavory nature of its subjects, and this approach clearly colors the methods for studying historical actors deemed dangerous.

In principle, Lay is right about the need to focus on Klansmen and Klanswomen as ordinary citizens. Klan members were not much different from their neighbors and friends, with the important exception that their hatred for certain others motivated them to commit acts of violence, economic terrorism, theatrical displays, and other more subtle forms of discrimination. However, the need to make Klan members appear ordinary is not my main goal, because Lay's work, among others, showcases the normality of the Klan in a number of communities. Re-creating the Klan's ideal vision of white Protestant America allows me to document how Klansmen and Klanswomen engaged and embodied intolerance and religious nationalism in rallies, marches, and protests, and, more important, through print and reading. While Lay is correct that these men and women were not wholly evil, their ideal world, their textual community, highlights how their religious vision and their commitment to intolerance impacted the Klan's discussions of the American nation. Engaging Klan print allows for me to reconstruct how members and leaders maintained the order and its vision of America through text and reading.

*Gospel According to the Klan* presents the official worldview of the 1920s Klan.[73] Leaders and members alike shared and negotiated the Klan's Protestantism and nationalism, and religion is a part of the social system that provides a set of scripts for its adherents.[74] Stepping into the worldview of the Klan illuminates what such scripts are and how they function for the order's members in their actions, beliefs, and lives. Klan print introduces those scripts in an ideal fashion that favors leaders' and editors' opinions and neglects any form of dissent. The official portrait demonstrates the complicated boundaries between the sacred and profane in lives of Klansmen and Klanswomen.

Klan studies have explored much of the profane, and a small bit of the sacred, but they have not approached how both are interwoven in the lives of Klan members. Scholarly reticence about how the sacred and profane interact hides the sacred aspects of Klan life.

To settle into the Klan worldview, I employ ethnographic methods to document, describe, and interpret. According to James Clifford, ethnography has the ability to make the ordinary strange and the strange familiar. Ethnography highlights the need for reflexivity and sensitivity to one's subjects. In the current ethnographic turn, ethnographers reach beyond a scientific model of studying subjects through a "microscope" and embrace a more dialogical model, which allows the subject to speak for him- or herself. Historian Robert Orsi argues for intersubjectivity in which the scholar places her world in direct dialogue with the culture studied to see similarities and differences. That transformative process allows for an awareness of one's own culture.[75] With its uplifting of informants, ethnography contains the risk that scholars might become the mouthpiece for those we study. Kathleen Blee has argued that the romantic assumptions embedded in ethnography and oral history, especially the desire to empower informants and tell their stories, should not apply to hate groups. For Blee, the question is why would anyone want to empower the Klan? She noted that to empathetically connect with the Klan violates the required boundaries for researchers, who work with so-called unloved groups.[76] Her main concern was that empathy and rapport might make scholars complicit in the "horrific" agendas of Klan members via description and study.

While Blee's concerns are legitimate, I would note that the study of unloved groups problematizes the focus on empowerment and empathy in ethnographic methods and oral history. Blee suggests a heavy dose of skepticism when handling unloved groups because of their obviously malevolent actions and intentions. However, I would suggest that ethnographic methods should apply skepticism to all informants rather than just those who make us uncomfortable. Ethnographic work should not be a venue to redeem our subjects, likable or not, but rather a method to understand how their worlds function for better or worse. Ethnographic methods allow glimpses of the Klan's world in a particular historical movement and how that world might operate.

Disgust at the order's actions might make us feel better, but that emotion does not allow for an understanding of how Klansmen and Klanswomen create and sustain their lives. It is not hard to imagine why many scholars refuse to work with unloved groups. In his work on conspiratorial worldviews, Michael Barkun complicates the view on how scholars should handle groups that are strange, bizarre, or downright hateful. "Failure to analyze" these groups "will not keep people from believing them." Moreover, Barkun writes that the study of "certain odd beliefs does not signify my acceptance of them."[77] Ann Burlein, in her study of the Christian right and Christian Identity, describes the ambiguity of projects in which we might be opposed to our actors, historical or otherwise. Her solution was to "see with" her conversants, which allowed her to engage but not slip into relativism when confronting their violence and intolerance. She strives to portray their words and actions but not to become complicit in their political agendas. According to Burlein, it is important to study those who make us uncomfortable, in spite of ambiguity and possible danger, because keeping silent or ignoring those we disdain could make those we oppose much stronger.[78]

For Karen McCarthy Brown, ethnography is neither for the faint of heart nor those in need of moral clarity.[79] To enter the world of ethnography is to enter the world of moral ambiguity. An ethnography of the Klan is not only morally ambiguous but also ethically challenging. The use of empathy on those who disgust us is an interesting problem. Examining the hate movement in particular by engaging how they see themselves is a large risk for a scholar who has to balance the Klan's worldview with historical incidents of hate and intolerance. Moreover, the study of these movements seems to force scholars into a position of judgment, in which the scholar must declare the evil intent and behavior of all of those involved. Scholars moralize and judge before they even begin to engage with the Klan's larger history and contemporary presence. In his revised edition of *Salvation and Suicide,* a study of the mass suicide at Jonestown, Guyana, David Chidester argues that as a scholar his place was not to judge the events at Jonestown. He claims we should not give in to the temptation to moralize, but rather strive to understand how a religious worldview functions for its inhabitants. He employs "structured empathy," a form of empathy molded by interpretative categories such as myth, symbol, and ritual. That particular method supposedly opens up a connection with the worldview of others and further allows the scholar to engage imaginatively with her actors to understand the appeal and logic of the religious movement.

While Chidester's form of empathy appears worthwhile, it is equally as problematic as Blee's skepticism. It forces engagement without recognizing the risks of engagement. First, as Chidester argues, it is necessary to see how religious worlds function for adherents. Previous scholarship has attempted to do this but often fails because of the overemphasis on the deplorable nature of unloved groups. Examining the unacceptability of a worldview often neglects the larger motivations and the appeal of a religious movement. Second, to simply render the world as members (of the Peoples Temple or the Klan) may see it yields a one-sided presentation, which reflects Blee's poignant concern. Understanding a movement from the perspective of members should not ignore how others, from the outside, engage the language, the symbology, and the believers of those movements. Blee's and Chidester's methods inform my attempt to find a more integrative approach to the Klan: to see with them and, more important, to recognize that this is only a partial presentation of the story.

Moreover, I am convinced by Michael Barkun's approach to movements generally labeled as fringe. Barkun insists that no matter how odd or repellant religious systems might appear, white supremacists still believe them to be true when they furnish a framework for supremacy's ends.[80] If supremacy movements maintained the legitimacy of their worldviews, then scholars must take seriously their claims no matter how extreme. The religion of the Klan should be seen as religion. The religious systems of the hate movement, believable or not, influenced their members and often supplied divine mandate for their racism, hate, and the purpose of the community. To recognize how those religious systems placed race, nationalism, and gender in the realm of the ultimate is not only necessary to comprehending how those groups function but also to how best to counteract similar movements. To study the Klan as a Protestant movement adds complexity to standard histories of the Klan and further explanation of how the order imagined the larger world.

In a strict historical work on the Klan, it might be easy to dismiss concerns of empathy, redemption, and my role as interpreter. I could easily just focus on the facts of the movement's rise and decline and the roles that Protestantism played in that history. However, because of my desire to step inside the worldview of the Klan, I have to engage more directly the ethics of allowing Klan voices to speak for themselves. By applying ethnographic methods to historical evidence, I attempt to re-create the religious lives of dead Klansmen and Klanswomen. What I do cannot neatly fall under the parameters of lived religion because I am re-creating the worlds of people who are gone. I have fragments of their lives cobbled together in print, and I use ethnographic methods to bind these fragments together into a cohesive whole. My work also engages the larger question of what happens when ethnography and history intermingle. Can we re-create the lives of dead religious actors? Are we truly presenting them as they see themselves, how they hoped to see themselves, or some mishmashed presentation of both? I am primarily interested in the complications that arise when we try to bind present and past tense, especially when the religious actors we study are at the very least unsavory.[81] By engaging and taking seriously the religious voices and actions of the dead, we are transformed by our work and our work can be transformative. Ethnographic methods both complement and complicate religious histories, but in my work it remains clear that this merger allows new stories to be narrated to provide richer, nuanced tellings of American religious history. This means that my study is neither a complete portrait of 1920s America nor a strict history of Klan actions. Instead, I present the worldview of the Klan by illuminating how the order characterizes faith and nation, as well as what members hoped, feared, and admired about American culture. To see through the eyes of members and leaders clarifies their understandings of religion, nation, race, and gender. My project is arranged thematically rather than historically, which means that each chapter centers on one component of the Klan's worldview to delve deeply into how the order represented itself and its vision of white Protestant America.

Chapter 1 revolves around the Klan's professed Protestantism. In an exploration of Klan robes, Jesus, and the retellings of Protestant history, the Klan's commitment to the faith appeared in terms of exclusion. The order employed a generalized Protestantism while simultaneously limiting the historical boundaries of the tradition. Building upon those presentations of Protestantism, chapter 2 explores the relationship between religion and nation in Klan print culture. For the order, white Protestants created America, and the burden of national maintenance fell solely upon their shoulders. Using material artifacts, like the fiery cross and the American flag, as well as the selective, historical accounts of amateur Klan historians, the order argued that the origins of the nation were explicitly religious. The battle for continued inclusion of the Bible in public schools became a religious brawl to safeguard the nation by guaranteeing that future citizens would have access to the sacred texts throughout their schooling.

Chapters 3 and 4 assess the place of gender, masculinity, and femininity in the movement. To be a citizen and a Protestant was to be masculine, which was the bedrock of being a successful Klansman. The order circumscribed the role of Christian Knighthood for members in addition to instituting the rhetoric of "real" manhood. Martyrdom emerged as the penultimate example of masculinity because the self-sacrificing act depicted strength, overwhelming allegiance to the order, and an emulation of the manly Christ. Whereas masculinity was crucial to the identity of the Knights, femininity proved to be a more ambiguous affair. Knights proclaimed the protection of white womanhood as slogan for the order, but women often contradicted the men's vision of the female roles and conditions. Klansmen represented women as defenseless, vulnerable, and endangered, usually by Catholics, but the Women of the KKK (WKKK) had different ideas about the nature of their womanhood. The WKKK asserted its members' rights as equal citizens in the Invisible Empire, whose dedication to nation and the perpetuation of the faith rivaled that of the men's order.

Chapter 5 delves into the Klan's presentation of whiteness and race by examining the order's reflections about African Americans and Jews. Through the account of "other" races, the traits of whiteness become more visible. In addition, the Klan traced the heritage of America to its Nordic and Anglo-Saxon roots to claim that the white race bore the responsibility for the development of the nation and Protestantism. However, the order's vision of racial alchemy, which created the American race, strained its commitment to racial purity.

Finally, the sixth chapter narrates the Klan–Notre Dame Riot of 1924 to show the order's devotion to nation, race, and religion as expressed in anti-Catholicism and its firm belief that Klan members were the victims of persecution in the riot and on the national stage. In South Bend, Indiana, the Klan sought to defend the nation and its true citizenry while also realizing how tenuous its own vision was. The order imagined a white Protestant America in print, artifacts, rallies, and speeches. The KKK stood at the crux of peril and promise for the beloved nation, and its worldview contained lament as often as hope. Warring factions, personified in the riot, attacked the nation from within her boundaries. The Klan was both soul and savior, the center as well as the defender, of its imagining of nation, but members also had to confront the fragile nature of the order's vision. To sustain beliefs and ideals, members turned to reading, robes, and fiery crosses. Those print artifacts tell the story of the 1920s Klan and its fervid persistence in maintaining white Protestant dominance.

## CHAPTER 1

*"Thank God for the Knights of the Ku Klux Klan"*: The Klan's Protestantism

*As the Star of Bethlehem guided the wise men to Christ, so it is that the Klan is expected more and more to guide men to the right life under Christ's banner.*
—H. W. EVANS (1925)[1]

*The real interpretation of the message of the angels who announced the birth of the Christ child . . . nearly two thousand years ago, was carried forth by the Klansmen and Klanswomen of the Altoona on the eve of Christmas day, and the lamp of happiness was lighted in more than fifty homes of the poor of the city and vicinity after the Ku Klux Santa Klaus had paid his visit to the said homes.*
—IMPERIAL NIGHT-HAWK (1924)[2]

In his *Modern Ku Klux Klan* (1922), Henry Fry, a former Klansman, described the ritual of naturalization, the process by which one became a member of the Invisible Empire. He observed:

> The Exalted Cyclops raises a glass of water and "dedicates" the "alien," setting him apart from the men of his daily association. . . . He is then caused to kneel upon his right knee, and a parody of the beautiful hymn, "Just as I am Without One Plea," is sung by those of the elect who can carry a tune. . . . When the singing is concluded, the Exalted Cyclops advances to the candidate and after dedicating him further, pours water on his shoulder, his head, throws a few drops in the air, making his dedication "in body," "in mind," "in spirit," and "in life."[3]

Previously a Kleagle for the order, Fry could no longer continue his membership when he encountered the naturalization ceremony. The ritual's resonance with Christian baptism proved unnerving to the author, especially since he considered the rest of the order's rituals "tiresome and boring . . . twaddle."[4] That ceremony convinced Fry that the Klan was a "sacrilegious mockery."[5] What proved most disturbing to Fry was how the Klansmen seemed to have no problem with the naturalization's proximity to the "sacred and holy rite of baptism." Naturalization made a "mockery and parody" of a Christian ritual that the author held dear.[6] For Fry, the ceremony confirmed that the Klan was a moneymaking scheme parading as a religious fraternity. Such blasphemy was more than he could handle. In a resignation letter to the order dated June 15, 1921, Fry listed his many complaints against the order:

> In defiance of your threats of "dishonor, disgrace, and death" as contained in your ritual—written and copyrighted by yourself—I denounce your ritualistic work as an insult to all Christian people in America, as an attempt to hypocritically obtain your money from the public under the cloak of sanctimonious piety; and, I charge that the principal feature of your ceremony of "naturalization" into the "Invisible Empire" is a blasphemous and sacrilegious mockery of the holy rite of baptism, wherein for political and financial purposes, you have polluted with your infamous parody those things that Christians, regardless of creed or dogma, hold most sacred.[7]

The Klan, Fry contended, was not a Christian order but rather a false rendition of a religious movement. Furthermore, the suggestion of baptism in its naturalization ceremony proved the order was blasphemous as well. Hiding "under the cloak of sanctimonious piety" might have served well the order's moneymaking schemes, but Fry denounced the so-called Christian beliefs that members professed. His book detailed the contradictions and dangers of the order, but nothing ruffled the author quite as much as the Klan's professed Protestantism.

Fry was not the only skeptic of the order's religious leanings. W. C. Witcher of Texas created a pamphlet exposing the hypocrisies and supposed scams of the Klan. Witcher opined that the Klan "seduc[ed] the preachers of this country into believing that they should encourage and support" the order and all of its actions. He also claimed that "to impress ministers with its sham benevolence . . . it adopted the old worn-out political trick of 'donating to the preacher.'"[8] The author suggested that the Klan would be rebuked rather than accepted by Jesus and that the Imperial Wizard, the leader of the Invisible Empire, was the "Ruler of Darkness."[9] To demonstrate the devious attempts of the Imperial Wizard to mold Jesus to the Klan's message, Witcher provided a fictional account of a chance meeting between the two. Witcher described the Imperial Wizard as a manipulative figure who sought to overcome Jesus by wooing Him with worldly things. In the account, the robed leader emerged as the Devil, in the guise of a Klan leader. His desperate attempts to entice Jesus with power and prestige ultimately failed, and the parallels between Witcher's tale and the biblical narrative of Satan's temptation of Christ were quite deliberate. Jesus berated the Imperial Wizard for his blatant manipulation and cunning. The Klan leader, a "cringing coward," "crumpled at His feet like a conquered beast before its master." Jesus had won, and the Klan lost the support of its savior. The order's deceptive commitment to the Christian tradition, at least for Witcher, became visible. He continued:

> The echo of that rebuke rings down through the centuries like the voice of a nightingale, and if these commercialized ministers who have prostituted their pulpits with the white-robed children of the Imperial Wizard were even susceptible of a rebuke, they would drive these character assassins from their services with the whips of scorpions. Judas committed suicide for the same kind of offense. My God! How long wilt Thou suffer these miserable hypocrites to insult Thy Name, and defile Thy Sanctuary![10]

Those vituperative statements affirmed the belief of both authors that the second revival of the Klan was not religious but heretical, devious, and dangerous. Witcher suggested that Klansmen who offered such false religion were no better than Judas, and he begged God to hold them accountable because of their defiance. He even advocated that members might want to imitate the suicide of Judas, since their actions were comparable to his. The author clearly found the Klan to be a significant threat to Christianity because of its declaration to be a Protestant Christian order. Both authors engaged the Klan's professed Christianity and quickly dismissed the possibility that the Klan and its members could be legitimately religious. Ultimately, they disagreed with the Klan's presentation of the Christian (Protestant) faith. They saw only "false" religion in the actions of the fraternity. In that way, their attacks highlighted how the Klan's allegiance to Christianity caused unease among critics and former Klansmen. Those authors, in particular, were nervous about the order's association with their personal faith tradition, and vitriol spewed forth. The order's practiced faith proved too similar to the faith of its detractors. The resemblance required both authors to demarcate the religion of the Klan as foreign from their own religious commitments. The Klan, in its founding, bound Christianity with Americanism, and members professed allegiance to both despite their relentless critics. In the order's white Protestant America, the order envisioned not only that members were the defenders of Protestant Christianity, but also that God had a direct hand in the creation of the order.

*They built in their crude altar greater than they knew.*

On the "bleak Thanksgiving night" of 1915, seventeen men climbed atop Stone Mountain, Georgia, with a purpose and a large wooden cross. They set the cross on fire, and under its light those "pilgrims" committed themselves to the U.S. Constitution, "American ideals and institutions," and "the tenets of the Christian religion."[11] The men built an altar of granite boulders and spread the American flag over the rocks. William Simmons, the leader of the ceremony, wrote that "they built in their crude altar greater than they knew."[12] The eerie glow marked the beginning of the second Ku Klux Klan. The new order harkened back to the Reconstruction Klan, but its founder, Simmons, proclaimed a new path of militant Protestantism and sacred patriotism.[13]

Simmons, who became the Imperial Wizard of the order, and his successor, Hiram Wesley Evans, promoted a vision of the Klan as a patriotic, benevolent, and Christian order. For Simmons, that altar on Stone Mountain was the "foundation" of the Invisible Empire, which was committed to "the preservation of the white, Protestant race in America, and then, in the Providence of Almighty God, to form the foundation of the Invisible Empire of the white men of the Protestant faith the world over."[14] Evans noted, "As the Star of Bethlehem guided the wise men to Christ, so it is that the Klan is expected more and more to guide men to the right life under Christ's banner."[15] The second incarnation of the Klan, therefore, was transformed and dressed in Christian virtue and metaphor. Protestantism served as the foundation of the movement, and the protection of its religious faith was a key component of the Klan's mission. The nation, it seems, functioned better in the hands of the faithful. The religious foundation of the order, as we have seen, was not without its detractors.

Robert Moats Miller, writing in 1956, argued that the relationship between the Klan and Protestantism should not be assumed, nor asserted, since denominational newspapers as well as national conferences condemned the Klan.[16] Miller utilized Christian journals to argue that Protestant churches were not bound to the order. National conventions and denominational governing bodies, for Miller, determined Protestantism. Yet local churches still proclaimed their affiliation to the Klan despite outcry from national bodies. Miller's study lacked detailed analysis of how religion functioned for the order, enabling him to conclude that Klansmen and Klanswomen were not authentically Protestant. The Klan specifically defined that term to match the parameters of its organization.

Interpreting the role of religion in the life of Klan members demonstrates clearly how the order defined the terms "Protestant" and "Protestantism." "Protestant" meant not only non-Catholic but also a recoded narration of Christian history. Questions still arise. How exactly did members and leaders define Protestantism? Were they evangelical, fundamentalist, both, or neither? Religious faith became crucial to the construction of the order by leaders, editors, and members. Protestantism undergirded the membership, the rituals, and the rites of the order, as well as imbued the pages of Klan print culture. My study of Klan print suggests a different conclusion than that reached by Miller: the Klan subscribed to Protestantism, and the order created their own definition, history, and vision of the faith for its members. That vision began with Simmons and flourished in the pages of the *Imperial Night-Hawk,* the *Kourier Magazine,* and other Klan papers. In the Klan's creation of a textual community, Protestantism emerges not only as the foundation of the order's structure but also as the larger nation.

In his writing and speeches, Simmons sought to create a super fraternity that not only appropriated the regalia and history of the previous Klan but also imported fresh symbology, which illuminated the importance of Americanism and Protestantism. As an ex-minister, Simmons combined faith with politics in his movement, and that faith washed over the pages of the *Night-Hawk.* Such might seem surprising to those who envisioned the Klan as a racist, anti-Semitic, anti-Catholic political organization, which it undeniably was. However, it was also an organization that required members to be Protestant Christians, who affirmed both Jesus as well as Americanism.

The Klan leadership crafted a religious organization, and the *Imperial Night-Hawk* (which became the *Kourier Magazine*), the Klan's official organ, molded a public persona that glorified its faith. Through weekly publication, the Klan presented the ideals of its community and attempted to fashion Klansmen to reflect those ideals. The *Night-Hawk* and *Kourier* created a unified order through text. Being a good Protestant was key to being a good Klansman or Klanswoman. The Klan's Protestantism was defined in a multitude of ways, from uplifting the literal meaning of the word ("to be a protestor") to aligning the Klan as successors of the Reformation who "cleansed" the church and provided Protestantism as a foundation for both democracy and religious freedom. Klansmen were to be "protest-ants" of systems of iniquity, deriving their example from Martin Luther. Additionally, the Klan envisioned its role as the "handmaiden" of the church because of its ability to unite Protestantism in the face of denominationalism and supposed enemies.

Moreover, the Klan rendered Jesus in its organizational image. Members employed Jesus' example as a model for their lives. In print culture, robes, and rituals, the order communicated its adherence to the Protestant faith and functioned to solidify the community in the face of threats to both faith and nation. It was a tenuous process to convince readers of the *Night-Hawk* to live the ideals and faith that the newsmagazines described.

The Reformation has taken residence in the Klan.[17]

According to Hiram Wesley Evans, the second Imperial Wizard of the Klan, "the angels that have anxiously watched the Reformation from its beginning must have hovered about Stone Mountain Thanksgiving night, 1915, and shouted Hosannas to the highest Heaven."[18] For Evans, the founding moment of the order was the second Reformation. Those joyous angels watched in awe as the order was born, and that event signaled that the church and society might be salvaged. Evans believed that the Klan had the potential to reform Christianity much in the same way that Martin Luther had "saved" the church within the first Reformation. The church was no longer able to lead such a movement because of fractious denominationalism, but the Klan, based on the Bible, with God and Jesus as its "soul," could bring about "universal and rock-bottom reform."[19] The Klan crafted its own form of Protestantism, which highlighted dissent (protest), individualism, militancy, and a strong commitment to the works of Jesus.[20]

Despite joyous angels and divine support, Klan leadership and newspaper editors expended much ink to make their case for the Klan's "protest-ant" heritage. Both the *Night-Hawk* and the *Kourier* contained lengthy articles about the Klan's Protestantism, which served to establish the Klan's place in Protestant history, to describe religious practice, and to demand Protestant behavior from Klansmen and Klanswomen. Imperial Wizard Evans even declared the 1925 Klan program was to promote Protestant Christianity. Evans beseeched the membership: "As the new year dawns, I, as Imperial Wizard of the Knights of the Ku Klux Klan, wish to call upon the Klansmen of America for whole-hearted, united, sacrificial service to the cause of Protestant Christianity. I ask you working through the several Protestant churches to which you belong, to make this a year of Christian devotion and high service."[21] The Klan both protested and proclaimed allegiance to Protestantism. Members sought, and often created, similarities between their movement and historical narratives of the faith. Klansmen hoped to place themselves directly in the lineage of both Jesus and Luther, as well as to define Protestantism in their own terms to reflect the purpose of their order.

A Protestant, in the most basic definition, is one who protests. For the editor of the *Kourier,* the protest could be directed at a person, event, or idea, and that protest was not confined to religious matters. The *Kourier* uplifted protest and dissent as important tools of both critique and change. Rather than limit the term to one who seceded from "the Roman Church," he suggested that severance from Roman Catholicism was not required. Instead, protest was more generally linked to reform. Jesus was a "Protestant" who employed that method to correct the ills of his day. His life was "one of unending protest."[22] According to the Klan, he contradicted priests and asserted the need for individual conscience. Jesus' ministry was "in open defiance to the religious monopoly that prevailed in Jerusalem."[23] He "believed" in free speech and the power of individuals to accomplish change. For the Klan, its use of Protestantism imitated Jesus' behavior and beliefs. Protestantism, then, suggested fair play, freedom of religion, and a more generalized vision of freedom.

The editor of the *Kourier* described fair play as the promotion of equality, love, protection, and concession. Rather than oppose ideas contrary to the order, Klansmen should protect the ideals of others as well as support their individual freedoms. The editor wrote that "while we find the teachings of Jesus to have been very positive and pointed, we do not find Him ridiculing these other religious expressions, nor placing a ban upon . . . the aspiration of the soul."[24] Since Jesus did not ridicule opposing expressions (except those of the priestly class), the order required Klansmen to respect other religious traditions. Interestingly, the Klan lauded Jesus' ridicule of "religious monopoly" in Jerusalem while still suggesting his tolerance for other religious beliefs. The Klan's savior, accordingly, had no problem with individual beliefs, just authoritarian religious systems. Fair play easily extended into religious matters, and the Klan argued that its Protestantism also uplifted freedom of religion. For the *Kourier,* Klansmen should not judge the "spiritual aspirations" of men, because all people claimed the spiritual legitimacy of their own religions. How could one determine whether those aspirations were false? Protestantism, then, allowed for men to aspire to the spiritual and guaranteed that "all men have the right to the individual expression of that aspiration."[25] That reflected Protestantism's commitment to individual rights, so individual liberty was embedded in this religious tradition.

The Klan's religious faith, then, rested on freedom, which reached beyond the varying conceptions of religion and also applied to civil society. Its Protestantism contained a celebration of liberty, at individual and religious levels, which allowed for religious groups to practice their beliefs as long as they were not forcing those beliefs upon others. Freedom implied the independence from religious tyranny in America. The Ku Klux Klan, "being Protestant, is fighting the battle of every religious sect and every religious denomination" in its attempts to assert America's freedom from religion as well as freedom of religion. For the order, the nation required protection from religious movements, which sought to inflict their traditions upon unwilling people. Such a notion of Protestantism demonstrated the Klan's acute concern over non-Protestant religious movements and especially Catholicism. The editor noted that the Klan was a "friend" of Catholics. That friendship, however, was fragile because of the Klan's fear that Catholics posed a threat to government and nation. The *Kourier* expounded, "Should Catholics seek to control this country to the exclusion of all other forms of religious expression, they will find the Klan fighting them until the last Klansman was [*sic*] dead." In regard to the threat to government, Methodists, Baptists, Presbyterians, or others might also find themselves on the receiving end of the Klan's wrath should they attempt to "usurp authority." For the Klan, Protestantism might have suggested freedom, but it still retained its anti-Catholic tone and militaristic nature to respond to religious groups who overstepped their bounds in civic life. Inclusion meant limits. Despite the suggestion that Klansmen would risk life and limb in the pursuit of freedom, the *Kourier* pleaded with readers to "throw aside pre-conceived notions about Protestants and Protestantism, and dig down to the root meaning."[26] That "root meaning" relied on notions of protest and fair play while simultaneously promoting exclusion, particularly for Catholics. Such notions of Protestantism resounded as more secular than religious. Freedom applied not only to Protestantism but also had larger parlance in American culture. Dissent, individual conscience, and freedom of religion did not necessarily originate from the faith tradition. Rather, the Klan newspaper sought to broaden understandings of Protestantism as a religious tradition and for the order. The Klan expanded the umbrella of Protestantism, so that it might encompass ideas that avoided the particularities of denominations. The order generalized its Protestantism for mass appeal.

The Klan's definition of Protestantism was not limited to a secular celebration of freedom. Protestantism did retain its spiritual aspirations. It was "the soul's religious declaration of independence" as well as "a law in the spiritual realm."[27] The soul was free, but to be Protestant suggested one's soul was truly unfettered. Jesus freed the soul from its fetters and reiterated the "spirit of religious law." He affirmed the "spiritual interpretation of religion" rather than "literal adherence, [which] resolves itself into formal ceremonialism." The spirit of the law negated the need for priests and ceremonialism. The Klan's Jesus reveled in disobedience toward the high priests. He taught his followers to rely upon their own consciences for religious practice. He taught that people "should be free to worship God, their Heavenly Father, in the way best suited to their liberated conscience, and at any time in accord with their conviction."[28] That law manifested again in Luther's reformation, which was a "re-formation" of Jesus' teachings.

Luther rearticulated the vision of Jesus that had been "abandoned" by the church. Both men emphasized the importance of the individual over the collective and criticized the role of priests in religious experience. For the Klan, Luther sought to reinstate Christianity to its original and pure form. The Klan's Jesus purported that salvation was in the hands of the individual, not through official ceremonies or formalism. Ceremonialism, however, was not the central focus of Luther's attack. The Klan found a certain belief to be more disturbing. The *Kourier* reported:

> The same belief exists today among millions of people who look to a human intermediary for their salvation more than they look to Almighty God. This is insidious priestcraft, and is tantamount to spiritual slavery. To break the people of His day from such enslavement, Jesus boldly declared: "Ye shall know the truth, and the truth shall make you free." He also declared to the people if He made them free, they would be free indeed.

Such was a veiled attack on Roman Catholicism. Its supposed "spiritual slavery" revolved around the issue of the pope, "a human intermediary" who stood between Catholics and God. For the Klan, the centrality of the pope demonstrated the Catholic Church's attempts to keep members bound in falsehood. The newspaper attacked the church because of its reliance on priests and the pope in spiritual affairs. Rather than criticize Catholicism outright, the article alluded to the similarities between ancient Judaism and the Roman Catholic Church.

Jesus' critique of Jewish priests proved applicable to the contemporary moment because the criticism echoed the detriments of the church. For the *Kourier,* the church tricked Catholics into believing that obedience to the pope was necessary for salvation and that personal interpretation was unnecessary and wrong. The *Kourier* lauded the example of Jesus, "who freely encouraged people to think for themselves."[29] The Klan, however, was quick to point out, despite its denouncements of Catholicism, "Klansmen are not 'against' the Catholics . . . but are 'for' Protestant Christianity *first, last and all the time.*" Perhaps the Klan and its leaders were not aware of the contradictions in their position on Catholicism; yet the Klan degraded that Christian tradition in an attempt to assert the importance of Protestantism. In Klan thinking, the freedom of religion for Catholics was tenuous at best. An Exalted Cyclops proclaimed, "The Klan is here, and it will remain until the last son of a Protestant surrenders his manhood, and is content to see America, Catholized, mongrelized, and circumcised."[30]

The vilification of Catholics was not unique to the order and had historical precedence in America. The Klan was embedded in a long lineage of American nativism and anti-Catholicism, which emerged in the colonial period and gained much ground in the nineteenth and early twentieth centuries. Historian Peter D'Agostino pointed out that by the eighteenth century there was "no shortage" of anti-Catholicism in America. He argued that the founders of the American nation maintained anti-Catholic prejudice, but they did not need to react to individual Catholics since they were a minority population in the new nation. If they had, D'Agostino noted, "anti-Catholic fangs would have surely shown themselves more frequently."[31] The early colonists and founders perpetuated that bias against Catholics. By the nineteenth century, the residual bigotry burst forth in the American cultural scene in magazines, newspapers, books, and associations. Protestants documented their so-called encounters with Catholics as well as Catholicism in Europe and America, and Protestant writers, historians, and everyday folks crafted Catholics in their imaginations as exotic and dangerous. For Ray Allen Billington, nativism was "the first American mania of hostility to Catholics."[32] David Brion Davis argued that the "anti" movements, including anti-Catholicism, were movements for unity of the American nation, in that they were the fruit of fears about internal subversion and conspiracy.[33]

Anti-Catholicism emerged due to the mass immigration of Catholics in the mid-nineteenth century and the fear that Catholics could and would change the American nation.[34] One consequence of that sentiment was the burning of an Ursuline convent in Charlestown, Massachusetts, in 1834. Anti-Catholicism was an imagined conspiracy. Catholics were the imagined enemies, but the consequences of those imaginings were very real.[35] In the 1880s and 1890s, the American Protective Association (APA) feared Catholic conspiracies. They also helped fuel those fears by giving lectures to Protestant audiences, during which they suggested that Catholics were taking the jobs of Protestant workers. Thus, the APA actually played a role in two major anti-Catholic riots.[36] Historian Mark Massa placed the second order of the Klan firmly in that lineage due to its use of "anti-Catholicism . . . as the most effective rallying cry." For Massa, the Klan proved to be the last bold presentation of mainstream prejudice until the outbreak of World War II. The order was one of the main promoters of anti-Catholicism. At the 1928 Democratic convention, the Klan attacked Al Smith's presidential candidacy because he was a Catholic seeking the nomination for the highest political office. Smith lost the nomination. Massa argued that the shallow victory signaled the end of the Klan because Catholic prejudice largely dissipated in American public life.[37]

For Massa, the Klan maligned Catholics and adopted anti-Catholicism merely as a rallying cry. However, the order's anti-Catholicism proved more sophisticated and illuminated the supposed alterity of the church. Its prejudice moved the order to refashion Christian history by excising Catholicism. To accomplish that goal, the Klan presented the Protestant Reformation not only as a movement to reform the church, but also as a movement that began with Jesus instead of Martin Luther. H. W. Evans argued, "*the* Reformation—started at the first altar that declared righteousness (right living)—has been, is and will ever be one cumulative urge toward Paradise Regained." That first altar was the mission and ministry of Jesus. Evans proposed that the Reformation had occurred as the result of many reformers who had strove "toward the right."[38] By marking the beginning of the Reformation with Jesus and its continuing influence with Luther, John Calvin, John Wesley, and other Protestant reformers, the Imperial Wizard sought to eliminate the Catholic Church's role in Christian history. His suggestion was that the Catholic Church's "corruption" of Christianity neglected the "real" message of Jesus. Moreover, Evans claimed that God was the "soul—the life—of the Reformation." God sanctioned and founded the reforming movements, and Jesus became the first reformer. Evans wrote, "Jesus therefore became the soul of the Reformation, and He will be its soul until it shall have accomplished its age-long task—that of restoring pristine relations between man and God, and between man and man; reproducing normalcy."[39]

The Reformation, then, restored Christianity to its pure form. According to a Klan minister, Martin Luther demonstrated that salvation did not come through the church but rather through Jesus. Luther substituted Christ for the pope to reclaim the "true" message of Christianity. He "maintained that Roman Catholicism had forfeited its right to support by its betrayal of Jesus Christ as the head of a Christian, or so-called Christian, organization." The minister continued, "Martin Luther blew up that doctrine [confession], and recrowned Jesus Christ as the great central object of our devotion and for our leadership in Christianity."[40] For the Klan minister, Roman Catholicism betrayed the mission of the Christian church, and Luther had corrected its errors. The Klan envisioned its members in the lineage of Jesus and Luther as the new reformers who would restore Christianity to its "originary" form. In retelling Christian history in a way that highlighted the importance of Protestantism, the Klan degraded the place of Catholicism. If God sanctioned the Reformation, then was the Catholic Church godless? If the Catholic Church "replaced" Jesus with the pope, were they really Christians? The Klan considered Roman Catholicism a failed attempt in Christianity. The *Kourier* noted that people were turning away from Catholicism because of its failure, and he wrote that the Klan's duty was "to show them the more acceptable interpretation of Christianity as held by Protestants."[41]

By minimizing Catholicism, the Klan strove to identify its own Protestantism. The Klan defined its Protestantism in opposition to "Catholics" as Protestants perceived them. That process of definition had historical precedent. In her work on Catholics in England in the seventeenth century, literary historian Frances Dolan argued that since Catholics were not easily distinguishable from Protestants, Protestants seeking to define Catholics as somehow different had to go to great lengths to make their case. For Dolan, the problem for Protestants was that they shared a common religious history and tradition with Catholics. To make their movement distinct, Protestants presented their own religious movement in oppositional terms. Protestants defined their Catholic brethren by what *could have happened* rather than what actually happened historically.[42]

The Klan participated in a similar process of differentiation. Whether or not the Klan was fundamentally opposed to Catholicism and Catholics was not always clear. The church, as an organization, served as a foil for all of the Klan's concerns about religion and nation. Klan members' relationships with flesh-and-blood Catholics proved more complicated. Their denunciations of the Roman Catholic hierarchy obscure how they related to Catholic neighbors (see chapter 6). Despite its vitriol, the Klan strove to portray liberating and tolerant perceptions of its faith. In presenting itself as a bastion of tolerance, the order made the Catholic Church the easy symbol of intolerance, backwardness, and authoritarianism. By showing the dangerous nature of the church, the order hoped to appear as more progressive and advanced. A Klan minister proclaimed: "Certainly Protestantism with its gospel of enlightenment, with its spirit of democracy, and with its idealism of the apostolic age of Christianity, has character, has righteousness, has purity of heart, has brotherhood, and certainly that type of Protestantism is at least two or three hundred feet higher than the darkness and the superstition and the rottenness and the tyranny of Roman Catholicism."[43]

Klan conceptions of Protestantism contained values like religious freedom and individualism while simultaneously drawing boundaries of exclusion. Catholicism became the representative of all the "rottenness" that Protestantism was not. Catholics and Catholicism became the foils to the "virtues" of the reforming spirit of the Klan. The order's anxieties about the church reflected more its unease with changing social norms than with actual Catholic actions or presence.[44] The negative portrayal of Catholics bolstered the Klan's Protestantism. The order also claimed its status as the promoter of the "true" form of Christianity. To present further its Protestantism, the Klan crafted Jesus as a savior, an exemplar for character and behavior, and as a likely member of its order. In presenting Christ, the Klan continued to use the church as a foil for the order's dedication to correct principles and, most important, correct belief.

*Jesus was a Klansman.*[45]

In the opening prayer of Klan rituals, the order proclaimed that "the living Christ is a Klansman's criterion of character." A Texas Klansman and minister, W. C. Wright pondered what those "magical, significant words" meant for the life of a Klansman. Wright wrote, "We desire to call attention to some of the outstanding characteristics of His life, as they pertain to the fundamental principles of Klankraft and the development of a *real*, dependable character." Jesus had an exemplary character, and the author believed that his experiences could relate to the experience of the ordinary Klansman. In the *Night-Hawk,* Wright pointed out that by knowing the character of Jesus, Klansmen could emulate his behaviors and principles for the betterment of themselves and for the good of the order. After all, "Jesus was a Klansman . . . a member of the oldest Klan in existence—the Jewish theocracy."[46] While the focus on Jesus' Jewishness might seem strange in that context, the Klansmen asserted that Jesus promoted Jewish supremacy much like the Klan supported white supremacy. The Jews, then, were just as concerned with maintaining racial purity as the Klan was. Jews "have been Klannish since the days of Abraham; and Jesus was a Jewish Klansman . . . by birth, blood, religion[,] . . . teaching and practice as well." Jesus was important as a savior and as a member of the Jewish clan. His "allegiance" to that clan resonated with Klan members. Additionally, Jesus "sought, first of all, to deliver the people of his own race, blood, and religion."[47] Interestingly, the order did not reflect upon Jesus' Jewishness; the savior, it seems, lost more of his ethnic identification the longer he was a Klansman. His ethnicity did not matter, only his membership in a clan. Instead, the Klan's Jesus reflected the values of the order. To bolster such, the Klan crafted the story of Jesus' life to fit its paradigm. The order engaged his example quite seriously.

By harkening back to Jesus' life, the Klan related his trials and triumphs to those of the order and its members. The Klan's Jesus overcame adversity, and he emerged from the Jewish clan to create his own clan, Christianity. After the resurrection, Jesus expanded beyond his previous "clan" and proclaimed a plan for salvation based on moral character rather than kinship ties. The trademarks of Jesus' followers

*God Is Our Refuge and Strength.* Georgia Klansmen kneel in prayer accompanied by the cross and flag. The 1920s order recruited ministers as members, leaders, and lecturers, and the Klan affirmed its Protestantism in prayer, creed, print, and robes. Courtesy of University of Georgia Hargrett Library, Athens.

were "spiritual, namely, a chivalric head, a compassionate heart, a prudent tongue and a courageous will, all dedicated and devoted to the sacred and sublime principles for which He had paid the supreme sacrifice." All of those were expected traits of 1920s Klan members. A Texas Klansman opined, "May every Klansman develop just such a character as He exemplified when He walked among men."[48] If members would follow the path of Jesus, their lives and their practice of "Klankraft" would benefit from his guidance.[49] That religion became "the Klan of Character" founded by Christ. Wright suggested that not only was Jesus part of a Jewish clan but also that Christianity was an extension of that previous clan. The 1920s Klan, then, "mimicked" the Christian clan. Wright attempted to renarrate early Christian history so that it reflected the structure of the order. To say that Jesus was a Klansman provided the order with religious legitimacy for its cause, and thus the order claimed Jesus as the role model for Klansmen's behavior.

The Klan's Jesus, then, was selfless, humble, meek, patient, and charitable, and he sacrificed himself for others. Thus, his actions inspired the Klan's motto, "Non Silba sed Anthar, not for self but for others."[50] Jesus' selfless nature inspired the Klan to be selfless. Members hoped that their actions would help others as well as strengthen the bonds of their community. Klansmen were to "be knit together as the members of our body, each co-operating with the other; so closely and vitally connected that when one member suffers the whole body suffers."[51] Wright employed Ephesians 4:16 for his rendering of Klan service, though his focus on suffering was absent from the biblical verse. Selflessness as a Klan virtue required a Klansman to discard his selfish impulses and deny glory for himself. Selflessness, then, led to equality. That corollary virtue urged Klansmen to be merciful and just to other members. The *Night-Hawk* declared, "Be hospitable to your fellow Klansmen, he is one of many who are many in one, devoted to a common pledge and pledged to a common cause."[52] As a part of the collective, the community, that common cause trumped individual turmoil. There were many in one body, and in practical terms selflessness afforded a way to circumvent the competing personalities of Klansmen. Selflessness emphasized the importance of cohesiveness in the order over an individual's desires and wants. It placed the order first and the members a distant second. In the printed pages, the uplifting of Jesus' example and the extolling of selflessness also illuminated members' charitable acts. Klansmen delivered baskets of food to the poor on Christmas, donated money to Protestant benevolent associations, and even created their own charitable institutions. In Altoona, Pennsylvania, the local Klan played Santa to poor children. For the Altoona Klan, "the real interpretation of the message of the angels who announced the birth of the Christ child . . . nearly two thousand years ago, was carried forth by the Klansmen and Klanswomen of the Altoona on the eve of Christmas day, and the lamp of happiness was lighted in more than fifty homes of the poor of the city and vicinity after the Ku Klux Santa Klaus had paid his visit to the said homes."[53]

The *Night-Hawk* reported that through such acts the Klan lived the "real interpretation" of Jesus' message. In Lisbon, Ohio, the Women of the Ku Klux Klan donated baskets to the poor with "a gift for each child." Christmas was not the only time in which the Klan exercised its charitable spirit. In Dallas, Texas, the Klan provided an $85,000 building as an orphanage for infants entitled "Hope Cottage." The Corpus Christi Klan started a Protestant memorial hospital in honor of a slain Klansman. The local klavern affirmed that a Protestant hospital was a much-needed addition to the town in which "the Roman hierarchy was in control." It was a memorial as well as proclamation of the faith. In Shreveport, Louisiana, the local Klan collected funds to start a "Protestant Home for girls," because in Louisiana the only homes for girls were Roman Catholic. That need came to the attention of the larger Klan organization when a young minister joined the Klan and hoped to "actively practice Klancraft." He revealed that a mother was prostituting her two young daughters and had the woman arrested. Discovering that there was only a Catholic home for girls, the distraught Shreveport Klan launched a fund-raising campaign for a Protestant home. That Klan hoped to build the home and provide it "to the State with the one proviso that it be conducted by Protestants and on Protestant principles."[54]

Additionally, the *Night-Hawk* established a fund for the widow and two children of Thomas R. Abbott, a murdered Klansman, so that his children could attain an education. The *Night-Hawk* encouraged Klansmen throughout the Invisible Empire to contribute money for the Abbott family. A Pennsylvania Klan even donated money to the building fund for a "Negro Church," as well as an ample number of Bibles. The Klan's benevolence could occasionally breach racial lines, but its charitable donations did not cross religious boundaries. Many local Klans, as demonstrated above, strove to uphold their pledge to selfless service. Imperial Wizard Evans affirmed that "Klanism is altruistic or it's nothing. Every benefit we seek not to monopolize, but to diffuse throughout our citizenship and to place, so far as may be, at the service of mankind."[55] In 1924 the national Klan instituted a charitable program. At the annual Klonvokation, Evans proclaimed, "It shall be the program of the Knights of the Ku Klux Klan (a program in line with the divine plan) that ten percent of all the monies that come to your National Organization shall be . . . applied to humanitarian service."[56] The Imperial Wizard also encouraged individuals to give 10 percent of their personal incomes to help those in need. The order constructed a tithe to aid others, but aid contained requirements. White Protestant organizations generally received such funds, and the *Night-Hawk* reminded Klansmen to review their donations to ensure that their "tithe" supported primarily Protestant organizations.[57]

Selfless service was only one component of Jesus' example. The *Night-Hawk* rendered their savior as a fighter. In print, Jesus was the "Master Christian, who stood unflinchingly for the cause that He knew to be right." The Master Christian "feared no man . . . never wavered, and . . . left to all mankind a heritage that you [a Klansman] may have for the asking." Each Klansman should take "stock of their mental and physical selves" in comparison with Christ. The *Night-Hawk* maintained that "the Pilot Imperial, Christ Jesus, whose teaching all Klansmen follow, believed in something better yet to come and threw himself into the cause of the future. He, alone, changed the universe. Klansmen . . . do reverence to Him, catch the Master's spirit."[58]

Klansmen embraced Christ's example. Christ's disciples were to be "fishers of men, who made their nets therefore of words and example to establish a principle of citizenship and duty and service to mankind." By following the example of the disciples, Klansmen could missionize more men for the Klan. Klansmen "engaged in the championing of principles of the organization co-operating as a solidified body of Christian Americans of one mind, of one purpose and one common understanding."[59] In that spiritual warfare, Klan members sought to convert others to the faith, through their personal examples. If the individual Klansman embodied Christ's spirit, in word, deed, and action, then he could be a "fisher of men" and bring more into the fold. He would spread the "holy principles of righteousness and truth" by following Christ.[60] The *Night-Hawk* urged Klansmen to do as Christ would have done, so the organization and the nation could benefit. Members' actions should reflect the Klan's teachings, and Klansmen's bodies, by conforming to the printed guidelines in the *Night-Hawk,* were to witness the Klan's Protestant core. Since each member represented the order, conformity was also a Protestant value.

Moreover, Jesus' crucifixion, as personal sacrifice, was also important for Klansmen because it demonstrated the lengths one man would go to for others. Members of the order were encouraged to remember Jesus' redeeming act. The cross, albeit a fiery cross, was an emblem of the Klan, which the order upheld because "the Cross . . . bore the Redeemer of the world, . . . the only begotten [son] of the Father." The light of the cross was a memorial to the model for Klansmen. An Indianapolis Klansman described the crucifixion and its significance in gruesome detail:

> Out from Pilate's hall, Jesus staggered down the steps to the narrow road that led to Calvary, and there under the burden of that rugged tree His physical strength failed. He fainted beneath its load—the blood clotting in His hair, the perspiration drying upon His face. He came out of the faint only to proceed to Golgotha, and there the cruel nails pierced through His hands and feet. The Cross was lifted and dropped with a thud into the earth, and upon it Jesus Christ gave Himself as a ransom for many.[61]

This Klansman hoped to remind his fellow members that Christ died for their sins. Members should follow Christ's path of righteousness and goodness. Jesus set the example for both service and sacrifice. Klankraft required a "living sacrifice," and Klansmen's bodies were to be living sacrifices for God's will. A column entitled "Christian Citizenship: The Gospel according to the Klan" reflected upon a verse from Romans 12: "I beseech you, therefore, brethren by the mercies of God, that you present your bodies a living sacrifice unto God." The *Night-Hawk* advised Klansmen to "present your bodies, a living sacrifice. If you are going to perform the reasonable service God demands you are going to use your body." Since Jesus' wounded body bore the sins of the world, a Klansman should offer his body in service of God through the Klan. A member should follow Jesus' example to a lesser degree by bearing witness to his path (as crafted by the Klan). It was not necessary to sacrifice one's life, but to sacrifice one's selfhood for the greater body of Klan membership.

The bodies of Klansmen bore the weight of Jesus' principles. The *Night-Hawk* advocated prayer but also "sacrifice on the altar, not only on Sunday and weekly prayer night, but week days and election days."[62] That living sacrifice was the "supreme test." A Klan minister wrote, "Man thinks more of his own body than anything else he possesses. He will gladly give up honor, glory, reputation, character,

Candidates for initiation into the Klan stand in front of an electric Fiery Cross, 1923. Photograph by W. A. Swift. Courtesy of Ball State University Archives, Muncie, Indiana.

friends, wealth, and even his own soul, to save his body." For the minister, the body was of utmost concern. He continued, "To lay our 'bodies,' yet living on the altar of service, is a supreme sacrifice. . . . This demands a clean, consecrated life. God will not accept an unholy offering."[63] Ideally, all Klansmen's actions should reflect Jesus' sacrifice, from charitable giving to political action to personal behavior. As a Klansman, life was no longer simply about one's self but also about the lives of others, as well as the reputation of the order. Through focusing on living sacrifice, the Klan required its members to follow the order's doctrines. Its rendering of Jesus was the archetype for behavior. To enforce the example of Jesus for Klansmen, the white robe, the uniform, contained a theology of its own. Wrapped in white robes, Klansmen presented their bodies for service.

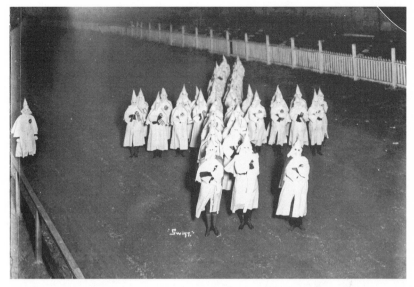

Indiana Klansmen create a "cross" formation. Photograph by W. A. Swift. Courtesy of Ball State University Archives, Muncie, Indiana.

*The white robe which is the righteousness of Christ.*

In the late 1860s, the Reconstruction Klan created the distinctive Klan uniform, which consisted of long white robes decorated with various occult symbols. Tall conical hats completed the outfit, and white fabric covered the individual's face with two openings for the eyes. The design supposedly imitated the ghosts of the Confederate dead.[64] The revival of the Klan in the 1920s appropriated the uniform, but its meaning changed. William Simmons, the founder, admitted that the initial purpose "in adopting the white robes . . . was to keep in grateful remembrance the intrepid men who preserved Anglo-Saxon supremacy in the South during the perilous period of Reconstruction."[65] However, the uniform proved more than a memorial. Simmons wrote: "Every line, every angle, every emblem spells out to a Klansman his duty, his honor, responsibility and obligation to his fellow men and to civilization. . . . All of it was woven into the white robes of the Ku Klux Klan for the purpose of teaching by symbolism the very best things in our national life."[66]

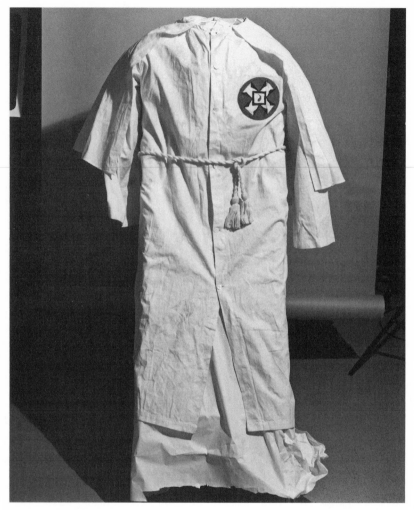

1920s Klan robe. Courtesy of the Indiana Historical Society, Indianapolis, Indiana.

No longer were the robes merely a ghoulish disguise. Rather, the clothing embodied a sacred meaning for Klansmen. According to Simmons, the new role of the costume was consistent with the symbolic function of robes in other religious and fraternal organizations. Moreover, Simmons asked, "Why should we the Knights of the Ku Klux Klan, be singled out and condemned for adopting a symbolism . . . to represent our particular service to the age in which we live?"[67] The

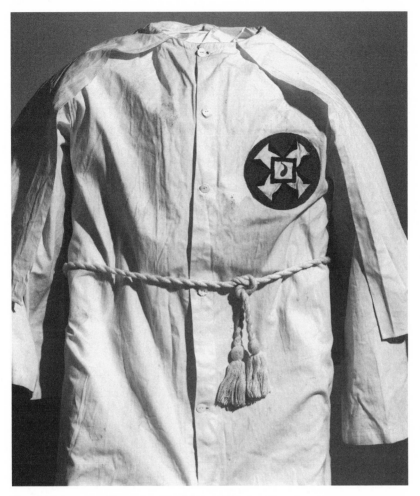

Detail of the 1920s Klan robe. The Klan emblem on the robes appears prominently, showcasing the white cross surrounded by a red circle. Inside the cross, a tiny blood drip signifies the blood Christ shed to save humanity. Courtesy of the Indiana Historical Society, Indianapolis, Indiana.

uniforms mapped patriotism, chivalry, and, most important, white Protestant Christianity on the wearer's bodies. The sacred folds of the uniform reflected the order's white supremacist notion of Christian virtue. The costume *displayed* the ideology and identity of the Klan.

The robes were the material presentations of the Klan's commitment to Protestantism and white supremacy. By 1923 Klansmen and

Klanswomen manufactured the robes in a Klan plant to guarantee homogeneity of the robes and to control how the product was made.[68] Since the robes had immense symbolic value for the Klansmen, the regalia factory controlled the manufacture of material artifacts, much like the *Night-Hawk* strove to monitor the image of the order. Despite its symbolic import, the uniform was quite simple. The average Klansman's uniform consisted of a belted white robe with cross insignia and a white hat with an apron, or mask, that covered one's face. The loose robes disguised the wearer's body, and the mask made one's face unrecognizable. The color white represented purity, racial and spiritual, as well as re-presented "whiteness" of the men "masked" by their uniforms (see chapter 5). The color of the robes displayed the requirements for membership: Caucasian, Protestant, and "native-born" American, all of which equaled whiteness.[69]

The cross insignia was a white cross in a circular field of red. In the middle of the white cross was a single red symbol that appeared to be a comma. The comma was actually a drop of blood that represented the blood that Christ shed for all humanity. The cross, then, harkened back to the Klan's Christianity and was a reminder of Christ's debt for human sin as well as his example of merit-filled action. According to the *Night-Hawk,* Protestant forces in the Middle Ages carried the cross "in their perilous efforts to rescue the Holy Land from heathen Turks," so it became a sign that the Klan, embodying Protestant Christianity, could conquer the "hordes of the anti-Christ" as well as the "enemies" of Americanism.[70] The robes functioned to represent the Klansman's spiritual purity and his commitment to Jesus.

A Klansman, then, could wear Christ's example, symbolized in the uniform, on his body. The white robes and the mask emerged as symbols of Christ's righteousness. The *Night-Hawk* noted that the robe was a "symbol of the robe of righteousness to be worn by saints in the land of Yet-to-Come." With Christ as their example, the robe was a sign that Klansmen were endeavoring to follow his teachings. A Klansman wore "this white robe to signify the desire to put *on that white robe which is the righteousness of Christ,* in that Empire Invisible, that lies out beyond the vale of death." Some "scoundrel" could attempt to wear the "sacred folds of the robe," but his soul was not a Klansman's soul. The robe functioned both as a purifying agent and a reminder of the sinless

Klansmen in Elwood, Indiana, 1922. Klansmen, both masked and unmasked, in the standard white robes with cross insignia. Klan leadership emphasized the need to keep one's apron (hood) down for protection of individual identity and the larger order. Photograph by W. A. Swift. Courtesy of Ball State University Archives, Muncie, Indiana.

perfection of Jesus as compared to the imperfect lives of the Klansmen. That material feature was the method for Klansmen "to cover here our filthy rags and imperfect lives with the robe," and members hoped "through the Grace of God and by following His Christ, [to] be able to hide the scars and stains of sin with the righteousness of Christ when we stand before His Great White Throne."[71] The robe cleansed their sinful impurities while uplifting the purity of Jesus.

The white-robed Klansmen also mimicked the white-robed figures in the Book of Revelation. A Colorado minister claimed that the white garments of the order echoed the characters in the biblical text. For the minister, Protestantism had "been groping back to that memorial room where those twelve men sat for the last time with their immortal Leader."[72] By examining Revelation, he applied the text and its prophecy to the current age. He noted a decline of Protestantism, but he conjured the image of the white-clad men who appeared before the throne of Jesus. Their robes were "washed" and "made . . . white in the blood of the Lamb." By wearing those robes, the men dedicated themselves to the worship of God and his service. The minister then noted the parallel between biblical narrative and the contemporary age: "I wonder if God did not notice the plight of His children . . . [and] He raised up a new order wherein all Protestantism could . . . promulgate the teachings of the Man of Galilee."[73] The men in the white robes not only represented Christ's example through their uniforms but also became reflections of the biblical narrative. For the minister, the Klan served to promulgate the teachings of Christ.

According to Rev. James Hardin Smith, Jesus would have worn the robes if he had had the opportunity. He proclaimed, "I think Jesus would have worn a robe such as they [the Klan] use, but because He did not wear a robe a mob came and took Him and crucified Him." Smith believed Jesus would have used the disguise to protect himself on missions of charity, much like the Klan employed the garments. Klansmen might have embodied the message of Jesus while wearing the uniform, but Hardin suggested that Jesus might have implemented the uniform as a tool for his own ministry. He continued, "I am not sure that Jesus would bid men to take off their robes."[74] In the Klan's rendering, Jesus was both exemplar of action and practical supporter of its disguise. Those garments were both sacred and practical: to uplift the Protestant message of the order and to mask the individual members of the order. According to Smith, Jesus would have supported both.

Through the sacred folds, Klansmen commemorated and lived the sacrifice of the "Master Christian," Jesus. Their robed bodies expressed the beliefs of the Klan.[75] The "hated mask" concealed the faces of members, making them part of a faceless, white-robed collective. The mask wiped away the last traces of the individual, which allowed a Klansman to become part of the larger body of the Klan. The *Night-Hawk* claimed that the masks functioned in two ways: as protection of the secrecy of the membership and as a symbol of the unselfish nature of membership. A Texas Klan leader wrote, "With the mask we hide our individuality and sink ourselves into the great sea

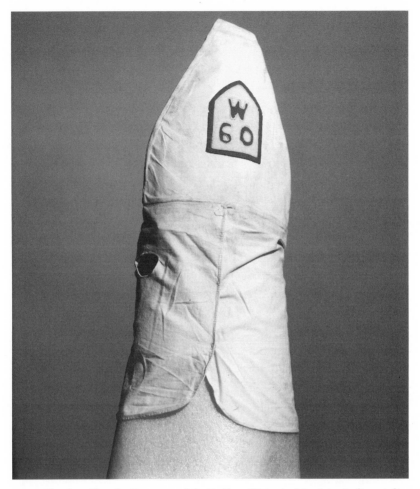

1920s Klan hood/mask. Courtesy of the Indiana Historical Society, Indianapolis, Indiana.

of Klankraft. . . . Therefore we hide self behind the mask [so] that we may be unselfish in our service." The individual Klansman sacrificed a sense of self to be a member. The mask eliminated distinguishing features, equalizing members and subsuming them into a collective. The Texan continued:

Who can look upon a multitude of white robed Klansmen without thinking of the equality and unselfishness of that throng of white robed saints in the Glory Land? May the God in Heaven, Who looks not upon outward appearance, but upon the heart, find every Klansman worthy of the robe and mask that he wears. Then when we "do the things we teach" and "live the lives we preach," the title of Klansman will be *the most honorable title among men.*[76]

For the Klan, the indistinguishable multitude presented its ideal of selflessness. The outward appearance reflected the collective. The Texas Klansman urged members to live by the Klan's teachings because the action of an individual could make the Klan more honorable or more loathsome.

Thus, the microcosm, the individual Klansman, was the symbol for all outsiders of the macrocosm, the Klan. Each Klansman represented the larger belief structure of the order, and the order struggled to control actions and beliefs of members. Imperial Wizard Evans issued an official position on the misuse of regalia, which warned that unofficial use of regalia was "a direct violation of the rules of this Order and must be discontinued." The *Night-Hawk* reminded readers that "untold damage might easily result from such practices."[77] The employ of regalia required regulation to maintain the ideals of the order and its public appearance. Moreover, Evans instructed Klansmen to keep their visors (part of their masks) down. Secrecy allowed a member to perform at his best as a Klansman. If a Klansman's identity was revealed by the careless act of lifting one's visor, he placed himself and his fellow Klansmen in danger. The enemies of the Klan could utilize that information to exploit members. Once a Klansman's identity was known, the enemy could easily discover who other Klansmen were by association. The *Night-Hawk* warned: "To expose your identity as a Klansman lessens your ability to perform constructive work for your country and your community. To divulge the membership of a fellow Klansman is nothing but the basest treason and under Klan law is punishable as such."[78]

The apparent anxiety in the print culture illuminated the organization's desire to control its message. That desire included monitoring the boundaries of textual and embodied community. Members mirrored the collective's ideals, and obviously there was room for human error. While wearing the sacred folds, one Klansman's actions could put the order's larger message of Protestantism in peril. The Klan crafted its own Protestantism, but individual members did not necessarily follow the dictates of the order. The white robes articulated the religious vision as well as the practical need for disguise, but that could not guarantee that Klansmen practiced in the method that the Klan preached. The order emphasized more than one's personal religious faith, commitment to Jesus, and collective Protestantism. The Klan hoped to unite Protestantism by moving past schisms within the faith and bringing Protestants together under one undivided banner of faith.

*Thank God for the Knights of the Ku Klux Klan.*[79]

According to the *Imperial Night-Hawk*, the Klan at its core was a "great American Protestant order."[80] To be eligible for membership, "one must have been born in the United States, of white parentage, be over 18 years of age and of the Protestant Christian faith." As we have seen, faith was a defining feature of membership beyond eligibility requirements. The order proposed that scripture was the basis of its principles, and Jesus was the criterion of character. The Bible was "the keystone of Klan principles." Moreover, the stated intent of the Klan was to be an auxiliary for Protestant churches. The goal of that auxiliary was to make Protestantism a more powerful force. A Louisiana Klansman remarked that one of the chief aims of the Klan was "to bring the different branches of the Protestant church into a closer relationship with one another as well as to preserve the United States as a Protestant Christian nation."[81] The Klan hoped to unite the forces of Protestantism by moving past the strictures of denominationalism. To accomplish that task, the Klan sought to make members more devoted to their personal Protestantism.

The *Night-Hawk* proclaimed that "one of the foremost duties of a Klansman [was] to worship God."[82] Klansmen should be religious and dedicated to their churches. "Every Klansman should have a Bible in his home[,] and he and his family should read it."[83] Ideally, membership in the Klan would improve the member's interaction with his church, his family, and his country—for "no man can be a good Klansman and not be a better citizen and a more consistent Christian by the experience." The Klan transformed men into inspired members who were good, churchgoing citizens.[84] A leader from Texas noted, "Klansmen are taught that they become much better Klansmen if they attend divine services regularly with their wives and families and support the Sunday Schools of their city."[85] An anonymous author asked, "How can any man presume to call himself a one hundred per cent Protestant if he does not give one hundred per cent support to Protestant churches?"[86] Good Klansmen became better men because of their devotion. Their worship made them familiar with some form of Protestantism and therefore, one hoped, more willing to campaign for a united faith.

Above all, Klansmen were expected not to be "Weak Kneed Protestants" who did not stand up for their beliefs. Rather, they were to embrace the Klan's version of Christianity as wholeheartedly as they embraced their Klan membership. According to the *Dawn,* a Klan newspaper from Chicago, real men "have long decided that sitting on the fence is not the place for a native born, white, Protestant gentile, who would save America from her enemies." The "man on the fence" should feel uncomfortable about his uncertainty about the order and its faith. Moreover, the *Dawn* proclaimed, "If you are on the fence get off today. Don't be like Mr. Weak Kneed Protestant."[87] The *Night-Hawk* also knowingly suggested that "the Klan is founded on the word of God: you're not ashamed of that are you?"[88] Both papers reverberated with defensive tones suggesting that white Protestant American men were not "REAL men" unless they belonged to the Klan.[89] According to contributors to both papers, Klansmen were strong Protestants as opposed to the other weaker Protestants. The Klan's logic proceeded that if Protestant men were not ashamed of God and knew the Klan's Protestantism, then they should join. The Klan's print culture contained a rhetorical style that goaded Protestant men into membership and shamed Klansmen into going to church. Individual Klansmen should have been defenders of the Klan's values, and the print culture served as a reminder of acceptable klannish behavior. The overemphasis on "true" religious behavior arouses suspicion about whether the Klansmen's behaviors were sullying the ideals of the order. After all, one author warned, "God hates nothing worse than cowardice in His cause."[90] Individual Klansmen were to be God-fearing men or face ridicule in print.

In addition to the demand for members to be "one hundred percent Christians," the *Night-Hawk* affirmed that Christianity was foundational to the structure of the organization. The twelfth chapter of Romans was the "Klansman's law of life," an example of how to live a Christian and klannish life. After reflecting on Romans 12, "the fundamental teachings of Christ," the *Night-Hawk* stated, "Klansmen should be so transformed, or different from the world, that [their] lives prove what is the will of God."[91] The Klan changed men, so that they were "new creatures" who were modest, active, never slothful, selfless, virtuous, persecuted, honorable, and just.[92] Klansmen became models of the will of God. A minister-defender of the Klan prayed, "May God help us, and Christ strengthen us to walk daily by the sublime law of the Divine will, that we, as Klansmen, may prove to our enemies, 'what is good, and acceptable, and perfect will of God.'"[93] Individual men were not only Klansmen but also moral exemplars for their faith. The order dictated the personal life of a Klansman, so the best, albeit masked, face could be put forward. Through print, the Klan strove to create God-fearing, white-robed men who, under the banner of faith, had the potential to unite the fragmented religious tradition.

Through those actions, the Klan endeavored not only to create religious Klansmen but also to bind together disparate Protestant groups. The *Night-Hawk* remarked that since the order was "composed of no one creed of the Protestant faith," Klan meetings furnished an arena for "many . . . branches of the Protestant Church [to] rub elbows at its meetings, form lasting friendships . . . as they work in a common and holy cause." A leader in the Texas realm of the Klan claimed, "A forward stride has been made for a United Protestantism which will present a solid front to those who would engender ill feeling among Protestants."[94] The Texan believed that the Klan allowed for a united faith, which enmeshed Protestant groups into a larger collective. The *Night-Hawk* hoped that the order would unite both the divided country and the divided faith. Due to the Civil War, Protestants tore the "Body of Christ by maintaining Northern and Southern convocations of their same sect." The weekly envisioned the Klan as the force to mend divisions of the country as well as among denominations. The *Night-Hawk* noted, "The Klan platform is broad enough to accommodate all Protestant faiths and strong enough to sustain their combined weight." The order sought to provide a program that emphasized the similarities rather than doctrinal differences of denominations. The program was the "united effort of Protestant patriots," who supported "one Lord [Jesus], one Faith, one Baptism."[95] The attempt to mend divisions rather than create new ones was an essential goal of the Klan. Unification did not mean that the Klan was attempting to be a church. For Rev. W. C. Wright, the Klan aided churches but was not a church in its own right. Instead, the Klan was a "Protestant Clearing House," which served all Protestant churches instead of affiliating with one denomination over another. Wright continued: "We cannot 'take sides' in religious controversies, and unprofitable wrangles; but we must strive to exalt the LIVING CHRIST as 'A Klansman's criterion of character,' and stress the twelfth chapter of Romans as 'A Klansman's Law of Life,' by constantly exemplifying these ideals in our daily conduct."

The Klan claimed to join "the forces of a divided Protestantism."[96] By providing an arena for Protestants to gather solely as Protestants, the Klan hoped to combat not only schisms but also enemies of Protestantism. One Klan minister suggested Martin Luther was actually responsible for the divisions. He argued, "Luther failed to secure permanent union in his own ranks." That lack of stability led to the fracturing of Protestantism. Moreover, the Roman Catholic Church had taken advantage of the divisions. Catholics were "banking on its destruction of this great Protestant organization [the Klan] that at last has arisen, under the glory of God."[97] The Klan felt that Catholics feared and criticized the order because of its efforts to mend the fragmented Protestantism. United Protestantism had the potential to save not only the faith but also the nation for Klansmen. The Klan's efforts at unity, however, were not appealing to all Protestants.

The religious and patriotic order strove to be an auxiliary for churches, yet some Protestant churches felt threatened by the order's reemergence. The order was also anxious about its relationship with churches, and that anxiety was well founded because of criticisms printed in the Christian press. The *Christian Century, Christian Work, Christian Herald,* and many local papers, like the *New York Christian Advocate* and the *Arkansas Methodist,* printed derogatory columns and opinions on the Klan, ranging from critiques of secrecy to claims of un-Americanism and un-Christian behavior.[98] A contributor to the

*Northwestern Christian Advocate* claimed any minister who supported or failed to criticize the secret organization "that plots its deeds in secret and executes its purpose cruelly and under mask was not worthy to preach the gospel of an open-minded and clear-breasted Christ."[99] For those religious presses, the Klan did not illustrate its religious legitimacy.

To counter the printed attacks, the *Imperial Night-Hawk* highlighted the aid the Klan supplied churches. The weekly reported, "where the Knights of the Ku Klux Klan are active, Protestant church attendance has shown notable increase and church work generally has taken on renewed vigor."[100] The contributors purported confusion at denunciations of another arena for Protestants to come together. One author wrote, "But if members of Protestant churches feel disposed to band together, merely for fellowship or for some more specific purpose, who is to deny them that privilege?" He continued, "Would hundreds of Protestant ministers retain their membership in an organization that is such a menace to Protestantism as is claimed?" After all, the author stoutly believed that the Klan "compare[d] favorably with that of any church in intelligence, morals, good citizenship, and even in Christianity itself." The order did not imagine itself as a threat to Protestantism. Rather, the *Night-Hawk* and its contributors argued that the organization was the opposite, a "secret society" that "advanced Christianity."[101] The tension was apparent between what the Klansmen thought their order did for their faith and the ways others perceived their actions. In the pages of the official organ, Protestant ministers defended the Klan and its good works for Protestantism. Rev. H. R. Gebhart of Indiana proclaimed, "God is surely with the Knights of the Ku Klux Klan." For the minister, the Klan was strengthening, not weakening, the faith. He opined, "I can see the hand of God more and more in this Klan movement. . . . The Protestant churches have lacked unity, but through this wonderful movement they are becoming united in a common cause. All I can say is: Thank God for the Knights of the Ku Klux Klan."[102] The Klan propagation of that worldview through its print culture proved members' participation in the "protesting" faith. After all, Gebhart believed that the churches should have been thanking God for the Klan's involvement in their cause.

The fashioning of a religious identity, the identity of the collective, was clearly undertaken in the pages of the *Night-Hawk,* which stressed, repeatedly, the Klan's worldview. The editor(s), the shock troops, seemed to paint the importance of Protestantism in page after page and volume after volume. The collective identity of Klansmen was what the pages *declared* rather than the individual experience of Klansmen. The *Night-Hawk* presented how a typical Klansman should act but not necessarily how Klansmen acted. The official sources occasionally demonstrated that members were not necessarily performing like good Protestants, but, overall, the editors and leaders were more interested in emphasizing how one could be a part of their burgeoning Protestant community. Those printed pages rendered members as part of a faith community by describing the evidence of Christian behavior. The most common script for Klansmen's behavior was Jesus' model of living sacrifice. Jesus was the ideal for their actions, and their uniforms mapped Jesus' message on their bodies. The Klan's Protestantism, then, was key to defining and understanding its membership as well as the ideals of the order. Evans, Simmons, editors, and contributors defined their generalized Protestantism through a genealogy including Jesus and Luther, as well as in more secular notions of dissent. The Klan's Jesus was crucial to how the order painted members as Protestant Christians. The burden of his example rested on individual Klansmen. The religious faith of the order was conjured for mass appeal, but individuals were to be believers who dedicated their lives to the righteous cause of the order. They were members of a religious community connected via reading and print. Official sources communicated expectations for members, who, through emulation, performed their commitment to Jesus and to their order. By being a Klansman, one proved his dedication to faith as well as nation, and he imbibed in the ideal worldview of the Klan. Leaders and members believed that God had smiled upon the Klan to unite the faith and save the nation. The order had God on its side. A Klansman from Arizona wrote a poem, "God in the Klan," sacralizing the movement:

> But then there came a Savior,
> With a face turned from the clod.
> The noble Knights of the Ku Klux Klan,
> Another form of God.[103]

For the poet, the Klan was arguably divine, and that sentiment would likely have troubled Fry and Witcher more than naturalization ceremonies and renditions of Jesus. To be a "form of God" suggested the Klan's reforms, ideals, and principles were legitimate, unchangeable, and dominant. Thus, its rendering of the faith was final and eternal, which proved to be essential not only in members' personal lives and actions of the order but also in their vision of the nation. Faith became the centerpiece of the Klan's nationalism. Moreover, faith imbued not just text and reading but also their construction and employ of patriotism.

## CHAPTER 2

*"Take the Christ out of America,*
*and America Fails!":*
The Klan's Nationalism

*My nature is serious, righteous and just,*
*And tempered with the love of Christ.*
*My purpose is noble, far-reaching and age-lasting.*
*My heart is heavy, but not relenting;*
*Sorrowful but not hopeless;*
*Pure but ever able to master the unclean;*
*Humble but not cowardly;*
*Strong but not arrogant;*
*Simple but not foolish;*
*Ready, without fear.*
*I am the Spirit of Righteousness.*
*They call me the Ku Klux Klan.*
*I am more than uncouth robe and hood*
*With which I am clothed.*
**YEA, I AM THE SOUL OF AMERICA**
—DAISY DOUGLASS BARR (1923)[1]

*Three times, on his bended knee, with his right hand raised to high Heaven, and his*
*left hand placed over his heart; in the presence of a sacred altar. Over the top of the al-*
*tar was spread the American flag, and on top of the American flag was laid the Holy*
*Bible open at the twelfth chapter of Romans; hanging aloof was the "fiery" cross, sym-*
*bol of the Christian religion; with still another American flag unfurled from a staff,*
*and the beauty and splendor of its wonderful standard blowing in his face. In this po-*
*sition he took the oath thrice binding him in solemn loyalty and serious pledge to sup-*
*port the laws of the city, state and nation. Therefore a Klansman, bound by patrio-*
*tism[,] which inspired him to become a member and then by a three-fold oath, is*
*pledged to the great government of the United States over and above any and every*
*government in the whole world. He pledges his life, if necessary, his property, and his*
*sacred honor to the unfaltering purpose of perpetuating our great American country,*
*the most dauntless lineage known to man.*
—"TO THE CITIZENS OF WAYNE COUNTY" (N.D.)[2]

On bended knee, each Klansman pledged allegiance to patriotism and
dedicated his life to the perpetuation of "our great American country."
Americanism, more particularly 100 percent Americanism, was a rally-

THE STARRY FLAG AND THE FIERY CROSS SHALL NOT FAIL

*The Starry Flag and the Fiery Cross Shall Not Fail.* Four Georgia Klansmen present the Fiery Cross and the American Flag, two of the seven symbols of the order. Courtesy of University of Georgia Hargrett Library, Athens.

ing cry for the 1920s Klan, and members prostrated themselves in front of altars of Americanism, complemented by the flag and the cross. Both the flag and the fiery cross were part of the "seven symbols" of the Klan. The American flag was an unsurprising symbol, one with an obvious and long-standing tie to patriotism.[3] The fiery cross, however, seemed to demonstrate more the order's uplifting of Protes-

tantism and religious belief than its national character. Yet the Klan
envisioned both of those material artifacts as signifiers of nation.

The flag, "purchased by blood and suffering of American heroes,"
articulated the "price paid for American liberties."[4] For the Klan, like
other Americans, it was a symbol of liberty, democracy, the Constitution, free speech, freedom of worship, and the rights of citizens. The
flag was a fabric symbol of American character. For W. C. Wright, a
Klan minister, the colors of that emblem presented American values
and history. The red stripes uplifted "the bravery and blood" of all
who fought for liberty. The white stripes symbolized "the sacrifice
and tears of American womanhood whose husbands and sons paid the
price, as well as the purity and sanctity of the American home." The
blue was "but a path of America's unclouded sky, snatched from the
diamond-studded canopy that bends above our native land." Finally,
the stars illustrated the union of the states.[5] Each component of the
flag communicated the character of the nation, its people, and its romanticized geography. The artifact provided a nostalgic view of the
country and its beneficence.

The *Kourier* reported that the flag was a gift from the forefathers
presented to subsequent generations as a representation of liberty.
The "Glorious Banner" connoted both liberty and law, yet the
monthly purported that Old Glory was denigrated by ignorance of
both. The monthly configured the meaning of the banner theologi-
cally. Red equaled devotion, which might have required "the shed-
ding of blood." The *Kourier* printed, "We love Jesus because He shed
His blood for us, and we love the Flag because it represents the blood
shed for our freedom." The white signified purity, intelligence, and
citizenship. The stars in the field of blue no longer indicated a commitment to the Union but instead the realm of the metaphysical. Those
stars "stand for Him Who is back of the stars in Heaven above." The
*Kourier* continued, "We may not all understand God alike, but we do
believe there is a God, and we must admit that the bases of America's
Laws are the great moral laws of God. When any man turns his back
on God[,] he turns his back on the Flag." Thus, the banner connoted
not only American history but also the relationship of God to the
American nation. The quintessential American symbol reflected divine guidance in American history, and it also affirmed that the belief

Two thousand candidates take the oath of the Invisible Empire in Marion, Indiana, 1922. Photograph by W. A. Swift. Courtesy of Ball State University Archives, Muncie, Indiana.

in God was essential to citizenship. The monthly, however, was not promoting a universal God that would be inclusive of citizens of all faiths. The *Kourier* understood Christianity as an important part of Americanism and expounded that "pure Americanism can only be secured by confidence in the fact that the Cross of Jesus Christ is the wisest and strongest force in existence."[6]

For the Klan, Christianity constructed nationalism, and the flag and the cross were artifacts of both religious faith and devotion to the nation. Daisy Douglas Barr, a Klan poetess, wrote that the Klan was "more than uncouth robe and hood"; it was "the soul of America."[7] The Klan was represented as savior and soul of the nation. The questions her poem begs prove intriguing: What if we take seriously the claim that the Klan was the "soul" of 1920s America rather than just the proclaimed "savior"? What if we understand that nativist movement as a nationalist one instead?[8] By overlooking the impact of Protestantism on the order's nationalism, previous historians have obscured the intimate relationship between faith and nation in 1920s America. Millions of Americans found resonance in the Klan's vision of white Protestant America, and they wore robes and burned crosses. They supported the Klan's homogenous, antipluralist construction of the nation and its people. Both presented the theology of the movement as well as its imagining of what America should be. Average, ordinary citizens found resonance in a movement that claimed to be "soul" and "savior" of American culture. Those people believed if the Klan was the soul of America, then faith and nation were inseparable. Robes, flags, and crosses demonstrated how the Klan welded Protestantism and Americanism together into a cohesive whole. To understand those artifacts and renderings of Americanism in Klan print complicates narratives of American religious history in the 1920s by suggesting that faith and nation were not as separate as we might like them to be. Religious exclusion and antipluralism were the foundations of this particular vision of the nation.[9]

Klansmen proclaimed Protestantism, and their Americanism reverberated with religious overtones. From their view, America was primarily Protestant, and the Klan romanticized the Founding Fathers and their "Protestantism" as the keystone in the creation of America. The *Night-Hawk* and the *Kourier* urged Klansmen to be defenders of the faith and Americanism by carrying the fiery cross. That faith dictated the behavior of members on personal and collective levels. The newsmagazines also confirmed the Klan's vision of the world, and its printed words sought to define a textual community of believers in homogenous faith and a particular vision of America. The cross, like the flag, articulated the order's form of nationalism, which emphasized faith as essential to the character of the nation.

*By the fire of Calvary's cross.*

William Simmons, the first Imperial Wizard, added the fiery cross to 1920s Klan's rituals, though Thomas Dixon's *The Clansman* (1905) introduced the idea of the burning crosses as a part of the Reconstruction Klan's mythology. In that literary work, the cross bound the American Klan to the Scottish clans of lore. Dixon used that connection to place the order to a larger history of Anglo-Saxons. More practically, in the novel the lit cross functioned as a tool for Klans to communicate with one another. Much like the robe, the 1920s Klan recrafted the fiery symbol from Dixon's staging to present its twin messages of Americanism and Protestantism. The cross harkened back to the Klan's Protestantism and the magnitude of Jesus' selfless sacrifice on the cross. It reflected the heritage of Protestantism as "the symbol of heaven's richest gift and earth's greatest tragedy."[10] As one of the seven sacred symbols of the Klan, "this old cross is . . . a sign of the Christian religion," which was "sanctified and made holy nearly nineteen hundred years ago by the suffering and blood of the crucified Christ, bathed in the blood of fifty million martyrs who died in the most holy faith, it stands in every Klavern of the Knights of the Ku Klux Klan as a constant reminder that Christ is our criterion of character."[11]

The cross magnified Christ's importance as the archetype for a Klansman's behavior. The wooden object was a memorial of Christ's debt for human sin as well as his merit-filled actions. In a poem praising the fiery cross, an Iowa Klansman noted that its light indicated that the universe was firmly under God's control and, moreover, that God would "redeem and regenerate the world."[12] For the Iowan, the cross suggested that "good," the Klan, would triumph over any "evil": immigration, alcohol, threats to the public school, attacks on Protestantism, Catholicism, Bolshevism, and Judaism, to name a few. The artifact reassured the Klansman that the universe was structured in the way he hoped. Its glow symbolized a world in which the Klan was the singular force of good and the order would triumph.

The fire signified that Christ was "the light of the world." That light vanquished the darkness and superstitions, though it was a beacon of truth for Klansmen only. (Victims of the order did not necessarily recognize the religious vision of the cross but rather the fear and terror the Klan inspired.) "The fire of Calvary's cross" purified Klansmen of their human sins. Much like fire purified the basest of metals, the purification process "burned off" vice, leaving only the glowing presence of virtue behind. An Exalted Cyclops reflected, "Who can look upon this sublime symbol, or sit in its sacred, holy light without being inspired with a holy desire and determination to be a better man? 'By this sign we conquer.'"[13] For the Exalted Cyclops, the cross inspired

Klansmen to become more religious, dedicated, and determined. The glowing light of the cross not only stirred members to be better men but also indicated their need to conquer forces opposed to them. To conquer, I think, was an obvious goal of the Klan. The order hoped to reconquer the nation in the name of Protestantism and "100% Americanism" and envisioned its battle as a crusade for the nation and its way of life. After all, members imagined themselves as Knights in white robes who marched under the glow of a burning cross. According to the *Night-Hawk*, Christ's light emanated from the fire, but the cross was also a sign that "rall[ied] the forces of Christianity" to conquer the "hordes of the anti-Christ," as well as the "enemies" of Americanism.[14] The artifact was both beacon and warning. For Klansmen, its glow provided comfort, but for those "enemies," the fire terrified.

The cross was explicitly bound to the cause of "100% Americanism." Its theology focused on the actions and death of Jesus as well as the exclusion of all those who were not (Protestant) Christian or American. Its glowing presence was an ominous signal to those who "threatened" the nation. The *Night-Hawk* claimed that the object was the "emblem of real Americanism" and "flashed its message of a Nation Reborn."[15] The "Nation Reborn" was one in which faith adhered to nation. The rebirth affirmed what Klansmen believed was the foundation of nation: white Protestantism. Faith built the exclusionary boundaries of its nation, which marked certain religious traditions and races as unable to assimilate. For the Klan, Catholics had allegiance to a foreign entity, the pope; Jews refused to assimilate; and African Americans were a "lesser" race that could never reach the great heights of the Anglo-Saxon. All of those groups proved threatening to the "glorious" nation. For Imperial Wizard Evans, a goal of the Klan was to preserve the "good government." He argued that preservation required "maintaining a Christian civilization in America." For Evans, "Pre-eminence is enjoined upon us by God and by our obligations to the world. If the Klan aspires to purify America and make her impregnable, it is not any selfish reason."[16] The reason, instead, was divinely ordained. America, in all its glory, needed to maintain its Protestantism or the future of the nation might be in peril. By wearing white robes and waving the flag under the light of the fiery cross, Evans and his Klan hoped to restore the faith in order to save America.

Their nation was in danger, and the only way to save it was to reconnect with the nation's religious foundations. The accounts of the flag and cross were purposeful discussions of what each should mean. Both artifacts articulated the Christianity of America to point citizens in the correct direction and to verse them in the Klan's ideology. To illuminate the correct path, the Klan defined its Americanism in opposition to cosmopolitanism in retellings of national history and in defense of the public schools.

*The Klan embodies the group mind of America.*[17]

In order to be a Klansman, a member had to follow the principles of "klannishness," which included patriotic, domestic, racial, and imperial klannishness. For patriotic klannishness, the Klansman had to devote himself to allegiance of pure Americanism, liberty, truth, and justice. According to Imperial instructions, "real, true Americanism unadulterated, [included] a dogged devotedness to our country, its government, its ideals and its institutions."[18] That nationalism required the uplifting of the country and government by all Klansmen, which also included the protection of the precious ideals. The order's message of Americanism contained menacing overtones because the nation appeared, at least to Klansmen, to be in grave danger. The speeches and articles of Imperial Wizard H. W. Evans tempered the hope present in the writings of Simmons. Evans feared the downfall of civilization and assessed the constant threats to American character. He argued, "We must look first at the crisis in our civilization, now near its height. Americans find today that aliens . . . instead of joining, challenged and attacked us. They seek to destroy Americanism." The nation was in crisis, and the Klan needed to confront those problems to save civilization and "the American stock." Evans continued, "The Klan embodies the group mind of America. It is representative of complete nationalism. It is not sectional, it is not personal, it is not selfish, it does not represent any private interest—it speaks for all America."[19] The Klan's goal was to be the voice of patriotism and to safeguard an imperiled nation. The order believed that it was representative of average Americans and their concerns.

Of course, the Klan was not representative of "all America." Instead, members presented their interests above the welfare of those who did not qualify as "true" citizens. Moreover, Evans characterized the Klan as the "group mind" of America, which suggested a collective spirit of all native-born citizens who molded their thoughts, actions, and words. Nationalism would not be effective without that group mind. Evans argued that America's particular nationalism contained six vital elements: the "fighting instinct," unity of kind, independence, public spirit, common sense, and conscience. Men of the "American race" were fighters who loved their "kind," meaning whites or Anglo-Saxons. The American was also inventive and independent, but that independence did not interfere with a sense of public responsibility. In regard to common sense, Evans penned, "Ours is no race to deal with fine spun theories, no race to allow our purposes to be thwarted."[20] And finally, conscience guaranteed the highest standards for home, faith, and nation. Those elements highlighted the superiority of both America and her people, but for the Imperial Wizard, the "Cosmopolitan movement" threatened her virtues.

"Cosmopolitanism" was an umbrella term for many of the movements that Evans and his Klan identified as threats. The term referred largely to various attempts to create understandings of a "citizen of the world unbounded" by national constraints.[21] For the order, Cosmopolitan movements included political ideologies (Communism, Socialism, and Anarchism) as well as religious traditions (Judaism and Roman Catholicism). For Evans, those Cosmopolitans all had group minds that proved oppositional to the American values. Evans relayed "four different types of people" who sought to destroy America: Jews, Celts, "Mediterranean peoples," and "Alpines." He noted material things consumed the Jews, who had their own form of ethnic and religious nationalism that trumped commitment to American nationalism. In his writing, the Celts, Mediterranean peoples, and Alpines were unstable, uneducated, and, above all, devoted to the Catholic Church. Because of their development in Europe, their lack of education, and their loyalty to the church, those groups differed too drastically from the American group mind, such that they could not assimilate to the norms and mores of the nation. Evans wrote, "The group minds of other races and other nations have developed differently from ours. Each nation has its own God-given qualities and its own mission."[22] Nationalism, then, was "the right of each nation to develop the genius and instincts with which God endowed its people." That understanding of nationalism uplifted patriotism, uniformity, common language, common religion, respect for the government, and common tradition as well as history. With his rendering of nationalism, Evans emphasized qualities that he thought were essential to the development and maintenance of a nation. Uniformity emerged as a necessity in order to avoid conflict and strife. He wrote, "True nationhood is essentially oneness of mind, and it recognizes certain beliefs held in common by its citizens. . . . No person who lacks them can be in harmony with the nation."[23]

Aliens, or foreigners, were the greatest threat to the unity of mind, or Americanism. For an Iowa Klansman, Americans were first and foremost nation builders; foreigners were not. Americanism fostered native-born Americans, and it was not was easily learned. He categorized an American as "one who lives in America, and lives for America and will die for America," and "whose oath of allegiance is to America above any other government, civil, political or ecclesiastical in the whole world."[24] "True" Americans upheld their country before other allegiances, and they were committed to fulfilling the destiny of the nation. Evans argued that Americanism "was bred into us—native, white, Protestant Americans—it was suckled with our mother's milk, absorbed in our homes, learned in our schools, breathed into the very air."[25] Americans were born, not naturalized. The Klan suggested that Americans could not be created through immigration legislation, since the group mind was akin to instinct. Klansmen knew American principles by nature and inheritance, which the order believed cemented members' roles as protectors of nation. The destiny of the nation depended on native-born Americans who had a clearer sense of their nationality.

That destiny included more than patriotic duty. It also included uniformity in (Protestant) Christianity and white supremacy. The Anglo-Saxon heritage of the Klan, and of America, directly resulted in the greatness of the nation, and racial purity ensured the maintenance and development of the group mind. Americanism, then, was not simply about democratic government but also about the racial superiority of whites. Aliens would destroy the group mind as well as democracy, a cherished American ideal. The Klan's vision was not pluralistic, for sure. The order noted that it was the representative of true Americanism. The Klan was "founded upon, and represents, those deep instincts and qualities of our race which have led us to high achievement." Klansmen also believed that their order was representative of the whole of Protestantism. Evans wrote: "This unity between Americanism and Protestantism is no accident. The two spring from the same racial qualities, and each is a part of our group mind. Together they worked to build America, and together they will work to preserve it. Americanism provides politically the freedom and independence Protestantism requires in the religious field."[26]

Protestantism was a central element of that form of Americanism because it proved essential in the creation of the nation. In addition, the religious movement helped define the all-important group mind. Freedom emerged politically from nation and religiously from Protestantism, a merger that produced the unique mind of Americans. Evans and Klansmen envisioned Protestantism as a major force in the history of the nation. They looked to its influence on the founders and other major historical actors as a sign of Providence in the formation of America. Americanism had sacred elements because God had made "the native Americans distinct from other peoples."[27] Americanism and Protestantism were unified because, at its core, America was a Protestant nation. To show that unity, the Klan strove to tell history in a way that reflected the divinity of the American mission.

*The soil of America was consecrated by the Pilgrim Fathers.*

A pamphlet entitled *The Menace of Modern Immigration* reported that God had favored America: "He [God] fashioned this land in surpassing beauty and placed in it and upon it a varied, exhaustless store of resources." The nation and its bounty remained hidden until the "best" settlers could arrive and cultivate the land. The pamphlet continued: "To this Eden journeyed the best and the bravest of the Old World. . . . There was a double refinement of these pioneer patriots, first through their strength and courage required for their emancipation abroad, and then in their triumph over the dangers and adversities of a virgin environment."

The focus on pioneer patriots, who conquered America with divine assistance, deemphasized the historical presence of indigenous peoples and the discovery of America by Christopher Columbus, a Catholic.[28] The pamphlet overlooked historical veracity to tell the story of America founded by patriots who were "physically, mentally and morally virile, with an inherent, kindred reverence for rightly established institutions."[29] The nation was a blank canvas ripe with possibility, which was painted skillfully by those settlers only. The "bane" of immigration had degraded the canvas, and the only way to restore the possibility and the beauty was for native-born Americans to realign with their destiny. Restoration and redemption lay in the hands of the native-born. Klan leaders, newspapers, pamphleteers, and ordinary members bore the responsibility of redemption. Through print media, the Klan avidly molded the history of the nation to reflect its values and concerns. The order sought to demonstrate that America, from inception, had been a Protestant nation and to illustrate how important historical actors held similar opinions to Klan leaders.

The *Imperial Night-Hawk* and its contributors analyzed the issue of Americanism and how it was intricately wed to the religious founding and destiny of the nation. In an article reprinted from the *American Standard*, the author reflected on the nature of 100 percent Americanism, and he produced a Christian foundation for that particular form of patriotism. He opined, "America's idealism, institutions, destiny, and affluence are written in the [B]ible, and upon this Book, the Work of God, America is founded." Americanism, then, was centered on the nation's religious foundation, and one could not be a citizen without recognizing that "truth." His article was a jeremiad, a lament about the decline of the nation and the forces aligning against it. For the author, the nation was in peril if Americans did not realize the sacred status of the peculiar place. All of the "great" documents (the Declaration of Independence, the Constitution, and the Monroe Doctrine) originated from the Bible, and "therefore these documents are the basis of the logic and demonstration of every American problem." Christianity thus permeated American culture, and the land became sacred as well. "The soil of America was consecrated by the Pilgrim Fathers with the words, 'IN THE NAME OF GOD, AMEN!'" The nation was exceptional in origin, doctrine, and even physical space. The distinctiveness did not entirely emerge from divine beginnings but rather from America's separation from the corruption of the "old world." The Monroe Doctrine proved significant because it "declare[d] the unique character of the American System and its inevitable separateness from the system of the old world." The author's emphasis alluded to his most important point: the labors of "white, Protestant, Anglo-Saxon Americans" created the country and nationalistic fervor.[30]

The greatest threat to the divine nation came from Old World machinations, in particular "the politico-ecclesiastical despotism of Europe" and "the Roman Catholic system of political control." The Roman Catholic political machine had an elaborate hierarchy: hundreds of thousands of lay members, Knights of Columbus, priests, "crafty Jesuits," cardinals, and a pope with the power to control them all. In the article, Roman Catholicism equaled tyranny and proved threatening to the promise of the New World. The author confirmed "the lives of the early fathers and their writings reveals [sic] that America was established by Christ . . . to put an end to 'their System' . . . Romanism." The Founding Fathers were opposed to that political system masquerading as religion. For America to survive and manifest her glory, Americans had to "break these alien bonds."[31] Divine providence was bound to the actions of white Protestant Anglo-Saxon Americans. In Klan retellings of American history, those true Americans were the heroes, and Catholics and others were excised from historical records. Americanism was Protestant Christian, and the order generalized the "forefathers" of the nation into Christian patriots.

For instance, an Arkansas Klansman presented the "builders" of America as "Christian pioneers." Those Christian men laid the foundations for all that was valuable in American life, including the freedom of speech and religion. For that Klansman, it was essential to look to the example of those founders because the nation was endangered. He wrote: "America is the great nation she is, because she was born of Christian ideals, and because she is in no small way moved by them. Take Christ out of America, and America fails! Take the freedom of the Protestant Christian religion from us and expect another St. Bartholomew's massacre."[32]

America was a nation that would suffer if Christianity was removed or denigrated. The Klansman noted the order's role to protect America from alien influences and preserve its Christian character. Not surprisingly, members observed similarities between their actions in the twentieth century and the actions of the forefathers. One Klansman observed that the Boston Tea Party might have been the "first Ku Klux Klan meeting on record." He reflected, "The members masked. They did a bit of night work, made an immense pot of tea, liberty tea at that. King George tried to break up the Klan."[33] The king, of course, did not succeed because of those patriots who masked themselves in the name of liberty. The task of the Klan, then, was to embrace the legacy of historical actors who molded the nation and its character. It did not just imagine historical actors as exemplars but also re-created various historical events to show continuities between those figures and the Klan.

In the October 1926 issue of the *Kourier*, W.A.H. compared H. W. Evans, the Imperial Wizard, to Abraham Lincoln to show striking commonalities in character. Both were "products of pioneer Americanism." They were fighters and leaders who preferred simple language. The author noted that both were fair. He affirmed, "Hiram Wesley Evans could well be called his [Lincoln's] reincarnation."[34] The purported eerie similarity was not as significant, however, as what Evans's relationship with Lincoln signaled. To make the comparison demonstrated that a Klan leader was wed to a quintessential American leader, which illustrated the Klan's ties with the mainstream as well as the order's place in American history. To further make the case, the *Imperial Night-Hawk* ran a series of articles about historical "One Hundred Percent Americans" that illuminated the resonance of Klan values with other influential historical figures. The Puritan sage, Jonathan Edwards, merited his own article, which emphasized his education, sermons, influence, and his removal from the Northampton pulpit. The *Night-Hawk* suggested, "Jonathan Edwards would have made a staunch Klansman" because "he preached the love of God." Moreover, he lived the Klansman's creed—"Be not overcome of evil, but overcome evil with good"—by not showing "any resentment" in his farewell sermon.[35] What was notable was not whether Edwards would have been a "staunch Klansman," though that might prove interesting, but rather that the weekly strove to convey his resonance with the order. Such was a blatant attempt not only to recraft historical actors to fit the Klan's mold but also to establish a longer historical lineage for the order. If the order and its members could trace the origins of its ideas to forefathers, the Pilgrims, Edwards, or even Lincoln, the Klan was the logical extension of mainstream cultural currents. The tactic gave the order cultural legitimacy and placed its members as the common inheritors of Americanism. In retelling history, Klan print culture crafted Klansmen and Klanswomen as the culmination of founding ideals, aspirations, and events. Those inheritors embodied the "legacy" of white Protestant Americans who created and fostered the nation from its earliest moments until the 1920s.

In that imagining of American history, the forefathers of the nation fought and spilled blood to create a country explicitly for native-born Americans. In a textbook for Klansmen entitled *Bramble Bush Government*, the author highlighted significant events and institutions for the country, including Moses's parting of the Red Sea, the settlement at Jamestown, the American Revolution, and the Civil War. Those events defined American character, and the parting of the Red Sea, I think, signified the divine heritage of the nation that could be traced from biblical origins. Each event proved notable because each was a moment in which Americanism was forged. Divine guidance, first settlements, and wars all changed the course of history, and the spilling of blood made values tangible and sacred. The bloodstained heritage made native-born Americans unique from their immigrant brethren because they were born and matured on consecrated soil. For the author, the native-born should have immense pride in their nationality and heritage because their nation was special and quite different. He wrote: "No people should be as proud of their heritage, their traditions and forbears as America's native sons. Why? Because in their veins run the courage of the Pilgrims, the bravery of Boone, the wisdom of Washington, sagacity of Franklin, the nobility of Lincoln and Lee. Surely the blood of kings and potentates could be no more royal."

Native-born Americans were part of an aforementioned legacy that made their nation singularly great, and they were to strive to preserve it from impurity. The author continued that the land, then, was not for "the refuse populations of other lands." The Pilgrim fathers worked and suffered to transform a "stern and rockbound coast" into a civilized country.[36] The "refuse" had not civilized the wilds of the nation: they hoped only to take advantage of the toil of the forefathers and pioneers. The author downplayed the fact that the builders of the nation, including the Pilgrims and the settlers of Jamestown, were immigrants as well. They were not born on native soil, yet those immigrants were coded as beneficial, while the other waves of immigration in the early twentieth century were viewed as "refuse." The early immigrants were transformed through alchemy. As soon as founding immigrants stepped foot on the soil that became America, they became the natural inhabitants of the land, which purified their Old World elements. The divinely crafted land was made just for them, and these "white, Protestant" settlers fashioned the nation. One of the faults of the founders was that they never created a movement to safeguard the nation; that responsibility became the burden of later generations.

The *Kourier* reported, "Our forefathers should have started a great Christian American citizen's movement, in connection with the new or American government. . . . But they did not do it, and the Klan got started very late in the process—but it is working day and night to save our civilization."[37] According to the monthly, the forefathers might have intended to create a movement that mimicked the order, but they did not. That responsibility, then, was left for the Klan. The creation of the order was fortuitous because the Klan and its leaders envisioned that they were continuing the mission of the founders to protect a white Protestant nation from the threats of Catholics, Jews, African Americans, and "hyphenated Americans." In the order's perusal of the American landscape, the providential nation was in threat of annihilation, and all along the landscape threats were apparent and imminent. They envisioned themselves as saviors of the nation, and the public schools quickly became a foremost battleground. By examining the Klan's dedication to the preservation of the Bible in the public school, one can see the order's commitment to a Christian nation and its rendering of national character. The threat to public education was essentially a threat to nation. To lose the schools would be a deathblow to the order's defenses. Schools trained future citizens, and the Klan wanted the public schools to remain firmly in the purview of white Protestants.

*The American Public School is the Safeguard of American Liberty.*[38]

Mrs. J. W. Northrup, a contributor to *The New Age*, lamented the decline of the public school, which she noted had to be "dear to all Americans." For Northrup, the public schools were "where tiny minds begin to soar, where great men and great women of this country first learn the alphabet that leads to fame." The public schools made children patriots, trained them for greatness, and informed them of the character of their nation. This patriotism, fostered and nurtured in the public school system, should have included Protestantism. Northrup's frustrated lamentation hinged on the lack of God in public education. She wrote vehemently: "Any intelligent Protestant knows when you educate a man to believe he can be saved without the living God, that he is *not* a true American citizen, for it is impossible to be true to this country and at the same time believe that his existence on earth and in eternity depends upon a foreign mortal. . . . Americans arouse yourselves; don't be cowards, for God hates nothing worse than cowardice."[39]

Mrs. Northrup's infuriated opinion piece crystallized the Klan opinion on the place of religion in public education. Her jeremiad was reprinted in full for the readers of the *Night-Hawk*. In her article, American citizenship was intimately bound to the belief in God, and American citizens could not be a people who believed instead in a foreign mortal (quite obviously the pope). Devotion was to be directed to divinity alone. She challenged her fellow Americans to move past their cowardice and protect "the little red schoolhouse." The Klan echoed Northrup's concern over public education in its print, and the order feared the removal not only of God from the schoolhouse but also the Word of God, the Bible. The public, or common, school became a sacred institution that inculcated children with a sense of American history, citizenship, and belief in God, and the Klan saw the public school as the front line to protect its threatened ideals.[40] In that battle, the order spilled much ink to show its textual community the danger to the public schools and the ramifications for its beloved nation.

Not surprisingly, the Klan's defense of the public school began with the forefathers of the nation. "The condition that existed in the early history of the Nation forced our forefathers to the conclusion that something must be done to unify the ideals of the people." The "early settlers" came to America for freedom and democracy, and thus they created a system that indoctrinated those principles and emphasized the unity of language. Moreover, the public school was instituted "so that the children of the rich and poor alike might have the same opportunity by being placed on a common level and so counteract that inequality with which birth or fortune otherwise produce." This ideal vision of the common school furnished opportunities to all children in spite of socioeconomic status and gave them a chance to absorb the value and character of America. It was equalizing, patriotic, and necessary. Yet this form of schooling did not materialize out of a vacuum; rather it had precedence within religious institutions. The *Kourier* observed that the earliest schools emerged from churches and that the schools in America "were clearly the fruits of the Protestant Reformation."

Specifically, the Reformation shifted the approach of schooling by uplifting the Bible as crucial to personal salvation. The reformers focused on personal salvation, which fostered the importance of personal responsibility, which stood in opposition to the "collective authority" of the Roman Catholic Church. More important, responsibility for one's salvation made reading a necessity because "one might know what the commands of God were and what was demanded of him."[41] If reading was essential for salvation, then schooling was required to train pupils in this religiously mandated skill. For the Klan, even the prominence of reading and schooling separated Protestants from Catholics. With reformers highlighting the need for schooling, the Pilgrims brought a commitment not only to religious freedom but also to education when they landed on American soil. They established homes free of "dictations of a paternalistic nature" and created "little town governments loosely bound together in colonial federations." Education was their project, which began as a voluntary endeavor and evolved into laws that "compelled children to be educated." For the monthly, the Pilgrims were essential to the development of American character because their "contribution" was an "institution so essential to her [America's] progress and welfare, The American Public School."[42]

The *Kourier* also examined the forefathers' contribution to the common school. The monthly reported that the forefathers "planned our public school system as one of the foundation stones of our liberties and claimed the right of the state to educate her children." The public school system was imperative to creating new American citizens well versed in the liberties they were guaranteed. That *Kourier* article did not focus on the religious basis for the school system but rather the function of schooling to create a solid American citizenship. The explicit aim of the institution was to foster "effective manhood and womanhood and prepare for good, useful citizenship in the various duties and callings of life." The school created good citizens, which affected the relationships of the nation to the rest of the world. The monthly argued that "the Public Schools of America have changed the mental equilibrium of the world" and produced "our best men, our strongest patriots, our sweetest daughters and our most devoted mothers."[43] Patriotism was a masculine act, but the schools also produced well-mannered daughters who became devoted mothers. The *Imperial Night-Hawk* lauded the public schools for evolving from the "schools of our fathers, wherein we taught the elements of education—loyalty to God and to our flag"—to more modern institutions. The common schools laid the foundation for patriotic citizenship. Schools taught children that God and flag were components of their lives and their future development. However, the Klan organ questioned the large amount of change in schooling and pondered, "Are our children developing Christian character? Are the right principles being brought to bear on their lives?"[44]

Modern schools appeared ill-equipped to replicate the values of the "schools of our fathers." The *Night-Hawk* called for school reform to align the current system with its predecessor, which emphasized loyalty to God and loyalty to nation. The development of the nation depended on children, and the *Kourier* noted, "The life blood of the Nation pulses no less in the veins of our children of the elementary school age, than those of adult life which fill the places of leaders, and of the rank and file in business, industry, commerce and professions."[45] The schools represented a safeguard to American ideals and liberties because those institutions inculcated a sense of nation in the young minds of their pupils. For the order, children became blank states to be molded into effective citizens in the venue of public education. Religious historian Robert Orsi noted, "Children represent the future of the faith standing there in front of oneself."[46] Children, then, were the new faithful, and they represented both peril and promise. In their small hands lay the fate of the faith and the nation. These small citizens had the ability to follow in the paths of their parents or shun them in favor of their own way. Children represented a future plagued with uncertainty. For the Klan, children embodied the future of the national ideals, and children proved to be a valuable resource for creating the nation that the order wanted. It is not surprising that the government did not necessarily educate children "for their own sake, but also for its own." Education molded the young minds in the dictates, values, and history of the nation, and the Klan wanted to make sure that what children were being taught resonated with the Klan's vision of America. Children were symbols of a future, and the order strove to influence public education to reinstate a Protestant Christian America in the minds and hearts of the nation's young citizens.

For Imperial Wizard Evans, children were "the greatest asset to the state" and the "hope for a glorious national future." The development and grandness of the nation rested on the small shoulders of American children, and the Klan's energies focused on those children learning certain historical events in the hopes of producing legions of patriotic children who would become patriotic adults. Evans continued, "What nation shall be the greatest among the nations of the 'New World'? That nation shall be the greatest that puts children first in its thought, in its politics, in its economics, in its ethics. The nation that accepts the leadership of little children."[47] The children were to be both immigrant and native-born, and their schooling would guarantee the nation's legacy.

The centrality of this legacy meant the Klan complained about educational funding, as it was so small compared with the benefits of enriched, future citizenship. In 1924 the Klan supported a law in Congress that would guarantee "every child, native, naturalized and foreign," would receive "a common school education." The Klan was not as progressive as it might have seemed. For the foreign children, the goal was "equipping these future citizens with the proper material for successful co-operation of American children in . . . the affairs of the country."[48] With the order's support of the educational bill, Klansmen assumed that Protestant native-born children would be more privileged. The Klan contributor opined, "It is natural to assume that the Protestant children of the United States will receive proper attention and adequate tutors will be provided with funds supplied by Federal authorities."[49] The equalizing vision of the early public school disappeared because of the overwhelming desire to protect white Protestant America. Protestant children were the backbone of the nation, and they were to be treated as such.

Yet those "little children" were not to be leaders in their own right. Rather, they were to be groomed by public education to be obedient, strong, patriotic, and devoted citizens. The Klan strove to craft the public education system to produce forbearers of nationhood. Upon small shoulders rested the fate of the nation, and the order did not take the situation lightly. Its anxiety over the school reflected paranoia about what would happen to the nation if the schools did not represent the intentions of the forefathers or Pilgrims. What would happen to the nation if the burden was too great for "little children"? The emphasis on child-citizens and their schooling highlighted the Klan's concerns about the absence of the Bible in schools and about the parochial school. Education inculcated nationalism, and the removal of the sacred text and the movement of students into parochial schools suggested that the Klan's preferred form of nationalism might be undercut or, more dramatically, attacked.

Education, in addition to patriotic leanings, was to provide moral teachings, in particular "the revealed will of the Bible," because a biblical focus would "make good citizens and will best promote the interests of the institutions under which they live and for which they are responsible hereafter."[50] For the Klan, the Bible, then, was not just central to public education; it was a necessity. Children could not fully become (Protestant) American citizens without biblical instruction.[51] The Klan's concern over the Bible in the public school arose over what the order perceived as threats to common schooling. Some wanted to remove the Bible from the curriculum, while others removed their children from the public school in favor of "sectarian" education. In an article titled "Patriotism" the author tackled the issue of the Bible in the public schools as a part of his system of nationalism. He wrote, "If we would keep this land of the free we must extend Christian principles. Let us keep the Bible in schools."[52] A *Kourier* contributor, a self-proclaimed former educator, explained why the Bible was so important. The Bible was "holy inspiration of the word of God to man as a guide . . . so regarded by all denominations of Christians." However, creeds and dogmas, according to the author, should be left out of the schools and instead taught in the home. For the "retired teacher," biblical instruction made good moral citizens dedicated to American institutions. He could not fathom why "one denomination alone objects to the reading of the Bible in the public schools" and how that objection caused the removal of the sacred text in many instances. The retired teacher wanted the text returned to the schools, so children would "become acquainted with their relations and obligations to the Creator." Additionally, he derided critics by noting that the Bible was not a "sectarian book," but rather that men placed sectarian theories upon it. The Bible was the center of the Christian faith, and the teacher did not see why Bible reading in schools would cause controversy. The contributor either lacked knowledge of the Douay-Rheims Bible, the Catholic Bible, or he did not consider anything other than the King James Bible to be a Bible per se. For opponents, it was a sectarian text—more specifically, a Protestant text. For the teacher and the Klan, the Bible was "the foundation upon which civilization itself and National liberty are based; it is more. It is the only guide that man has to lead him upward to God. Without it the future is all darkness and the present all gloom. It is the ray of light emanating from the throne of God that illuminates the destiny of man beyond the grave."[53]

This sacred text was a necessity for education because civilization and national liberty were at stake with its removal. The character of nation would be changed not for the better but to reflect the concerns of one denomination, Catholicism. The Klan did not acknowledge the concern that a generalized Protestantism might indoctrinate Catholic children. The nation had caved to sectarian interests instead of uplifting the nation's heritage and the lineage of the common school. Moreover, the foundation of religion and nationalism civilized children. Because of the emphasis on education as civilizing, Imperial Wizard Evans noted that the public school could provide an aid to the lawlessness that he believed was overrunning the country. Evans lamented that the public schools no longer followed the approach of Horace Mann, a prominent educational theorist. Mann, "the immortal sponsor and patron saint of education in America, believed that *national safety, prosperity and happiness could all be attained through free public schools, open to all, good enough for all and attended by all."* If public education had followed Mann's direction, Evans believed that the nation would be free of anarchy and crime. The schools in their longevity had become somehow inadequate. The Imperial Wizard voiced his concerns that the schools "have not the institutional standing to which they are entitled; they do not prevent illiteracy, not always promote patriotism; too often they teach a divided allegiance."[54] The schools had been corrupted, and the removal of the Bible was only a piece of the puzzle. The Klan's enemies surrounded the sacred institution.

J. S. Fleming, a Klan author, reported, "Our enemies would bar Jesus Christ and His Bible from our public schools, in order that we may forget them and thus enable aliens to cunningly substitute the pope and his creed as our God and Guide." Without the Bible as guidance, Fleming was afraid that immigrants might be able to subvert "traditional" American culture by focusing on the pope and Roman Catholicism. Fleming conveyed the magnitude of Bible reading as part of common education, as did the contributors to the *Kourier*. He contended that the biggest threat to education was Roman Catholicism. Fleming wrote, "Subjects of the Roman Catholic government cannot avail themselves the benefits of our American public schools on account of the contaminating influence of religious heresy over their children." In Fleming's opinion, Catholic worldview contaminated children, and the public school might not prove effective for them. Like Evans had maintained, those children faced a "divided allegiance." Catholic students would not have the experience of public education because they were enrolled in parochial schools operated by the church. The parochial school was particularly offensive to Fleming because Catholic religious tenets were taught there, and the Bible was supposedly missing "because it is dangerous to the moral and religious welfare of the children of its subjects." Fleming did not acknowledge that the Catholics used their own Bible, the Douay-Rheims, which shows at best a lack of understanding about Catholic worship and practice. The crux of the issue for the author was that Catholic parochial schools, which taught Catholicism, were receiving some funding from the government. Fleming lamented that the government "cannot yet legally force loyal Americans to pay for the training of children into a religious hatred of everything American."[55] The Klan envisioned the parochial school as a vehicle that might destroy national character because Catholic children were not being taught the correct form of American citizenship.

For the order, the parochial school was an affront on American culture. For one missionary, the Roman Catholic Church was replacing the necessary state education with Catholic forms of education. The missionary argued, "Evidently Rome believes that there is a radical difference between Catholic education and that given by the civil government, else her leaders would not be so bitterly opposed to the public schools." What most concerned the writer was the "obvious" plot by Catholics to put American children in parochial schools and then to take over the educational system as a whole. Catholics obeyed the pope, and their priests "[forbade] their members to send their children to our schools," as well as threatened "them with hell-fire" if parishioners sent their children to public schools.[56] The writer envisioned Catholics as oppositional to the ideals of democratic government and questioned their ability to maintain parochial schools. Sectarian schooling was unnecessary since state schools were created with the explicit purpose of educating the nation's children and youth. Parochial schools supposedly taught papal infallibility, ecclesiastical law over civil law, "inferior" moral codes, and limited subject matter.

The missionary warned, "We have only to wait until they have duly trained five or ten millions of their youth to find ourselves worm-eaten with a close-knit constituency pleaded to a system of politics which is entirely subversive of our liberties." In the order's thinking, the parochial schools were breeding grounds for un-American ideas and foreign allegiances, and those schools created youth and children versed in an alien religious system. The Catholic Church and its schools were, then, a direct menace to the Klan's America. The "Romish education" robbed the government's right to educate children and taught "immorality and anti-democratic doctrine." Moreover, Catholic teachers could not be trusted in the public schools because of their allegiance to their church. The missionary ended his article by affirming that "no Protestant Church holds or teaches such anti-democratic and iniquitous doctrines."[57] What becomes clear is that the missionary, like many other contributors to Klan newspapers, believed that Catholicism was an inherent threat to the nation. Catholics did not use the same Bibles as Protestants, and they often educated their children in parochial schools rather than the public schools. Their children, thus, were pedagogically dissimilar to Protestant American children, and future generations of citizens would not be trained on how to be citizens by the common school. How could Catholics and their children be trusted? They did not absorb the mandated patriotism of the public schools, nor were they aware of whom the "forefathers" were. Catholic opposition to common schooling was coded as an enemy's attack on sacred liberties. For the Klan, those Catholics preferred not only the degradation of public education but also the destruction of national foundations.[58]

Despite the Klan's attempts to present the parochial school as opposed to citizenship and real Americanism, Catholics envisioned the parochial school as "a solid bulwark of good citizenship." Writing in *Our Sunday Visitor*, T. L. Bouscaren presented the Catholic concern with the public schools in similar terms to the order. For Bouscaren, the problem with common schooling was that it excluded religious instruction because those schools were open to all citizens. Since a variety of students from diverse religious backgrounds attended school together, teachers could not force a particular religious belief on them. He wrote: "Americans have always been, and are still a religious people. Even in the public schools, many of the most prominent teachers and directors have been either ministers of religion or at least sincere and earnest Christians. They would be shocked at the idea of regarding religion of Christ as something un-American."

For the Jesuit, religion was not antithetical to Americanism but rather a crucial part of nationalism. The problem was in the public schools' attempts to be nonsectarian. Excluding religion proved detrimental for students and the nation. That absence of religion was why Catholics preferred parochial schools for their children—they guaranteed that their children would receive needed religious instruction. Bouscaren noted, "The public schools would be better and truly American if they included much-needed religious instruction."[59] American citizenship still needed religion from a Catholic perspective, and the public schools were sorely lacking. In spite of the similar concerns about the absence of religious instruction, the Klan did not see the parochial schools as beneficial for the nation. In addition, the order believed Protestantism to be the only religious tradition bound to patriotism. Bouscaren supported the place of religion in schools, but only if Catholic students learned about Catholicism and other students learned about their own faith traditions. For the Klan, that was not a viable plan because students then would not have access to the white Protestant version of American history. In Oregon, Klansmen mobilized around the issue of compulsory public education to combat the influence of the parochial school. In 1922 the Oregon Klans supported a statewide initiative that required attendance at state schools.[60] The hope was to diminish the impact of the parochial school and bolster the beloved public school. Americanism was defined in general Protestant terms, and the school proved to be the battlefield not just for local communities but also for the larger nation.

*The spirit of Americanism and the spirit of Protestantism are one and the same.*

For the Klan, "The spirit of Americanism and the spirit of Protestantism" were not just similar but "one and the same."[61] To protect America required a defense of Protestantism against all those reprehensible forces that would weaken or denounce the faith. The Klan's attack on immigration, its religious intolerance of Catholics and Jews, and its campaign to keep the Bible in the public schools emerged because of concerns about the relationship between faith and nation. Immigration introduced millions of non-Protestants into American culture, and the Klan feared that those immigrants might not assimilate to the Klan's version of American culture. Evolution was blasphemy in the face of God, and the Bible belonged in the schools because good citizens needed to experience God as part of their patriotism. Many of the Klan's "enemies" of Americanism were supposed enemies of the predominantly Protestant culture of 1920s America. Protestantism was an essential facet of the Klan as a movement, and it shaped the order's approach to the nation and the many different peoples within it. American culture was changing, and the Klan wanted to save its vision of the *only* America, white and Protestant. For Imperial Wizard Simmons, "The cross of Christ must be exalted and sustained, or our splendid civilization might be doomed."[62] America's fate was intimately wed to the place of Protestantism in the nation. For Imperial Wizard Evans, the only choice to protect America was for Klansmen to step forward, proclaim their religion, and protect their nation. The Klan was needed to "sound continuously its certain Protestant note in this Protestant country." Evans wrote: "The Klansmen of the nation, unafraid and undeterred, strong in their faith in God, cherishing an open Bible, loyal to the Klansman's Christ, firmly believing in the principles taught by Him, *rejecting all traditions and opinions of men contrary to His teachings*, will continue to contend to establish these principles in *Protestant America*."[63]

Exclusion and homogeneity defined both faith and nation. The Klan's virtues and theologies hinted at the more nefarious side of the organization. The order hoped to be the savior of the nation, "a civic Messiah" to lead Protestant Americans in their reclamation of America.[64] To save the nation, the Klan defined the nature of true Americanism, in opposition to all groups who were not white and Protestant, and retold American history with a selective sampling. It also fought fiercely to keep the Bible in schools. To protect the nation, the order felt it must keep the country Christian in the face of foreign as well as domestic threats. The Klan envisioned members as Christian knights defending faith, nation, womanhood, and the race in the battle against all of its enemies. They strove to preserve the white Protestant nation and the order's enduring vision at all costs, but masculinity and manliness could not solve the problem confronting the second order. The challenge to the Klan's vision was already in place, and encroaching diversity of religion and race made its white Protestant America tenuous at best.

# CHAPTER 3 *"God Give Us Men"*: The Klan's Christian Knighthood

*God give us men, sun-crowned and strong, with their heads above the fog.*
*Give us men whose hearts beat true to the principles of personal decency*
*and whose souls are filled with the love of Jesus Christ.*
*Remove from our makeup the bane of human selfishness*
*and broaden our usefulness to God and man.*
—IMPERIAL NIGHT-HAWK (1923)[1]

*Dear Lord, help me to do all I can*
*To raise my boy to be a real man*
*Who is kind to children, gentle to the old*
*Who loves his friends and God more than gold*
*To keep him brave and sweet and clean*
*Never stoop to do a thing that's mean*
*To teach him to love this land so dear*
*And if ever it need be in time of strife*
*To defend his Country—with his life.*
—MRS. P. B. WHALEY (1923)[2]

In the *Dawn*, a Klan publication from Chicago, a Klan cartoonist sketched a challenge to fellow Protestants. His cartoon, "The 'Man on the Fence' Becomes Uncomfortable," depicted "Mr. Weak Kneed Protestant," a dejected figure sitting on a fence with his head in his hands. On one side of the fence, Klan figures represented the different facets of "100% Americanism," including liberty, white supremacy, protection of womanhood, Christianity, law, and freedom. On the other side of the fence were supposed Americans, enemies in disguise, from Catholics and "Negroes" to "corrupt politicians" and "bootleggers." The anonymous cartoonist chided the weak-kneed Protestant, who lacked the "courage and faith to join the ranks of those whose strength he doesn't know." The popular opposition to the Klan confused the poor fence straddler. Yet the caption reassured: "Fortunately there are not many real men in the position of Mr. Weak Kneed Protestant. The REAL men have long since decided that sitting on the fence is not the place for a native born, protestant Gentile."[3] For the *Dawn* and the cartoonist, the message could not be clearer: real Protestants were *real* men who belonged to the Klan. The enemies of American culture, illustrated or in the flesh, did not sway them. Real men did not sit on the proverbial fence about the order.

The miserable cartoon figure signaled the trajectory of uncertainty and ambivalence about the Klan. The *Dawn* proclaimed, "If you are on the fence[,] get off today. Don't be like Mr. Weak Kneed Protestant."[4] A Louisiana Klansman continued the *Dawn*'s attack by targeting not only the weak-kneed Protestants but also the "'jelly-bean' Americans [who] are willing to forego [*sic*] Bible reading in the public school, surrender their religious convictions and, if necessary, deny Jesus Christ to avoid offending the Roman Catholics and the Jews." According to the Louisianan, what America really needed was the Klan's form of manhood. The Klansman was not just "a one hundred percent American, but an honest law abiding Christian gentleman and a real 'he-man.'"[5] The order attempted to make Klansmen who were strong patriots and dedicated Protestants to protect the order's faithful nation. They remade knighthood and their savior, Jesus, to showcase the importance of manliness in nation with both weak-kneed Protestants and effeminate enemies. The order was clearly a continuation of muscular Christianity and fraternal norms. Through discussions of Jesus, martyrdom, militarism, and boyhood, the Klan argued that masculinity was essential not only to the order but also to the defense of Protestantism and the American nation. Christianity created and informed Klan masculinity; Klansmen were to be Christian Knights who protected the high ideals of the order. The textual community was to be faithful, patriotic, and manly. Yet both men and boys struggled to meet the Klan's expectations of exemplary Christian knighthood.

*To become Christian "knights" in a brotherhood.*

An ex-minister, William Simmons, was the architect of the 1920s Klan. His inspiration appeared in the form of D. W. Griffith's film *Birth of a Nation* (1915), based on Thomas Dixon's *The Clansman* (1905), a romanticized rendition of the Reconstruction Klan. Simmons dreamed of a supreme fraternity.[6] Influenced by the success of Dixon's novel and its film adaptation, Simmons drew figures of Klansmen, created a new organizational structure based on the previous Reconstruction order, and developed new terminology for the fraternity.[7] When he regained his health, Simmons constructed a new Ku Klux Klan in 1915. Simmons and later Imperial Wizard Hiram Wesley Evans culled their membership from the white middle class: bankers, lawyers, dentists, doctors, ministers, businessmen, and teachers. Religiously, Klan members were Baptists, Methodists, Church of Christ, Disciples of Christ, and United Brethren, as mentioned before.[8] The order was critical of liberal Protestantism—in particular, the feminized Christ they believed it engendered. The Klan spanned the rural and urban South, the urban North, the Midwest, and even the Pacific Northwest. Klansmen and Klanswomen appeared much like their neighbors but were more than willing to express their disdain with the larger nation.

The order proclaimed allegiance to 100 percent Americanism, Protestantism, the purity of white womanhood, white supremacy, and democracy. The order mobilized around those campaigns, and Klan newspapers urged members to fight for the order's beloved nation and protect her from all of America's supposed enemies. For this fight to be successful, the order required dedicated white Protestant men and women. The Protestant men belonged to an order that claimed auxiliary status for Protestant churches. A Louisiana Klansman remarked that one of the chief aims of the Klan was "to bring the different branches of the Protestant church into a closer relationship with one another as well as to preserve the United States as a Protestant Christian nation."[9] To accomplish that task, the Klan sought to make members more devoted to their personal Protestantism.

The *Imperial Night-Hawk* proclaimed "one of the foremost duties of a Klansman [was] to worship God."[10] Klansmen were to be religious and dedicated to their churches. "Every Klansman should have a Bible in his home[,] and he and his family should read it."[11] Membership in the Klan improved a member's interaction with his church, his family, and his country. For "no man can be a good Klansman and not be a better citizen and a more consistent Christian by the experience."[12] A leader from Texas noted, "Klansmen are taught that they become much better Klansmen if they attend divine services regularly with their wives and families and support the Sunday Schools of their city."[13] An anonymous author asked, "How can any man presume to call himself a one hundred per cent Protestant if he does not give one hundred per cent support to Protestant churches?"[14] Worship made Klansmen familiar with some form of Protestantism and possibly more willing to campaign for a united faith.

If Klansmen became more masculine and religious through their interactions with the order, opponents of the order were neither religious nor masculine. The Klan emasculated opponents in print. The *Kourier* derided proponents of tolerance as those with "dulcet voices of flattery" who indulged in "pious platitudes" while "folding" their hands. For the order, tolerance was "the free, frank, manly, clear-eyed facing of facts, issues, and conflicts and disagreements without frenzy, prejudice or fanaticism."[15] Since Klansmen were manly and analytical, their opponents were weak, frenzied men who either lacked the ability to be manly or willingly stood against the Klan's ideology (which signaled a lesser form of masculinity).

The masculine ideal avoided weakness by emulating a manly Jesus and chivalrous knights of lore. The Klan was, after all, a fraternity, and the Knight was its fraternal symbol of choice. The order had all the trappings of a fraternity from extensive ritual to elaborate costume and symbology to an obsession with secrecy. According to Mark C. Carnes, fraternities allowed men to journey from the realm of childhood into the realm of manhood through ritual. Though Carnes primarily explored the world of nineteenth-century fraternal orders, his understanding of those orders was that they primarily served to instill masculinity and to transition young men into manhood. Such was accomplished through ritual that rehashed familiar religious norms, which, in Carnes's example, was evangelical Christianity.[16] Carnes affirmed the widespread appeal of fraternal orders for American men: by the turn of the twentieth century between 15 and 40 percent of men belonged to orders.[17] The fraternity offered a sacred space for men to avoid the "feminized" religion of the Victorian Age.

The second incarnation of the Klan in the 1920s embraced the fraternity as a realm in which men could reaffirm their religious faith and their patriotism in the face of an ever-changing world. Cloaked in secrecy and filled with ritualism, Klan members became real men. White American men found a sacred space that confirmed their fears and

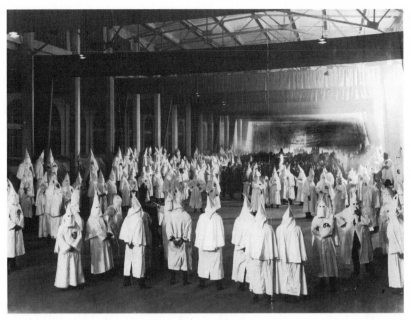

Klan group photo. Courtesy of University of Georgia Hargrett Library, Athens.

hopes for the nation and allowed them to reclaim a "militant" spirituality that they believed was lost. In the guise of Christian knighthood, Klansmen became the exemplars of American ideals.[18] The Knight, in white robe with face covered, became the symbol of the order as well as the ideal for manly behavior. The Knight was chivalrous yet militant and dominating because, above all else, he was a symbolic figure of a soldier and protector. Robert J. Higgs argued that in both European and American history, the Christian knight functioned as a masculine archetype who fought and won both physical battles and the battle of beliefs and ideals.[19] The Klan was not necessarily a physical army; rather, they were locked in a clash of wills against "weak-kneed Protestants," Catholics, Jews, and African Americans. These enemies wanted the destruction of the nation and the degradation of the national (Protestant) religion. Similar to Carnes's example of preceding fraternities, the Knights of the KKK also feared that its religiosity was in danger of becoming effeminate and soft.

The Klan continued calls for a "muscular Christianity," though the members and leadership never specifically used the phrase. The hey-day of muscular Christianity was 1880–1920. The proponents of the movement lamented the more visible place of women in society and feared "feminization" of religion and society.[20] The Men and Religion Forward movement (1911–1912) emphasized "More men for religion. More religion for men."[21] They sought to masculinize religion from the clutches of overly sentimental women and the ministers who catered to them. The unifying assertion of muscular Christians, ranging from the Men and Religion Forward movement to Bruce Barton and Billy Sunday, was that Christianity needed to be more masculine. In particular, Jesus should not be portrayed as a soft, feminine savior. Billy Sunday, the "baseball evangelist," emphasized that Jesus was the "Manly Redeemer" and perhaps the "greatest scrapper that ever lived." According to Stephen Prothero, Sunday derided the "sissified Jesus of the feminized crowd."[22] For muscular Christians, Jesus became the ideal of Christian manhood: a hardworking carpenter and a fighter. Even the Social Gospeller Walter Rauschenbusch called for men "to become Christian 'knights' in a brotherhood." They were to fight "on behalf of their women, their families, their country, and their Savior" to "achieve a just social order they called the Kingdom of God."[23] Rauschenbusch's Christian knights fought to protect their society, their religion, and their nation from forces that opposed them. The Klan's Christian Knights sought to protect their homes, country, and God as well, though their Kingdom of God was not Rauschen-busch's. Rather, the Klan embraced the masculine ideals found in both Protestant Christianity and in nationalism to proclaim its vision of what American society should and should not be.

The Klan's manly Jesus resonated with muscular Christianity. Jesus' act of self-sacrifice became the penultimate representation of a "real" man. Klan martyrs laid down their lives for the Klan's twin messages of Protestantism and nationalism. The martyrs, like Jesus, were symbols of Klan manhood that each member was supposed to emulate. Militarism pervaded the structure of the order. Leaders described Klansmen as members of a "crusading army." Masculinity and militarism were intimately bound together in the hierarchical structure of the order and informed understandings of how Klansmen should act.

*The living Christ is a Klansman's criterion of character.*[24]

In the *Kourier* the pseudonymous "G.W.W." proposed, "God wants men." For G.W.W., even God had criteria for acceptable masculinity for Christian men. The divine "measurement of a man" required faith, patience, courage, sweetness, and fairness. Not surprisingly, those were all similar traits to the Klansman's ideal man.[25] Klansmen needed faith in God and faith in their own abilities. Patience would allow the Klansmen to wait for the reforms that they were trying to cause, which would require sacrificing both their time and energy. Courage was the requirement to keep up the long fight rather than giving up in the face of opposition and criticism. Klansmen should also "keep sweet," which meant they should watch their tongues by being kind rather than caustic. Sweetness was the only "measure" that did not seem to fit within the order's conceptions of manhood, because the term usually signaled effeminacy. The focus on sweetness, however, allowed G.W.W. to warn members to watch their words and actions because they represented the order. Sweetness was the temperament that they all were expected to cultivate to guarantee good public behavior. Members also promoted fairness, because "the real man, the real citizen in the truest sense, the true Klansman, will not stoop to little and the low and the vile."[26] G.W.W. emphasized that Klansmen should follow the example of Christ as practicing Christians. He wrote, "You cannot get too much of God in your life, if you intend to make the emblem of the sacrifice of His Son your standard."[27] Klansmen needed God in their lives, and Jesus was their moral example. His example was the standard by which Klansmen could judge their behaviors, but that model proved to be an unreachable ideal to match.

Jesus was selfless, benevolent, and patriotic, the model of manhood. W. C. Wright, a Klan minister, congratulated Klansmen on their "manly decision to forsake the world of selfishness and fraternal alienation" by joining the order. He also urged members to embrace the example of Jesus, "the Klansman's criterion of character." For Wright, Jesus established a pattern for Christian manhood, which included courage, compassion, chivalry, and sacrifice. "Christ was a man of honor," so Klansmen were to be honorable. Wright pointed to Jesus' courage when he drove the money changers out of the temple. For the author, Jesus did not flinch at that duty, nor did he fear the outcome. Wright asserted, "Christ was the living example of moral manhood. . . . His life was clean, chaste and pure as any woman. He never swore or cursed, by taking God's name in vain." The minister continued, "We blush to admit that Klansmen too often indulge in such things. . . . We have heard Klansmen curse like troopers. Klansmen, lest we forget, let's remember Christ and His moral example."[28] Wright chastised members using Jesus' example as a corrective to their own bad behaviors. He chided them into being manly. The Klan's Jesus was strong, full of conviction, courageous, and fearless, and he was the epitome of Klan manhood.

Moreover, the Imperial Wizard Evans, Simmons's successor, and his Klansmen balked at the representations of Jesus in larger culture. They believed that the "popular conception" of Jesus did not match with his biography. Evans wrote:

> The usual picture of the Christ is effeminate, whereas the word-pictures of Him in the New Testament reveal a virility which challenges the admiration of all who place themselves in a position to comprehend it. Jesus was a robust, toil-marked young man who conserved both His physical and mental strength—in our modern way of putting it, "He was fit." In other words, He was prepared for life—able to think straight, to hold His propensities in leash, to endure the strain of arduous service, to bear the burden of trial.

Jesus was "a man among men," able to handle any situation with which he was presented. He was not "effeminate" or weak. He was a man of thought as well as action. Evans continued, "Jesus was The Man—full orbed." For the Klan, Jesus was a reformer as well as a virile savior. By using his example, Klansmen could "dethrone Wrong and enthrone Right," but the "initial task" of the order was to make "bright and attractive its own manhood." The Imperial Wizard Evans worried about false representations of manhood. He was afraid that most men did not look to Jesus as an exemplar man, but rather they saw manliness represented in vice. Drinking, cheating (in politics or business), and bullying were supposed hallmarks of masculinity. Additionally, those men also used profanity and told "licentious" stories.

That, for Evans, was false manhood and the "lowest culture."[29] In her study of evangelical men in revolutionary Virginia, Janet Lindman Moore noted the need for evangelical men to assert new forms of masculinity to counter public expectations of masculine behavior. In Virginia, masculine reputation was wed to the public sphere and public expectations of men, which included racing, drinking, or gambling, and any men who did not live up to these expectations were regarded with suspicion. Those religious dissenters added manly characteristics to their religious experience. The white male evangelicals created masculine archetypes of suffering saints and Christian soldiers, and the new form of evangelical manhood focused on the ability to abstain from worldly pleasures and behaviors. For Lindman, those white men molded evangelicalism to complement their role in society. This re-creation of manliness led to the popularity of dissenting Christianity because it affirmed the role of white men in society.[30] Evans's rhetoric of manliness echoed these earlier attempts to re-create Christian manhood. Evans's description of false manhood functioned as a foil for the behavior of Klansmen, who were supposed to be Christian knights.

Thus, real men discarded debauchery and embraced the example of Jesus. Evans believed that his Christian Knights represented the Christian soldiers mentioned in the Book of Revelation. Those soldiers marched "through the centuries—at war with the evil in their own inclinations and in the world about them." More important, aware of their baser tendencies, they fought valiantly against them.[31] Evans's Christian soldiers mimicked the path of Jesus and the figures in Revelation who would do away with evil in the world. Biblical text foretold Evans's order, and through dedicated manhood and the example of Christ, his white-robed soldiers could right the wrongs of the world.

Other Protestants did not generally accept the Klan's Christianity and rendering of Jesus, and the *Christian Century,* the liberal, nondenominational journal, took offense at the Klan's purported faith. Sherwood Eddy, in a piece on the Klan for the *Century,* labeled the order both a "prostitution of 'Protestantism'" as well as a "travesty of 'Pure Americanism.'"[32] Despite the criticisms and condemnations of the order, the contributors to the journal created a similar understanding of a masculine Jesus.[33] The renderings of Jesus in the *Imperial Night-Hawk* and *Kourier* resounded in the pages of the *Century.* Both sought

a masculine Jesus to counter effeminate portrayals of their savior.[34]
James I. Vance argued that art moved one away from "the virile and
rugged simplicities" of Jerusalem and even feminized the crucifixion
with halos and radiance rather than its gruesome reality. Art removed
the blood and toil from the cross, which eliminated the brutality of Jesus' sacrifice. For Vance, Christianity was a "rugged religion," and he
feared that Christianity might become "so soft, so artistic, so dilet-
tante, so lacking in grim reality, so empty of the rich red blood of Calvary." Vance, similar to muscular Christians, asserted the inherent
masculinity of the faith and critiqued the sallow and soft understanding that was supposedly predominant in American culture. Moreover,
he noted that Jesus "never meant for his disciples to dwindle down
into a race of relic-hunters and site worshippers."[35] Vance's Christianity was rugged and masculine in comparison to the soft and effeminate
Catholicism apparent in the use of relics and pilgrimage. Catholicism,
thus, created the lingering effeminacy of Christianity, and Vance countered the Church's influence by lauding a masculine Christ and the return of the rugged religion. Looking at the history of the tradition, he
documented the religion's "red-blooded virtues," which included
"common honesty, unpurchasable integrity, uncompromising conviction, zeal for righteousness, and a devotion to truth which does not
back down at death." Such faith also demanded duty, even if it required sacrifice, and heroism produced a certain kind of saint, one
who was not "a sallow face under a dim halo, but a heart courageous
and a soul heroic."[36] Jesus was a hero who should have been venerated
as such.

Other contributors to the *Century* emphasized the courage and wisdom of Jesus, and some warned against the "dangers of softness" for
men.[37] What became clear to one contributor was that Jesus served as
the medium for "each culture and civilization . . . to authenticate its
most cherished ideals."[38] In a critique of Bruce Barton's *The Man Nobody Knows* (1925), the *Century* derided Barton's conception of Jesus as
a "regular he-man" who "loved outdoor life." Barton's Jesus became a
hero of "physical vitality" as well as an exemplary advertising execu-
tive.[39] To illuminate the masculinity of Jesus meant his religious principles were diluted. The *Century* contributor found the masculine Jesus to be troubling rather than inspiring or comforting. Another

*Century* contributor, Kirby Page, challenged the notion of whether Jesus could be a model patriot, much less a beacon of manliness. Page explored Jesus' commitment to his race as well as his commitment to freedom. Moreover, the author argued that Jesus relied on love and forgiveness as part of his ministry. For Page, Jesus could not be a patriot if patriotism was defined in a "narrow nationalistic and militaristic sense." However, if patriotism was understood as the "love of one's countrymen and devotion to the highest ideals of one's nation," then Jesus could be patriotic. Page continued that for "real Christians," patriotism required "genuine affection for one's people" and "wholehearted allegiance to the noblest ideals of one's nation." Page envisioned a patriotism of love rather than hate, and he admitted that patriotism had been "prostituted to unholy ends."[40]

The patriotism of Jesus would not allow hate, evil, or revenge but would model the actions of the savior, including suffering, humiliation, and possibly death. The Klan defined its patriotism in a similar way and understood its actions as devotion to the country and beloved faith. Jesus was a patriot for the Klan as well. Yet I am not sure that Page would have found correspondence between his rendering of Jesus and the order's. The order's focus on devotion to country and religion through the exclusion of others would have struck Page as harmful. Thus, the rhetoric of manly Christianity and Christ by some contributors did not imply that the *Century* understood Jesus in the same fashion as the Klan despite the similarities. The Klan's loyalty to nation and religion centered upon exclusion, while Page emphasized Jesus' ethic of love. Yet for both Page and the order, sacrifice was essential to Jesus' message, and for the Klan the sacrifice of one's life represented the ultimate masculine ideal.

*A faithful brother—who gave his life to the cause.*[41]

Jesus' example included his "living sacrifice." As noted in chapter 1, Jesus sacrificed himself for the sins of the world, and the fraternity expected Klansmen to offer themselves as living sacrifices. At the first annual meeting of the Grand Dragons of the Klan in 1923, the order reflected on the example of Jesus' sacrifice and what that action meant for membership. Jesus "came not to be ministered unto, but to minister, and to give His life a ransom for many. He, therefore, Who is the Klansman's Exemplar, sets the example to all Klansmen."[42] That particular kind of sacrifice "calls for a living body placed upon the altar of Service, utilized by man and dedicated to God."[43] Jesus had died for noble principles, and members of the order were at the least expected to live their lives in unflinching service to him (and thus to the order). There was also an expectation that Klansmen might die in service to the order. Brown Hardwood, the Imperial Klazik (the second vice president of the order), noted, "But, if our cause is worthwhile, if our principles are right, if the objectives for which we strive our worthy, though we may have our martyrs and the pernicious persecution prompted by insidious forces . . . right will prevail eventually."[44] The Klan, after all, was a crusade to right the wrongs present in Protestant America, and the fraternity had its fair share of enemies. Klansmen expected persecution at the hands of their enemies. For Brown, the martyrs were casualties in a war in which the Klan would ultimately prevail, as Jesus had prevailed over sin. Some Klansmen gave their lives. Sacrifice emerged as a masculine trait embraced and re-created in the selfless act of Jesus. When Klansmen were martyred, the *Imperial Night-Hawk* was quick to report their deaths to its reading community.

The *Night-Hawk*, however, rarely discussed individual Klansmen or Klanswomen in its pages. Rather, the editors and contributors described how to be (and not to be) the ideal Protestant, patriot, and Klansman. Klan martyrs, however, provided an interesting exception to the rule. The newspaper glorified the individual stories of martyrs because of their selfless service and ultimate sacrifice for the Klan. This glorification was not necessarily a memorial of the individual *but* a restating of the Klan ideals that the martyr supposedly died to protect (regardless of whether he actually died to protect those ideals or not). In death, the bodies of these men represented the principles of the order, and Klan martyrs became rallying points for membership as well as affirmations of the importance of manly behavior. The martyrs also offered "concrete" examples of the supposed persecution that the "American, Protestant order" faced.[45]

Accusations of persecution permeated the pages of the *Night-Hawk,* and most articles contained at least one reference to the resistance the Klan encountered from other newspapers, Roman Catholics, Jews, Bolshevists, Communists, employers, businesses, the government, state legislatures, "unenlightened" Protestant churches, the police, Congress, immigrants, African Americans, Socialists, the Knights of Columbus, and proponents of evolution and secular schools, to name several. For instance, the *Night-Hawk* reported that "anything [was] permissible in slandering and vituperating this great American order by newspapers who pander to the tastes of their Catholic and Jewish advertisers."[46] As evidence of that resistance, the weekly reported on anti-Klan groups who attacked, and sometimes injured, Klan lecturers. In Kemblesville, Pennsylvania, an anti-Klan group mobbed Dr. D. J. Hawkins with fists and stones flying. They shot his car, and his "automobile certainly showed many marks of the bullets."[47] This persecution occurred because the Klan argued that the meaning of its organization had been distorted. A minister from Maine commented: "But how it [the Klan] has been willfully misrepresented and maligned by its enemies! It was to be expected that hindrance and hatred would be heaped upon this fraternity by the age-long merciless enemy of all things Protestant."[48]

The enemy assumed many forms, and the Klan alleged members were victims of merciless persecution. The *Night-Hawk* reasoned that the Klan faced persecution because of its antipluralist commitment to keep America white and Protestant. Klan martyrdom was the pinnacle of persecution because those cases affirmed that Klansmen confronted death because of their membership in the order. Two Klan martyrs, Fred Roberts and Thomas Abbott, emerged as symbols of the order.

Fred Roberts, a Klansman from Corpus Christi, Texas, was "one of the foremost and best beloved citizens of Texas," and he died while coming to the aid of a friend. Frank Robison, the "Roman Catholic sheriff of Nueces County" and the supposed enemy of Roberts, "because of his activity in behalf of Klan principles," murdered Roberts. According to the *Night-Hawk,* the sheriff harassed an elderly friend of Roberts, G. E. Warren, and the police department offered neither assistance nor protection for Warren. Roberts made it his duty to check on Warren at his store. On one fateful visit, Roberts entered into the store while the sheriff remained at "the front" and "paced back and forth." "While consoling and comforting his friends [Warren and his wife]," Roberts caught the eye of the sheriff. When Roberts returned to his car to leave, the sheriff shot him as he sat "unarmed and defenseless, one hand on the steering wheel and the other resting on the back of the seat." The *Night-Hawk* bemoaned, "his life was snuffed out by the one sworn to protect and shield him from harm." Roberts became a martyr because he was "the exponent of all that is best in the highest type of Christian citizenship." His name would "adorn the pages of history as a martyr to the cause of one hundred per cent Americanism." In the print, his life and death embodied the ideals of the Klan: clean government, religious liberty, the protection of womanhood, free press, and free speech. His death did not directly pertain to any of the ideals, but the newspaper molded the events to reflect his dedication to the order. He died "because he stood valiantly and unafraid for these great ideals."[49] His sacrifice reflected the life he had led as a "good man" loved by his friends and hated by his enemies. The *Night-Hawk* memorialized Roberts because he lived and died by Klan principles. The Texas Klan even built a memorial hospital in Roberts's name. Under the firm control of Protestant trustees, the hospital would use its revenues to help "suffering Klansmen and their families."[50] The memorial hospital reflected Roberts's generous spirit and established the importance of martyrdom for the order.

The *Night-Hawk* also venerated Thomas Abbott, who was killed during a Klan ceremonial parade, in three issues. The weekly proclaimed: "MOURN, Klansmen, a brother lies dead. The Cross, symbol of Christian sacrifice and hope, is stamped and broken in the mud of a little Pennsylvania township. . . . Yes, Klansmen, mourn. Drape your altars in black. Honor the memory of a simple and humble American who laid down his life unafraid and unshrinking for the cause which is yours."

On August 25, 1923, Klansman Abbott participated in a large naturalization ceremony (an initiation service). According to the *Night-Hawk,* more than 25,000 thousand Klansmen participated in the event held in Carnegie, Pennsylvania. It was a "peaceable gathering." As Klansmen paraded home, "gun fire broke out" from a nearby Catholic church. An Irish undertaker, Patrick McDermott, "emptied the magazine of an automatic pistol into the ranks of the white clad Klansmen. Klansman Abbott fell, shot through the head." For the *Night-Hawk,*

Abbott's martyrdom "was merely a typical instance of the intolerance of malign forces which would grind Americanism and Protestantism into the dust and make a mock of men who are striving to live and act cleanly."[51] Abbott died for a "noble cause"—his participation in the order—and his death demonstrated to the Klan the reality of the persecution that members faced. The sacrifice of Roberts and Abbott should have "renewed" Klansmen with "energy for the right."[52] Those men should have been examples to engender Klan action. To show their commitment to the order and Abbott, possibly thousands attended the funeral of Abbott to pay their respects to the Klan exemplar.

The funeral was held in Atlasburg, and a Pennsylvania Klansman documented the event for the weekly. The *Night-Hawk* noted that the account was *"printed here so that Klansmen may realize that their brother did not die for their cause in vain."*[53] Abbott was "a faithful brother—who gave his life to the cause." The Klan funeral attendees were "wonderful and courageous men" who signified a "higher type of manhood." Abbott became a hero. The Pennsylvania Klansman also observed the graveness of his "sad-eyed widow" in her effort to control her tears. At the funeral his widow, between sobs, stated, "Tommy . . . met his end bravely and will be rewarded. He always loved the Klan and honored its principles. He will receive his just reward in the great beyond."[54] In spite of their grief, the widow and her two children appreciated and accepted his sacrifice. The *Night-Hawk* established an educational fund for Abbott's children.

Not surprisingly, the weekly even redescribed Abbott's murder to emphasize his martyrdom: "Klansman Abbott, marching beneath the flag and the fiery cross at Carnegie was shot down by a cowardly assassin who lurked in the shadow of a Catholic church. He laid down his life willingly and unflinchingly for the cause of Protestant American Christianity—the cause for which the Knights of the Ku Klux Klan stands."[55] For the newspaper and Klansmen, Abbott died because of his commitment to the fraternity. He faced his death with courage, which exemplified his manly virtue. He was a "true martyr to the cause, hopes, and beliefs of Protestant Christianity." His death transpired, above all, because he was a Klansman. Klan martyrs were the fruition of Klan persecution. Abbott's death was an extension of the hatred that Klansmen faced because of their principles. The attacks on these men were larger assaults directed at the collective goals of the order. Their bodies began as targets for Klan enemies, and their *dead* bodies symbolized the ideal path of a Klansman.

These martyrs were rallying points for Klansmen. The *Night-Hawk* urged Klansmen to be "fortified by the example of Tom Abbott of Pennsylvania and Roberts of Texas, and the others who have died and suffered for our cause, go forth and work and live with renewed energy for the right."[56] The deaths also bolstered the Klan's collective agenda. The dead bodies, emptied of selves, energized the cause of the Klan because martyrdom glorified its holy cause.[57] Their sacrifices demonstrated the virility of the order because men would willingly give their lives.

However, the *Night-Hawk* did not discuss those individuals to venerate their lives. Rather, the paper used their examples to glorify Klan membership. Roberts and Abbott became representative Klansmen, manly Protestant Americans, and the *Night-Hawk* crafted their stories to portray such. Their memories became klannish. Death allowed only a static presentation of Klan ideals on men's bodies. Those men became the ultimate Klansmen, real men, but only in death. However, living Klansmen proved more difficult to control, thus the order relied on a military structure to keep its members in line.

*A soldier in our ranks because of his beliefs.*

In a document for the Exalted Cyclops, the "supreme officer" of a local Klan, the order instructed the officer to use a "COMPLETE MILITARY SYSTEM" not just to organize leadership but also to run meetings, political campaigns, and membership drives.[58] The *Klansman's Manual* (1924) admitted that the Klan's form of governance was not "new" but was meant to impersonate the army. The manual, intended to be a textbook for members, noted, "As the United States Army is duly organized with its various officers and troops, so is the Knights of the Ku Klux Klan welded together as an organized force for fulfillment of its patriotic mission." The Imperial Wizard was the commander of the army while there were also commanders of division and region (Grand Dragons), provinces (Grand Dragons), local Klans (Exalted Cyclops), and all of the officers under the command of that hierarchy. For the Klan, democracy proved unwieldy and possibly ineffective. The leadership argued that the militarism of the order was a necessity for efficiency and mobilization, and the officers watched over their members, or soldiers, to keep them organized and loyal. Each member was aware of the rank of the officers, as well as his own rank in the organization. Moreover, that form of governance allowed for "the whole movement to respond as one unit instantly and effectively to the call" of local, regional, or national leaders.[59] The *Manual* documented the failure of other fraternal and patriotic movements because they organized around democracy. The militarism supplied "efficient leadership, effective discipline, intelligent co-operation, active functioning, uniform methods, and unified operation," without which even the Klan would decline into a society obsessed with ritual but ineffectual in its larger goals. Moreover, the militaristic government was key to the preservation of "true, patriotic Americanism" because it guaranteed successful action. The *Manual* stated emphatically, "Both experience and history demonstrate the fallacy and futility of a so-called democratic form of government for any such movement as the Knights of the Ku Klux Klan."[60] Democracy proved inadequate in the face of the mass mobilization that the Klan wanted to garner, and, interestingly, autocracy provided the venue through which the leadership and faithful members protected their nation and democracy.

Paul Etheridge, the Imperial Klonsel (attorney), was perhaps concerned with the message of militarism over democracy. He argued that the Klan constitution was democratic "in principle" and valued democracy, but it was militaristic and autocratic in practice. The order vested the Imperial Wizard with ruling authority, and he organized the order in the hierarchical fashion. Etheridge repeated the problem of democracy presented in the *Klansman's Manual:* a truly democratic order would have lacked the organizational power of a militaristic hierarchy. He pointed out how other organizations with valuable aims were lost to history because they lacked structure and efficiency. The Klan attorney even lauded the efficiency of hierarchy in the Roman Catholic Church because "no form of government . . . has developed such proficiency in handling the masses as the Church of Rome." The Catholic Church could manage large amounts of people in her form of "government"; thus, to organize a mass of Protestants in the Klan a similar form of government must be utilized. Democracy was a principle upheld by the Klan, but hierarchy supplied a mechanism to organize masses of men to accomplish the Klan's goals. However, Etheridge cautioned that the Klan would use militaristic hierarchy as a method for good rather than the "destructive and inimical" purposes of the Catholic Church. The Imperial Klonsel further asked, "Is there any good reason why the same . . . plans should not be perfected for the accomplishment of the good [and] . . . operate along constructive lines with the same degree of effectiveness?"[61] The Klan's hierarchy implemented greater goals and accomplishments than the supposed machinations of the Catholic Church. For the leadership, the lack of democratic methods within the order was not a dismissal of the American form of government but a necessary means to further the purpose of the order in the most effective way possible. Militarism also proved useful because the Klan was locked in battle with enemies of religion and patriotism.

The Klan was a crusade for Protestantism and Americanism. "Military discipline" was required to maintain the order in the battle for the nation. For Etheridge, the Klan would remain a "militant, fighting organization" until the goals of the order had been accomplished.[62] Alva Taylor, writing on behalf of the *Christian Century,* believed that the empathetic patriotism and militarism were just "post-war reaction" held over from World War I. Taylor discredited the Americanism of the Klan as "short-circuited patriotism" and its method as "a great menace."[63] The *Christian Century* author did not see the benefit of militarism, nor did he recognize Klansmen as crusaders despite their attempts to claim that mantle. Imperial Wizard H. W. Evans purposefully conjured the image of the order as crusaders for American society. For Evans, crusaders were noble, heroic men who attempted to "rescue the Tomb of our Lord from the power of Saracens," and Klansmen were contemporary crusaders, an army of soldiers prepared to fight for another momentous cause. Each Klansman was "a soldier in our ranks because of his beliefs." They represented the "mind of America" and sought to fulfill "their Divinely appointed task."[64] They led Americans to better government, law enforcement, and "cleaner public thought." Evans noted, "No man becomes a Klansman and

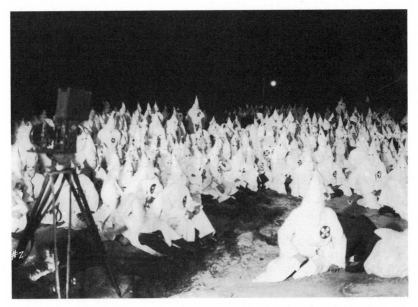

Klansmen sit outside for a group photo. Courtesy of University of Georgia
Hargrett Library, Athens.

stays a Klansman without becoming a better citizen, a better Protestant, a better husband and father, a better man."[65]

The Imperial Wizard believed that the "manly" manhood of the fraternity improved members and the larger society. He feared that aliens, or immigrants, would trample upon American masculinity as they had upon the American mind. Evans thought that aliens had almost destroyed the American mind by scoffing at the "greatness" of American pioneers. Aliens had attempted to make Klansmen, and Americans in general, "ashamed of being American" and envious of "the slick, soft, degenerateness which they call art and culture." Evans lamented, "Forgetting that manhood is the greatest thing in the world, and that all else is valuable only if it can be added unto manliness, but [art and culture] is damning if it replaces virility."[66] The alien enemies of the Klan emasculated American culture by removing its inherent virility. Masculine virtue informed the pioneers of American culture. Enemies were presented as "slick" and "soft" to demonstrate their threat to rugged Americanism. Masculinity, then, was a crucial component of both patriotism and faith, which made both more legitimate and valuable. Manhood and militarism sustained the improvement of nation and the order as well as (Protestant) Christianity.

"Militant Protestantism" was a battle cry for the Klan, and an Exalted Cyclops noted that the nation needed a "militant Protestant organization." The Klan would necessarily be involved in religious warfare, but it guaranteed that the religious faith would be protected. The leader worried that Protestantism might lose its "genuine" principles because of the actions of Protestants. He wrote: "Theologians may continue to split tenuous hairs; pulpit dilettantes may go on pronouncing their pretty little essays; sweet-scented sentimentalists may list their puling denunciations of the Klan; . . . shrinking, timorous, paling souls may deprecate the temerity of men who are bold to proclaim their Protestant Knighthood."

The Exalted Cyclops (regional leader) recognized the divisions within the faith, especially the reaction of "dilettantes" and "sweet-scented sentimentalists" to the Klan's militant Protestantism. For him, the Klan had to continue the practice of its faith by cherishing the Bible and the "Klansman's Christ." Those Protestants acted unmanly in their faith while the Klan was boldly supporting its call to "Protestant Knighthood."[67] Militancy was required in both nationalism and religion to preserve America and her Protestant heritage. The fight required men who were not timid, pale, or sentimental but bold and committed. For the Exalted Cyclops, opponents derided the Klan because of its manly action. To protect those ideals, Klansmen sounded the battle cry. Relying on the example of Jesus, martyrs, and militarism, the Klan crafted its masculine image. But in the creation of the Junior Order, the image fell flat for younger recruits.

*Be militant knights of the religion of our Lord and Savior, Jesus Christ.*[68]

For the Grand Dragon of Oregon, one of the pressing issues that faced the Klan was the thousands of degenerate and delinquent boys in America. Delinquent boyhood was not usually included as a rallying cry for the 1920s Klan.[69] The Grand Dragon noted, "Our boys are the masters of posterity, we must win them for this glorious cause." Boys left in delinquency would likely become degenerate men, presenting a problem for the nation because they lacked proper understandings of citizenship and hindered the nation's progress. Most important, boys were the future of the order and the nation. According to a Klan poem, "Your reputation and your future are in his hands. All your work is for him, and the fate of the nation and of humanity is in his hands." The poet continued, "So it might be as well to pay him some attention."[70] The method to move past that degeneracy was to create a Junior Order of the Klan for boys. The Junior Order provided "serious work of character building through right thinking, by ways and means of klannishness which will appeal most strongly to the boyish heart." The Grand Dragon believed that Klan principles coaxed boys into becoming men of character and hoped that the model of knighthood would appeal to them. The Junior Order provided the "average Protestant boy" with "the incarnation of all manly virtues, a knight."[71]

The program guided boys in the "critical and trying years of boyhood," ages twelve to eighteen, to become manly, nondelinquent men. A Klansman would be a hero to them and would hopefully inspire by his example. For the Grand Dragon, the Klan auxiliary benefited the nation and Protestantism by "making" better boys. Boys became assets to their communities and their nation through lessons on how to become a principled man, "the maker of his own character" and the "molder [sic] of his own life."[72] The Grand Dragon received his wish when the Klan instituted the Junior Order in 1923. By 1924 fifteen states had chapters of the order for boys.[73] The Klan hoped that the auxiliary would provide "strength" and numbers. The Grand Dragon insisted "that it is the highest duty of Klansmen . . . to do everything that is right and practicable for the betterment of boys, and through them, ennoble and bless the entire manhood and boyhood of our nation."[74] The training of boys as Knights reflected the desire of adult Klansmen to also embody that manly model. The adult men articulated their vision of knighthood to the boys who joined the Junior Order. The Knight was the epitome for both adult and adolescent behavior, and the adults communicated their vision of masculinity through ritual materials.

The *Kloran* for the men's, women's and Junior orders provided the script to Klan rituals, such as inductions, funerals, and other ceremonies. The *Kloran* for the Junior Order of Klansmen explained the centrality of knighthood to the young members of the order. In the manual for boys, the ritual of induction summarized the importance of knighthood for the applicants. All the officers of the Junior Order were boys, not adults, so they also ran the rite of induction for prospective members. In the ceremony, the "Worthy Lieutenant" of the Junior Klan praised the applicants for their decision to become Knights, but he warned that they must receive instruction in virtues of knighthood.[75] According to the *Kloran,* the Knight foundationally was a "gentleman," which implied one "who is not a brawler or a noisy person." "Gentle" signified a willingness to be "thoughtful and considerate." A Knight was also to be courteous and obedient.[76] Moreover, knighthood included generosity, hospitality, honesty, courage, purity, and loyalty. Another officer, the "Worthy Capitan," urged the boys to be courageous in the face of adversity. The boys were to fight for things that were good but avoid bullying. Loyalty was the most important virtue. The Knight was indebted to God, country, vows of service, and his fellow members. The "Worthy Knight" echoed the sentiments of his fellow officers: "He [the Knight] fought for God and his native land, he honorably lived up to the promises he made when he was admitted into Knighthood, he kept secrets that were entrusted to him by his Order and its members, and he let no one and nothing tempt him to be disloyal to these things."[77]

In the ritual of induction, the young Knights encountered the dictates of their Junior Order as well as their future involvement in the Klan. The importance of the Knight highlighted the order's masculine values, to fight for what one believed, and to revere loyalty above all other commitments. The Junior Order prepared young men for their full involvement as Christian Knights who fought for religion and for country. Interestingly, adult Kleagles created the ritual manual, and the Junior Order eventually dropped the rituals because they were too long and complicated.[78] Adult men tried valiantly to express the values of knighthood, but the rituals proved unappealing to teenage boys. The adults had great hopes that the boys would embody the manly ideals of the Junior Order and would become "real" men in the adult order. Thus, the adults actually articulated in the *Kloran* a vision of what they desired a Knight to be. The ideal Knight would fill the ranks of the Klan's crusading army, but he was not a tangible hero for the boys. The order's articulation of masculinity failed to live up to its promise of better men because the requirements of virility were too much to bear.

*God give us men, sun-crowned and strong, with their heads above the fog.*

In the poem "God Give Us Men," an anonymous author describes the type man the Klan needed:

God Give Us Men! The Invisible Empire demands strong
Minds, great hearts, true faith and ready hands . . .
Men who possess opinions and a will;
Men who have honor; men who will not lie;
Men who can stand before a demagogue and damn his treacherous
    flattering without winking!
. . . .
Men who serve not for selfish booty,
But real men, courageous, who do not flinch at duty;
Men of dependable character; men of sterling worth;
Then wrongs will be redressed, and right will rule the earth.[79]

The Klan's "man" is portrayed here, with clarity and rhyme, as courageous, selfless, faithful, and dependable. The God-given men were patriotic and noble, and they were easily discernible from the weak-kneed and "jelly-bean" men who neglected the Klan. In practicality, the Klan needed men to fill the membership rolls, but the order communicated a lofty goal of finding "REAL" men, who would not be indecisive, selfish, dishonorable, or soft. Those men served the valiant role of a Christian Knight, protector of Protestant America, and his sons trained in the values of the order.

For Brown Harwood, the Imperial Klazik, the "great movement" had found some men of the caliber they required, and the "hearts and souls of [these] manly men thrilled with such great emotion for a righteous cause."[80] They embraced the chivalry, patriotism, and Protestantism of the order, and they became bound to Klan principles and could not help but join. Klancraft encouraged "thousands of big, manly men into . . . filling the pews of Protestant churches throughout America."[81] The *Night-Hawk* and *Kourier* documented these emulations of the masculine Jesus and faithful service to the order. The Klan newsmagazines also memorialized the valiant souls that died for the cause, who sacrificed in support of the fraternal order. Men could not be good patriots, Protestants, or fathers without emulating a muscular Jesus. For Imperial Wizard Evans, virility enhanced everything from dedication to nation to the practice of religious faith, and Klan enemies assaulted virility by stripping away the "rugged" nature of America and replacing it with soft, artistic understandings of culture. Klan masculinity helped preserve the white Protestant nation. Enemy actions, on the other hand, rendered Jesus impotent, and the Klan struggled to re-masculinize him in order to rejuvenate the faithful. While other men wallowed in their shallow imitations of manliness, the order claimed that real men strove to save both America and Protestantism. God wanted men, and the Klan provided.

In the pages of the *Night-Hawk,* however, the Klan did not actually offer "real" men. Instead, the order showcased idyllic exemplars of masculinity. From the Christian Knight for boys, to the rugged Jesus for adult men, to the rigid militaristic order, to martyrs transformed into quintessential Klansmen, the Klan presented manly members with unreachable ideals. The adults created rituals that emphasized the virtue of Knights, but the rites were too complicated to interest teenage boys. Jesus was the bastion of masculinity, but there were glimpses that Klansmen did not emulate him. The support of militarism to breed masculinity and efficiency degraded a central tenet that the order upheld: democracy. Martyrs were not celebrated as the individuals that they were; they were celebrated because their deaths allowed the *Night-Hawk* to emphasize manliness and exemplary behavior. Above all, the order crafted a narrow masculine model via print. The Klan wanted members to be rugged yet gentle, sacrificing yet tough, and virtuous but militaristic. Virility was injected into faith and nation because the Klan sought a method to reclaim its hold over both.

The emphasis on manliness conveyed the fraternity's anxiety about the role of white Protestant men in the American nation. The leadership feared that the "weak-kneed Protestant" might have had the upper hand, which placed patriotism, faith, and masculinity all in question. The Klan's uplifting of real men reflected its growing concerns over an America that was beginning to seem more strange than familiar. Real men tried to save their religion and their nation from impending peril. Most important, Klansmen did not want to become the men on the proverbial fence. That defense and decisiveness rendered male members as protectors of not only the nation but also the home and family. The order's muscular Christianity hoped to do the impossible, guard a white Protestant nation that already was no longer homogenous. Masculine warriors lost the battle before they had even begun to fight. The Klan, however, was not just composed of men. The Women of the Ku Klux Klan staked out their place in the battle as well. Klanswomen believed they were essential to the fight for nation, but they faced the added complexity of the Klan trying to define and limit women's roles in national culture. Vulnerable white womanhood might have been a rallying cry for the men's order, but the WKKK proved that they were just as interested and motivated as the men in preserving the order's vision.

CHAPTER 4 *"The Sacredness of Motherhood"*:
White Womanhood, Maternity,
and Marriage in the 1920s Klan

*We women believe that the Klan is to America what a loyal wife and mother is to the
home. Her work is in a sense invisible to the eyes of the world. Yet she is ever on the
lookout and ready to meet this need and to care for that one. She is the spirit of protec-
tions, of love, of idealism, of discipline and of life itself in the home.*
—ROBBIE GILL COMER (1925)[1]

*We believe that under God, the Women of the Ku Klux Klan is a militant body of
American free-women by whom these principles shall be maintained, our racial purity
preserved, our homes and children protected, our happiness insured, and the prosperity
of our community, our state and our nation guaranteed against usurpation, disloyalty,
and selfish exploitation.*
—IMPERIAL NIGHT-HAWK (1924)[2]

In Thomas Dixon's *Clansman* (1905), the inequality of Reconstruction
for Southern whites as well as African American enfranchisement
causes the birth of the Ku Klux Klan. The pivotal plots of the novel focus on the danger that African American men, now in positions of
power, pose to vulnerable, white women. Dixon creates many female
characters, but two, Elsie, the plain and kind Northerner, and Marion,
the "shy elusive beauty," are essential to the action of the novel.[3]
While playing her banjo in a veteran's hospital, Elsie encounters Ben
Cameron, the Confederate hero. Moved by his mother's desperation to
save her son, Elsie secures a presidential pardon for the handsome Ben
and promptly falls in love with him. However, her father disapproves
of Ben's Confederate background, and their romance is thwarted
throughout Dixon's tale with increasingly sappy prose. Dixon describes her with "warm amber eyes" and "fair skin with its gorgeous
rose-tints of the North paled."[4] The tale documents not only the Klan's
rise to prominence but also Elsie and Ben's growing love for one another, her eventual embrace of Southern culture, her growing disdain
for African Americans, and Ben's interpretation of Reconstruction.

Marion, on the other hand, is Southern by birthright, and her
beauty and gentle nature enchant even Elsie's cantankerous father. On

her outings with her horse, "every boy lifted his hat as to passing royalty, and no one, old or young, could allow her to pass without admiration," because she "had developed into the full tropic splendor of Southern girlhood."[5] Blonde and fair, dainty and graceful, Marion is the example of a Southern woman. She is the epitome of white womanhood metamorphosed into the tragic symbol of Southern loss in Reconstruction. When Gus, an African American, rapes her, Dixon alludes to the loss of not only a white woman's purity but also the white men's power. The rape demonstrates that white men are no longer able to protect the honor of their women in the face of African American "brutes." Because of their dedication to racial purity and her reputation, Marion and her mother react with horror to the rape and lament the loss of innocence. They decide that suicide is a far better option than allowing anyone to find out about the terrible act. The mother and young daughter throw themselves off Lover's Leap. When their broken bodies are discovered, Ben and others recognize the brutal attack on Marion.

Several white men, including Ben, seek to avenge Marion's demise and to take back control of their region. They gather together as a clan in white robes and helmets to protest the ruin of white womanhood and their imperiled South. During their first gathering, one member utters, "Brethren, I hold in my hand the water of your river bearing the red stain of life of a Southern woman, a priceless sacrifice on the altar of outraged civilization."[6] The loss of Marion's virginity and her death haunt Ben, and he is convinced that the Klan has to combat "dangerous" African Americans. Vulnerable and in need of constant protection, Elsie and Marion represent white womanhood at its finest—exemplifying virtue, loyalty, and love—and both women impact Ben in his journey to save the South. The defense of white womanhood was a banner for the first Ku Klux Klan in the 1860s and 1870s, and the concern over the fragility of white women resonated in the 1920s Klan. However, the characterization of women changed with the second order.

In George Alfred Brown's *Harold the Klansman* (1923), a novel about the 1920s Klan, Ruth Babcock is not only the central female character but also the heroine. Ruth has a career as a stenographer, and she works very hard to support her aunt and her father, who has been injured in a car accident. In the early pages of the novel, the author traces her lineage through her mother's family, who is of Confederate stock. Like Dixon's female characters, Brown's Ruth is also attached to the South, which informs her decisions throughout the novel. In addition to her career and domestic duties, Ruth is also the love interest of Harold King, an architect and the Klansman for whom the novel is titled. The novel is an elucidation of Klan principles through fiction to provide "entertainment" as well as "a greater appreciation of the Invisible Empire."[7] To accomplish his goal, Brown uses discussions between Ruth and Harold, as well as Ruth and other characters, to flesh out Klan principles. Ruth, "a girl with a kindly heart and plenty of grit," eventually falls in love with Harold and embraces the order.[8] However, she struggles greatly as she slowly becomes aware that Harold and the Klan are the man and the order she supports. She is a woman of honor and modesty, and Harold's admiration for the heroine grows page by page. He, of course, is the exemplar of manhood: hardworking, kind, courageous, and dedicated to his order. The plot also follows the opposition he encounters as a Klansman from the larger business establishment, which is under the control of Roman Catholics and Jews.

Interestingly, Ruth proves to be a more developed character than either Elsie or Marion because she has more agency. In a pivotal moment in the novel, she terrorizes an African American janitor at the bank, where she works, by donning a robe and a mask. Rastus, the janitor, is significantly behind in his tithing, and Ruth uses her costume to terrify him back into financially supporting his church and pastor. Rastus's pastor is supportive of the Klan, and Ruth believes the janitor needs a little encouragement in the form of terror to back the white-robed order. Unfortunately, her bold action brings negative press upon the Klan, who, Brown reminds readers, never committed such dastardly acts. The heroine eventually confesses her actions in an affidavit to a local newspaper to guarantee that the press did not malign the order, which marks Ruth's transformation into a proponent of the Klan. When her other suitor, Chester Golter, who is also the nephew of Ruth's prosperous boss, Stover, impugns the Klan, she quickly defends it: "I believe in the principles of the Klan; I believe that a good class of men belong; that they are doing many charitable acts, and in many places have created more respect for law and order. If I were a man I would join this order of real red-blooded Americans."[9]

Her support of the Klan displeases Golter, who opposes the fraternity and Ruth's newfound admiration for the Knights. More important, her desire to join the order, if she were a man, reveals her commitment to the fraternity and its politics. That commitment emerges again when her friendship with Harold imperils her job. Stover demands that Ruth end the friendship, but she refuses. Despite Stover's threats and later cajoling, Ruth quits. In that moment, Brown describes her as "a type of noble womanhood," determined, daring, and loyal. The heroine's actions enchant the author and hopefully his readers.

However, Ruth is not a complete agent in her literary destiny. Harold saves the floundering heroine by finding her a new job and uncovering that Stover stole her father's fortunes. The novel ends with Stover's arrest and Ruth's marriage to Harold in a nearby town. On the way back to their hometown of Wilford Springs, they spot a fiery cross in the landscape, which signals the sanctity of their marriage. Unlike Elsie or Marion, Ruth surfaces as a strong female character but still requires a Klansman's protection. She works to take care of her family, upholds her principles, and finds comfort in marriage to her protector. Harold, of course, rescues her and restores her father's dignity (and wealth), but Ruth proves responsible for her actions. The plucky heroine might require defense, but she also has agency, which Dixon refuses to provide to Elsie and Marion. Ruth signifies the paradox for the Women of the Ku Klux Klan (WKKK): women claimed their agency but also negotiated the gendered expectations and constraints from their male brethren about the required roles of women in American life.

In the 1920s Klan, defense of white womanhood was a slogan for members. Yet with the advent of the WKKK in 1923, women were crusaders for the order as well as supporters of their husbands, brothers, fathers, and sons who were members. For Klansmen, Klanswomen were to be virtuous white women in need of defense and protection, but those women strove to define their service in their own terms. They used their roles as wives and mothers to articulate their entrance into the order while men sought to circumscribe their roles. Motherhood was a primary feature of a woman's role, along with undying support of Klansmen. Yet Klanswomen had their own notions about

Women of the KKK, New Castle, Indiana, 1923. Photograph by W. A. Swift. Courtesy of Ball State University Archives, Muncie, Indiana.

the role of women within the order and in the larger American society. They called for political equality for white women, echoing the Klan's concerns over the sanctity of the home and the virtue of white womanhood.

To articulate their positions on gender, the WKKK relied on Protestantism and nationalism to showcase the important role women played in domestic and public spheres. While the men's order limited the place of women to wives, and most significantly mothers, the Klanswomen attempted to prove that motherhood made them more apt than their male counterparts to protect the nation the Klan held dear. The WKKK were "conservative maternalists" who deployed the Klan's expectations about motherhood and womanhood to their advantage. Drawing upon beliefs about inherent differences between the sexes and women's special role in producing young citizens, the WKKK, like other conservative women of the 1920s, manipulated their gender role to help promote the Klan's political aspirations but also to critique the men's order.[10] Both Klansmen and Klanswomen uplifted the home as a sacred altar that stoked the fires of religiosity and patriotism, and this

Women of the KKK in regalia. Courtesy of Ball State University Archives, Muncie, Indiana.

emphasis on the special status of the home and domesticity furthered the order's preoccupation with women and marriage. The Klan supported lecturers, who were supposed ex-nuns, ex-priests, and ex-Catholics, to demonstrate the pressing danger of Catholics toward young women in both the confessional and the convent. The 1920s Klan, then, perceived a pressing Catholic threat to the bonds of Protestant marriage because of the reinterpretations of legitimate marriage by the church's hierarchy. This threat signaled that Catholics, once again, were dangerous to nationhood and faith, and that the danger was most significant for white Protestant women, who were the supposed targets of the church's convents, priests, and marriage reforms.

*American women are the uncrowned partners of American men.*[11]

For W. C. Wright, a Klan minister, the first Klan came into existence because of the "negro domination" of the South. His narrative echoed Dixon's portrayal of Reconstruction, and he argued the "Klan saved the South from negro domination, protected the chastity of Southern womanhood from black brutes in human form."[12] The 1920s Klan was partially a memorial to celebrate the achievements of those original Klansmen, especially their desire to defend chaste white women. The second revival of the order sought "to promote good morals," which required the protection of "the chastity of womanhood, the virtue of girlhood, and the sanctity of the home."[13] This morality was bound to womanhood. The defense of white women was essential for the order as well as for its predecessor, and the 1920s Klansmen lamented the degradation of white womanhood that they found in popular culture and society at large. The 1920s, after all, was the era of the flapper as well as the establishment of women's right to vote (1919), which provided women with political power in the form of the ballot.[14]

Historian Nancy MacLean noted that Athens Klansmen wrung their hands over the behavior of young women, their treatment by the men in their lives, and their need of protection because of female fragility and vulnerability. MacLean pointed to the Athens press as the cause of such anxiety, because the newspapers documented the prevalence of unwed mothers, deserted wives, the abuse of women by husbands and fathers, and, most disturbingly, defiant young women who did not heed the warnings of their mothers or fathers.[15] These women were in dire need of protection not only from societal ills but also from themselves. Thus, Klan newspapers, speeches, and other print asserted the proper characteristics and roles for women to correct those documented ills. The Klan's reading community became versed in the proper places for women in American society and acknowledged the order's crucial role in preserving those places and spaces.

In the *Kluxer,* a Klan weekly from Dayton, Ohio, the pseudonymous C.B. reflected on the essential nature of women, who possessed the "most wonderful kind of heart created." For C.B., humans first had to acknowledge that our hearts were "inclined to do evil," but by following the path of Jesus, one could have a change of heart. Once members realized that truth, then they could not disagree that the hearts of women might possibly be divine. Women were the more spiritual yet delicate creatures. C.B. continued:

Do you realize women, that on our every side, to the North of us, to the South, to the East and to the West of us are precious young ladies with hearts as pure as gold, and with a conscience as tender as a baby's, which are about to blossom forth with all the splendor, and the beauty of the purest lily growing. O God, how can I say it—it grieves my heart to know it is so, but here in America, a nation of Christian people, these precious young lives are taken in beauty and innocence with no regard for their feminine timidity, with no respect for their sense of shame, and in a cruel and pitiless manner, their lives are wrecked forever.[16]

Women had hearts "as pure as gold," infantile consciences, and beauty. For C.B., the fairer sex was essentially childlike and in need of defense. Men deserted, abused, and maligned these pure and vulnerable women, so women lacked the care they rightly deserved. C.B. was astounded that in "Christian America" the cruel treatment of women existed with no attention to their "timidity" and gentle qualities. Heartbreak, cruelty, prostitution, and suffering "wrecked" young women. C.B. lamented the burgeoning "white-slave traffic," which created despairing and piteous women. Only "white-robed figures" could protect the white woman with "girlish figure and innocent eyes." The Klan was the only organization that could remedy the poor state of womanhood. The author purported that the "God-inspired army" of the Klan could guarantee that the "Heart of Woman" would never suffer again. C.B. urged the men of the Klan to be a part of that campaign, and he also encouraged the WKKK and ordinary young women to take a stand against such travesty. The author pleaded with American women to take up the "banner of purity" to assure "fair young creatures have their liberty too." Those women should offer prayers to ensure the safety of all women in the supposed Christian nation. C.B. proclaimed, "Let us push forward and clean things up, for the protection of pure womanhood in America."[17]

Such protection was crucial not just because women were delicate creatures in peril but also because women were a valuable resource for nation and order: 100 percent American women were needed just as much as 100 percent American men. C.B., however, painted a disturbing portrait of fragile, timid women confronted by danger lurking around every corner and the inability to provide protection for themselves. The men of the Klan had to supply much-needed defense for white women.

In spite of women's "inherent" fragility, the order lauded women who embraced the traditional roles of wives and mothers and maintained the home. In "A Tribute and Challenge to American Women," the Grand Dragon of Arkansas observed "the word 'Woman' always arrests the attention of every true man at once."[18] That was not because of the sexual attraction of women. Rather the Klan leader professed that no man could forget his loving and wonderful mother. Mothers, sisters, wives, and daughters were all noble beings who supported and fostered their men. Yet their nobility was often ignored, and women were treated as lesser than men. For the Grand Dragon, women throughout history had faced prejudice, ignorance, and superstition until Jesus "discovered" woman and started "her on the upward road." The presence of Christ undercut that ignorance. Christianity served to advance women in society, and despite the Catholic attachment to Mary, the author argued that the "mother of our Lord" should be reevaluated, even if America sought to expunge Catholic ideology from its history.[19] Jesus called upon women in his ministry and demonstrated that they had the ability to impact their individual societies and the larger world.

The Grand Dragon continued that the American woman shaped the "destiny of America" as much as the American man because she reared children. Women were more than "help-meets"; they were "help-mates" who helped build homes, churches, and schools.[20] American women were the "uncrowned partners of American men." For the Klan leader, they could no longer be limited to the domestic sphere. More important, with the right to vote women could support the Klan ideals and principles through the ballot box, a mandate that provided women with a voice in the nation's development. The Grand Dragon remarked that his "tribute" to women came from his "tenderest recollections of a mother's solicitude" and the "constant inspiration of a wife's undying affections."[21] Women fostered him, and he believed that the Klan should encourage women to participate in the political process to repay their kindness. Additionally, he challenged women to stand beside "one hundred percent American men in their stride to restate, and reinstate, great American principles in this, our God-given Country."[22] Men needed to protect women, but their female counterparts were to be partners in the Klan's endeavor to bolster Christian America. Women had the ability to help reclaim the American nation.

*The sacred remembrance of their glorious mothers.*

Despite the equality offered by the Grand Dragon of Arkansas, the Klan, overall, glorified women as mothers rather than as political participants. In a letter to the Exalted Cyclops and Kligrapps in Indiana, a Klan official reminded fellow officers of Mother's Day, "the sacred remembrance of their glorious mothers." The director of the Department of Propagation wrote, "When God opened the gates of heaven and gave to all the world MOTHER, it was his greatest blessing to all humanity outside of Jesus Christ."[23] Mothers were a blessing who were only surpassed by Jesus in their significance, which clearly demonstrated the magnitude of ideal motherhood for Klansmen. Motherhood equaled love and support, and, more important, motherhood was God's gift to humanity. The director continued:

> She knows how to kiss away the sorrow of the heart, her hand knows just when and how to stroke a weary brow. Her sweet, soft voice gives the loving word of counsel and sympathy needed but—oh, how we miss her when she is gone. She has waded into the jaws of her death for her offspring and is willing to lay down her life again if need be that their lives might be spared. She has spent the long weary night in taking care of the babes, watching over them during their growing school days, planning the meals, mending the clothes, bandaging the hurts, following them closely up to young manhood and young womanhood, and then she gives them to some one else to have and to hold. THAT'S A MOTHER'S LOVE.[24]

For the director, mothers were counselors, sympathizers, and supporters who guided their children from "babes" to adulthood. They gave up sleep and time for their children, and likely those adoring women would hand over their own lives for the lives of their children. A mother's love was defined by self-sacrifice because women raised their children only to lose them to the adult child's husband or wife. The director encouraged Klansmen to reflect on their own mothers and to write notes that echoed the love that they had received. Contemplating a mother's example "shall do much to strengthen the morale of our Klaverns."[25]

New Jersey Klansmen celebrated Mother's Day in an Ocean Grove auditorium. The event, which the *Christian Century* called a "bed sheet revival," began with a Kleagle's speech on the "sacredness of motherhood, the services of the [K]lan in the protection of motherhood, and the despicableness of the persons—presumably not white Protestant gentiles—who do not love their mothers as they should." The main speaker, however, was a "lady kleagle," who was excited to speak to young women in the audience. Those young women were the "mothers of tomorrow."[26] She also reiterated the Indiana director's vision of motherhood by asserting that mothers were the second gift from God (because Jesus was the first). She even suggested that she would rather "hold the office of motherhood than be a President of the United States of America."[27] All her positive attributes, she claimed, came from her very own mother.

The Kleagle's mother, by inculcating Klan principles in the life of her daughter, served to further the order. The Klan idealized motherhood and uplifted the primary role of women as mothers for that very reason. Women had the power and influence to raise their children by Klan principles. They taught their boys and girls a love for religion, nation, and the order—the mother's primary and most imperative role. This power over one's children, however, also gave the men's order pause. If women could produce better white Protestant citizens, then they also had the ability to create lackluster and problematic citizens too.

The *Kluxer* warned that a mother's influence could prove dangerous to her children. In a morality story for its readers, the publication confirmed the unspoken dangers of motherhood. A young man with "the Ku Klux germ," which grew into a burgeoning sense of Americanism, almost neglected the Klan because his mother did not want him to join the fraternity. The young man was "manly" and "a native born Protestant" who admired the order and its "wonderful" reputation. Yet he feared that he was a "slacker" for both his country and Christianity. His mother, however, was against his membership. The *Kluxer* reported that she was a nervous creature, and "when that young man told his mother that he intended to join an organization and that he would be away at meetings at night, it nearly killed her." His mother did not deny the efficacy of the order. Instead, she wanted to hold on to her son a bit longer. She, unlike the ideal mother, was not prepared to sacrifice herself for the betterment of her son. The young man joined the order against her wishes. Like "the heroes of fiction . . . are willing to sacrifice their loved ones for the common good," that young man decided to fight for Americanism.[28] Through his noble example, his mother forgave him, and she eventually embraced the order that her son loved. Her son's commitment changed the heart and mind of his mother. Mothers, then, wielded much influence, good or ill, over the lives of their children.

In "American Mother's Prayer," published in the *Imperial Night-Hawk,* Mrs. P. B. Whaley emphasized her crucial role as a mother to her son. She instilled a love of nation, religious faith, bravery, and manhood. She prayed to God to make sure that her son would become a Klansman because that was her utmost duty as an "American mother." Mrs. Whaley, unlike the mother from the *Kluxer,* understood what was expected of her in the maternal role. Whaley was the example, and the unnamed mother was the exception. The Klan portrayed the exemplar mother motivated by self-sacrifice in the face of her children's needs. Mrs. Whaley's submitted poem emphasized how women desired to guarantee that their children, especially their sons, turned into "real" American citizens. The wishes of the unnamed mother, the most pressing of which was to keep her son at home, were cast aside in the face of her child's needs and her responsibility to raise white Protestant citizens.

Mothers were supposed to be supporters, but they were not sustained in their own wishes and desires. The Klan's vision of motherhood revolved around the female figure, who sustained the order and fostered her children regardless of her own interests. She was deserving of Mother's Day praise while the order cautioned less devoted mothers about their harmful behaviors. The expectations the Klan placed on motherhood were unattainable. Relationships with one's children defined the archetype of maternity, but the model woman had her own desires and wants relegated behind her maternal duties. For the Klan's textual community and its vision of nation, women became mothers only, but the order expressed its deep concern over the power women could wield when they ignored the Klan's larger ideals and goals. The relegation of women to maternity and domesticity occurred because of the mother's relationship with the sacred home. Mothers helped create, maintain, and preserve the home, the order's foundation of faith and nation. Mothers, much like masculine Knights, inhabited a tightly inscribed role, and the Klan tried valiantly to keep women within it by emphasizing the significance of the home to its vision of America.

*God's greatest earthly institution . . . the anteroom to the Mansion in the Skies.*

Regard for the home appeared in domestic klannishness, a term employed by the first Imperial Wizard, William J. Simmons. Domestic klannishness was one of the "four-fold" applications of the order, and the main goal was the protection of the "sanctity of the home" by Klansmen.[29] The Klan warned members of the danger posed to the sacred institution, which served as the building block for both religious faith and nation. For Imperial Wizard H. W. Evans, the fate of the national government rested in the "quality" of the American home. The Imperial Wizard argued that the home was "the highest and soundest expression of both personal and public welfare." The strength of its homes supported America, and the failed countries were those "whose citizenship worshipped not at the fireside."[30] The nation, for Evans, was like a home that previous Americans built and current citizens protected. A citizen's personal home directly impacted the national home. And families were equally as important. The love of individuals for their homes and families produced love of nation. Familial love transformed into national love. According to Evans, the defense of the home and family life was a necessity because the home was the arena where future citizens learned patriotism.

Texan judge Felix D. Robertson outlined the duties of citizenship in a public speech reprinted in the *Night-Hawk*. He saw the home as pivotal to the formation of better citizens. Robertson argued that America should actively put God in history and trace the presence of God through momentous events, from Mount Sinai to the Civil War. The way to guarantee recognition of God's presence in American history, he believed, was to emphasize the matters in the "American home."

Robertson called the home "God's greatest earthly institution . . . the anteroom to the Mansion in the Skies." The home represented the path to salvation for individuals and the nation. Robertson suggested each home should contain an "old style Family Altar[,] that sacred place around which every American family ought to meet in humble supplication to the God of their Fathers twice each day." The family altar served as a place of worship that would produce "that high and noble type of men who built our Government on its solid foundation of reverential faith." The physical altar should contain the "starry banner" and the Bible, which were symbols for human liberty and God's promise respectively. The altar functioned as a material artifact to show the family's dedication to the Christian nation. Interestingly, Robertson focused primarily on the rearing of sons to become patriots. But he ignored the daughters as potential citizens despite the fact that the mother was responsible for both education and maintaining the altar. The critical feature for the betterment of the nation for Robertson was the family and the home, yet he neglected women in his plan to restore national consciousness of religion. To foster a religious and patriotic environment in the home would lead to better citizens and the restoration of a "Godly land."[31]

The godly land, however, included female citizens who wanted to do their part for the nation and their families. Women hoped to participate in the Klan's restoration, and the women's order allowed them to become active participants. In their creed, the Women of the Klan affirmed the American home as the "foundation upon which rests secure the American Republic, the future of its institutions, and the liberty of its citizens."[32] The home, the domestic space over which women had such power, was essential for citizenship, and the WKKK did not take that role lightly. They, unlike Robertson, recognized the power of women to foster the order's vision. They saw themselves as soldiers for the cause, much as Klansmen were, and they articulated their position in both religious and patriotic terms.

*We believe in the mission of emancipated womanhood.*[33]

In 1923 the Klan established the Women of the Ku Klux Klan as an order. The national officers adopted a creed similar to the men's order,

Klansmen and Camelias on parade, 1923. Three thousand Klansmen and Klanswomen paraded with 60,000 onlookers. Photograph by W. A. Swift. Courtesy of Ball State University Archives, Muncie, Indiana.

but it contained key differences. Both the men's and women's creeds emphasized Christianity, the separation of church and state, public schools, racial purity, freedom of speech, freedom for the press, freedom of worship, the Constitution, and the protest of foreign influence in American government. The women's creed also emphasized political and social equality for men and women, as well as a call for "emancipated womanhood freed from the shackles of old-world traditions and standing unafraid in the full effulgence of equality and enlightenment."[34] Not surprisingly, the Klan did not focus upon rights for women but did appreciate the potential power of white women as voters. The WKKK stressed that both men and women had built the nation together, and so they could restore it together. They advocated their role in protecting and fostering national culture, and they endeavored to be active participants. Like their male counterparts, they focused on benevolence as well. Klanswomen in Alabama founded a

Klanswomen attend a funeral in full regalia. The deceased's uniform rests on the coffin. Photograph by W. A. Swift. Courtesy of Ball State University Archives, Muncie, Indiana.

Protestant orphanage named Klanhaven, which connected children with Christian families.[35] The founder was an exemplary Klanswoman known for her religious faith as well as her mothering skills. The orphanage was just one example of the power of Klanswomen and their organizing ability. More important, such a benevolent action signaled that the WKKK claimed leadership ability from the members' power to nurture.

The WKKK was "organized by women for women" with the aid of the Knights of the Klan. Previously, women could only help the men rather than have their own order.[36] The WKKK was headquartered in Little Rock, Arkansas, under the command of Lula A. Markwell, the Imperial Commander, and Robbie Gill (later Comer), the Imperial Kligrapp (who eventually became the Imperial Commander after Markwell). The WKKK was an order of "white, Gentile, Protestant native-born women of America, imbued with the high ideals of patriotism and love of home, school and country, [who] recognize in the new order the agency wherewith they may make secure the emancipation for which they have been struggling from the beginning of time, and which the last few years have actually began to realize."[37]

Klanswomen imagined their order not only as a mechanism to fight for their country but also as a vehicle for women's rights. In Kathleen Blee's *Women of the Klan,* she provided a much-needed monograph on the role of women in the WKKK, as well as how the men's order envisaged the women's auxiliary. Blee examined the tension between the men's and women's orders as well as how the Klan understood the home and women differently from the WKKK. She wrote, "The W.K.K.K dissented from the idealized view of home and family that was such a powerful symbol in the men's Klan. Instead, Klanswomen described the home as a place of labor for women."[38] She found that the WKKK called for political equality as well as social equality. Yet she downplayed the religious emphasis of that order. Blee focused on their drive for women's right to vote and defense of said right while ignoring the resonance between the men's and women's orders on the place of Protestantism in women's equality.

Rather than rehearse the support of women's suffrage, I choose to explore how the WKKK and their commander, Robbie Gill Comer, understood the role of religion in women's equality. Blee wrote that the WKKK "appropriated the Christian emphasis of the Klan and used it to support an agenda of women's rights."[39] Rather than examining the purported Protestantism of the women's order, Blee, unfortunately, dismissed the faith as appropriation. The WKKK imbibed in the religious faith of the men's order. Protestantism and nation defined the women of the Klan as much as it did the men.

*God gave him woman to be his [Adam's] comrade and counselor.*[40]

In "American Woman" (1924), Robbie Gill explored the relation of her order to the men's Klan and reflected upon the place of women in America. This speech, given at the Second Imperial Klonvokation in Kansas City, Missouri, proved to be very popular, and it was reprinted several times in the Klan press. Gill began her speech by admitting her hesitancy of speaking before Klansmen about the power of a woman.

She admitted that the men might have already realized their "inability" to function "regardless of her [a woman's] whims and annoying ways." The Imperial Commander showed deference to the men in her audience, but she continued with her theme of female power. She traced the ability of women back to the Garden of Eden. God provided Adam with Eve as "his comrade and counselor," and Adam was her "lord and husband." Eve was the partner of Adam, but he was the head of household. Gill, however, centered upon Adam's name for the "first" woman. Gill observed: "Gentlemen, that name he gave his wife on the morning of their nuptials is worth all the lectures on women ever written since. Adam . . . called her Eve, which in our language is *Life*. . . . Eve was intended to be not only the mere life of humanity, in its literal import, but the life and spirit of all true and genuine civilization."[41]

God's place, then, for Eve was represented in women, who were the lifeblood of society. Rather than emphasize men's control over women, Gill explained how women were essential for both men and the larger culture. Not surprisingly, she ignored Eve's participation in the exodus from Eden and instead relied upon the significance of Eve's name. For the leader of WKKK, such action signaled that God never intended for women to be slaves to men. Women were to be equal participants in society, which she purported was the divine intention, although they had been treated poorly throughout history. For Gill, women had achieved their full freedom under the influence of Protestant Christianity. She argued that women were "better educated, more refined and more honored in Protestant countries than anywhere else—in Protestant countries, under free governments which are the fruits of Protestantism." Gill lauded America, a (Protestant) Christian nation, as the country that most supported and recognized the rights of women.

Even the flag symbolized the national commitment to women. The red stripes signified the "manly blood" spilled for "women's protection." The white stripes represented both the purity of men and women. Each stripe "bears silent testimony" of the men, who would protect the "honor and chastity of our home-builders—our women." Finally, the field of blue indicated both "loyalty and royalty," which included loyalty to country and home, as well as Gill's assessment that women in America were like royalty. Comparing American women to the "queens" in a deck of cards, Gill noted that they toiled (spades), disciplined husbands and children (clubs), and basked in their wealth (diamonds), but more important, all of these women were queens of hearts who loved.[42] Their love fostered their husbands and children. Such love encouraged women to support their men because women's power rested in men's dependence upon them.

Eve might have been Adam's helpmeet, but she had the ability to persuade him because of her support. Gill suggested that women yielded power over their husbands, and she reminded Klansmen of their dependence and need for their female counterparts. The Imperial Commander also acknowledged that men had provided women with an honored position as well as the ability to vote—a crucial step in the right direction. Gill assured her listeners that she would not continue to bore them with the virtues of women, and she congratulated her audience on their commitment to suffrage for women. Gill's apology only rang partially true because she attempted to dismantle stereotypes that her audience, primarily men, had about their female companions. Her compliments to her audience masked her intent. Gill wanted to prove to the Klan that women would take suffrage seriously and that women actually had stronger political convictions than men. The conservative maternalism of the WKKK emerged in Gill's speeches and convictions about the ability of women to reform American society.

These convictions emerged from the life stories of individual women who had experienced the detriment of alcohol, unlawfulness, and gambling because they had husbands who were drinkers, gamblers, or supporters of some other vice. Their families were at stake, and the power of the ballot gave women the voice to protect their families. The underlying message was that American women were victims to the men in their lives. With the ballot, women had the power to correct societal ills to make their own lives better, which meant they would not be subjected to the rule of detrimental husbands. Gill's message was that those women would be involved in the political process, but what were the men doing? She affirmed that the WKKK supported the Klan's program of Americanism and Protestantism, and she stated, "We believe with gripping conviction that a rediscovery of Jesus Christ . . . will be the only thing that will save our nation in these days of unrest and disturbance."[43]

Yet Gill turned her attention to the men in her audience to point out that her membership had pressing questions about the men's order. She wanted direct answers about its objectives, so that both Klans could demonstrate what they had accomplished for faith and nation. Interestingly, Gill compared the Klan to a "loyal wife" and mother, and she suggested that the Klan's relationship to the nation was similar to the wife's relation to the home. The maternal endeavor was not always visible, yet the mother handled the needs of the home. The Klan fulfilled the maternal role for the Invisible Empire. However, she still wondered whether the Klan was living up to the goals that the order cherished. Gill wanted objectives for action. She questioned, "Are we going to be Christlike in our relationships with all men, showing to the world just why Protestant Christianity is better for it than any other religions? Or, are we going to reveal the spirit of bitter intolerance in condemning the intolerance of others?"[44]

Gill interrogated the religious ethic of the Klan, and she affirmed the need to be "Christlike," which she believed matched the true religious spirit of the Klan. Gill's pointed questions revealed her frustration with the actions of the Klan, but she still deferred to the men's authority by suggesting that Klansmen needed to provide a strong direction for both orders. In her speech, women, like Eve, were still helpmeets. She used her convictions to question their authority, but they did not give her the ability to rule the men's order. The women wanted to put their God-given power behind the Klan, but they needed instructions to follow. Again, Gill emphasized the role of women to support. She asserted:

We women of America love you men of America. We believe in the things that are high and good and holy. Our homes will be kept as sanctuaries for you. . . . We will mother your children, share your sorrows, multiply your joys and assist you to prosper in the way of this world's good. In return, we expect you to recognize our power for good over your lives, and in the nation. We expect you to be men of no ulterior motive, of no double-dealing, of no base conduct. . . . We pledge our power of motherhood to America. We can instill the spirit of our forefathers into the lives of our boys and girls. Our knees can be the altars of patriotism to them, and our homes the shrines of idealism where liberty can be fostered. The old saying that "the hand that rocks the cradle is the hand that rules the world" is true.[45]

Klanswomen offered their support, but Gill again hinted at the power of women over men. She also affirmed the power of those women to change the world. Such God-given power gave Klanswomen the ability to stand beside Klansmen in the fight for the nation. Moreover, Gill relied on Klan-sanctioned roles for women as mothers and wives to influence the development of the home and the nation. But her message was more radical because she alluded to the influence that women held over their children as transformative power over the larger world. White women were crucial for the implementation of the Klan's vision of Protestant America, and Gill's speech made such clear.

The *Kourier* continued to praise women for their attachment to the home. As in Gill's speech, Klanswomen were important as homebuilders and supporters for the Klan. The home, again, served as a foundation for nation, and a woman, "in all her purity and virtue," made the home a sacred space. The monthly reflected not only on the connection of femininity with home but also the ability of women to engage the political realm. The *Kourier* noted that the amount of control women possessed over the domestic sphere might be applied to government and politics. The monthly argued that women had historically played an indirect role in government, motivating husbands and sons, until the passage of the Nineteenth Amendment. "Woman gave to the world her greatest leaders, and is it at all out of place that she should now come to the front, proving her sex is fully capable of performing arduous and important duties?" Since the fairer sex gained the responsibility to pull their "share" in government, the *Kourier* affirmed the practicality of women in an age of radicalism. The hope was that white women would bring their abilities from the domestic sphere into the political realm. The "home builder" could become a nation builder.[46] Not everyone was supportive of the new political power of women, and the *Kourier* reported that some denounced the ability of women to act in the political process.

In 1926 Robbie Gill Comer (who married) deflected criticism of her women, who were accused of not employing the ballot as many deemed they should. Comer had to explain the poor showing of women in electoral politics as well as to defend her own order.[47] At the Third Biennial Klonvokation, Comer gave a speech that provided explanation. Comer focused on the mistreatment of women throughout history and argued that women faced a "handicap." In her narration of women's history, women started out as slaves to men, and later wives became "toys" to men, playthings who were at the whim of their male counterparts. As women began to assert their influence in the lives of their husbands and children, "Christian Europe," with the emphasis on chivalry, allowed for women to advance forward. Chivalry placed women on "a pedestal of reverence and respect," which Comer recognized as "unsatisfactory" for her female contemporaries. She remarked, "In the vow of Knighthood, to defend beauty, virtue, and the gentleness of womanhood, was the practical beginning of that respect in which, in Christian lands, woman is held today." Men still lorded over women, but there was slow progress. A woman "was still the keeper of the fires, and her voice was heard only beside the fires."[48]

Women continued to be the "keeper of the fires," and the true destiny of those keepers occurred in America. For Comer, America was not just an advanced civilization but a country that advanced because of Protestant Christianity. The Imperial Commander narrated American history from the *Mayflower,* to the Puritans, to Salem, to the founding of the Republic by emphasizing the role of women in the nation's development. Pilgrim mothers tended the fires of their husbands and endured unbearable hardships because they sought to found the nation beside their men. Comer observed that men ruled women in the beginnings of the American nation and neglected women's education because they did not realize that women could be their equals with education. Such was the crux of the issue for the leader of the WKKK: how could men expect women to use the ballot and learn the political system when they had been systematically held back for years? She questioned, "If we go slowly, in our share of the Nation's management, stumbling sometimes because the path is strange, can we be blamed, whose feet were seldom set and guided in that path?"[49] The denial of equal rights for women had caused adversity, which meant women had yet to embrace their political duty. Confined to domestic spaces and denied access to education, women faced nearly insurmountable odds that led to their ignorance of politics.

Comer was not, however, overly negative about the potential of women. By using the examples of pioneer women and heroines in American history, she suggested women could overcome the prejudices they faced and embrace the power of the political process. Comer pointed to Ann Hutchinson, "a woman of ambition and some brains," and Mary Dyer, a martyr for religious freedom, as two influential women who, though persecuted in their eras, laid the foundation for religious freedom.[50] Moreover, Comer stressed that men and women founded the nation together, so that while men used "swords of liberty," their female counterparts continued to tend the fires. Women fostered the men in their heroism and bravery. Comer proclaimed:

> Then—and since—woman taught her sons, encouraged her husband, held up the hands of her fathers, in the case of justice and liberty. What to her are the risks and suffering necessary to save men? She forever endured risk and suffering that men may be born. What fear does women know when her loved ones are in danger—woman—whose love has neither measurable length, nor breadth, nor height nor depth. Hers for countless centuries has been the tending of the fires. Hers forever shall be the duty that the fires she has helped to build shall not go out.[51]

Women tended the flames of liberty, and for Comer, women, in America at least, had reached a stage of equality. Her rhetoric echoed to the Klan's rendering of American history, in that she selectively uplifted examples of patriotic women as an example for her Klanswomen. She used national history as evidence of women's impact on American culture. Comer continued to rely on the language of women as helpmeets to the Knights of the Ku Klux Klan.

At her urging, Klanswomen were to "go about our business of helping Klansmen feed and keep bright the fires of true Americanism" rather than take charge of the push for liberty.[52] The professed equality for women did not match Comer's assertion of women's support of men. Despite the calls for equality, the KKK and the WKKK imagined women as essential to the domestic sphere, while men remained the active participants in the public restoration of Christian civilization. Women taught sons and encouraged husbands in the pursuit of liberty. Where did their daughters fit into that paradigm? Were they taught to tend the fires like their mothers? In her discussion of a

Klan Parade, Muncie, Indiana, 1923. Thirty thousand people attended the initiation of 600 candidates. Photograph by W. A. Swift. Courtesy of Ball State University Archives, Muncie, Indiana.

mother's power, girls were absent. What about the "virtue of girl-hood"? Comer talked directly to Klanswomen as mothers, so that Klan daughters might have been viewed as future mothers. A "lady klea-gle" from New Jersey was more direct. In her speech, she noted that the "girls of today are the mothers of tomorrow."[53] Girls were impor-tant as potential mothers who would foster and support their hus-bands and sons, but their possibilities in other initiatives for the order fell short. In spite of her rhetoric of equality, Comer affirmed the Klan's conflation of womanhood and motherhood, and she ignored the roles of girls as patriot citizens by centering only on sons. Klansmen and Klanswomen were not quite prepared for an active female citizen-ship, and Comer stressed that women would remain primarily the sup-porters of their male counterparts.

In 1928 Comer addressed the Fourth Imperial Klonvokation in Chicago, and her speech once again centered upon the American woman, her progress, promise, and problems. In her opinion, women had advanced. New professions as well as social and economic equalities were now open to American women, and she believed that women would not return to their previous, lowly positions. She critiqued "women extremists" who alleged that women had no physical limitations. For the Imperial Commander, women were still essentially "child bearers" who were "busy through a part of their lives with the reproduction of humanity unless the race is to die and the earth become as unpopulated as before the Almighty breathed into the nostrils of the first man the breath of life."[54] Even though she emphasized child-rearing as the main role for women, she questioned the supposed superiority of men by suggesting again that historically women faced more limitations than men. She interrogated the assumption that women needed men's governance. The burden of such history rested squarely on the shoulders of women, who were not able to rid themselves of those bonds. That burden plagued Comer, and she admitted it "rests upon my soul." Due to the critical nature of her speech, she claimed hesitancy for fear of being misunderstood by both women and men. Her speech trod over familiar themes of previous speeches and leaned toward the theological. Women had to free themselves from "our progenitor's mental servitude" to recognize their true potential.[55] Moreover, she stressed that God established the ability of both sexes:

> Woman is half the created kingdom of mankind, which is of the Kingdom of God. He made mankind in His own image—male and female created He them. That they should be fruitful and multiply was the Divine command, and each sex has its share in obeying that mandate, with women the mothers of the race and theirs the duty to exercise care and watchfulness over the sons and daughters of the race during the years when character is formed.[56]

By divine mandate, women were to reproduce the race. Motherhood, again, emerged as the most important role for women because it involved the molding of children into citizens. Comer admitted that not all women would be mothers, but all women had instincts associated with the divinely ordained role. Womanhood and motherhood became one and the same for Gill Comer and the men's Klan. In that speech, she also reiterated that women were to be helpmeets to men.

Together, men and women could create a better world in partnership than men had created alone. Such was crucially important because Comer lamented the state of the nation, particularly the youth. She noted that boys and girls had "taken a bit of control into their teeth" and were "dashing almost unhindered toward a future of unbridled selfishness and unhappy irresponsibility."[57] Parents provided bad examples. Mothers who lacked modesty produced immodest daughters, and children and parents embraced irreligion. Daughters became a pressing concern when they behaved immorally, as such behavior was a threat to citizenship. As potential mothers, their behavior directly affected their offspring. Divorce was on the rise, which suggested the collapse of the home, the sacred foundation of nation and religious faith. There were good men and good women who could restore the nation, and women would be on the front lines to combat immorality in their ranks.

For Comer, women directly impacted American life more than their counterparts in any other nation. With newfound equality, they could assist the men more than ever before. Men and women together could restore religion and order to the nation. Perhaps to assuage the minds of her male listeners, she emphasized that such equality would not mean that a woman would "neglect the home-building and home-keeping for which she is not only more experienced but better fitted than man."[58] It was even possible that women might move from helpmeets to true partners to their husbands with their new abilities. That partnership would lead to a better country for their children. Speaking for the WKKK, she pledged that the order would protect the government, which was "established Christian, Protestant, and white," to make sure that it remained so. Additionally, the members would raise children that supported those values to safeguard the American home. Women would be the helpmeets who worked to protect the Klan's vision of a religious nation. Her vision of partnership proposed men and women could accomplish their goals together. Her rendering of equality was a limited one, and it conformed somewhat to the Klan's vision of white womanhood. Klanswomen might be strong, active participants in faith and nation, but they were still bound first and foremost to traditional roles. Comer struggled to voice equality for herself and her order, but she conflated womanhood and motherhood similarly to her male brethren. In that conflation, women remained the supporters of their husbands and sons. She made it clear that her women wanted to protect rather than to be protected, but the defense of white womanhood required that Klanswomen employ their roles as mothers to claim authority. The ability to nurture and sacrifice remained the uplifted norms for the women's order.

However, the Klan was concerned not only with the protection of Klanswomen but also with American women more generally. Klanswomen might be able to protect themselves because of their affiliation with the order, but other American women were vulnerable to threats that they were not aware of. For the Klan, threats to white womanhood took the form of Jews, African Americans, and Catholics who might harm the purity of those delicate women. The order seemed most concerned with Catholics and their institutions. The order articulated its fear of Catholics as the danger to white women from both the confessional and the convent, and anti-Catholic lecturers, who gained popularity in Klan circles, stoked those fears to show that Catholicism was a personal as well as political threat.

*There is a continuous cry going up, from the lips of thousands of wives and daughters, to be delivered from the terrors of the confessional.*[59]

Comer asserted that Protestant civilization uplifted women, unlike other religious cultures. Klansmen and Klanswomen feared the influence of other religious traditions on young Protestant women, and the order often sponsored lecturers who documented in gruesome detail the hazard of Catholicism to the minds and bodies of young women. According to Kathleen Blee, the Indiana Klan in particular focused on "graphic tales of female enslavement and sexual exploitation" by Catholic institutions. Klan lecturers and various Klan publications obsessed about the celibacy of the priesthood, the treatment and character of nuns, and the stories of Protestant girls captured and enslaved by secretive convents. Blee contended that the apprehension about the sexual morality of white women gave the Klan a large following among Protestants, who were at best ambivalent about Catholics.[60] However, such trepidation was more than just an attempt at public legitimacy. After all, white women were seen not only as vulnerable and delicate targets but also as potential mothers essential to the creation of national character. Attacks on white women were harmful to the national body. The Catholic threat revolved around issues of morality and decency, but it also concerned the centrality of women to the formation and reformation of the Christian nation. They kept the fires of patriotism burning and provided religious education for their children. If the purity of white women was at stake, then the Klan's ideal nation was in danger.

Lecturers claimed that Rome targeted and captured Protestant girls. They affirmed the exaggerated fear and distrust that many Protestants and Klan members had about Catholics. As mentioned earlier, the order labeled Catholics as a menace to the Protestant foundations of the American nation as well as dangerous to the American form of government because of their allegiance to the pope. Their allegiance affirmed what the Klan believed all along: Catholics aligned with the papacy instead of their nation. The message perpetuated by Klan lecturers that Rome targeted women for slave labor and debauchery cemented the church's status as a possible foe to the American way of life. On the Klan lecture circuit, Klansmen and Klanswomen heard the tales of horror, which motivated both orders to protect white womanhood at all costs. Two of the most popular lecturers were Helen Jackson, "the escaped nun," and L. J. King, a self-proclaimed "ex-Romanist." King became a Klansman in the early 1920s, and he and Jackson often lectured together for Klan events. They even staged revivals for the Klan in many towns in Indiana while lecturing on the depravity of priests and nuns.[61]

Helen Jackson's popularity emerged from her *Convent Cruelties, or My Life in a Convent,* which was published in 1919. The volume had seven editions between 1919 and 1924. Jackson documented supposed cruelties at a number of Catholic convents in Pennsylvania, Michigan, and Kentucky, and her tale targeted Good Shepherd convents as particularly heinous. According to her own accounts, Jackson was raised in a Polish Catholic family, and from age thirteen she desired to be a nun. Her mother was adamantly against her decision and forewarned, "Helen dear, I do not want to stop you from going to be a nun and go to hell for your lost soul but you will understand me some day and think of what your Ma-me said." Jackson ignored her mother's warning and claimed, instead, that the nuns somehow hypnotized her into making the decision. Even more, she reported that membership in a convent might exempt her "from hearing these embarrassing questions that were asked of me at my first confession."[62]

The first convent she entered was a Felician convent. Jackson quickly realized that the nuns were not the kind, enchanting nuns she knew previously. Instead, they were cruel and vindictive to their charges. They punished her for many indiscretions, from disobedience to questioning the nun's authority to attempting to help other girls. Such was the major thrust of her "memoir," which recorded not only the punishment that the young Jackson faced but also the harsh penalties imposed upon the other young girls at convents. She even escaped, but determined nuns forced her back into the convent against her will by "pinching, punching, and nearly pulling me into pieces."[63] At various points in her narrative, Jackson turned her attention to the reader, especially after egregious acts by the nuns. She asked, "How many girls are struggling in those convents today, so you know? Is your daughter one of the victims, or perhaps your friend's missing girl? If so, I advise you to do your duty according to the fundamental principles upon which this great republic was founded."[64]

The most important principle was liberty. Jackson asserted that the convent, a Catholic prison, blatantly ignored the founding ideal. Convents enslaved girls in secretive places, and the enslavement denied their liberty. She encouraged her readers to save these girls from the injustices they encountered. Moreover, Jackson demonstrated that the abuse impacted Catholic and Protestant girls because priests prided themselves on kidnapping Protestants. The reasoning behind the kidnappings remained obscure throughout her "memoir," especially the logic for abducting girls. One Protestant girl attempted to escape by rappelling down the side of the convent, but her rope snapped. In her plummet, she broke her leg, and her screaming alerted the nuns. However, the police saved her because she told them she was Protestant and did not belong in the convent in the first place.[65] For young Jackson, the Protestant girl was lucky because she was able to escape when so few other girls ever had the chance.

To make obvious the gruesome punishments inflicted by the nuns, Jackson recorded the broken and bruised bodies of the girls. Body lice

afflicted them as well. The nuns punished Jackson, now Lena, for refusing to wear an overly warm dress while working in the laundry.
(Jackson asserted that the girls' names were changed, so their families
could not locate them.) Her hands and feet were bound, and she was
tossed into a small room where she licked up her sustenance "like a
dog."[66] Many girls were also dunked in a bathtub full of cold water
and lashed with "sewing machine straps," which left many bruised
and unable to walk.[67] Jackson reported that the nuns often did not inflict the punishment themselves but had their young charges commit
the crimes. The diabolical scheme meant the nuns could not be accused of wrongdoing. After the death of her mother, the nuns allowed
Jackson to return home to her family. Unfortunately, her reprieve was
short-lived because a priest re-kidnapped her and sent her to a different convent.

The rest of her tale focused on the cruelties she and others faced
until her successful escape. Jackson described the deceptive machinations of the nuns. If there were visitors in the convent, the nuns tied
up the faces of girls with black eyes to fake a toothache.[68] A dear
friend of Jackson, Modestus, died because of her chastisement. The
nuns intended to give her a "cold water ducking," but instead tossed
her into a "tub where they soaked the sanitary clothes of about one
hundred and eighty girls."[69] Modestus's dying wish was that her family would find out where she was located. Reflecting on the death of
her friend, Jackson stated:

> Oh, what would you do if your loved one was sick and dying away from
> home, longing to see you? Would you broaden the dividing line or grant
> their request? Yet this girl laid here looking as if she would like to see
> some one for the last time. Do you ever wonder why so many of our girls
> are missing? I say "Our Girls," because they are American girls; and if they
> are not American girls then it is un-American to treat them like that. Why
> tolerate such slavery and devilish practices in this country.[70]

She questioned how those practices could happen in a nation that
no longer tolerated slavery. Jackson's enslavement, however, came to
an end. She managed to escape with the help of her friend Vivian.
Mrs. Graeff, a Baptist, saved the girls by hiding them in her house.
Jackson then wrote about the horrors that she had faced in many con-

vents. She hoped that her book would lead readers to suppress convents in America and to save female inmates from the experiences that she faced as a young, vulnerable girl. On the lecture circuit, she regaled audiences with those tales of horror and reported on infanticides that covered up priests' illicit relationships with nuns.[71] Jackson's "memoir" primarily verified the damage to the bodies of young women and the intolerable cruelty of supposed Catholic prisons.

Her comrade on the lecture circuit, L. J. King, wrote pamphlets and gave speeches on similar topics, but he perceived the threat to American women to be primarily the confessional, which he argued ruined the female mind as well as the body. King claimed to be a former Catholic who was privy to knowledge the average Protestant might not have, and he asserted that the confessional was a den of iniquity for women because of the immodest questioning they faced. The crux of the issue for King was that the Roman Catholic Church required celibacy for their priests, and that requirement led to debauchery. For King, "horrible disorders, seductions, adulteries and abominations of every kind . . . have sprung from this practice of auricular confession."[72] King painted the penitents as "young, beautiful, and interesting females," and the priests as men "young and vigorous, without the grace of God in their hearts, burning with fires of passion, and in many instances wrought to a frenzy by the vow of celibacy."[73] The Roman Catholic Church thus created a problem because the priests were passionate and the female penitents had to answer indecent inquiries. According to King, such questioning led to dubious behavior between the two parties. The "ex-Romanist" maintained that confession was not a practice of which young women could abstain because it was one of the seven sacraments of the Catholic Church. He wrote: "All her faithful must pass through this cesspool of iniquity. Rome had decreed that her pious shall not escape; but that all should be bound . . . by the relentless irons of the confessional in order to reduce and enslave them to the will and wishes of her priest craft."[74]

The practice of confession guaranteed obedience of the faithful. It compromised the purity and modesty of American women. Abstaining from confession was a path to hell, so that the soul was at stake if one neglected confession. The church forced women into the dreaded confessional as part of their religious practice. King affirmed that the inquiries of priests proved detrimental to both the priest and the women. The supposed questions concerned the sexual experiences of the penitents, which he purported often led to relationships between priests and women. Basically, King envisioned the confessional as a tool used by the priests to seduce female congregants, married or single. The "depraved" questioning demoralized the women and made them vulnerable to the "lecherous" priests.

To demonstrate his claims, King used selections from other "former" nuns and priests, including ex-priest Chiniquy and Maria Monk. Using Chiniquy's text, King claimed many noble and modest women fell victim to vile priests. Between 1874 and 1875, Chiniquy wrote *The Priest, the Woman, and the Confessional,* which supposedly documents confessions he heard as a priest in Canada. Bishop Duggan from Chicago, however, excommunicated him in 1858 because of his previous indiscretions with female congregants.[75] Nevertheless, King still culled examples from Chiniquy's works to provide a general description of what occurred in the confessional. For example, he describes the penitent in her struggle against the priest: "She grows pale and trembles like an aspen leaf, her bosom heaves, showing the terrible storm within; her lips quiver, then move as she pleads to be spared the ordeal. She pleads, pleads for self-respect and chastity." King characterizes the priest as "the bachelor confessor" who seeks to "uncover every secret chamber in the soul of the penitent."[76]

Not surprisingly, the priest wins the battle of wills because of his claim that the woman must confess every sin or vile thought to be absolved. King laments that "every garment of modesty is torn in twain and the last vestige of self-respect has gone down leaving the heart bare, and open to his unhallowed gaze."[77] Using the metaphor of rape, King suggests that the priest is able to conquer the heart and minds of the women in the confessional. Through the confessional, priests seduce women, which leads to illicit sexual relationships, illegitimate children, adultery, and perversion. The confessors destroy female virtue, a requirement of confession rather than a consequence. Moreover, he also asserts that nuns and priests use the confessional as a cover for their sexual relationships. The "ex-Romanist" urged husbands and fathers to protect their wives and daughters from such evil, arguing that Catholic machinations ruin women, putting female modesty and virtue at stake. King implored Catholic women to turn away from the "deceiving words of the church of Rome" and embrace "the invitations of our Savior, who has died on the cross, that you might be saved; and who along, can give rest to your weary souls."[78] He felt they should convert to Protestantism to protect their modesty. Not surprisingly, Catholics did not welcome King's message. He claimed that the Knights of Columbus and Catholic mobs attempted to kill him multiple times because of his exposés on the church.

The writings and speeches of King and Jackson reverberate with themes of anti-Catholicism from the nineteenth century. Both Marie Anne Pagliarini and Tracy Fessenden argue that anti-Catholicism functioned as a method for Protestants to renegotiate gender norms in the nineteenth century. Pagliarini points out that the abundance of anti-Catholic literature declares the sexual immorality of Catholicism.[79] Building upon Jenny Franchot's work, she reasons that Protestants imagined the Catholic priest as sexually depraved because Protestants believed Catholicism represented "a threat to the sexual norms, gender definitions, and family values that comprised the antebellum 'cult of domesticity.'"[80] Anti-Catholic literature focuses on the importance of the purity of American women, and such literature has a pornographic quality that appealed to Protestants while also reestablishing the importance of sexual norms. The tales portray young women defiled by priests or convent life and serve as a lesson that Catholicism endangers both young women and family life. For Pagliarini, the sexually perverted priest and the dangerous convent are pitted against the pure American woman whose greatest asset is her sexual purity. Catholicism emerges as a path to sexual immorality that not only endangers individuals but also families and the larger society. Tracy Fessenden proposes that anxiety over gender roles drove the Protestant attack on Catholics.[81] Nuns and prostitutes surface in nineteenth-century literature as women of sexual excess.

In particular, Fessenden maintains that anti-Catholicism helped create and preserve the Protestant woman's sphere in opposition to the realms of prostitutes and nuns. Protestant women defined their sphere by placing boundaries between themselves and other women. Anxieties overflowed in their characterization of liminal women because nuns were enshrouded in secrecy, and prostitutes participated in behavior that was too public.[82] Catholicism was, once again, the imagined enemy by which Protestants sought to define themselves and project their anxieties about society.

The rhetoric of anti-Catholicism reified the gender norms that Protestants embraced and maintained the domestic sphere. The tales of convent horror and lecherous priests affirmed notions of what womanhood should be, and King's and Jackson's works uplifted similar themes. The depraved Catholic of the convent, or confessional, illuminated the delicate nature of Protestant womanhood and emphasized the fact that white Protestant women could not protect themselves. In their respective works, King and Jackson solidified the Klan's representation of white womanhood as fragile, vulnerable, and defenseless. The nuns and priests proved to be the villains in their stories, emphasizing the harm that women constantly faced.

The careers of both lecturers were born of fears of the Catholic Church. However, Catholics did not ignore the sordid tales and called into question the legitimacy of the narratives. *A Record of Anti-Catholic Agitators* listed all the known anti-Catholic lecturers as well as other Catholic detractors. The pamphlet included Jackson, King, and various leaders of the Klan (notably H. W. Evans). Jackson surfaced as a fake ex-nun sent to the House of the Good Shepherd in Detroit because of her own misconduct, including questionable behavior with young men. King was exposed as a fake ex-priest whose lecture tour proved controversial, and he had been charged with assaulting a woman in Indiana because she protested a portion of his lectures. He was also arrested for inciting riots and resisting arrest.[83]

Both King and Jackson were accused of acting in ways that they publicly disdained in their writings and lectures. Jackson acted immodestly, and King had harmed a woman. Whatever their indiscretions, however, they were both popular on the lecture circuit for the Klan. They confirmed the Klan's worst suspicions about the Catholic Church's treatment of women. They also demonstrated the helplessness of white women and their need of protection from Rome. Their stories of terror and debauchery echoed the Klan's unease about white women and the menace to the American home. Cruel convents and lecherous priests were not the only attacks by Rome on white womanhood. Catholic hierarchy's approach to marriage proved threatening to the virtue of Protestant women as well, because the Klan believed that Rome's next line of attack involved the sanctity of marriage.

*To change the established American customs concerning marriage would produce social confusion, discord, and finally civil war.*[84]

According to Imperial Wizard Evans, "Homes and family life are the warp and woof of America." Patriotism was the "overflowing of family life in National life," and Evans found that "spiritual autocracy" damaged the sacred institution. Rome, he accused, alleged the only right to preside over the marriage ceremony. The implications of Catholic jurisdiction over marriage were frightening because the order believed that the home would be "entirely under their control."[85] That would mean that Catholics would have a religious as well as political advantage over Protestants, and the nation might bend to Catholic influence. For Evans, marriage, and the laws surrounding it, proved to protect the "chastity of American women" and the "honor of the mothers of America who have been united in the holy bonds of matrimony by any person authorized by the law to perform the ceremony."[86] A challenge to marriage equaled opposition to the honor and purity of American womanhood, and the Klan needed to act to stop any religious group from harming the American home. Changing "American customs" of marriage would prove disastrous because of the potential for social upheaval.

Moreover, Evans reported confusion as to why religion needed to be a part of a legal agreement like marriage. He wrote, "It is inconceivable to me that religion enters into the ceremony of marriage by and beyond adding approval of Almighty God to any union formed in accordance with the law of the land." The approval from God, he asserted, likely emerged from Christian tradition because it contained no legal benefit. What troubled Evans was that Catholic practices would somehow degrade Protestant marriages. If the Protestant marriage bond was not valid, then the women in those marriages would lose all claims to honor and virtue. The American home might be disrupted if Protestant marriages were declared null and void.

Evans also feared the "intrusion of the Roman hierarchy" in the home because of a required "contract from the parties marrying when they are of different religious faiths, that the children born of marriage shall be raised in the Roman Catholic Church." For Evans, this was another example of the Catholic attack on religious freedom because of "the religious control of minds yet unborn." The parents in "mixed" marriages promised their children to the Catholic Church without the child having a say in his/her religious faith. To protect the home and the nation, Evans urged the Klan to "plead for the enactment of laws to protect the religious liberty of unborn Americans."[87] Catholic control over marriage could lead to Catholics' control over the nation if they were continually promised the religious adherence of the unborn. In Evans's logic, the unborn would become citizens under the auspices of Rome.

A Grand Dragon of the Klan put the matter a bit more bluntly. He asserted the arrogance of the Roman hierarchy in the realm of marriage, and he criticized the "Catholic" position of marriage being lawful only if performed by priests. He boldly stated, "I believe any person . . . who, by any means whatsoever, questions, denies or slurs marriage by civil law . . . should be heavily fined and sentenced to a long term at hard labor in State's prison." The Grand Dragon reported that an attack on marriage by civil law would lead to "millions of worthy American men and women" being branded as "libertines and harlots" and their children as "illegitimates." The Grand Dragon called for a federal law to defend "the sacredness of our marriages performed either by our civil magistrates or clergymen other than the Roman Catholic priesthood."[88] The Klan argued that members needed to prevent Rome's offensive on marriage before the compromise of American liberties occurred. The order's acute concern over the status of marriage was intriguing because one might wonder what caused their uproar.

Both the Klan and the WKKK lamented the decline of the marital bonds. Robbie Gill Comer derided the younger generation's careless entry and exit from the marital bond. She declared, "To tens and hundreds of thousands of our young men and young women, 'for better or for worse, till death do us part' has ceased to have any binding force whatever."[89] The "breakdown" of the home was possible because marriage was no longer forever, and divorce was becoming an option for the younger generation. With marriage in peril, the sanctity of the home was at risk.

However, much of the concern over marriage emerged from the annulment of the Marlborough-Vanderbilt marriage. In 1926 the *Christian Century* pondered, "When is a marriage not a marriage?" The article centered upon the annulment of the Marlborough-Vanderbilt marriage by the Catholic Church. The "salient facts" were that at age seventeen Consuelo Vanderbilt married a man with a "British title," Charles Spencer-Churchill, the ninth duke of Marlborough, due to her mother's cajoling. Two Episcopal bishops presided over the service, and the bride's father, as part of the marriage contract, received an income of $100,000 annually. The bride and groom remained married for twenty-five years, and they had two sons. Then the wife acquired a divorce and remarried. The duke entered into a new marriage as well, but he wanted to convert to Catholicism. Moreover, he wanted his new union to be considered valid by the Catholic Church. In "ecclesiastical court," it was determined that his first marriage "was not a marriage at all." "He was never married at all until he was married to the lady whom he now calls his wife." According to the *Century,* the Episcopal Church was offended by the fact that another church would "deny the validity of a marriage performed under its sanction."[90]

The Catholic Church defended its actions as not meddling with a non-Catholic marriage, but rather helping a person who wanted to become a member. Moreover, the church also asserted that the children were still legitimate. The *Century* argued that the case demonstrated people could be married according to the state but not according to the Catholic Church. The duke and his wife were "married enough to have legitimate children" but "not married enough to interfere with another marriage after an intervening divorce." The periodical continued, "And all this is in the interest of maintaining a professedly higher standard of domestic morality and a level of purity in family life to which the state and the [P]rotestants do not attain!"[91] By disdaining divorce, the Catholic Church supposedly upheld a higher moral standard than their Protestant brethren, but the *Century* writer called that assumption into question. For the *Century,* the crux of the issue was that the case seemed to suggest that Catholic marriages were superior to non-Catholic marriages, so much so that a non-Catholic marriage could be deemed not a marriage after all. The periodical stated that the

Catholic Church's action implied that its religious dictates were superior to the laws of the state.

The Klan also dwelled on the Marlborough-Vanderbilt case, and the Grand Dragon of the Georgia Klan disdained "the arrogant assumption of authority by Rome to interfere in the marital relationship of persons outside the church." The Klan leader questioned why Rome had the authority to interfere with a marriage contract performed in the United States, much less the ability to judge the legitimacy of said contract. For the Georgia leader, the annulment signaled the Catholic Church's obvious belief that the church led by the pope was superior to the state. Thus, the church claimed the sole responsibility to define when a union was actually a marriage. That not only impacted the husband and wife but also led to confusion as to whether or not the children were legitimate. According to the Grand Dragon, the Marlborough children became illegitimate with the annulment. Additionally, he reported that the church claimed the ability to regulate the marriage of all baptized persons. The leader questioned what that meant for all of the people who were the fruit of Protestant marriage. He stated, "It means that you and I, unless we were so unfortunate as to have been born within the Roman Church, which thank God the writer was not, are within the eyes of the law of the Roman church, of illegitimate birth, or to use the plain word, bastards."[92] For the Klan leader, Rome had judged all children of Protestant marriage as illegitimate; Protestant women were no better than harlots; and the home was an illusion that lacked moral foundation. If Rome became the dominant church in America, Protestants would lose their religious freedom and their claims to legitimacy. Such was the Catholic attack on the sacred marital bonds of Protestants, and such degradation could not be tolerated. For the Klan, the church clearly targeted the home, via marriage, to further its conquest of America.

While the Klan warned of the Catholic threat to marital bonds, Catholics attempted to show that their sacramental view of marriage had no bearing on their Protestant brethren. *Our Sunday Visitor,* a Catholic newspaper from Huntington, Indiana, ran a series on the Code of Canon Law (1918) and its relationship to marriage to illuminate what Catholics actually thought about marriage. Rev. H. C. Hengell wrote eight articles on the canon and marriage for the readers of the *Visitor*. Marriage was a sacrament entered into by two baptized persons. He noted, "There can be no valid marriage between baptized persons, whether baptized Catholics or baptized Protestants, which is not at the same time a Sacrament."[93] However, Hengell quickly stated that Protestants had valid marriages performed by ministers or civil officers. Catholics, then, did not believe that Protestant marriage was somehow illegitimate or lesser than the Catholic bond. The Klan misunderstood Catholic notions of the marital relationship, and its rendering of the Catholic threat to marriage represented their own concerns. The Klan was nervous about the status of marriage in the 1920s because of rising divorce rates and the "rebellion" of the younger generation. Catholics provided a foil to the apprehension of white Protestants about marriage and white womanhood.

Such anxiety about the status of womanhood presented in sharp relief the Klan's fears about the American nation. The protection of white womanhood was a rallying cry in a time when white women were asserting their rights, including members of the WKKK. Those women wanted to be partners in the struggles for nation while the Klan (and the Imperial Commander of the WKKK) stressed the importance of women as helpmeets to their men. The perception of white womanhood reflected the Klan's ideal for how the nation should be constructed. Women were home builders responsible for nurturing children and cherishing the domestic space. Motherhood equaled womanhood, and the order idealized Klanswomen and other American women in that role and chided them if they did not nurture and embrace sacrifice. Young women were potential mothers to be protected by the order of Knights to guarantee that the home remained a stronghold for citizenship and religious instruction.

The home, as mentioned again and again in Klan literature, was the foundation of faith and nation. The possible destruction of the home represented fault lines in their ideal nation. To protect women from Catholics, illegitimate marriages, and even themselves was crucial to maintaining a Protestant nation that harkened back to the ideals of the founders. Those Knights, in all their masculine glory, protected women so that the nation they envisioned could be perpetuated. Klansmen were soldiers, and Klanswomen were the keepers of domestic fires. In Klan print, both men and women in those roles guaranteed the continued control of white Protestants over national culture. The control of white women also signaled alarm with the perpetuation of the race and vitality of white supremacy for the order. White supremacy was another fixture for the movement, and the trepidation over racial purity molded the order's vision of nation and faith. Racial politics and supremacy, much like gender, were essential to upholding the Klan's particular vision of an exclusive, white Protestant America.

CHAPTER 5  *"White Skin Will Not Redeem
a Black Heart":*
The Klan's Whiteness, White Supremacy,
and American Race

*We avow the distinction between the races of mankind as same has been decreed by
the Creator, and shall be ever true in the faithful maintenance of White Supremacy
and will strenuously oppose any compromise thereof in any and all things.*
—H. W. EVANS (N.D.)[1]

*The group minds of other races and other nations have developed differently from ours.
Each nation has its own God-given qualities and its own mission: but each can do its
own work only if the racial and group qualities, which depend upon the blood of the
race itself, are preserved relatively pure. If any nation is mongrelized, that nation will
lose its distinctive quality and its power to contribute to civilization.*
—H. W. EVANS (1924)[2]

In the *Imperial Night-Hawk,* a Klan cartoon declared the "planks" of
the movement for 1924. In the middle of the cartoon, a white-robed
Klansman holding a fiery cross sat atop a similarly costumed horse. In
the background, the sun was rising, which suggested a new day
dawned for the order. Surrounding the archetype of a Klansman and
radiating from the sun were the various issues the Klan supported, including Protestantism, clean politics, and restricted immigration. The
Klan, as the cartoon indicated, was neither shy about its politics nor
the love of race, but white supremacy was noticeably absent. Such was
surprising because the 1920s Klan was historically infamous for its
racial politics. White supremacy was a slogan of the order, so why was
it excluded from the planks? On the other hand, in another cartoon
from the *Night-Hawk,* an Irish figure and a small band comprised of
two African American men marched down the streets of Atlanta. All
were grossly stereotyped with exaggerated racial features. The "Negro" figures wore marching band attire and almost appeared to be in
blackface. The Irishman appeared as a Leprechaun with a jaunty hat
and a flag in hand. Lining the streets were thousands of robed Klansmen who appeared ready to menace or attack the interlopers in the

Southern city. The caption read, "St. Patrick's Day in Atlanta, Georgia," and the cartoon implied that the Klan, at best, was unhappy with the small parade as the white-robed figures grimaced in frustration.

*Life* magazine originally published that particular cartoon to poke fun at Klansmen, but the order employed it to comment on race. The order did not appreciate or respect nonwhites. Moreover, as the cartoon made apparent, the figures signified a threat to the wider American culture. The cartoon signaled the order's view of race in general and the uplifting of the whiteness of members. In the 1924 cartoon, the ideal Klansman, surrounded by rays of light, indicated the beginning of a new era in which white supremacy would reign (even though white supremacy had already been a force in American cultural currents). The cartoon rendered the Irish and the Negro as backward races who lauded a foreign holiday. All of the figures seemed ignorant of the dominance of the white men who happened to be masked and robed.

Moreover, the cartoon displayed that those outsiders were the minority when compared to the prowess of the white-garbed figures and their dominance in American culture. The 1924 cartoon lacked the mention of white supremacy because that superiority was assumed. White superiority was truth for the Klan and for many sectors of the general populace. The 1920s Klan embraced white supremacy as a founding value of its order to protect both faith and nation from the perils of lesser races and miscegenation. Klansmen were not alone in supporting that position. White superiority, like Protestantism and native birth, emerged as an element of legitimate citizenship. Klansmen embraced the privileged status of white skin, but whiteness was an invisible, though occasionally visible, racial category for them. The Klan was hyperaware of its racial heritage and hypervigilant about racial boundaries—parameters that maintained racial purity and national purity. For the fraternity, white skin equaled "real" American citizenship.

William Simmons, the Klan's founder, opined, "We are here to grasp the great problems that confront us as a people, as a Nation, as the white men of the world."[3] The role of the Invisible Empire was the "preservation of the white Protestant race in America." For Simmons, a nation of white men eagerly awaited "the proclamation of the principles of the . . . Klan," because "the sons of the white man's breed were feeling the tremendous pressure that threatened to crush out the An-glo-Saxon civilization."[4] The Imperial Wizard affirmed the assault on white men and advocated that the fiery cross was their beacon of hope in a dangerous world. Simmons's rhetoric demonstrated that the Klan confirmed its racial dominance while simultaneously fretting over its demise. While uplifting the place of white Protestant men in the American nation, the founder also feared that those powerbrokers would lose control because of immigration and enfranchisement for African Americans. "Alien" elements threatened the purity of the nation, which amounted to racial purity for the order.

Membership in the Klan assuaged concerns over the threats to racial heritage. As a unified white movement, those men could maintain their hold on the national culture and on the nation's soul. The development of the order allowed for white men to come together, strategize, and renew their prowess over the nation. For Simmons, the "invisible phalanx of patriots" stood "as impregnable as a tower against every encroachment upon the white man's liberty, the white man's institutions, the white man's ideals, in the white man's country, under the white man's flag." The Klan was an organization of white men who believed that the race was in peril. The founder articulated a vision to members of the centrality of white race to the development of American liberty and principles, so that danger to the race equated with hazard to the nation.

White supremacy proved vital to the Klan's mission and motivation. While most Klan scholarship has recorded the emphasis on white supremacy in the 1920s Klan, it overlooks how the Klan crafted its whiteness and how members apprehended the creation of racial categories and norms. It assumes the whiteness of members without recognizing how the racial category impacted the Klan's rendering of nation, religion, and gender. It also neglects how whiteness and racial awareness intermingled with religious faith and nationalism in the order's print, speeches, and monographs. Exploring the Klan's proclaimed white supremacy demonstrates how the order envisioned whiteness as a category in opposition to other races and ethnicity.

The Klan claimed a theology of whiteness, in which the divine created divisions within humanity, and the fraternity proclaimed that racism was ordained, expected, and sacred. Enforcing the boundaries of racial purity fueled understandings of other races, primarily Jews and African Americans, as models to disdain. Despite the concern for racial purity, the Klan also articulated a vision of an amalgamated American race in which hybridity led to strength and tenacity of the American character. That racial alchemy complicated its vision of divine whiteness and highlighted the order's struggle to affirm nation, faith, and race as one and the same in its worldview.

*It is clear that our most important work is to preserve the white American race as a unified, integral and undiluted body.*

Racial heritage, much like faith, defined Klan membership, and whites joined by proving their racial purity. The order barred all who were rendered nonwhite from admittance. Imperial Wizard Simmons consciously prepared his organization as such. Various rules regulated Klansmen's behaviors, aims for the betterment of (white) humankind, and membership. Simmons prepared the *Kloran,* the constitution of the Klan, and several pamphlets to describe the "true" intentions of the Klan. The Klansmen's Creed detailed the correct beliefs of Klansmen:

I believe in God and in the tenets of Christian religion and that a Godless nation cannot long prosper.

I believe that a Church that is not grounded on the principles of morality and justice is a mockery to God and to man.

I believe that a Church that does not have the welfare of the common people at heart, is unworthy.

I believe in the eternal separation of Church and State.

I hold no allegiance to any foreign government, Emperor, King, Pope or any other foreign, political or religious power.

I hold my allegiance to the Stars and Stripes next to my allegiance of God alone . . . I believe in law and order.

I believe in the protection of pure womanhood.

I do not believe in mob violence but I do believe that laws should be enacted to prevent the causes of mob violence . . . I believe in the limitation of foreign immigration.

I am a native born American citizen and I believe my rights in this country are superior to those of foreigners.[5]

The creed illuminated the order's worldview that was Christian (Protestant), anti-immigration, patriotic, and anti–mob violence, but, more interestingly, the creed declared who was not included in the fraternity.

One had to purport belief in the creed to become a member of the Klan, which was markedly different from the Reconstruction Klan. Simmons's Klan revolved around rituals and symbols that expressed white Protestantism as well as patriotic sentiments. The order actively recruited Protestant ministers and offered them the Klan publications for free.[6] Protestant theology imbued Klan symbols and actions. The emphasis on whiteness resonated in the 1920s Klan, though Klansmen were no longer free to enforce their forms of vigilante justice in the newly bureaucratic order.[7] Simmons regulated meaning of the order as well as the racial hue of its members. Simmons wrote, "The Klan, organized to protect and advance the cause of our native institutions, is therefore exclusive in the restriction of its membership to white native-born Americans."[8]

H. W. Evans revised the creed, and race became a more explicit feature that was bound to theology. It stated, "We avow the distinction between the races of mankind as same has been decreed by the Creator, and shall be ever true in the faithful maintenance of White Supremacy and will strenuously oppose any compromise thereof in any and all things."[9] The Creator legitimated those distinctions, and white men were on top of the paradigm. The supremacy of whiteness was divinely mandated in the revised creed, but the racial threat remained for Klansmen. Catholics, Jews, and African Americans posed religious, patriotic, and racial threats to the principles of the order. The original creed asserted the rights of the "native born American citizen" as superior to others, and the order maintained the centrality of white dominance in its print culture.

Race was a binding concern for the organization, but the Klan carefully crafted the creed not to appear overtly racist, possibly to distance the 1920s Klan from the prejudice of its Reconstruction predecessors. The underlying sentiment of both creeds was that white citizens were in charge of the nation, and their rights should therefore be superior to all others. Racial superiority guaranteed dominance. Supremacy to other racial, religious, or ethnic peoples defined whiteness. That, however, was not an inclusive understanding of whiteness, in which one was white by virtue of the color of one's skin. For the order, not all whites were "actually white" unless they embraced white supremacy. White supremacy, a phrase that the Klan employed in print culture, was a crucial feature of the order's worldview. Klan authors painted several images of what the phrase should mean.

White superiority assured that whites maintained their dominance in American culture and abroad, so white supremacy guaranteed that vision. White supremacy, much like Americanism and Protestantism, faced the challenges of immigration, foreign ideas, and foreign religious movements. The white fraternity sought to preserve the racial purity of the nation and to protect the advanced racial traits of whites. For a Louisiana Klansmen, the supremacy of whites demonstrated that other groups were simply inassimilable. He believed that since Catholics and Jews already had their own "all-Catholic and all-Jewish societies," white Protestant Christians also had the ability to organize their own orders to laud the lofty character of their racial heritage. Despite the precedent of exclusive orders, the Klan did not appreciate the practice for others. Exclusivity signaled the inability to blend into white American culture. Catholics aligned themselves with a "foreigner or foreign institution" (the pope), and Jews did not accept Christianity. Neither set of religious peoples, then, could embrace the American nation. Additionally, the "Negro," who was not foreign, was "an inferior race," meaning "Klansmen were sworn to protect him, his rights and property and assist him in the elevation of his moral and spiritual being and in the preservation of the purity of his race."[10] The Louisiana Klansmen implicitly showed that the white race was superior, especially to the Negro, by noting that the Klan's duty was to keep pure not only the white race but also the Negro race. Such supremacy echoed the "white man's burden," in that Klansmen had to protect inferior races from themselves by guaranteeing that they abided by racial boundaries. Such was the burden of being a Klansman but also of being the superior race. To be white equated with "natural" superiority and dominance.

Louisiana Klansman W. C. Wright further defined white supremacy as having three main tenets. First and foremost, the white race proved superior to other races, and the race was "the advance guard of all great civilizations and must ever be the leading race of people on earth." Wright espoused the special place of whites in the advancement of global, not just American, culture because of unique talents, specifically leadership, gifted to whites. Second, the minister affirmed that America was primarily "a white man's country, discovered, dedicated, settled, defended and developed by white men." The superiority of white founders and members of the nation fashioned the national character, and the subtle notion behind Wright's commentary was that the nation would only continue to advance if guided by the hands and minds of white Americans. And third, the minister proposed that divinely imposed distinctions between the races signaled the necessity of racial purity.

Wright presented a vision of white supremacy in which white men were to be the rightful leaders of the world because of their advancements. Wright's commentary alluded to his understanding that America needed to maintain a racial caste to continue its greatness. The Klan minister also noted that race was not a natural construction, but supernatural, which meant God legitimated those distinctions. Parameters of race could not be questioned or challenged. According to Wright, God favored the white race, which meant that other races lacked divine support.

Imperial Wizard Evans also affirmed the vitality of white superiority. He noted, "The Klan law, requiring that its members be white men and women only, is an expression of this deep racial quality. It is clear that our most important work is to preserve the white American race as a unified, integral and undiluted body."[11] He noted that uplifting whiteness was one of the most important campaigns for his Klan brethren, because the downfall of the white race guaranteed the ruin not only of the nation but also of the world. Domination was a characteristic of that race, and the tenuous grip of whites on that dominance indicated the collapse of civilization. The Imperial Wizard affirmed the position of other Klan authors, including the centrality of skin color to membership, the leadership of the American nation, and the need to control and protect nonwhite peoples. White control and preservation demonstrated the order's pride in its racial heritage, as well as its fear that members would lose their prominent place in society.

The pamphlet *Fifty Reasons I Am a Klansman* declared the importance of preservation and perpetuation. The pamphlet asserted that "duty of every white, Gentile, Protestant, American citizen" was to "preserve the purity of his race and religion by choosing a mate of like color and creed."[12] White Protestants bore responsibility of religious and racial homogeneity to their nation. The duty of citizenship was the perpetuation of the white race to ensure the continued superiority of national character and national progress. That character was at stake due to the immigration of foreign people, ideas, and religions, as well as domestic threats residing within the nation's boundaries. Visions of the assimilative melting pot were not beacons of American progress for Klansmen but nightmarish visions of the demise of civilization. The order's nativism was part and parcel of its defense and perpetuation of whiteness.

*Immigrants are streaming into cities to make modern Sodoms and Gomorrahs.*[13]

For historian Matthew Frye Jacobsen, nativism emerged in the nineteenth and twentieth centuries as a crisis of defining whiteness. He argued that the 1790 naturalization law provided an open and inclusive definition of white persons, which nativists attempted to redefine from the 1840s to the 1920s to limit whom could be considered a white person. Moreover, immigration legislation in 1924, the Johnson-Hartley Act, "segmented the community of 'white persons' and ranked its disparate members—the arrival of desirable 'Nordics' continued to be favored, whereas the number of 'Alpines' and 'Mediterraneans' would be dramatically curtailed."[14] Through the act, legislation redefined whiteness. The Klan of the 1920s was a major proponent of the Johnson-Hartley Act. The *Imperial Night-Hawk* broadcast Klan opinions in its attempts to guarantee passage. The *Night-Hawk* as well as Klan pamphleteers weighed in on the dangers of unrestricted immigration. On the cover of the Klan pamphlet *The Menace of Modern Immigration,* a dragon appeared at the top of the cover climbing from the recesses of a dark cave. Instead of shooting fire from its mouth, the dragon vomited a stream of immigrants who oozed down the cover in a jumbled mass. Legs and arms twisted and tangled. Clothed in various forms of ethnic dress, with kerchiefs and caps upon their heads, the immigrants' feet dangled haphazardly underneath the title. The image made the pamphlet's position on immigration immediately discernible. Immigrants appeared as the bile from the belly of the dragon, and the printed words of the pamphlet did not improve upon the grotesque imagery.

"God never imposes insuperable burdens and obstacles upon his children," maintained the pamphlet. The burden of immigration was one that Americans could bear. The *Menace* argued that America was a "superior Christian civilization" in which a "smaller superior element" gave impetus to national character.[15] That element, of course, was white Protestant Christians. After lauding the "natural" state of American character, the pamphlet turned to jeremiad. The *Menace* stated:

> We are the melting pot of the world, a problem and a responsibility faced by no other people. Into it has been poured, almost promiscuously, perhaps in recent years designedly, every dross ingredient of citizenship that the earth produces. The good and bad have haphazardly been thrown together, to be turned out as the nation's human metal under the same conditions. No account has been taken of the different degrees of refinement required, nor of the unmergeability of basically conflicting elements.[16]

The melting pot was not a metaphor that lauded the benefit of Americanization and assimilation but rather signified the jumbled combinations of people of the nation. Additionally, those who praised the melting pot imagery ignored a basic fact, according to the pamphlet: not all had the ability to assimilate. The melting pot, instead, was a "cauldron of chaos and disaster."[17] The *Menace* proposed that Americans needed to decipher what God intended in the terms of immigration. Failure to interpret divine intention would lead to catastrophic combinations of cultures and races. According to the pamphlet, when assimilation was occurring, it was definitely not beneficial.

A Grand Dragon from South Carolina echoed those concerns in the *Night-Hawk*. For the South Carolinian, America was devolving into a ruinous state by becoming a "nation of nationalities chattering all the tongues of Babel."[18] Immigrants overran the nation, and the leader pleaded with the Klan to take action for immigration reform. He begged Klansmen to safeguard the nation from the destitute and unwashed masses. Moreover, he quoted a poet to emphasize his point: "O Liberty, white goddess, is it well / To leave the gates unguarded?"[19] Liberty was white, and the Klan was her defender. Her purity faced numerous assaults. By opening her gates, the hue of Liberty moved away from snowy white to a less desirable shade. For Imperial Wizard Evans, the "new" immigrants were the center of the problem. The first immigrants on American soil had been dedicated religious men of correct racial stock, and the new immigrants were the "diseased and festered sinners of despoiled and broken Europe." Evans continued, "These immigrants, far from being the Anglo-Saxon or Scandinavian types of fifty years ago . . . are mostly scum of the Mediterranean and middle European countries." They were "Italian anarchists, Irish Catholic malcontents, Russians Jews, Finns, Letts, Lithuanians and Austrians," who all created "the present horde of immigrant invaders."[20] Such vituperative language gave Evans's sentiments clarity. The "horde" of immigrants was a danger to the supposed homogeneity of American culture. Those aliens were of a different racial caste, and Evans feared their influence would create a "polyglot nation," which would challenge white Protestant America.[21] Assimilation might be not only the downfall of the Klan but also the death knell of the nation that Evans held dear.

In an interview for Chicago's *Daily News,* Evans's beliefs about immigration came to the forefront. Evans argued that before 1890, 95 percent of immigration was Nordic, and those immigrants were "kindred, desirable, easily assimilable people." But, only twenty years later, immigrants were "utterly and eternally hopeless from the American point of view." He continued: "What Nordic greatness has wrought in this country, if the Ku Klux Klan has anything to say and it is going to have something to say—neither shall be torn down by political madness nor shall be dragged down by disease and imbecility."[22]

Because the "new" immigrants were of lesser racial stock and mind, Evans and contributors to Klan print envisioned immigration as an evil to be stamped out. Assimilation was iniquity because it chipped away at the homogeneous white Protestant culture. The Klan supported the development and eventual passage of the Johnson-Hartley Act. Under the banner of "America must be kept American," the *Night-Hawk* monitored the work of Representative Albert Johnson, who was the chairman of the House committee on immigration. Moreover, the Klan organ documented the opposition to the bill by "Catholics, Jews, Italians and foreigners of all nations."[23] When President Coolidge signed the bill into law, the *Night-Hawk* declared that patriots reaped the rewards. Moreover, the passage of that law meant "the purification of the American citizenship" and protection from diseased bodies and minds.[24] The nation could maintain its roots.

Yet the Klan's lament over immigration did not end because of new, more restrictive legislation. The *Kourier* continued the well-worn attack against immigration. In an editorial entitled "Bramble Bush Government," the monthly reiterated the lingering fear that America was devolving into a "polyglot" nation instead of reaffirming the central white Protestant voice. Moreover, the "aliens" poisoned the minds of the young with their foreign ideologies. The order continued to be on guard against the evil of immigration. To show that the Klansmen were the preferred choice as guardians, the *Kourier* traced the racial and religious lineage of Klan members back to the founders:

> The Klan is a protest against the injection of non-American elements into our government to our hurt. Since the Klan is a movement of protest, Klansmen are, therefore, Protest-ants. Since our government sprang from Anglo-Saxon and Nordic races we are, therefore, as Klansmen, Anglo-Saxon Protest-ants. And since every signer of the Declaration of Independence was a member of the white race and since it is the ambition of the Ku Klux Klan to hold this government true to the fundamentals of the signers of the Declaration of Independence, therefore, Klansmen are of necessity, white Anglo-Saxon Protest-ants.[25]

The *Kourier* wanted to prove not only what the preferred national stock was but also that the Klan was representative of America in all its white, Anglo-Saxon glory. The lament about polyglotism reflected the Klan's anxiety about how immigrants would change the face of its beloved nation from pristine white to a cacophony of colors. Since the Declaration signers were white, according to the KKK, the nation should remain so. Immigrants menaced the purity and racial makeup of the nation, and the order sought to stop the flow of immigrants before the creation of another Babel, the illustration of divine disfavor.

Immigrants were poison because they had the ability to transform the character of the nation. The immigrants were considered nonwhite because of racial distinctions and incorrect religious and political backgrounds. The Klan's poignant trepidation about the purity of the white race echoed in their concern about immigration and their desire to limit membership in the order. The protection of whiteness not only entailed protecting the national borders from foreign elements but also the denunciation of domestic "interlopers" who presented themselves as American.

*Remember, my fellow Klansmen, that white supremacy . . . is not based upon the brawn of the brute but upon the superior culture, more, social and spiritual.*[26]

The concern over the purity of the white race and the assumption of its superiority were not unusual for the time period. The Klan gained popularity because of the changing social climate in the United States. Immigration, urbanization, and the migration of African Americans bolstered the Klan's national appeal. Klan meetings and gatherings appealed to white folks, who could gather without the fear of integration.[27] The paeans to white supremacy mobilized white communities, who voiced similar concerns about the possible demise of the nation in the face of immigration and African American enfranchisement. The banner of whiteness solidified a community of citizens.

The visibility of whiteness emerged in the clear demarcation of Klan identity in opposition to other groups. Klansmen, after all, were members of an Invisible Empire, and that invisibility meant that whiteness was sometimes less than tangible in the order's print and spoken words. The white identity of members became quite visible in the face of Klan enemies. These foes were hazardous to everything that the Klan championed and loved. The Klan identified not only how the groups were unfit for membership in the order but also how they were unfit citizens. Catholics, Jews, and African Americans emerged as the canvas for the Klan's religious and racial ideologies. As discussed, the order labeled Catholics as menacing to Protestantism and America because the Catholic, "if he honestly believes in the Pope" as a divine agent of God, "would first hold allegiance to the Pope and then allegiance to America."[28] The Jews were inassimilable and "indelibly marked by persecution with no deep national attachment," as well as strangers to the "emotion of patriotism as the Anglo-Saxon feels it."[29] In the Klansman's mind, Jews and Catholics proved to be dangerous to (the Klan's) American way of life. "American" was synonymous with "white" in the order's vision of nation.

More important, the Klan believed that both groups had willingly separated themselves from American life. Neither group participated in assimilation. The Klan's nervousness about these groups centered on their inability to assimilate, but the order insisted it was neither "religiously intolerant" nor showing racial hatred by criticizing Catholics and Jews.[30] Rather, the fraternity protected America from those "aliens" who could cause damage. The exclusion of such groups was necessary because the nation belonged to white men. Klan leaders noted again and again that Jews and Catholics had already identified themselves as different. Members, thus, reacted to the exclusionary practices of the other groups. Their reaction to Jews and African Americans, however, can be telling.

According to Imperial Wizard Evans, "the good qualities of the Jewish character" were well known even by him. Jews had faced persecution in many times and historical places, but Evans affirmed that America was a "better home . . . than almost any other land in which he [the Jew] had lived."[31] Evans and other Klansmen appeared to have begrudging respect for Jews because of their self-imposed exclusion to maintain racial purity. Blood and religious heritage were required conditions of "membership." A Klan minister lauded the Jews: "The Jews are a wonderful people: the remnant of a God-chosen race. Whatever may be said of them, one thing is sure: They have never forgotten God's law on marriage. Through nearly forty centuries they have maintained the purity of their racial blood, refusing to intermarry with others races; because God forbade such marriages."[32]

Their focus on racial purity and their denial of intermarriage made Klansmen appreciate the Jewish community's emphasis on segregation. The Jews understood that God forbade intermarriage, and they remained closely allied with his mandate. Despite such respect, Jews were still suspect in the Klan's larger racial ideology. Their focus on racial purity did not guarantee the Klan's acceptance. Rather, Evans documented supposed Jewish racial traits: "Law abiding, healthy, morally alert, energetic, loyal and reverent in his home life, the Jew is yet by primal instinct a Jew, indelibly marked by persecution, with no deep national attachment, a stranger to the emotion of patriotism as the Anglo-Saxon feels it."

In spite of Evans's somewhat positive list of Jewish characteristics, he still found them completely incapable of true patriotism because they were not white. Anglo-Saxons could feel patriotism, and their racial hue placed them in harmony with the needs of the nation. Moreover, Evans continued that the Jews' "jealously guarded separatism unfits them for co-operation" in the Klan's movement to unify "dominant strains in American life."[33] *The Menace of Modern Immigration* affirmed that the Jew was "alien and inassimilable" and provided a laundry list of the Jews' faults: "the evil influence of persecution is upon him," careers in banking and finance (which somehow conflicted with the agrarian emphasis on land-owning), and materialism.[34] The *Menace* called upon popular stereotypes of the Jews to show their inability to assimilate to larger culture. Their ethnicity, religious practice, and careers defined them as other and nonwhite. The undergirding assumption was that white Americans were not "money mad," and they had attachments to the land instead of profit. Moreover, the pamphlet confirmed that Jews could not become proper citizens through assimilation because if the "melting pot [were] to burn hundreds and hundreds of years," the Jews would still remain distinct from Gentiles.[35] For the Klan, the Jews proved to be too distinct to assimilate. The impulses of the Jewish race were supposedly opposite of the instincts of white citizens.

The *Menace* also turned its attention toward the Negro as inassimilable. The Negro was a lesser race than the Anglo-Saxon, and the "low mentality of savage ancestors" coursed through the veins of the "colored race in America."[36] The criticism of African Americans was more scathing than the denouncements of Catholics and Jews. Imperial Wizard Simmons noted that Negroes still spoke "the jargon of the jungle," and they were "but one generation removed from savagery." For the Klan founder, Negroes lacked the capacity to reach a developmental stage that would make them eligible for citizenship. The citizenship in the "great white man's Republic" was so valuable that "lower" races could not attain it. Simmons lamented the fact that "the black man from Africa" could be "clothed and vested with all the rights and privileges that the white man can claim, and are solely the white man's heritage."[37]

The *Kourier* warned that the approach to the Negro should disband prejudice because they could not reach the standards of white men. Dr. F.L.L. noted that the "Negro in America" was an "American problem that only white Americans can solve, if it can be solved." For F.L.L., the Negro was "a benighted race intellectually and morally" who proved to be a "burden" in national life.[38] To prove his point, the contributor provided a catalog of the Negro race's problems, including crime and the impact of enslavement. He also listed the very few Negroes who had remarkable ability, including W.E.B. DuBois and Booker T. Washington. F.L.L.'s list functioned more as accusation to prove the inferiority of the best and brightest Negroes when compared to whites. The author continued his offense by suggesting inferiority led to African enslavement. His conclusion ignored that white Europeans and Americans willfully enslaved Africans against their will for economic gain and advancement.

For F.L.L., there were only three options to handle the Negro conundrum in America: slavery, extermination, and amalgamation. The first two he ruled out as impossible. He observed that slavery had existed once, and it was not likely to be reinstated. Extermination was also impossible, but not because of the barbarity of the suggestion. Rather, Negroes were "breeding too fast." Luckily, according to F.L.L., Negroes were also prone to disease, which kept their booming birthrate under control. Finally, amalgamation was unacceptable to the contributor because the inferior race breeding with the superior race was a violation of nature. He noted that "the younger generation of Negroes are beginning to dream white dreams of amalgamation," but that dream was unattainable. F.L.L. turned to science to prove his point. Natural law, he argued, was explicit about the danger of racial amalgamation. Those laws of nature demonstrated that "wherever colored blood mingles with white blood it's always caused a degeneracy of the white blood." Proponents of racial mixing could not see the untold dangers to the white race if the practice was condoned. Racial mixing would bring the downfall of white superiority, and that was an egregious crime for F.L.L. He wrote, "If 'White Supremacy' is to be maintained in America, then white Americans must insist that the white peoples remain white and black peoples remain black."[39] The Negro should have remained in his lowly position.

Moreover, the contributor expressed his confusion over the Negro's understanding of his race. F.L.L. could not fathom how "millions of the black race in America have been deluded into the false belief that they—already—are 'just as good as the white man.'"[40] Such was impossible because of the supremacy and advancement of whites. Through the Klan's presentation of the Negro and the Jew, its support of white supremacy becomes tangible. The white race was all that those other races were not. Whiteness included mental and moral superiority, racial purity, aversion to crime, patriotism, and civilization. The Klan's whiteness was visible in the denunciations of Jews and African Americans, and those condemnations bolster white superiority. Yet the question remained: Why were whites understood as superior? For the Klan, the answer was found in religious renderings of the origins of races and nations.

*That we avow the distinction made by the Creator between the races of men and are pledged to forever strive to keep white Caucasian blood pure and undefiled.*[41]

In February 1926 the *Kourier* issued a terse reply to Dr. Glenn Frank, a contributor to the *Christian Century*. In December 1924 Frank had written "Has the Ku Klux Klan a Right to Celebrate Christmas?" The issue most pressing for the *Kourier* was Frank's presentation of the Klan's position on race. Frank wrote, "The Klan has no right to celebrate Christmas as long as it holds to its dogma of racialism." The monthly's cheeky response was "When did the *Century* become the guard that protected the 'Babe of Bethlehem'?" The *Kourier* attempted to show that Frank really had no understanding of the Klan's position on racialism, and instead, like many others, caricatured the Klan. Frank misrepresented the so-called racialism of the order. First, the monthly affirmed that the Klan supported white supremacy and opposed the "deluge of aliens."[42] The support of white supremacy was, therefore, different from racism because it was the love of one's race

rather than a hatred of another. Second, the *Kourier* questioned
Frank's interpretation of biblical text. Referring to a speech in which
Paul claimed all nations were made from the same blood, Frank as-
serted that the Klan could not be racist and Christian.

The monthly argued, "Grant that God 'made of one blood all nations.' Paul also decreed the bounds of their habitations. This clearly
shows that God did not intend the races to intermingle."[43] To press the
point further, the *Kourier* confirmed that Frank's position on intermarriage of the races was quite similar to the Klan's. Perhaps the author
and the order did not hold such different positions. Frank did not support the complete embrace of intermarriage but instead thought the
journey to that process should be slow and cautious. Moreover, the
*Kourier* laid out yet another Klan defense of white supremacy in its attack on the *Century* contributor: God created race. The divisions between the races originated from the divine. How could Frank argue
with the religious backing for separation of the races? By putting race
in the realm of the divine, the *Kourier* used religious reasoning to
counteract his argument against the Klan. For the monthly, the order
had divine support, but it was questionable whether Frank or the
*Christian Century* did as well.

The *Kourier* and the larger Klan understood racial boundaries to be
instantiated by God. The white race, in that particular vision, was the
pinnacle of civilization, and protecting the purity of whiteness reflected divine mandate. George Alfred Brown contended that Christianity was inherently white: "Christianity was born of the white race
and promoted by them, and while it is destined to become universal,
yet if the institutions which support it should be controlled by pagan
people the source of the supply of missionaries and Christian teaching
would be destroyed."[44] Christianity, then, was a white man's religion.
Klansmen alleged that whites were the superior race created by God.
Christianity was the order's religion, which supported the divine favor
of its race and advancement of white Christians over "darker" peoples.
The Klan racialized the so-called universal religion and normalized its
superiority in the process. As the *Kourier* reported, Paul believed God
had made racial distinctions. Whiteness demonstrated that God favored the order and its members. That was why keeping the white
race pure was paramount. The Klan had divine backing not only for

its religious choice but for skin color as well. For Brown, "the mainte-nance of white supremacy" required "the propagation of the ideals and institutions that experience has shown to be best for the race."[45] The Klan followed the will of God, and Klan authors noted such to show the magnitude of maintaining white supremacy through racial segregation.

To show the hand of the divine in race, F.L.L. quoted Gail Hamil-ton, who said, "If God made the white man white, the yellow man yel-low, the brown man brown, the red man red, He no doubt intended them to remain that color."[46] He believed that to be enough evidence to shun the practice of miscegenation. For F.L.L., if God made those boundaries, it was the duty of all races to uphold them. Interestingly, the author used science to show the travesty of miscegenation. W. C. Wright, a minister in the order, also supported the divine view of racial creation in his pamphlet on Klan ideals. For Wright, the Klan maintained "the distinction made by the Creator between the races of men," which meant that members "pledged to forever strive to keep the white Caucasian blood pure and undefiled." The minister also im-parted that those divine differences between the races meant the Klan was "unalterably opposed to intermarriage of whites and blacks, or the amalgamation of the races in any way." Wright continued that the "crime of the age was miscegenation."[47] White supremacy was crucial for the minister because it preserved the distinct characteristics of each race. Wright further suggested that "the mixing of racial blood is a violation of Divine Law." To prove his point, Wright expounded that the "flood on the world in the days of Noah" was a consequence of that particular sin.[48] The Klan minister also questioned the idea that everything created was made by God. He wrote, "God did not create a mule or a yellow negro. They are products of men's sin and shame." To prevent God's law from being broken, Wright proposed a law "to pre-vent the marriage of whites and blacks."[49] He articulated the position of many Klansmen: racism was divinely mandated, so miscegenation was a sin. When white blood degraded, amalgamation meant the deci-mation of the race and its advancement.

For the Klan, God created racial distinctions for the preservation of all the races and their unique qualities. To follow divine will required accepting those distinctions, even if they were paramount to racism. A

Klan pamphlet maintained a similar position to Wright and stated, "It is the duty of every white, Gentile, Protestant, American citizen to preserve the purity of his race and religion by choosing a mate of like color and creed."[50] As a part of citizenship, racial and religious purity had to be preserved. The pamphlet noted that patriotism was also based on uplifting as well as preserving religious and racial purity. Patriotism, then, could also be harmed if amalgamation was allowed. Miscegenation, too, was a national threat. Other Klan pamphleteers and editors were stringent as well in their denunciations of intermarriage and their uplifting of divine will.

In another Klan pamphlet based on a series of interviews by a national magazine, the message was more strident. In response to the question "What is the basis, then, for the distinctions which the Klan draws against members of these races and religions?" the answer was "Americans must face the fact that God Almighty never intended for the social equality of the negro and the white man."[51] The races were distinct because of divine mandate, and equality was far from guaranteed. Moreover, such distinction signaled that God definitely did not allow for intermarriage if equality was not even acceptable. The *Kourier* affirmed that opinion in response to Frank. *The Menace of Modern Immigration* upheld a position akin to Wright's, stating "there could never be intermarriage between whites and blacks without God's curse upon our civilization." Since God created the divisions, transgression would be punished harshly. The *Menace* wanted Klansmen and the general populace to know the danger in miscegenation: the ruin of the American civilization.

Imperial Wizard Evans also explained the divine reason for the disparity in the character of the races. For Evans, the issue revolved around the fact that each nation or race had "its own God-given qualities" and "its own mission"—but they only functioned properly if the "blood of the race" remained pure. He wrote, "If any nation is mongrelized, that nation will lose its distinctive quality and its power to contribute to civilization."[52] Moreover, the Anglo-Saxon race, the white race, had the most to lose in disobeying the divine separation of the races. The purity and the advancement of the white race would decline with miscegenation. The anxiety over racial purity and the tenuous nature of white supremacy was apparent even in the texts in which the Klan emphasized God's role in the race's development. The sin of miscegenation was not only the sin of violating racial purity but also the sin of dismantling the superiority of the white race. Miscegenation and amalgamation put fear in the hearts of Klansmen because they might lose their status as the divinely favored race. The violation of racial purity was the most disastrous sin because it signaled the declension of the white race. The anxiety over the purity of white womanhood echoed that sin.

Miscegenation also led to the violation of white women. In *Harold the Klansman* (1923), the heroine, Ruth, makes her disgust of racial mixing known. Ruth reads a novel in which a young woman is about to marry a white cultured gentlemen, only to find out before their wedding that he is one-sixteenth Negro. "In the end love triumphed and the girl married the man with a strain of colored blood in his veins." Ruth reacts vehemently to the conclusion by tossing her book to the floor and proclaiming, "Rot, rot, that makes me sick!"[53] Pearl Gardner, a fellow employee of the bank, witnesses the violent treatment of the book and questions the heroine's reaction. That, of course, allows Ruth to become the mouthpiece for the Klan's view of race. She argues that love cannot conquer racial distinctions because "love that violates the racial instincts, that runs counter to the experience of mankind, that does violence to the highest social standards—is love run wild and does not lead to the greatest good."[54] Poor Pearl does not realize the dire consequences of intermarriage, and Ruth lays them out for her. Most important to Ruth, a white woman falling in love and marrying a Negro man is a violation of "the racial instincts within her as well as the social standards of the race."[55] Ruth attempts to convince misguided Pearl that the white race is damaged through miscegenation, that the Klan preserves the integrity and the purity of race through this racial ideology, and the protection of the race equals the maintenance of the home. Ruth explains to Pearl that the "American home is a home that is based on the love of one man for one woman and requires a freedom of choice in marriage which is seldom found among the dark races."[56] For Ruth, the Klan protects the white race from amalgamation and helps other races reach their potential separately. Through a fictional character, Ruth, the author resounds the previous arguments about racial distinction. The threat of miscegenation might lead not only to the damage of racial stock but also to the ruin of the home.

According to Imperial Wizard Evans, miscegenation signaled race suicide, which ultimately would cost whites their positions of power in American culture. Evans argued by allowing "the crowding in of foreigners," "America's own sons and daughters . . . cannot support large families."[57] In other words, immigration and amalgamation stunted white births. Pointing to various studies, Evans confirmed that Anglo-Saxons were already in decline. Moreover, he agreed with "some observers" who argued that "every alien landing upon American shores prevents the birth of a native white American."[58] Therefore, miscegenation and immigration together, for the Imperial Wizard, caused race suicide. In the face of such threats, the dominance of white supremacy would no longer exist. Evans and his Klan feared that the rule of native white Americans might come to an end. Just because God mandated the division of the races, such did not guarantee protection of white dominance. Whites were under attack by immigration, African American enfranchisement, and miscegenation. Even though the divine stipulated racial distinction, the Klan worried its supremacy and homogeneity might no longer be valued. For Evans, white people encountered persecution, and intermarriage was just one prong of the attack. Persecution, as much as purity, described the experiences that they encountered.

*We white folks protect all these folks in their rights.*[59]

Klansmen envisioned themselves not only as the defenders of Americanism and religious beliefs but also as white victims surrounded by hostile minorities. Catholics, Jews, African Americans, and various other groups victimized the Klan. As discussed, the protection of the community was paramount in the face of so-called persecution, and that protection occurred in two ways: the public image of the Klan and the masked identities of individuals. The Klan had many newspapers dedicated to describing the merit-filled actions of Klansmen and klaverns (local chapters of the Klan). The *Imperial Night-Hawk,* the *Kourier Magazine,* the *Dawn,* and the *Fiery Cross* documented the order's actions. As we have seen in previous chapters, the production of print was one way to prove to an often-hostile audience the good works and "true" meaning of the Klan. The explicit purpose of the *Night-Hawk* was "to keep Klansmen informed of the activities at the Imperial Palace in their behalf and of the progress and advancement" of the Knights of the Ku Klux Klan.[60] It was also a way to demonstrate the order's victimized status.

For instance, the *Night-Hawk* reported the *Catholic Union and Times*'s slanderous remarks about the character of Klansmen. The paper supposedly called Klansmen "murderous bigots who work like rats in the dark," which led the *Night-Hawk* to point out that such commentary was "not the least bit bigoted."[61] The Klan became the target of bigotry as well as encountered accusations of prejudice. The publications presented the attacks the Klan faced as an organization that defended America, Protestantism, and whiteness. Catholic police and legislators cracked down on "peaceful" Klan meetings, Jewish rabbis petitioned the removal of Christian songs from schools, and despotic enemies destroyed Klan residences.[62] The weeklies and pamphlets deplored the Catholic, Jewish, and later Communist enemies as well as explained the problems that each of the groups caused for America and its defender, the Klan. The true meaning of the order was under fire, and the enemies disseminated faulty information.

In 1923 Imperial Wizard Evans documented the persecution of his members and their various attempts at peaceful assembly. In particular, an attack on the Klan in Carthage, Pennsylvania, where Thomas Abbott became a Klan martyr; a riot in Wilmington, Delaware; and a Catholic attack on a meeting in New Jersey. These events were unfathomable to the Klan leader. Why couldn't Klansmen assemble without being victimized? How were Klansmen different from any other fraternal order? To convey his surprise at the malicious attacks, he said:

> You never heard of a meeting of negroes being jumped on in the South; you have never heard of an assemblage of Jews being bothered, did you? We white folks protect all these other folks in their rights. Bless your soul, they [Catholics] were going to hold a meeting of the Holy Name Society in a place over in New Jersey and asked for police protection . . . [from]

Klansmen. Within twenty miles of there gathered five, six, or seven thousand rabid Catholics and rocked and wrecked the building which Klansmen were gathered about their own business.[63]

For Evans, this event provided a clear example of the persecution the Klan met as an order of white men. Groups asked for police protection from the Klan. Yet the order needed protection of law enforcement to guarantee the safety of its members. All other groups could organize peacefully, but enemies assaulted the order's meetings and gatherings.

According to David Goldberg, the second incarnation of the Klan faced much more violence than it doled out. In 1923 and 1924, anti-Klan forces employed violent tactics effectively against Klan rallies, marches, and demonstrations. From Chicago, Illinois, to Steubenville, Ohio, to New Castle, Delaware, to Carnegie, Pennsylvania, anti-Klan forces bloodied hooded Klansmen, destroyed electric crosses, and even killed Thomas Abbott. The martyrdom of Abbott, in particular, was a clear example of vicious actions against Klansmen by Catholics. In Carnegie, Klansmen fled the scene as they were being pelted with bricks. In Perth Amboy, New Jersey, "6,000 counter-demonstrators forced Klan members to seek refuge in a local Odd Fellows hall."[64] What Goldberg demonstrated was that the persecution the Klan faced was not completely imaginary. The order had its fair share of enemies who hated its racial, religious, and national politics. Anti-Klan forces did not view their countermeasures as persecution but retribution for what the Klan inflicted upon them.

One dramatic example of persecution was an explosion at the *Dawn* publisher's former office. The *Dawn* was a Chicago Klan weekly, and the bombing supposedly occurred at the time when the paper normally would have gone to press. Additionally, bombings occurred at a business that had recently advertised with the *Dawn,* as well as the pharmacy of Alfred Kurrasch, who was accused of being a Klansman by the newspaper *Tolerance.*[65] The *Dawn* ran one story on the bombings, accompanied by a picture of the wreckage and the title "Was This Tolerance?" The article began, "This picture shows the extent to which religious or racial fanaticism may be carried when lashed to the furious expression by propaganda." The Klan was clearly the target of the explosion. The *Dawn* squarely placed the blame on *Tolerance,* the newspaper of the American Unity League (AUL). Despite its title, the publication "aroused these passions through misrepresentations, calumnies, and lies." Moreover, the *Dawn* noted that after working up its readers, the magazine committed the egregious act of giving "them the names and addresses of Klansmen." That meant "the sick-brained religious fanatics and morons with a race inferiority complex might know whom and where to attack." For the *Dawn*, the irony was that *Tolerance* did not actually promote tolerance but seething hatred for the order. *Tolerance* maligned the Klan and Klansmen in its false accusations, which led to outright persecution of the order. Such inspired those with a "race inferiority complex" to create an attack on a beloved Klan publication. The *Dawn* noted:

> When those enemies of the Klan, masked in darkness more disguising than the pure white robes of a Klansman, slunk forth to murder and destroy they took a step which religious hatred although artificially inspired, made inevitable. That it did not lead to the murder of innocents . . . can be due only to the miraculous intervention of a good God who, even in his omnipotence must wonder what his mis-guided children mean by "Tolerance."[66]

The weekly reported that through the intervention of the divine no one was hurt. Members encountered persecution for the color of their skin and their dominance in the social structure of America.[67] However, the Klan blamed *Tolerance* and the AUL not only for the bombing but also for other large-scale assaults on the order. The AUL, composed of Catholics, Jews, and African Americans, attacked the order where it was most vulnerable: the League revealed the names of members. Blatant attacks on the Klan published in their journal generally were a nuisance, but the revelations of membership proved to be more damaging. According to Goldberg, the AUL should have been recognized for their "tactical ingenuity," because they "infiltrated the Klan, staged break-ins at various Klan offices and gathered information supplied by disillusioned former Klansmen." The AUL used the order's commitment to secrecy as a key part of their campaign. They revealed the names of members, including "over 23,000 Klan members in Illinois and Indiana alone."[68] The Klan fired back at the AUL for the malicious attacks, but the League formed under the banner of tolerance hit upon a Klan sore spot. Those attacks also gave much credence to the need for robes and masks to protect white members from dangerous minorities.

From the perspective of leaders and the membership, their enemies portrayed the KKK unfairly and should rely upon Klan publications to understand its goals and works. Their publications presented the new Klan as separate from the rough and rowdy types of the Reconstruction Klan. No longer were Klansmen supposed to be rogue vigilantes; rather, they were white Protestant men who upheld American values and freedoms. Klansmen were virtuous Knights in the Klan weeklies, cloaked in white fabric and wearing masks. The robe and mask became the most identifiable symbol of a Klansmen, and the costume was also the most contentious. It hid the individual identity of each Klansman while reinforcing the collective identity of the white, faceless, and homogenous mass. Because of the attacks by various anti-Klan forces, the white costumes of Klansmen became a necessity. The robes protected members and served as religious symbol and racial signifier.

Imperial Wizard William Simmons confirmed that the initial purpose of the robes was "in grateful remembrance [of] the intrepid men who preserved Anglo-Saxon supremacy . . . during the perilous period of Reconstruction."[69] The white robes for white men illuminated the second revival's purported allegiance to white supremacy. The garments linked the 1920s Klan to the Reconstruction Klan in one similar goal: the maintenance of white dominance. For the Reconstruction Klan, the costume allowed them to claim to be vengeful ghosts from hell to frighten African Americans.[70] However, the 1920s Klan did not attempt to frighten enemies by recalling that approach. The sartorial sign instead emphasized the purity of the order and protected members. Photographs of 1920s Klansmen capture their homogenous presence and their facelessness rather than their ghostly qualities. Photographs usually construct an identity for an individual, but the images of the Klan showed shapeless, indistinguishable figures.[71]

The photographs in Klan newspapers were primarily group pictures in full regalia, and the venue for personal autobiography became a method for representing a white-hooded collective. It was almost as if members displayed themselves as they wanted their America to be: white and homogenous. The order documented its presence in the robes for others to see in the print culture. The images depicted mem-

UNDER THE FIERY CROSS

"Under the Fiery Cross." This cartoon represents the Klan's official planks, including militant Protestantism, law enforcement, clean politics, and greater allegiance to the flag. *Imperial Night-Hawk* 1, no. 40 (January 2, 1924): 8.

bers in full regalia at picnics, rallies, demonstrations, and their own klaverns. The process of wearing the uniforms was the process of assimilation to Klan ideals and goals, but, more important, the robes served to reinforce the race of their wearers and to communicate the ascendancy of whiteness.[72] Caucasian hands peaked underneath the shapeless visage. Members in their robes presented a snowy-white

Muncie Klan Band, 1923. Photograph by W. A. Swift. Courtesy of Ball State University Archives, Muncie, Indiana.

movement that uplifted the superiority of their racial heritage through the racial and religious exclusion of other groups. Robes affirmed the race of the wearers and the "white" religion of Protestantism.

By putting on the robes, Klansmen magnified their racial whiteness. Robes provided a visible whiteness to invisibility of membership. The Invisible Empire became quite visible and tangible in the images of men wearing the white cloth, which demonstrated the numbers of members but not their identities. All of the members were Caucasian, of course, but with their faces hidden their stock became less apparent. The white cloth emphasized racial heritage, and the tall, conical hats made each Klansman a towering figure, echoing the theme of superiority. The whiteness of the robes magnified their racial caste as well as their spiritual righteousness.[73] The robe harkened back to the whiteness of Christianity, mentioned by Brown and others, but I would argue that the whiteness of membership was also emphasized by the focus on protection of identity.

The Klan needed robes to guarantee the secrecy of the order and the confidential nature of membership. The robes were fundamentally

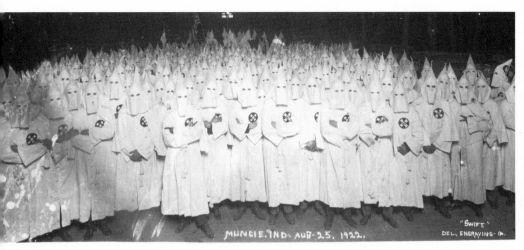

Muncie Klan, 1922. Photograph by W. A. Swift. Courtesy of Ball State University Archives, Muncie, Indiana.

related to the Klan's interpretation of persecution. The garments defended Klansmen against those who would persecute them for their ideals or skin color. The garments showcased the racial homogeneity of the order and protected Klansmen from being victimized for guarding their race, their religion, and their nation. For Imperial Wizard Evans, the mask guarded "scores of thousands of our members from intimidation, sabotage and worse." The begrudged mask guaranteed that "the organization of native born white American Protestants" could continue to be "bent upon saving American traditions from the mongrelized and criminalized foreign deluge."[74] The disguise allowed white Americans to save their nation despite the adversity they faced. The robes allowed Klansmen to be saviors of nation without becoming obvious targets of persecution and hatred.

The importance of the cloth manifested in the manufacturing of the crucial sartorial symbol. Evans established a factory for the production of KKK regalia, which only white hands crafted so as not to taint the garments and the membership. Heretofore, private companies employing Klansmen had created the garments, but Evans wanted the Klan to benefit economically from their production.[75] Only Klansmen could be trusted in providing robes to each klavern and its members. The uniform and the print culture demonstrated the Klan's clear vision of its persecution and how it related to the white skin of its members. Supremacy emerged through the race's need for protection and the order's reliance upon secrecy. Along with its focus on racial purity and persecution, the Klan also constructed an American race that needed protection from menace and harm, a construct that complicated the order's previous racial renderings because it emerged from hybridity.

*We have inherited . . . the God-given qualities that have made the native Americans distinct from other peoples.*

According to historian Edward Blum, in the nineteenth century "almost every aspect of American Protestantism was permeated by whiteness."[76] Blum further argued that nationalism after the Civil War uplifted whiteness and a common Protestant heritage to mend the wounds caused by sectional strife. Nationalism and faith in American character combined whiteness, Protestantism, and patriotism to signify who American citizens really were. Klansmen defined real citizenship in similar terms. Not surprisingly, the America the Klan safeguarded was the America that reflected the order's own racial and religious values. Members codified their understanding of nationalism in their characterization of the American race. Thus, America was a divinely created and guided nation. The Klan was an agent of the divine, which was why the order answered the call to save the nation and its institutions. Imperial Wizard Evans noted again and again that America was under attack, and only those of American stock were fighting for the soul of the nation. The order marshaled against those threats because the members "had faith in nationalism under which our racial qualities and our national genius should grow to perfect fullness."[77]

The white race honored nationalism and perfected it as well. Evans believed that the Klan's actions "came from the instincts with which God endowed our race." The order proposed that the Creator gave the white race special traits, which bolstered superiority and talent over other races. However, Evans understood race beyond the categorization of whiteness, and he envisioned an American race that combined racial and religious features. The American race was native-born, white, and Protestant. Religion played an equal part in his rendering of a special race endowed with "the greatest heritage ever given to a race of men." The peculiar race gained land abundant in resources, "a home where racial qualities can have the fullest development," an advanced legal system, and a slew of traditions and customs that fostered nation-building. Evans wrote: "We have inherited, together with a religion under which each man may hold direct communion with his Maker and consider for himself the great problems of life and death, the God-given qualities that have made the native Americans distinct from other peoples."[78]

The racial category included a personal relationship with God and the benefit of divinely ordained traits that guaranteed the success of the race. However, the race and its national home faced the threat of alien ideas, peoples, and attempts to redefine American nationalism, which Evans noted was only suitable to the racial character of whites. "American blood," however, did not ensure one would agree with the Klan because many of the racial caste were swayed by immigrant propaganda. The American race, for the Klan, contained a larger history unbounded by the continent.

Interestingly, the racial heritage of white Americans was a history of amalgamation. Evans argued that "there is a clear history of the peoples who were blended into what is called the Anglo-Saxon race, who were blended again in America with the blood of the Northern races of Europe." Evans painted the process of amalgamation in which white Americans gained all the worthwhile traits of the various (white) races, making them truly special. He traced all the races and their inherited traits to show the hardiness and unique abilities of Americans, starting with the so-called Northern races, who likely were Scandinavian. The severity of the climate molded them into "hardy, industrious, persevering, level-headed and independent" peoples who conquered Rome and England, "where they settled and were welded into one race."[79]

In England, the racial mixing continued. According to the Imperial Wizard, "this little island" allowed for the "mixture of Angles, Saxons, Danes and Norsemen." The amalgamation created a people who fought against tyranny and "Cosmopolitanism." This was only the beginning of what would become the American race. The English bloomed, which was pivotal to the development of Evans's beloved nation. The English peoples imbibed liberty and fought against the tyranny of the Roman Catholic Church. Moreover, Evans suggested that although Protestantism emerged out of Germany, the English adopted the religious movement and brought it to its fullest potential. The "little island" nurtured Protestantism, whereas France, Spain, and Southern Germany fell under the purview of the Catholic Church. England's pivotal role in creating American stock was due to English influence: "Protestantism is today synonymous with Anglo-Saxonism." Because of England's embrace of the religious movement, Protestantism became racialized. The Imperial Wizard proposed that "all Protestants are blood cousins" of the same racial stock. However, despite the importance of liberty in England, the country was not "free enough for the Protestantism that built America."[80]

As a result, the Puritans became the creators of American Protestantism. "Their faith in their religion and their race" drove them to leave England in search of a place where they could worship freely. They wanted freedom to worship their Calvinistic brand of Protestantism, and the Klan leader uplifted the color of their skin. To gain freedom, Puritans settled in Holland, a country that proved to be beneficial for worship. Evans argued that they left that country "because they could not maintain there those racial qualities which were dearer than life." They journeyed to America "to face starvation, cold and constant warfare that they might preserve their religious faith and racial integrity." Evans claimed: "The history of America is the story of how those pioneers, impelled by the same heroic qualities which had brought them to America, spread across the continent. They were joined, as time went on, by the like-minded of other races—closely allied in blood and spirit with Anglo-Saxons. A new race, the American, was born as it marched across the continent—building schools and steepled churches."

The American race, then, was born of Nordic and Anglo-Saxon traits, English Protestantism, and the experience of the new land. From white civilization, America formed her greatest liberties and accomplishments, including democracy, religious freedom, and public education, and the future of America depended upon the presence of whiteness. As Evans declared, "Just as this Western march built

America, so it must save America."[81] To protect its heritage, the order fought against "alien blood" that might erode the greatness of the white American race.

The order, according to its leader, must be cautious of four groups: Jews, Celts, Mediterraneans, and Alpines. Jews were a threat because they were "a people apart." Celts could assimilate, but only "a slight mixture of Celtic blood is valuable to the Anglo Saxon race." Moreover, Celts allied with the Catholic Church. Mediterraneans were of "mixed blood," which made them incompetent and lazy, and they too owed their allegiance to Rome.[82] Finally, the Alpine was Catholic, which meant he lacked "leadership, initiative, and independence." Each of those peoples would only harm the American race. For Evans, "if any nation was mongrelized, that nation will lose its distinctive quality and its power to contribute to civilization."[83] The threat of "mongrel blood" proved disastrous to the nation built by white Protestants. Furthermore, Evans believed the "Klan's peculiar mission" was a "divinely appointed mission—to work in every way for the fulfillment of Americanism, and for the protection and correction of America."[84]

Evans's predecessor, William Simmons, emphasized that the continent was made for the white race. He also envisioned the danger of alien immigrant elements on American culture. Simmons lauded the Anglo-Saxon as the foundation for the American race. He wrote that the Anglo-Saxon "sailed untried seas and wrote his compact of white supremacy while the angels hovered in the rigging of the Mayflower."[85] The Pilgrims, for Simmons, were the bearers of white supremacy as well as notions of religious freedom. Yet Evans placed more importance on how the white race created both Americanism and Protestantism. According to him, "The unity between Protestantism and Americanism is no accident. The two spring from the same racial qualities, and each is a part of our group mind. Together they worked to build America, and together they will work to preserve it. . . . We serve God best by serving mankind, and our greatest service is rendered through the building of a unified nationalism."[86]

Race was the foundation of the twin ideals of the fraternal order. Evans spilled much ink to prove that point. The Nordic (white) traits of Americans provided liberty and democracy. In another speech,

Evans argued that "Protestantism has found a real home only in the souls of men and women of Nordic races." The unity between Protestantism and the Nordic race meant that attacks on America by alien foes could lead to the untimely death of the religious movement. The Imperial Wizard proclaimed, "It is only through the maintenance in America of native, white supremacy . . . that Protestantism itself can be saved."[87] The religious movement was bound to the superiority and dominance of whites, which if challenged would lead to the downfall of Protestantism as a whole. White supremacy and the religious tradition were symbiotic; the ruin of one would equal the destruction of the other. Whiteness was the lynchpin of America's Protestant Christian society. The Imperial Wizard believed that the "greatest gifts" of being white Americans were the "racial qualities and instincts" of the Nordic. The racial stock of (white Protestant) Americans was the foundation of the nation's success and progress. He continued:

> From all these things we have in spite of our individual differences, inherited a national character, a national mind, and a joint understanding of and grasp upon the problems of life which are different from the ideas of any other race. *This national mind, which belongs to every member of our American group, and which is based upon our God-given and inbred instincts and traditions, is our most priceless inheritance and our most valuable possession.*[88]

God provided whites with this priceless gift as their rightful inheritance. The Klan's task was to shield the dominant position of whites in American society. For Evans, danger lurked in the form of unchecked immigration and foreign ideas. Neither nationalism nor the race could reach full potential with the presence of aliens.

There remained, however, a vexing problem. Evans and his Klan lamented "mongrel blood," yet the foundation of the great American race he proposed originated from the alchemy of races. Various traits materialized from the diverse white races: the Northern races of Europe, Nordics, Anglo-Saxons, and occasionally the Celts. How could the American race be pure as well as being a mixture? The core of Klan white supremacy was the purity of the blood. In his attempts to claim the heritage of Americans, Evans culled together various racial stocks that when combined created an elevated race, despite the heated Klan warnings about the danger of amalgamation for whites. How could Evans have argued vehemently for both? Could various white races have merged to create the American race? How did that reconcile with Evans's previous assertion about the addition of any lesser races leading to mongrel populations? This precarious position of the American race demonstrates that Evans obviously imbibed in racial theory popular in the nineteenth and twentieth centuries in America.

According to Matthew Frye Jacobson, Daniel Ullman, a leader in the Know-Nothing Party in New York, articulated a similar paradigm for America in 1868. Ullman believed that God had "hidden the continent of North America from Europe's 'civilized races' until they were properly prepared to undertake the bold experiment of self-government." Ullman favored Germanic races, the Anglo-Saxons, and the Teutons as the racial groups that influenced the formation of America. Those great races combined to form an American race, but Ullman still argued that an American race could be ruined through assimilation.[89] Scholar Carol Mason also noted that race often appeared as a matter of "character" as well as color in the early twentieth century. For Mason, "the semantic slippage between being 'colored' or not, having good character or not, and belonging to a particular place . . . began in the early twentieth century when determining what it meant to be American was debated in terms" of whiteness. Mason observed that President Theodore Roosevelt uplifted the melting pot while lamenting race suicide. The American race was a key phrase for the president, and "it effectively became a euphemism for 'the white race' despite his outspoken admiration" of race theories that viewed some forms of miscegenation positively.[90] Even Roosevelt maintained the contradiction that white miscegenation should be affirmed, but other varieties of race mixing should not.

Obviously, Evans promoted logic similar to Ullman and Roosevelt, but the contradiction still remained. How could one form of amalgamation be beneficial and the other detrimental? According to Evans, as soon as the American race was formed from various white races and their mingling with Protestantism, it somehow transformed into a pure white race separate from its amalgam origins. The American race was the pinnacle of civilization because of this forging of similar racial elements. As a result of this process, which was tempered through the encounter with American geography, the white American race was superior to all other racial castes. Whiteness was only diluted through its encounter with lesser "darker" races. The American race, in all its pure whiteness, stood the most to lose with assimilation.

Evans, however, did not correlate the racial mixing that created the race he loved with other forms of miscegenation. Those two appeared like foreign processes. Evans's trepidation about certain racial mixtures appeared in the Klan's pamphlets and newspapers alongside his praises of white supremacy and dominance. The creation of the American race was the only beneficial mixing. For the Klan, America was a white man's nation with the white man's religion, Protestantism. Evans's American race communicated that to the membership. White saviors in robes defended the "true" American race to stave off the ruin of national civilization and culture. White men had to save the American race from all those who did not qualify.

The white race was marching toward its destruction, despite divine favor and superiority, but white supremacy ensured the protection of the nation, the faith, and the place of white men and women. To demonstrate the fragile position of whiteness in larger culture, the Office of the Grand Dragon in Georgia relied on "lamentation of a full blood Indian over the passing of his race." Under the dramatic question "Shall the prophecy come true?" the poetic jeremiad was a warning to Klansmen about the vulnerability of their race.

> For hearken you Anglo Saxon,
> Though your belching guns may boom,
> You shall follow our father's footsteps,
> And your remnant shall march to its doom.
> You shall stand with us in the sunset,
> You shall follow our dying race;
> In the house that your fathers builded,
> An alien shall stand in your place.[91]

Whiteness was another component of the Klan worldview and demonstrated how the order's concerns with racial purity were bound to understandings of nation. White supremacy functioned to inform the true Americans of their lineage and the need to protect the nation's heritage. To protect the race and the nation, the Klan primarily fought rhetorical battles via text and print. In May 1924 the battle became physical as Klansmen fought Notre Dame students in the town of South Bend, Indiana. The Klan–Notre Dame Riot of 1924 demonstrated how the Klan actively sought to define membership and citizenship against the un-Americanism and supposed brutality of Notre Dame students. Anti-Catholicism reared its ugly head in the order's documentation of the riot, and the Klan's retellings of the event signal how the order's view of America intermingled with faith, gender, and race.

CHAPTER 6 *"Rome's Reputation Is Stained*
*with Protestant Blood"*:
The Klan–Notre Dame Riot of May 1924

*"It [the Indiana Klan] has never been accused of violence," says Mr. Frost, "and in a recent riot which I happened to see at South Bend the aggression was entirely from the other side. That bloodshed was prevented was due to the strenuous efforts of Klan leaders."*
—*THE TRUTH ABOUT THE NOTRE DAME RIOT* (1924)[1]

*Because of the intolerant views held by Rome, thousands of Protestants have been murdered in the past, and until Rome proves that she has discarded those murderous policies, Protestants will do well to fear her.*
—*IMPERIAL NIGHT-HAWK* (1924)[2]

In *Roman Catholicism and the Ku Klux Klan* (1924–1925), Charles E. Jefferson seeks to explain why the hooded order opposed Roman Catholicism. The pastor of the Broadway Tabernacle in New York, he makes it clear that he is willing to criticize both movements for their critical flaws in his effort to inform the American public about the Ku Klux Klan and to be a meditating presence between the Klan and its foes. In a sermon of the same title as the book, Jefferson examines why "the Roman Catholic Church . . . excites the Klan's antagonism."[3] According to Jefferson, the Klan was not essentially an anti-Catholic order. The numerical lack of Catholics in states under the banner of the Invisible Empire did not justify such behavior. He reasoned that since Catholics only made up "one-seventieth" of Christians in Georgia and one-fourth in Texas, the Klan could not be opposed to them just because of their presence. By Jefferson's logic, it would make no sense for the order to expend its energies on such a small population. Numerical absence, however, did not mean that Catholics were ignored either. Catholics, the pastor admitted, proved to be quite troublesome to the order because of their supposed lack of patriotism. Jefferson noted that the order was primarily a patriotic reform movement that sought to improve America for Americans.[4]

Catholics stood in the way of this reform. The pastor centered on the Klan view of Catholics because "the Ku Klux Klan gives the impression that a certain class of Americans are being discriminated against because of their religion." After asserting that he was not a Klansman, he argued that the Klan was not entirely religiously intolerant. The author explicated the Klan's complicated position on its Catholic neighbors. First and foremost, the KKK did not oppose Catholics because of their worship, even if it was "Christianity in Italian dress."[5] Jefferson wrote, "Americans have no objection of Catholics making use of candles and incense, holy water and the sanctus bell, and the gorgeous robes of the priest." Additionally, he wrote, Protestants did not mind Catholic doctrines, including transubstantiation, papal infallibility, purgatory, or the adoration of the Virgin Mary. He further argued that Protestants have no problem with Catholics believing such doctrines if they were able to actually believe such things.[6]

The quarrel between the Klan and Catholics lay firmly in the realm of politics. The Klan opposed the government of the church and hierarchy because of the threat of mass mobilization under the command of the pope. The New York pastor upheld the KKK position on the Catholic Church. The danger of the papacy and the hierarchy was one that Jefferson agreed all Americans should be aware of. Moreover, Jefferson asserted that Rome was partly to blame because the church ignored and disdained Protestants, which practically forced Klansmen to take up their hoods to protect white Protestant supremacy in America.

Despite his attempts to understand the Klan's relation to the church, Jefferson approached the issue differently from his Klan brethren. He urged his listeners and readers to recognize the patriotism and dedication of Catholics throughout American history. He pleaded with them to think of Catholicism at its best rather than obsess over the church. Such obsession made them the "victims of hysteria" who inhabited a "whole world [that] swarms with enemies." For Jefferson, that conspiratorial thinking elicited a divine response. Anxiety was "the penalty that God inflicts upon men who always think of their fellow men at their worst."[7] The pastor wanted to comprehend the Klan's persistent fear of Catholics, and he alluded to the many portrayals of Catholics present in Klan print culture. The hierarchy and the influence of the pope made Jefferson nervous, but he did not fully agree with the order's presentation of the church as an enemy of Americanism. Jefferson instead looked for the best in Catholic neighbors and their institution rather than condemning outright the religious tradition. The order, however, did not allow such a gracious interpretation.

The KKK feared Catholics because of their allegiance to an opposing religious movement, their ties to immigration, and the hierarchy of the church, which appeared secretive and possibly dangerous. Catholic strangeness caused the order's anxiety. Catholics were the perfect foil to the Klan's white American Protestantism; they epitomized all that the Klan hoped not to be. The Klan's imaginings of the church and her members showed acute concerns with nationalism, religious orientation, womanhood and manhood, and whiteness. The church symbolized all that could lead to the downfall of the Protestant nation.

On May 17, 1924, a riot broke out between Notre Dame students and Klansmen that actualized the Klan's fears about Catholics and their place in America. In the streets of South Bend, young men from the Catholic university attacked and ripped robes off of Klansmen who had gathered for a rally. Klansmen fought back. The rioting lasted for a total of three days and finally came to an abrupt end.

For the KKK, the battle quickly metamorphosed into a fight over American ideals. In the order's accounts, Catholics resorted to attacking Protestants in the streets. In his *Notre Dame vs. the Klan* (2004), Todd Tucker employed a Catholic narrative of the riot, in which the men of Notre Dame not only won that battle but also won the larger war. For Tucker, the riot in South Bend stopped the nefarious organization in its tracks.[8] Despite Tucker's earnestness, Klansmen being disrobed and threatened by Catholic students did not lead the order to the brink of destruction. Rather, in some ways the riot emboldened Klansmen and their fellow Protestant brethren in their verbal and printed attacks on Catholics.

The riot was significant and underplayed in the history of the 1920s Klan. While Tucker's work examined both the Notre Dame and Klan experiences of the riots, he overlooked the Klan's religious mooring. Moreover, he assumed, like much of the literature on Klan-Catholic relations, that the Klan simply hated Catholics. The riots, and the press surrounding them, tell a dissimilar story. The order feared Catholics as a threat to nation and to white Protestant dominance, even as Klan members claimed a place in larger culture. For the 1920s Klan, Catholics were powerful enemies, but Protestant citizenry still dominated American life. The Notre Dame–Klan riots elucidated Jenny Franchot's hypothesis that Protestants were attracted to and repulsed by Catholics in her work on Protestant-Catholic relations of the nineteenth century. The Protestant KKK was both attracted to and fearful of its enemy.[9]

Tucker's provocative work, then, overlooked the intricacies of the riots as well as the rhetoric of Americanism employed by both sides. Those riots demonstrated how both Catholics and Protestants in South Bend utilized the rhetoric of faith and nation in very similar ways. The men of Notre Dame struggled with the issue of being Catholic in America, and the Klan lamented the decline of Protestant America because of the presence of Catholics and other outsiders. Both were concerned about the character of nation and how their religious affiliations affected their citizenship. To explore the riot in detail demonstrates how ideas of American nation intermingled with religious ties and white supremacy. Moreover, the examination of the riot and its place in Klan print culture highlights how the Klan worldview functioned. Protestantism, whiteness, gender, and nationalism coalesce in Klan renderings of the riot and allow one to see how those fixtures function together to define the order. The Klan's characterization of Catholics, as a menace to American culture, explains why both sides interpreted the riot in such stark terms.

*Rome's reputation is stained with Protestant blood.*[10]

The *Imperial Night-Hawk* claimed that the Klan was "unalterably opposed to religious intolerance," but the news organ also professed common suspicions of Catholics held by Protestants. As the *Night-Hawk* noted, the "infallibility of the church," its disdain for Protestant marriages, and its belief that "all Protestants are heretics" led many to "dread its power." Rome proved to be intolerant and inflexible, not the Klan. The weekly reported that "Rome's reputation is stained with Protestant blood." The provocative statement said much about how the order interpreted and reinvented the Protestant relationship with Rome. Rome became the active oppressor of movements that it supposedly considered heretical. According to the *Night-Hawk,* the Catholic Church had a crimson-tinged history. Until the church reckoned with that history, how could Protestants feel anything but dread? Protestants could not trust the intentions of the church. The article continued:

> It is regrettable that there is a religion in America, that cannot be trusted. It would be satisfying to feel that no religion considers our wives concubines or our children bastards. It would be equally gratifying to know that no religion stands for murder and devilish cunning in its dealings with other religions. And, it would also be pleasing to feel that no church in America wants to limit freedom. But, until Catholics prove that they do not stand for such principles . . . safety demands that Protestants stand together, not to molest Catholics, but to protect themselves.[11]

The *Night-Hawk* insisted that Catholics must be watched to safeguard Protestants and American liberties, and such precautions were preventative measures. As the editorial made clear, Catholics could not to be trusted because at best they were saddled with a bad reputation, and at worst they were still an active threat to Protestants. If Catholics had control of the nation, Protestants would lose their constitutional guarantee to religious freedom and control over their own marriages. The *Night-Hawk* painted a dire image of the nation under the firm control of the hierarchy. A Texas Klansmen concurred with the weekly's assessment. He argued that "Romanism" sought to "lay its slimy, blood-stained, murderous hands" upon the public schools, Protestant marriage, and the government.[12] Romanism—more loathed than Catholicism because of its political rendering of the Catholic Church—could potentially corrupt American institutions.

While the order proved highly critical of the hierarchy, its stance did not necessarily affect members' views of ordinary Catholics and beliefs. Individual Catholics garnered protection for the freedom to worship. Imperial Wizard H. W. Evans emphasized that the Klan had no quarrel with the individual's right to worship. He argued, "The right to worship God according to the dictates of one's own conscience is necessarily one of the fundamental principles of human liberty." However, that right could be compromised if religious practitioners intruded upon the state. Evans affirmed that those "devotees" would have to "abstain" from political behavior for "their own protection."[13] The order grudgingly admired the efficiency of the hierarchy and employed it as a model for the Klan's own bureaucracy. The difference, of course, was that Protestant bureaucracy would be on the side of good intent, unlike the Catholic counterpart.

In a position paper on Roman Catholic hierarchy, H. W. Evans pinpointed one particular threat. The position of the pope within the tradition unnerved Evans, especially the pope's supposed challenge to the separation of church and state. He wrote, "The individual Klansman recognizes the right of the individual Catholic to worship God, pope, or idol . . . but the claim of the pope that he is God's divinely appointed . . . representative on earth complicates" the Catholic position in the nation. Evans believed that the pope's position gave him special power over the state. As God's human agent, the pope might hold more sway over the minds of practitioners than calls to patriotism by national governments. For the Imperial Wizard, this indicated that Catholics would be loyal first to the pope and then to America. Catholics, therefore, supported faith over government, which meant that they might not be prepared to support the state in all necessary arenas because of their religious allegiance. Evans, who was more subtle and cautious than his predecessor, observed that "the Knights of the Ku Klux Klan do not believe that persons of the Roman Catholic faith necessarily are un-patriotic, or in any way inferior to people of other beliefs, but we do hold that a system of Church government which claims dominance over state governments is dangerous to the state."[14]

The Klan fretted about the church because of its potential for political interference. In the Klan view, the church's system of teaching and government contradicted American principles and values. Individualism and religious liberty were not foundations of the Catholic tradition; rather, they were created, with difficulty, for Catholics to fully embrace the character and heritage of the nation. Bound by hierarchy and dominated by priests, bishops, and the pope, Catholics were unable to make their own decisions or to embrace fully American institutions. Evans feared that Catholics would destroy sacred American liberties because of the pope's influence on their hearts, their minds, and especially their votes. Through the pope's dictate, the faithful might block votes, which could prove ruinous not only to democracy but also to the sacred separation of church and state. To protect the nation from the church might be viewed as intolerance. Evans believed it to be a defense of all that he held dear: "For the Roman Catholic as a man we are sorry, for the Roman Catholic hierarchy as a semi-political religious organization we have an antipathy bred into us from the loins of our forefathers, the men who conquered the wilderness and built a nation, and set ablaze the beacon fires of liberty that all the world might see by that light the true road of happiness."[15]

Evans was not demure in his denunciation of the church's political organization, and he made it clear to his Klansmen that Catholics were a threat to the liberty of their Protestant nation. Interestingly, this logic could have legitimated Klan persecution and intolerance of Catholics, but the print culture remained remarkably silent about the Klan's actual treatment of the church and its members. Various Klan journals denounced Catholicism in their pages, but there was no documentation of how the Klan reacted to adherents of the faith.

Instead, the print highlighted the persecution of the Klan by Catholics. The order's opposition to the hierarchy led to the maltreatment of the Klan at the hands of the hierarchy and some willful individuals. Evans warned his members that "the heavy weight of Catholic persecution . . . is a cross we will bear," and bear they did.[16] The *Night-Hawk* documented various incidents of Catholic harassment of the Klan. In New York, Catholics and Jews supposedly championed the Walker Bill, which applied only to the order, instead of broadly to all secret organizations. The Walker Bill required antimasking, filing membership lists with the state, and limiting mailing and political participation of the order. Walker, according to the weekly, was a supposed Catholic or at least sympathetic to the Catholic cause.[17] The support of the bill demonstrated to Klansmen what they had believed all along: their foes were out to get them.

In one bizarre instance of Catholic harassment, Nelson B. Burrows claimed that the Klan abducted him and branded the letter *K* on three different body parts, including his forehead. At first, Burrows, a Catholic convert and a member of the Knights of Columbus, received support from his community of Rochester, New Hampshire. However, once the attorney general began questioning him on the attack, it became apparent that Burrows concocted the whole scheme to place the blame on the Klan. He staged the hoax and branded himself. The *Night-Hawk* reported that Burrows hatched the elaborate plot to harm the reputation of the order in Rochester because of a recent spike in Klan membership. Burrows, who fancied himself a religious martyr, hoped to turn the public against the order. The *Night-Hawk* noted that many people attempted to blame the KKK, but "the truth always comes out, sooner or later."[18] This plot, in particular, represented the fanatic persecution that the order confronted not only from the hierarchy but also from rogue individuals. Moreover, Burrows was a member of the Knights of Columbus, a fraternal order that the Klan believed was full of nefarious intentions toward Protestants in general and the Klan in particular. Thus, if Catholicism made the Klan anxious, the Knights of Columbus (KC) proved more menacing. The fraternal order, an organization of Catholic men, appeared harmful to the purpose of the order. Klan leaders conspiratorially noted that the KC engineered schemes against them.

To demonstrate the hazard of the KC, an Arkansas Klansman submitted an article from the *Memphis News Scimeter,* which detailed the dangers of Catholicism as well as his own analysis of the threat, to the *Night-Hawk.* The *Scimeter* pointed to the creation of two new American cardinals and the prowess of the KC. The addition of cardinals made visible Rome's encroachment on America. However, he proved more concerned about the possible power of the KC. Overall, the Arkansas Klansmen's position was similar to the standard line about the Catholic Church being a "master of political intrigue, masquerading under the guise of religion." More important, he uplifted the threat of the KC as the "militant arm" of the church. He pondered, "Or is it true, that the Roman Catholic Church . . . has so organized its militant arm . . . that it is now ready to remove its mask, throw down the gauntlet and defy patriotic American Protestants to do their worst?" America, in all her focus on liberty, created "a Frankenstein monster which now shamelessly threatens to devour its benefactor." By allowing freedom of worship and immigration, the nation had opened its doors to the church, its political apparatus, and varied missionary attempts. The church was powerful, and its fraternal order might have proved to be the most powerful in America, according to the Klansman's rendering. Catholic Knights took their orders directly from Rome, and the protection of the hierarchy was their central goal. With the power and support of the KC, the Klansman dreaded that the church might be unstoppable. However, the KKK's opposition meant that the hierarchy could not maintain reprehensible plans for America. The order imagined that its Protestant Knights were the only ones defending the nation from Catholic danger. To differentiate the order from other Knights, the Klan sought to demonstrate that it was the truly American order with the "blood of pure Americanism coursing" through its members' veins.[19] The other Knights, by default, were not actually American but rather pawns of a foreign interloper.

American or not, the KC had to be exposed to show its militant intentions and its hatred for Protestants. To further document the menace of the KC, the Klan issued a pamphlet titled *Knights of the Klan versus Knights of Columbus*. The pamphlet represented the issue in stark terms. One could either be allied with "the Roman Catholic hierarchy as representative of the Pope of Rome, or with the Ku Klux Klan representing Americanism in this country."[20] This "with us or against us" stand, according to the pamphlet, was no fault of its members. Catholics had caused the divisive rift by attempting to take over American government. The Catholic Knights were the strength behind that attempt. Additionally, the KC was to Catholicism what the Klan hoped to be to Protestantism: a militant, religious army fated with the task of protecting the faithful. Interestingly, the order ignored that they were parallel organizations and instead demonized the other Knights and their hypothetical practices. The KC was dangerous precisely because members sought to defend Catholicism, which was ironic considering the Klan envisioned itself functioning in the same but legitimate way for Protestantism. The defense of the faith was a virtuous task, but the defense of other religious movements was represented in the order's writings as harmful and intolerant.

To present the motivations of the KC, the aforementioned pamphlet contained a supposed KC oath interspersed with various images presenting Catholic torture of Protestants, supposedly from the Inquisition. The images of Catholics hanging, burning at the stake, and generally threatening and harming Protestants provided the visual evidence for the legitimacy of the oath. The images made the claims of the oath tangible and concrete, and Protestant readers might have been duly convinced by the depictions of torture. The interlacing of words and images clarified the Klan's intentions: to malign the Catholic fraternal order. The oath declared:

> I will defend this doctrine [Roman Catholic positions on Jesus, the Virgin Birth, the papacy, etc.] and His Holiness's right and custom against all usurpers of the heretical or protestant authority. . . . I do further promise and declare that I have no opinion or will of my own or any mental reservation whatsoever, even as a corpse or cadaver . . . but will unhesitatingly obey each and every command that I may receive from my superiors in the militia of the Pope, and of Jesus Christ. . . . I do further promise and declare that I will when opportunity presents, make and wage relentless war, secretly and openly, against all heretics, Protestants and Masons, as I am directed to do, to extirpate them from the face of the whole earth; and that I will spare neither age, sex, or condition, and that I will hang, burn, waste, boil, flay, strangle, and bury alive these infamous heretics: rip up the stomachs and wombs of their women and crush their infants' heads against the walls in order to annihilate their execrable race.

The graphic words made the images appear tame. The oath avowed the destruction of heretical Protestants in grotesque and visceral methods. It proved what the Klan had believed all along: the hierarchy was waging secret and open wars against them. The oath confirmed the Klan's worst fears about the KC, including its unquestioning devotion to the pope. Catholics, again, became the unthinking followers of a powerful religious leader. Additionally, the pamphlet provided "evidence" that Catholics harmed heretical Protestants as well as the permissible violence committed by the KC under the dictate of the larger church structure. Men, women, and children were not safe from the Catholic fraternal order and its wicked intentions. The violence was not limited to Protestants, however. If a Knight of Columbus was weak or uncommitted, the oath detailed his fate as well. The member might have "his brethren . . . of the Pope cut off my hands and feet and my throat from ear to ear, my belly opened and sulphur burned . . . and my soul shall be tortured by demons in eternal hell forever."[21] For the Klan, what more evidence could one need to show the violent tendencies of the KC, or of Catholics in general? The oath served as a warning to those who did not align with the order that if Catholics conquered America, torture might await all Protestants. It was clear that unlike Pastor Jefferson, the Klan wanted to view Catholics at their worst, even if it was an imagined worst.

Not surprisingly, Catholics responded to the KC Oath and asserted its falsehood. *Our Sunday Visitor,* a national Catholic weekly, denounced the fake oath and its continued popularity. The "bogus" oath continued to be used despite "a committee of prominent Masons," who vouched that "no such obligation forms any part of the ritual work" of the KC. The fraternal order even published the real oath as a countermeasure. The *Visitor* noted that the *New York World* proclaimed the oath was fake and documented that "paid organizers of the Klan" circulated it. Moreover, the *Visitor* questioned the Klan's own oath as dangerous and harmful.[22] For the weekly, the Klan willfully used a bogus oath to malign Catholics while its own oath recorded the threatening nature of its order. To support those denouncements, the *Visitor* offered a $1,000 reward to anyone who could prove the oath was "genuine." The reward was also offered for any documentation of "misstatement of facts concerning real Catholic belief and practice on subjects treated."[23] For the weekly, the Klan's persecution of the Catholic Church actually helped the church in its cause. The church could not change bigoted minds, so Klan membership demonstrated who the bigots really were.

The *Visitor* reported that the church benefited from all of the negative press and argued, "The more Protestantism espouses the Klan, the more its cause is sure to be injured, because where the Klan disgraces itself, Protestantism must be disgraced." The order, in its attempts to discredit other religious movements, was presenting a seamy side of its own faith. Protestants, then, had to repudiate the Klan or suffer a fall from grace at the hands of the order. Additionally, the *Visitor* claimed that those tactics actually helped the church because members and new converts came to its defense. The weekly reported, "In a nearby city, where the Klan became very powerful, every Catholic became zealous; the Knights of Columbus Council initiated one hundred new members" and "a wealthy Catholic donated a home to the Knights." Klan actions, according to the weekly, actually led to growth of the KC, which was obviously not the order's intention. The *Visitor* also responded to Klansmen in a gentler manner than the hierarchy was treated in Klan newspapers. The weekly affirmed the order's anti-Catholicism, but "we must not presume that every person who has joined the Klan has anti-Catholic antipathies in advance."[24] The motivation to join was not necessarily driven by that antipathy, and the *Visitor* sought to give Klan members the benefit of the doubt.

The order was not so gracious in its renderings of the KC or the church as an institution. Klansmen were at best ambivalent about Catholics and their position in the nation and in the world. Their condemnations of the church and the Catholic Knights bordered upon hatred and were fueled by deep mistrust of the church's intentions. The order was on the defensive, watching and waiting for the despicable intents of Rome to become public. Catholics repulsed and attracted Klansmen, and more often than not the order chose to interpret the church as a political organization in religious clothing. The order feared what impact Catholics might have on the political realm, yet much of the ambivalence about the church revolved around the Klan's professed Protestantism. To prove the distance between the religious movements required exaggeration and accusation.

The riot in South Bend proved to be a candid example of Catholic intolerance and persecution for the Klan, as well as evidence of the order's fight to uphold true Americanism. The battle in the streets became a canvas colored by Klan fears and anxieties about Catholics. For many Klansmen, that event proved that even ordinary Catholics could have despicable intentions toward the order. It was a self-fulfilling prophecy that allowed the order to present all that it upheld under vicious attack. Much like its understanding of the KC, the Klan portrayed those events to fit previous narratives about Catholics and their avid loathing of all things Protestant and American. The riots, similarly, gave "evidence" to Klan claims about the peril of the nation.

*Students of Notre Dame College . . . are the latest to commit an outrage against citizens of the Invisible Empire.*[25]

The *Fiery Cross* reported the following about the Klan–Notre Dame Riot of 1924: "In South Bend, Indiana, while it seems impossible, students of Notre Dame, a Catholic university, burning with hatred,

Klansmen on parade. Courtesy of Ball State University Archives, Muncie, Indiana.

attacked men and women . . . and trampled under their feet the American flag."[26] The riot became a pitched battle between Protestants and their fierce attackers, Notre Dame students (who represented the whole of Catholicism). The order viewed the event as indicative of Catholic affronts on Americanism, their hatred for Protestants, and their continued persecution of the Klan. In essence, the riot proved to Klansmen that their beloved nation was under attack, and they were the victims as well as defenders of the noble heritage of the nation. Their depictions, then, present their victimization. Moreover, reports of the rioting served as a rallying cry to mobilize the white Protestants not only of South Bend but also of the nation. The riot legitimized the Klan's worldview and demonstrated that its concerns were tangible and real. The assault by Notre Dame students illuminated that Catholics were a menace that needed to be stopped.

Interestingly, the riot in many ways was unremarkable. It was cataloged as one of many incidents of persecution. For the Klan, the event

# Students Rout Klansmen

*Masked and garbed in full klan regalia, guards directed visitors at a klan festival in South Bend until fifty university youths descended upon them. The students ripped off the robes of the guards and then paraded the streets with the captured costumes.*

A 1924 newspaper clipping from South Bend, Indiana, describes the initial skirmish between Klansmen and Notre Dame students. The students disrobed several Klansmen and then proceeded to wear the "captured costumes." Courtesy of the University of Notre Dame Archives, Notre Dame, Indiana.

was only the "latest outrage" faced by "citizens of the Invisible Empire," which suggested the normality of persecution that the Knights faced. According to the *Night-Hawk,* May 17 started as a mundane Saturday. Klansmen gathered in South Bend for an ordinary ceremony and parade. The villains of the weekly's rendering were the Notre Dame students, who opposed a "peaceful assembly of one hundred percent Americanism." Those students uncovered the location of the Klonclave, the assembly, and they "booed and hissed" at all the men who had gathered at the hall. The *Night-Hawk* characterized the beginning of the riot in the following terms:

> At about half past eleven, when the students realized that the Klansmen intended to carry out their purpose in a quiet and orderly manner, they [the students] became violent and began to stone an American flag hang-

ing from the Klavern window and to smash the windows of the building. As the Klansmen left the hall, they were pounced upon[,] beaten and cursed by the students of Notre Dame. The Klansmen, as is their custom, refrained from fighting back those who opposed their movements and actions, again proving to the world that they are law-abiding citizens, willing and ready to let the law take its course.[27]

The Klan news organ presented the Klansmen as innocent victims of many indignities. According to the weekly, the police did not come to the order's aid because much of the police force was Catholic. Those sectarian police officers did nothing to halt the student escapades. By late afternoon, Protestant policeman joined the fray to protect their kindred citizenry of South Bend. Interestingly, the *South Bend News-Times* described the police presence as more substantial in number. According to the paper, all available police reserves were called in to quell the riot. Policemen wielded clubs indiscriminately at both parties and arrested Klan and anti-Klan factions.[28] The order, however, emphasized not only the lack of police presence but also the larger motivations of the rioters: to assault all the Protestant citizenry. By the order's accounts, the students enlarged their attack to include any Protestants, whether they were affiliated with the Klan or not. All white Protestants became potential targets and victims of the rowdy students.

On May 18 the rioting was quieted by rain, and the students returned to the university. However, the street clashes began fresh on Monday, May 19, until Father Matthew Walsh, the president of Notre Dame, intervened. According to the *Night-Hawk,* students mercilessly trampled American flags and harmed the citizenry. From the order's perspective, the riot boiled down to attacks on Klansmen, Klanswomen, and civilians because they were Protestant and American, and their enemies, the students, lacked patriotism.

To document the persecution, the *Night-Hawk* described the event and the order crafted a pamphlet, *The Truth about the Notre Dame Riot.* In the twenty-one-page document, the Klan inserted editorials, eyewitness accounts by Klan and non-Klan writers, and opinion pieces. The pamphlet documented the injustice Klansmen faced at the hands of riotous Notre Dame students and a cover-up by the media that revealed the press's support for Catholics. It also provided a time line from the first attack to the development of "general rioting." In the so-called general rioting, students attacked Protestant men, women, and children. Students trampled flags, accosted women, destroyed robes, and even harmed the young and the elderly in the fray. The students were clearly on a rampage. Robes "were torn from them and torn into strips," and students tied "the strips about their arms" and gave "them to girl sympathizers to mark them as friends."[29] One eyewitness, Wingfoot, noted that the students quickly outnumbered the Klan. The order decided not to hold its parade, not because of numerical disadvantage but because members feared more bloodshed.[30] Wingfoot also reported the savage beating of an elderly couple. He wrote, "One of the most distracting scenes was the beating of an old white-haired couple who carried small American flags." The elderly woman was injured.[31] According to the *Fiery Cross,* police sustained countless injuries, and "hundreds of women suffered the injured indignities of receiving threats and scurrilous names."[32] In one incident mentioned again and again in the pamphlet, a student accosted a baby girl in the tumult. One account rendered the story most dramatically:

> Finally, at one of the cross streets, I saw several of them [students] run across the street and surround a woman who was pushing a baby carriage on which was fastened a small American flag. One of them tore the flag from the carriage and pulled out the baby. He slapped the baby first on one side of the face and then on the other, and threw it, literally threw it, to the woman I suppose was the mother.[33]

According to Wingfoot, that was one of the "worst outrages of the day," because the "baby girl was struck in the face by a student and her mouth was badly lacerated." According to the Klan, one student stooped so low as to slap a baby because her carriage sported a flag. Such showed the desire of the students to attack any Protestant Americans no matter what age. The elderly and the young were full-fledged targets. The assaults were not limited to people and included symbols of Americanism. Students trampled, ripped, stomped, and otherwise desecrated flags. Wingfoot reported, "When appeals came from American citizens not to stone and trample flags, students cursed and said they 'were not American flags.'"[34] In excerpts from the *Noble Country*

*Democrat,* a purported non-Klan editor commented on the calamitous events and the defilement of the flag. The editor of the *Democrat* disdained the South Bend police as Catholic and as "appear[ing] to be more ignorant than they sound." He also interviewed "a very gentlemanly Catholic" who claimed "he didn't like Klansmen," but "he could not condone the desecration of the flag." The editor continued at length to make sense of the riot and the possible Catholic responsibility for the event:

> We much prefer to think this whole disgraceful affair at South Bend was fostered by that small thirty to thirty-five per cent of the students who do not owe allegiance to this country, but facts ascertained by close investigation do no bear this out. They—the foreign element—were undoubtedly of the mob hurled on a peaceful citizenship from the gold-domed college, but they were not all of it. They were augmented and assisted and undoubtedly directed by religious fanatics who are citizens of the United States, but feel called upon to disgrace the flag of this free land just because it is given a place of honor in an organization they oppose.[35]

By trampling the flag and rioting against the Klan, Catholics proved that they showed no allegiance to nation. In the editor's opinion, they were fanatics who possibly did not deserve the honor of citizenship.

Notre Dame students, then, showed their true colors in the riot: they did not support the peaceful nation, which provided "the foreign element" a home. According to the pamphlet, the students were not patriots. Moreover, the Klan impugned the faculty of Notre Dame, who supposedly did nothing to punish their students for the "outrage." Wingfoot reported that the riot lasted a full day without response by the faculty "to stop thugs who were beating women and children, dishonoring the American flag and causing riot." He also reported that the "gates" of Notre Dame had been locked down with no reason given.[36] According to an eyewitness, the institution had not sufficiently punished the students for their malfeasance and their apparent lack of patriotism. The students had harmed innocent bystanders, including vulnerable women and children, and defiled the flag. Yet no action was taken. To add insult to Klan injury, Mayor Seebirt of South Bend requested the Klan "lower" its emblem from the order's headquarters. A Klan officer rebutted that "the Knights of

Columbus display their emblem at lodge halls . . . and that Roman Catholic churches display crosses." According to the account, the mayor did not continue his request.[37]

Despite the uneventful end to the riot, various authors of the Klan pamphlet affirmed that the persecution did not end with these events. Rather, the press attempted to cover up the students' actions in South Bend. According to the *Fiery Cross,* the reactions of the press made it more apparent to the residents of South Bend that the Klan stood for law and order. Residents witnessed the dramatic events of the riot and read local newspapers that "made an effort to gloss over the actions of the mob." One "prominent business man" questioned whether the press could ever be trusted to fairly represent the Klan since the actions of the Notre Dame students were hidden.[38] To show the prejudice of the local papers, the Klan paper pointed to an article on Edward Dinneen, a Notre Dame student who supposedly lost his life in the riot. The article placed the blame for the riot squarely on the shoulders of the order and claimed the students protected themselves and their university from the attack.[39] The story was evidence of the press's bias against the Klan and the distortion of the events to benefit Catholics. Klansmen were the victims in this event, but the press defended the unpatriotic Catholics. Even though the persecution continued, the Klan adamantly believed that they had won the war, even if they had lost this particular battle to the students.

According to the *Night-Hawk,* the riot led to a boon in applications in Indiana. The "state organization" was "clogged by applications from American citizens seeking membership in the Klan." Additionally, the states nearest to Indiana also gained in membership applications. From the Klan's perspective, the riot proved to be beneficial because it demonstrated to white Protestant Americans the real threat of Catholics and Catholicism to the nation. The riot, in some ways, proved that the church actively maligned the Klan and Protestants. The Klan, despite the beatings, flag trampling, and robe ripping, had won a significant battle against the enemies of Americanism who might have altered the face of its beloved nation. For Catholics, however, the order impugned the Americanism and dedicated patriotism of not only the Notre Dame students but also all Catholics. Both the Klan and the students interpreted the riot as a battle for Americanism, but each side believed they were defending national pride and culture.

*There is no loyalty that is greater than the patriotism of a Notre Dame student.*[40]

In the May 17, 1924, *Notre Dame Daily,* an editorial titled "Heads, Not Fists" reported that an "organization formed of men who do not think deeply nor well plans to parade in South Bend this evening." The organization was obviously the Klan, and the *Daily* reported that Mayor Seebirt forbade the order to parade and beseeched "the Notre Dame men to remain at the university on that evening so possible trouble could be avoided." Moreover, Seebirt confirmed that South Bend's officials had the situation under control. The *Daily* warned Notre Dame students that ignoring the mayor's request would only cause trouble. The editorial continued:

> Some children need to be whipped, but the approved correction is an appeal to growing intellect. The approved correction is a means, not of administering bruises that surely pass with time, but of impressing mental blows that do not pass but remain to germinate. Tonight, we are sure, Notre Dame will give some shallow-minded ones an example of respect for the law. Tonight, Notre Dame men will use their heads and not their fists.[41]

The *Daily* reported that the students who planned to march against the mayor's order would not provoke the Klan. Instead, they would provide a shining example to the order of how to be law-abiding. The president of Notre Dame, Father Matthew Walsh, also issued a bulletin on the Klan rally and parade, which was reprinted in the *Daily* on May 18. He noted that Notre Dame was "interested in the proposed meeting of the Klan," but the university planned not to interfere. Interference in Klan events, according to Walsh, led the order to "flaunt its strength," which "resulted in riotous situations, sometimes in the loss of life." Walsh also acknowledged why Notre Dame students might feel the need to react to the order:

> However aggravating the appearance of the Klan may be, remember that lawlessness begets lawlessness. Young blood and thoughtlessness may consider it a duty to show what a real American thinks of the Klan. There is

only one duty that presents itself to Notre Dame men, under the circumstances, and that is to ignore whatever demonstration may take place today. . . . It is my wish that the Klan be ignored, as they deserve to be ignored, and that the students avoid any occasion coming into contact with our Klan brethren during their visit to South Bend.[42]

Unfortunately, some Notre Dame men did not heed the warning of Walsh to stay on campus. According to Todd Tucker's account, curiosity motivated some Notre Dame students to disobey the directives of the president. The Klan gathering and parade could not be missed. For Tucker, the events began when Notre Dame students scared, attacked, and even disrobed Klansmen in alleys and on the streets. One student Tucker chronicled, William "Bill" Foohey, even had his picture taken in a tattered Klan robe. The fun quickly turned violent as Klansmen decided to arm themselves with handguns underneath their official costumes. Tucker noted that deputy sheriff John Cully, a Klansman, called the governor in hopes of mobilizing the Indiana National Guard.[43]

From that account, the students had caused a full retreat of timid Klansmen, and they began to gather at the Klan headquarters. Luckily for the students, the first floor of the headquarters housed a grocery, from which the creative students plucked potatoes and took aim at an electric fiery cross that was mounted atop the building. Tucker wrote:

The first potato shattered the third-floor window that shielded the cross, showering a few pedestrians with glass as they ran for shelter. A fusillade of potatoes followed. Each time one hit its target, a red bulb would burst with a pop and a shower of golden sparks. Occasionally, an angry-looking Klansman would peek out through a window, but a barrage [of potatoes] would quickly drive him back into the shadows. Soon, only the top bulb of the cross remained glowing. Throw after throw fell short. The men had exhausted their arms trying to hit the bulb, and their throws were becoming weaker and wilder. The remaining red bulb mocked them from above.

Eventually, Harry Stuhldreher, a Notre Dame quarterback, burst the final bulb.[44] Some students decided to enter into the headquarters, and according to their accounts one Klansman confronted them with a gun. Tucker noted that priests from Notre Dame attempted to have the

William "Bill" Foohey, a Notre Dame student, wears a stolen Klan robe in 1924. Courtesy of the University of Notre Dame Archives, Notre Dame, Indiana.

chief of police intervene in the riot, but he was dismissive of their concerns.[45] Luckily, rain dampened the excitement of the day. *Our Sunday Visitor,* in agreement with the *South Bend News-Times,* noted that a "thunder shower" kept the violence at bay and made Sunday a day of rest.[46] However, by Monday, May 19, Notre Dame and Klan forces again clashed in the streets.

The *News-Times* reported that the rioting began again when the Klan hung a fiery cross from the window of its headquarters. Police stationed near the headquarters noticed "500 members of the anti-Klan forces began a march." Faced with such a large presence of Klansmen and Notre Dame students, "policemen charged the crowd and wielded their clubs at random members of both factions." In the process, the police clubbed some "innocent bystanders." Fights broke out all over the city. Even "railroad detectives" were called in for reserve. The police force arrested both Klan and Notre Dame rioters, and members of both groups sustained injuries in the brawl. Catholic students claimed that they "were attacked with clubs, bottles and other weapons carried by men who wore white handkerchiefs as arm bands."[47] The order eventually removed the fiery cross, and the crowds dispersed somewhat. For the *News-Times,* the appearance of Father Walsh calmed the calamity. The Notre Dame president talked to the students in an attempt to hamper their tempers and soothe bruised bodies and egos. Walsh stated:

> Whatever challenge may have been offered tonight to your patriotism, whatever insult may have been offered your religion, you can show your loyalty to Notre Dame and to South Bend by ignoring all threats. . . . If tonight there have been violations of the law, it is not the duty of you and your companions to search out the offenders. I know that in the midst of excitement you are swayed by emotions that impel you to answer the challenge with force. As I said in the statement issued last Saturday, a single injury to a Notre Dame student would be too great a price to pay for any deed or any program that concerned itself with antagonisms. . . . There is no loyalty that is greater than the patriotism of a Notre Dame student There is no conception of duty higher than that which a Notre Dame man holds for his religion or for his university.[48]

# N. D. Students Pledge to Leave Klansmen Alone

South Bend, Ind., May 20.—[Special.]—Notre Dame students today pledged themselves to refrain from further rioting with the Ku Klux Klan in South Bend. The declaration of the students followed addresses by Knute K. Rockne, director of athletics, the Rev. Matthew J. Walsh, C. S. C., president of the university, and other officials.

A 1924 news clipping reports that after the intercession of Rev. Matthew Walsh and athletic director Knute Rockne, Notre Dame students pledged to leave the Klan alone. Courtesy of the University of Notre Dame Archives, Notre Dame, Indiana.

Walsh's measured statements affirmed the indignities that the students faced at the hands of Klansmen and the dismissal of their patriotism. He argued that it was not necessarily their fight to correct the ills of the Klan but rather to focus on their own loyalty and duty. Notre Dame men were patriotic, and they did not have to assault members of the order to prove their dedication to the nation or their local community. The *News-Times* did not comment on Walsh's statement about the patriotism of the students but rather summarized the events of the three previous days, saying that the order had scheduled a Klan parade, students and Klansmen clashed in the streets, rain prohibited further rioting on Saturday, and Monday proved to be the day of most vigorous fighting. Finally, Walsh stepped in to save the day.[49]

What the accounts show is that the Notre Dame students were culpable. They did antagonize Klansmen, and Klansmen returned the favor. Both sides were involved in the street fights, and neither could really claim to be victims. The Klan narratives present wild-eyed college students attacking Protestants, and the Catholic version of events do not necessarily support the students' actions. What started out as pranks led to destruction of personal and public property, injuries within both factions, and chaos in the streets of South Bend. The event was calamitous, to say the least. Patriotism was an issue for the Notre Dame students as much as it was for the Klan. For some, Notre Dame's victorious football season in 1924 showcased that they had won the larger battle with the Klan and established their place in American culture.[50]

Walsh attempted to show the students that street fighting did not necessarily affirm their patriotism. Some students, however, believed their attacks on the Klan were retribution for the order's degradation of Catholic loyalty to the nation. To Walsh, the KKK was not powerful enough to impugn the patriotism and duty of his students. Rioting did not legitimate the Catholic presence in South Bend or the nation. Despite Walsh's sentiments, the events caused some members of the community to question further the Catholic university's commitment to nationalism.

Walsh received letters decrying Notre Dame's role in the riot. In a letter from Toledo, Ohio, J. E. Hutchison admitted that he was shocked to hear of the events that took place in South Bend and that previously he had admired the university in its educational efforts. However, the destruction of the flag by students swayed his opinion. He believed that the particular incident could have happened in a foreign country, but on American soil it was unbelievable. He ended his letter, "This Un-American demonstration has lost for Notre Dame University many ardent Protestant supporters in this section."[51] A letter from a self-proclaimed "Kluxer" noted that Walsh should "thank your lucky stars" that Klansmen were not as destructive as "your bunch of lawless Anarchist students." If they were, the author wrote, Notre Dame might have been razed to the ground. For the Kluxer, Klansmen were law-abiding, as opposed to the "Anarchist Ruffians" of the university who had attacked him and showed obvious disregard for the law. The Kluxer explained that Walsh should start teaching patriotism to those Catholic students who "tore the American flag to bits." He wrote:

I have heard the Knights of Columbus deny that they have took such an oath as has been circulated among the public, but after reading in history of the bloody murders during the French Revolution, and knowing conditions as they exist today under Catholic domination in South America, and seeing with my own eyes some of the things that the bunch of Mackerel Smacking Anarchists from Notre Dame did last Saturday, I can easily believe that every world of the K of C oath is true.[52]

For the Kluxer, the Notre Dame riot proved beneficial because more Americans would realize the present danger of the Catholic Church in America. The Klansman had his previous impressions of the church and the KC confirmed by the students' actions. The Klan's renderings of the events were palpable to some who might have already wanted to believe the worst about Catholics.

But *Our Sunday Visitor* did not take the matter lightly. It produced its own version of events, in which the Klan ignored pleas and requests to call off its parade. Klansmen, then, "assumed the places of regular traffic officers," which led students to disrobe some members of the order. Most important, the claims of "flag desecration" by students concerned the weekly. The *Visitor* responded that desecration was "only an embellishment of fervid minds, which, in their pipe dreams, take every rebuff to the Klan as 'an outrage of the flag.'"[53] Such was an unfounded allegation created by the Klan. Notre Dame students were patriotic and loyal, and they did not destroy flags. By Tucker's account, the students won the battle, showing Klansmen that Catholics were a force to be reckoned with when their patriotism was on the line.

*We could go and raze Notre Dame University, but that is not what the Klan teaches.*[54]

Accounts of the events on May 17, 18, and 19, 1924, vary widely. What is likely is that each contains some truth and a good amount of exaggeration. The Klan's audacity to hold a gathering and parade in such close proximity to the university incensed Notre Dame students, and Klansmen believed that they were physically, spiritually, and intellectually beleaguered. What the riot most clearly highlighted was the Klan's understanding of its worldview in one particular incident.

The Klan envisioned a world in which Protestantism and nationalism needed defense from foreign ideas, religious movements, and races. The riot gave credence to that way of viewing the world. Catholics, who loathed the Klan's faith and nation, attacked Protestants in the streets of South Bend. As students ripped robes off the bodies of Klansmen, Protestant theology was also trampled. The riots were an all-out religious war happening on native soil. White women, children, and flags faced indignities. All the ideals that the Klan held dear seemed fragile in that moment. The order's print culture had warned of various threats, and they were actualized in the eyes of Klansmen and Klanswomen in the days of the riot. If the Klan was attacked, the nation was actually in peril. The order understood its members as the only real citizens because of their religious affiliation, their race, their commitment to patriotism, and their protection of gender roles. The street battle signaled the failing dominance of white Protestant men. In the tumult of the street battles, all of the order's principles appeared to be harmed. The students besmirched patriotism, disgraced white womanhood, and accosted the faithful in the street brawls. The Klan's worldview, in which a dedicated white Protestant citizenry populated and ruled the nation, appeared tenuous at best.

The physical manifestations of the order's slogans, robes, flags, and the bodies of white women were molested. Vicious Catholic enemies tampered with the physicality of the Klan's beliefs. Its anti-Catholicism, which appeared primarily in the printed word, gained justification because the students confirmed the order's worst imaginings. The Notre Dame students became the foil of the Klan's desires and fears in that historical moment. After the chaos passed, the Klan again imagined the nation as its members preferred to. Time and distance reaffirmed its worldview, and Klansmen and Klanswomen embraced their previous positioning. Members did not hate or fear Catholics. They definitely did not accost Notre Dame students with weapons. They faced persecution because of their beliefs and their proclaimed Protestant identity. Instead of reacting with hate, they responded with tolerance and love. Members did not attack the university for vengeance but returned to the gracious principles of the order. The *Fiery Cross* enumerated the order's position:

Klansmen . . . are truly taught to obey the law, to love their fellowman re-gardless of what their fellowman may believe. The acts of the Klansmen showed naught but love. The tolerance displayed by misused Klansmen might well serve as a criterion for all Americans. Klansmen could have done that which the man quoted said they could have done [harm the uni-versity]. But they did not; did not in the face of the fact that as American citizens they had a perfect right to assemble as they did. Every law, moral and otherwise, had been broken in the attack against them, but, remem-bering their pledge to uphold the laws of America—which give those Ro-man Catholic students the right to worship as they please—they were not swayed by hatred; they were held steadfast to American principles and, in the face of demoniacal hate, exhibited naught but love.[55]

Love, not hate, was the defining feature of the order. Yet in the vis-ceral renderings of the events of May 1924, the Klan appeared in its most intolerant form. Members' anger at the Notre Dame students' au-dacity to assault the order rang clear. Anti-Catholicism materialized through the eyewitness accounts of the riots as well as the "fake" Knights of Columbus oath. The order imagined the church and its faithful at their worst, and these particular events confirmed such.

The Klan accounts of the assaults were not personal but national. The assaults were larger than torn robes and slapped babies because they were acts of violence against the nation, the faith, and the race. The Knights of the KKK visualized themselves as quintessentially American. Thus, harm to the Knights was harm to the nation at large. Each Klansman was a symbol of the larger image of America. In the or-der's imagining, America was a nation founded, fostered, and actively crafted in the hands of white Protestant men. The white-robed visages were symbols of that heritage. Destroyed robes signaled racial and re-ligious intolerance as well as national peril. True 100 percent Ameri-canism could only be found in the hearts, minds, and bodies of white, native-born Protestants. The Klan's envisioning of beloved nation was exclusive and stark, so that African Americans, Jews, and especially Catholics could not really be citizens but only interlopers. They were hazards to body politic because of supposedly foreign ideas, religious movements, and the possibility of miscegenation. In foreign yet famil-iar hands, the nation would become heterogeneous, loathsome, and corrupt. American values and liberties would be decimated, and Liberty, the white goddess, would be tainted irreparably. The riot was a small representation of the larger battle, and the Klan had to win to guarantee the sanctity not only of the Indiana town but the whole of the nation.

*"Guardians of Privilege"*:
What the Klan Tells Us about
American (Religious) History

*In most of the United States the Klan served as an ordinarily peaceful defender of
white Protestant morality and power.*
—STANLEY COHEN (1994)[1]

*The Ku Klux Klan believes in keeping America true to the ideals of those noble patriots
who gave their lives that this republic might be founded upon liberty, justice and freedom. The Klan believes in America being run by genuine Americans at heart, cost
what it may.*
—REV. I. M. HARGRETT (1923)[2]

In 1925 the end of the Ku Klux Klan, much like its fabled beginning,
emerged because of the death of a white woman. In 1913 the death of
little Mary Phagan mobilized the Knights of Mary Phagan to claim retribution through the lynching of Leo Frank, and the second Ku Klux
Klan sought to be a white men's order tasked not only with the protection of vulnerable white womanhood but also of nation, faith, and
race. Twelve years later, the death of Madge Oberholtzer at the hands
of a former Klan officer made the order and its members seem more
dangerous and terrible. In the wake of another young white woman's
death, the ideals of the hooded order appeared disingenuous at best.
For some, the Klan, its secrecy, and its reach for political power enabled Oberholtzer's death. Thus, little Mary and Madge became the
bookends of the Klan's American saga, idealistic strivings countered
by tarnished realities. William Simmons was responsible for the creation of the white Protestant men's order, and David Curtis "Steve"
Stephenson, the Indiana Grand Dragon convicted of the murder, was
one force behind the Klan's decline in the mid-1920s.

In November 1925 Stephenson was convicted of the second-degree
murder of Madge Oberholtzer. Before the trial and subsequent conviction, Stephenson had made a name for himself as the leader of the Indiana realm, among others, having recruited 25,000 Klansmen in Indiana in only six months.[3] Stephenson appeared a model Klansman who

gave speeches on the importance of Protestantism and nationalism, reinvented the *Fiery Cross* (an Indiana Klan newspaper), and hosted large Klan rallies with parades and picnics. He was a charismatic charmer, and he became one of the public faces for the 1920s Klan. Yet Stephenson was also an alcoholic and a womanizer with a questionable past whose relationships with women showcased abuse and abandonment. For the Indiana Klan, however, Stephenson integrated the order into statewide politics by helping to elect several Indiana politicians supportive of the general Klan platform of 100 percent Americanism and Protestantism, in addition to Stephenson's personal legislative agendas. In particular, Ed Jackson, the Indiana governor elected in 1924, owed his victory to Stephenson's influence. Stephenson sought to pass legislation, including the prohibition of religious garb (aimed at Catholics), the adoption of Bible reading in the public schools, the public display of the flag, and the disbandment of the parochial schools. The Indiana legislature of 1925 became known as the "Klan legislature" because of the dominant Klan presence.[4]

The so-called Klan bills by and large failed in the legislature, though a bill on flag display in public schools passed. Historian M. William Lutholtz noted that the Klan's inability to impact the political culture perhaps led members to be "disenchanted" with the order.[5] His public persona and sensational trial made Stephenson a ready symbol of the 1920s Klan, which naturally brought about criticism of the larger order due to his personal behavior. In recounting Stephenson's rise and fall, journalistic accounts and histories conflate Stephenson's personal history with the history of the national order. His downfall becomes the fall of the Klan.

Stephenson's rapid rise in the Klan ranks was ultimately derailed by his fascination with Madge Oberholtzer. In January 1925, Stephenson met Oberholtzer at a dinner party at the governor's mansion. Her job at the Indiana Young People's Reading Circle in the statehouse helped support her family. Journalist Richard Tucker described her as "not a femme fatale, but rather a plain brunette who wore her hair in the careless upswept style of the times."[6] Her friends described her as ambitious and intelligent. Oberholtzer was an Indiana native who attended Butler College but did not finish her degree. She was the manager of the state library program for teachers. Historian William

Lutholtz described her as "an attractive and ambitious young woman, though not, as some reporters would later portray her, either particularly striking or beautiful . . . quick-witted and intelligent, according to her friends, and she knew how to hold up her end of a conversation. In a word, she was interesting."[7]

Whatever her virtues or faults, Stephenson found Oberholtzer attractive and compelling. In character with his previous treatment of women, his pursuit of this librarian culminated in her kidnapping, rape, and slow death. On March 15, 1925, Stephenson's secretary, Fred Butler, called Oberholtzer with a request to see Stephenson immediately. Because she was away from home for the evening, she did not receive the message until late evening, and she decided to see Stephenson because his message seemed urgent. The events that follow appear more fitting as a plot for a soap opera rather than historical narrative. Stephenson forced Oberholtzer to drink alcohol and board a train bound for Chicago. Stephenson essentially kidnapped and then raped her. Her body bore his bites and marks, and he refused to let her go home after the brutal evening.

In her dying declaration, Oberholtzer explained that she devised a dangerous plan for escape. She convinced Stephenson that she needed a new hat for their trip, and he allowed her to go to a pharmacy with one of his employees in tow. At the pharmacy, Oberholtzer bought a new hat as well as mercury bichloride tablets. To escape Stephenson, Oberholtzer willfully poisoned herself. However, Stephenson, upon learning of the poisoning, refused to take her to a hospital unless she married him. Oberholtzer did not acquiesce to his demands, and eventually one of Stephenson's friends returned her home. Absent medical treatment until her late return home, Oberholtzer eventually died due to infections of her wounds and the impact of the poison.

Stephenson's trial revolved around his responsibility for Oberholtzer's death, with his attorneys claiming Oberholtzer committed suicide. However, Oberholtzer's family secured lawyers who had the foresight to record a dying declaration from their daughter and her accusations against the Klan leader. Prominent newspapers, including the *New York Times,* covered the sensational trial and its Klan connection. A young woman dead by the hands of a Klan official made prominent headlines and enabled journalists to air their opinions of not only Stephenson but the larger order.

Not surprisingly, this distasteful tale proved interesting to journalists, the general public, and historians alike. Stephenson's brutal attack on Oberholtzer, her ingestion of mercury bichloride tablets, his refusal to take her to a hospital, and then her prolonged death from both the poison and the injuries from her rape made rich fodder for headlines. Stephenson's violent actions and blatant disregard for Oberholtzer's health suggested the brutality of the larger Ku Klux Klan as well. A model Klansman, Stephenson demonstrated to the nation the inherent corruption and violence of the order, and his downfall wrote the closing chapter in many popular newspapers and Klan histories of not only the Indiana klavern but also the national Klan.

The *New York Times* declared in February 1926 that "the Ku Klux Klan is definitely on the wane."[8] The *Times* conducted a survey of entrenched Klan states illustrating the decline in membership in Klan strongholds in the South, Midwest, and urban North. It was a fitting end to an order that once was lauded by the national press as a much-needed addition to American society before later emerging as a threat to national conscience.[9] The fears about the Klan were realized in Stephenson's criminal behavior and trial. Stephenson not only abused women and murdered Madge Oberholtzer; he also manipulated elections, produced a Klan legislature, and created his own separate Klan organization when his power was threatened by the national order. This one Klansman illuminated the danger of the Ku Klux Klan.

Yet, the Klan did not disappear from the American cultural scene in 1925 or 1926. In 1928, the Ku Klux Klan appeared in opposition to Governor Albert "Al" Smith of New York, the Democratic presidential nominee. Smith, a longtime target of Klan ire, had lost the Democratic nomination in 1924 due to the chaos created by the Klan at the Democratic National Convention. Catholic historian Mark Massa notes that Smith would have likely been defeated without the Klan's opposition, but the Klan helped convince other voters of the danger of the Catholic Smith as the president of the United States. Both Republican and Democratic opponents of Smith exploited the Klan in their campaigns against him.[10] If the Klan appeared to be an important force in the

1928 election, why is the end of the Klan so often dated in 1925 with the Stephenson trial?

Stephenson's decline provides an apt and tidy narrative for the rise and fall of the Ku Klux Klan. The Klan supposedly emerged in 1915 in response to the brutal murder of Mary Phagan, and other burgeoning social ills, and ended in 1925 with the equally brutal rape and murder of Madge Oberholtzer. D. C. Stephenson's actions and trial appear to make a mockery of the Klan's supposed commitment to the virtue of white womanhood, Christianity, and civic virtue. Historian Wyn Craig Wade makes this sentiment about the Klan clear: "It championed morality and sanctity of womanhood, while its most successful Grand Dragon was convicted of the most sordid rape-murder of the decade. It revered the teachings of Jesus, while its hopes and endeavors may be called the least Christian and certainly the least charitable of any American popular movement."[11]

The order's long suspected vices become apparent not only in this moment but in the entirety of the second revival of the Klan. Stephenson becomes synonymous with the order. While it is tempting to assume that Stephenson was representative of the whole Klan membership, it is a misstep to do so. Imperial Wizard Evans had even banned Stephenson from the national order in 1924. Stephenson attempted to craft his own Klan organization to counter Evans, and his reputation with women and alcohol caused the national leadership pause. The story of the 1920s Klan ends with Stephenson as proof of the nefarious intentions and actions of the order. Stephenson's violation of the order's ideals somehow proves that Klansmen were never actually virtuous, but rather collectively deceitful and dangerous hypocrites like the Indiana Grand Dragon.

With the convicted Grand Dragon, Klan virtues imploded under the weight of hypocrisy, shameless politicking, corruption, and desperate power grabbing. His conviction illuminates the dangerous nature of the Klan, from its celluloid portrayal and its new start on top of Stone Mountain to Stephenson's prison sentence, which becomes the fitting, theatrical end to the spectacle-filled order. The historical message appears clear: movements that perpetuate intolerance, hate, and racism often end as quickly as they begin.

Yet the order did not end after the Stephenson trial. The *Kourier* was published by the national order until 1936, and its final issues still trumpeted the dangers of immigration as well as the materializing threat of Communism. Klansmen mobilized against the candidacy of Al Smith for president in 1928, and a much smaller Klan existed until the early 1930s with Imperial Wizard H. W. Evans still at the reins. Furthermore, not all the members of the order were cut from the same cloth as the disgraced Stephenson. Instead of making Stephenson the metric to judge the order's actions and members, perhaps the Grand Dragon is more a cautionary tale about the danger of manipulating political power and believing one's self to be above the law, both locally and nationally, and hiding behind a veil of secrecy.

The order was indicative of the common prejudice and privilege of whiteness in the 1910s to 1930s. Historians are correct that membership did decline in the late 1920s. Local klaverns shut down, and many Klan members distanced themselves from the hooded order. Relying solely on membership numbers leads to the conclusion that the order effectively ended in the 1920s. Indeed, the 1920s Klan was the last unified order, and its other twentieth- and twenty-first-century manifestations are fractured and many.

However, the ranks of membership are not the only evidence of the Klan's presence. I would argue that the 1920s Klan organization ended with the end of the *Kourier,* and that this end was affected by Stephenson's trial and the national press coverage. Yet, this is simply the end of the unified Klan. The order's lasting legacy, instead, is its combination of Protestant Christianity, nationalism, and intolerance in its rhetoric and printed materials. Furthermore, obsession over the various Klan revivals obscures the longevity of a particular Klan-inspired brand of political and religious language and action. Political scientist Allan Lichtman argues convincingly that the end of the Klan did not result from Stephenson's trial and conviction, declining membership, or lack of interest. He asserts that instead the order became too successful. While the Klan lost members and faced scandals, "America restricted immigration, unions declined, and white Protestant Republicans and southern Democrats ran the nation." The Klan's campaigns succeeded in protecting a certain vision of the American nation, and the nation aligned with the Klan's larger vision of white Protestant dominance. Yet Lichtman writes: "By framing its appeal in overtly religious, ethnic, and racial terms the Klan limited its potential for expansion and sparked a backlash. . . . Yet the Klan survived, more as a brand than as a movement. As generations of promoters on the fringes of the right proved, there was money and fame to be made in marketing hate, no less than other mass-produced goods."[12]

The unified order ceased to exist, but Lichtman argues that the Klan's brand of religious nationalism, prejudice, and intolerance outlived the 1920s order. Yet Lichtman's analysis can be pushed further than its applicability to the "fringes of the right," as the Klan's antipluralist, Christian, and intolerant rhetoric emerged as a crucial component of American political and public culture. The order's prejudice, nationalism, and faith were part of the dominant white Protestant culture in the United States; the Klan in all of its vice and perhaps virtue was indicative of national political and religious culture. In the 1920s, the Klan was not a movement of the right-wing fringe but a movement of white Protestant citizens who wanted to protect their dominance and their culture.

Lichtman further includes the second Ku Klux Klan as a manifestation of American conservatism, but he characterizes the order as more extremist than others in the fledgling movement of the American Right. The Klan could be a manifestation of conservatism, but it was not indicative of the larger history of American conservatism because of the order's methods and strategies for accomplishing their vision. White robes and burning crosses signaled the Klan's difference from the patriotism of the American Legion or the Daughters of the American Revolution. While Lichtman's work attempts to historicize the emergence of the Klan in this larger history of American politics, he still relies on a conception of the order as outside the mainstream. For Lichtman, the modern Right emerged

> out of a widespread concern that pluralistic, cosmopolitan forces threatened America's national identity. Those Americans most inclined to protect what they perceived as embattled traditional values came from all parts of the nation. They lived in every type of community, worked in numerous occupations, attended many different churches, or even lacked for-

mal affiliation with a church. *The vanguard of American conservatism in the 1920s, however, shared a common ethnic identity: they were white and Protestant and they had to fight to retain a once uncontested domination of American life.*[13]

If this is indeed the ethos of modern American conservatism, then the Klan fits the bill. The order sought to protect an embattled nation, to preserve white Protestant dominance, and to maintain racial supremacy. For Lichtman and for me, the Klan is a part of the lineage of the American Right. I would also argue that the trajectory of the American Right becomes more full-fledged and complicated with the Klan's inclusion. The 1920s Klan is the lynchpin between the nativistic political movements of the nineteenth century (the Know-Nothings, American Protective Association) and the emergence of full-fledged American conservatism after World War II. If the Klan is included in this legacy, then, we can see how movements concerned with white Protestant dominance evolved in their tactics, concerns, and political strategies from the nineteenth century to the twenty-first century. Its short life not withstanding, the Klan represented one of many organizations tasked with battling "un-American radicalism" after World War I. For Michael Kazin, these movements relied on public outrage, patriotism, discipline, and religious faith in their skirmish over the nature and character of America.[14] Leonard Moore writes that the "Klan movement and the 1920s generally" are the "starting point" for the history of the American Right. For Moore, the elevation of "white Protestant cultural hegemony and an inflamed populist opposition to the growing power of political, economic, and culture elites" were essential to the second Klan, much in the same way that they are essential to conservative and other movements of the Right in the contemporary period.[15]

The 1920s, then, marked the beginning of the mythical culture wars, and the Klan's lament about the decline of a white Protestant nation echoed throughout the twentieth century to the twenty-first. Declension, family values, nationalism, Protestant faith, affirmation of traditional gender roles, racial supremacy, and intolerance appeared prominently in the Klan's print culture. The order's reclamation of the nation for the white Protestant faithful added to a brand of politics that conservatives still embrace, one which seeks to return and restore an America in which white Protestants and other moral arbiters are the cultural guardians. The fragmentation of American culture that the Klan feared was apparent, and the order's lament continued despite its organizational end. Scholars of American conservatism do not usually include the Klan as the beginning of this political movement, but the Klan's legacy, its brand, appears plainly in conservative political and religious movements.

Nancy MacLean argues that the lasting legacy of conservatism is the defense and promotion of white privilege. These "guardians of privilege" strove to negate the reforms of the New Deal, return "America to the business domination of the Gilded Age and the 1920s," and defend imperiled white supremacy.[16] After World War II, conservative thinkers, politicians, and promoters all emphasized myriad threats to the larger nation, from abortion to civil rights to environmental protection and welfare. Upholding white privilege became more important than consensus. Conservative religious faith impacted conservative political ideology, and American families and women's bodies became the battlegrounds for an ideological war. The 1920s Klan imagined themselves as guardians, or Knights, of an endangered culture, and this vision of imperiled defenders protecting tradition, faith, and family appears again and again, from the so-called Christian Right to neoconservatives to the Fox News Network.

The question, then, is why the order is excluded from the larger history of American conservatism and what is at stake in the Klan's inclusion as a legitimate part of the American Right. While Moore, Kazin, and Lichtman readily admit that the Klan might be not only a conservative movement but also one of the forbearers of contemporary American conservative thought, this is not the common historiographical praxis. Klan historian Wyn Craig Wade argued that the Klan "mentality" could be found in the Christian Right, specifically the Christian Coalition of the 1980s, because of their use of "slander and backhanded methods" and "endeavors to elect candidates who support its right-wing views."[17] Historian David Bennett asserts that the Klan is part of not just the Right but also the Far Right. The Klan was just one of the many permutations of the Far Right, beginning with nineteenth-century nativists to the militia and white supremacist movements of today. These self-proclaimed guardians sought to preserve an older, moral, and political order and to save an imperiled America from alien immigrants, foreign ideological systems, and interlopers in our midst.[18] Bennett's work is indicative of how the Klan's inclusion with the American Right usually includes labeling the order as fringe. The Klan becomes not a movement of the Right but the Far Right, which signals its unusual intolerance when compared to the whole of American history. By shifting the Klan to the far instead of the near, the order and its members are represented as a one of many short-lived movements of intolerance and bigotry, strands of American culture but not representative of our culture as a whole. By labeling the Klan as a movement of the Far Right, its unsavory nature does not taint narratives of the Right. Thus, we scratch our heads and ponder how such a movement gained momentum in our clearly tolerant culture.

Yet John Corrigan and Lynn Neal, in their documentary history of intolerance in America, showcase how banal and present intolerance is in American culture from the colonial period to the twentieth century.[19] Intolerance is as American as ideals of tolerance and freedom, and the Klan is a clear case of the presence of intolerance in not just the Far Right but also the Right and our larger political and public culture. Just like the tidy narrative of the Klan's rise and fall, placing the Klan in the margins protects equally tidy narratives that laud America's long history of tolerance and inclusion. If the Klan is part and parcel of American conservatism, what does this show about our current political moment and the history of our recent past? The 1920s Klan and its brand of religious nationalism and intolerance emerges in our contemporary guardians of privilege—religious, racial, and otherwise. This showcases that while our national virtues might be noble, our common practice is still not. Klan historian Kenneth Jackson was correct in his assertion that "to examine the Klan is to examine ourselves."[20] Analyzing the Klan as a legitimate component of the American conservative movement illuminates the continued presence of intolerance and exclusion in American nationalism and how Protestantism still provides the moral compass to cultural guardians. Understanding the Klan's significant place in American history and American religious history helps explain the permanent presence of religious intolerance in our national culture. By learning from the

Klan's lessons, we can move beyond our collective history and recognize the danger of the Klan's brand in our current moment.

*Neither villains nor noble souls.*

In his groundbreaking study of old Christian Right, Leo Ribuffo examines Christian fascists who created ministries based on fear and anti-Semitism in the Great Depression and through the Cold War. The ministers he analyzes take part in the Klan's brand, and Ribuffo showcases how even those on the Far Right can overlap with the so-called mainstream. Most important, Ribuffo notes that most scholars studying conflict in American history "share a signal flaw with consensus scholars whom they criticize." Both types of historians are hesitant "to take seriously groups that retard 'progress.'"[21] For Ribuffo, the past contains heroes, heroines, and villains, and our histories are not complete with the inclusion of all of these groups. While I share Ribuffo's sentiment, my approach to another set of villains, the 1920s Klansmen and Klanswomen, is quite different. While I will readily admit that the Klan encapsulated and promulgated the malevolent, proclamations of historical actors as heroes and villains make me uneasy. My approach was to "see with" the Klan and its approach to religion, nation, gender, and race. Villainy surfaces in my narrative, but this is not a tale of villains and/or heroes.

Rather, this is the story of the 1920s Klan as the men and women of the order understood and personified themselves in print, for better or worse, and the Klan's story shows more ambivalence than good or evil. Contemporaries of the Klan also sought to understand the order as dangerous, benign, or something else. In 1921 the *Evening News* characterized the men and women who joined the Ku Klux Klan:

Already you hear large numbers of people declaring that the K.K.K. is an organization made up of villains and smaller numbers of people declaring that members of the organization are noble souls who are determined to elevate the morals of society. Members of the K.K.K. are of course neither villains nor noble souls. In this they all resemble other members of the human race; for villains and noble souls belong in fairy books, along with griffins with three heads and fairies who give you an enchanted ring.[22]

Members of the Klan were ordinary people who joined the order because it proved useful in their daily lives and confirmed their vision of nationalism, race, and religion. After all, the planks of the 1920s Klan asserted the centrality of white supremacy, Protestant Christianity, the purity of white womanhood, and clean politics, among others, and its message appealed to white Protestant men and women who feared immigration, women's equality, foreign ideas and religions, as well as changes to the social order of American society. The Klan's well-crafted message of white Protestant dominance and the possible ruin of said dominance resonated among those citizens. The order's language and presentation of those threats convinced white men and women to read Klan newspapers, attend rallies, and even burn crosses. They joined the order because of spectacular displays and the order's coherent and familiar worldview. Men became Knights—defenders of the nation, religion, and women—and women became helpmeets in the cause rather than just passive supporters.

To examine Klansmen and Klanswomen in their banality reflects more accurately their understandings of themselves and their membership in the order. In *Women of the Klan,* one of Kathleen Blee's informants argued that the "better people" joined the Klan to defend the nation, the schools, and their families.[23] Those who did not join the Klan, then, lacked either the initiative or the foresight to see that the nation was in peril. Most of the women she interviewed did not report their hatred of Catholics, Jews, or African Americans but rather focused on the value of their membership, the social gatherings, and their work in the order, which these women believed improved the nation in the face of the foreign. They did not see the detriment of their actions. Some even longed for the camaraderie of membership and the sense of belonging the order instilled. Her conversants understood their work for the order as necessary and crucial for the protection of the nation, faith, and white women. They were defenders, not perpetrators, of violence and maliciousness. Even when confronted by the history of the order's more violent offspring, members still imagined themselves as part of a righteous cause rather than a harmful movement.

This belief, however, does not abdicate Klansmen and Klanswomen of the damage they inflicted, but it does illustrate that members did not willingly recognize their roles in an organization known for terror and violence. The women Blee interviewed did not join the order spe-cifically to cause harm or because of their own evil tendencies. They joined alongside their neighbors, relatives, and loved ones. Joiners took up the cause of the Klan because of the familiarity of the order's politics and pointed laments about the fall of American society. They were not villains. As the case study of the Klan illuminates, ordinary people can do what most would feel is extraordinary without realizing the magnitude or danger of their actions. Ordinary people commit physical and rhetorical acts of violence for movements that claim benevolent and righteous intentions, whether or not their intentions prove to be malicious. Klan members embraced the order's anti-Cathol-icism, anti-Semitism, and racism as necessary defenses of national character and complexion. They donned hoods and masks to show their allegiance to the order's ideals and values and to intimidate their supposed enemies. The case study of the 1920s Klan shows that ordi-nary people commit heinous acts without evil intentions and that they can promote a worldview founded on intolerance even as they de-scribe its tolerance.[24]

To recognize that humans commit atrocities against other humans without being willfully malevolent means that we cannot condemn members of movements like the Klan as wholly evil, deranged, or ab-normal. If we label the order as evil, we run the risk of ignoring the wide appeal of the order and the various reasons people chose to join. Such labeling leads to simplistic and useless renderings of complex movements. Wicked people were not the only ones who joined the Klan. Mothers, fathers, sons, daughters, and grandparents embraced the Klan, and we need to understand their motivations (benevolent, malevolent, or ambiguous) to harvest an accurate portrait of how that hate movement gained such popularity in a particular time period. Condemnatory accounts gain nothing because they obscure why mil-lions joined the Klan in the 1920s. Moreover, blatant judgment hides how the Klan was representative of 1920s America in its white su-premacy, anti-Catholicism, anti-Semitism, and other vices. Historian David Bennett characterized the Klan's popularity as appealing in a time of change: "It was the Roaring Twenties, and as mores changed, as traditional social arrangements were overturned, as skirts went up and speakeasies flourished, as the movies and radio made their mark with Tin Pan Alley songs . . . , the Klan found a way of identifying these disturbing developments . . . [by] standing up for America by assailing yet another band of un-Americans."[25]

The order and its members were products of American society, and they showcased the seamier side of that culture through robes, fiery crosses, and inflammatory pamphlets. The order voiced the fears of a nation by employing dramaturgical methods and illuminated the fragmentation of the white Protestant rendering of America.

If condemnation is not an analytical option for approaching the Klan, then historians must find other ways to assess Klan members and leaders in the second revival of the order. This study of the Klan demonstrates the complexity of the order's ideology and its white Protestant nationalism. The place of historical judgment in this narrative becomes paramount.[26] One could easily label Klansmen and Klanswomen as morally bankrupt for perpetuating prejudice, racism, and strife in their writings and in the public square. Alternatively, one could rely upon stereotypes of Klan members as rural, uneducated racists who burned crosses to inspire fear and dread. The order obviously contributed to a divisive atmosphere that questioned the loyalty of Catholics to the nation, degraded the intelligence and worth of African Americans, and reified traditional gender roles in an attempt to limit women's participation in larger society. Unlike their neighbors who might have embraced similar positions, Klan members publicly campaigned against such groups and causes, and they employed white costumes to protect their identities.

Such a theatrical style brought much criticism from the mainstream press and much attention to the order's actions and politics. The supposedly secret order attempted to maintain the supposed white Protestant dominance of American society while the nation became more diverse and heterogeneous. Yet judging these historical actors as harmful and immoral is too easy and dismissive. By focusing on the Klan's depraved nature, we assert the order's otherness and unfamiliarity to other historical movements and actors. Klansmen and Klanswomen become anomalies who drifted away from the morality and good standing of other American citizens.

That conclusion, however, obscures the Klan's similarity to the mainstream. Other Americans recognized the same dangers and threats that the order purported. They campaigned against immigration, women's rights, and the removal of the Bible from schools. Are these actors not depraved and prejudiced as well? By judging the Klan, we can distance Klan members from the general public, and we can heap disdain upon their actions while overlooking the fact that non-Klan members also acted in such despicable ways. The Klan envisioned a moral nation, and its Knights were not the only ones defending such a vision. The order showcased its own version of morality in which maintaining the religious and racial caste of the nation justified prejudice and hateful rhetoric. The ends, for the order, justified the means. To protect the nation and the faith required unsavory action and words. What might be immorality to the historian can be the paramount example of morality to the actor. Religious and racial hatred might be clear to the historian, but the actors found divine justification and legitimation for both.

The worlds of historians and actors do collide, but time and space can separate judgments from perspectives. It is easy for me to condemn the Klan, but it is more important for me to place the order in the context of its historical time and place. My own history colors my judgment, and the Klan's judgments contain the same historical weight. What is at stake is context of the order's actions and what that says about America in the 1920s. By understanding how the Klan envisioned morality, we can see how the order fit into mainstream America and how the order is more indicative of the development of American nationalism than we might be comfortable with. We can "see with" them even if the Klan's moral universe is offensive to us. Seeing with the Klan does not mean that we have to like its rhetoric, agendas, or politics, nor does it mean that we need to avoid criticism and analysis.

In *Upon the Altar of Nation,* religious historian Harry Stout argues the case for moral history that showcases the distance between what historical actors ought to have done and what they actually did.[27] Stout imbues his narrative of the Civil War with moral judgment based on just war theory. Such moral history judges historical actors in their historical milieu and their reactions to the atrocities of war. To craft a moral history of the Klan, one could evaluate ought versus actuality. The Klan ought to not have burned crosses as a method of intimidation. The Klan ought to have organized as public citizens rather than behind the white robes that inspired terror. They ought not to have been prejudiced toward foreign ideas, peoples, and religions. In actuality, Klansmen and Klanswomen adopted such tactics and ideas because of their morality. Religion and ethics inspired them to do all of those things to protect the nation that they loved. Their religious nationalism fostered their morality. The order believed its cause was righteous and acted in ways that bolstered that righteousness.

Moral history, in this instance, becomes the history of the Klan's morality in a particular time and place. Those historical actors believed they were the moral agents, while the rest of American society embraced immorality and vice. The actor's vision of morality must be assessed in our narratives. Otherwise, we leave undocumented a vital part of that person's history. Judging the order and its members as evil neglects the moral and religious worldview of the 1920s Klan. If we are to do moral histories, they must reflect the complexity and particularity of moral systems and recognize that just because we as historians cannot reconcile our own morals with those of our actors does not mean that morality is somehow absent. Klansmen and Klanswomen developed their own form of what they ought to do. To move beyond stereotypes of the order (often based on moral judgment) allows a richer history of the Klan and its place in narratives of American culture and American religious history. To see how morality influenced them gives a clear sense of how religion and nationalism were bound together for the order. It also shows that religious people do not necessarily embrace principles that would better humanity. Rather, religious actors are complicated and contradictory, and they use their religious beliefs and actions for the benevolent as well as the malevolent. The Klan as a case study showcases how religion in the United States has not always been a force for civic good or progress, and adding the Klan to the American religious landscape illuminates the seamier side of American Christianity.

The second revival of the Klan positioned members as defenders of faith, nation, race, and womanhood to guarantee the homogenous complexion of Liberty. To study the worldview of the Klan illuminated the intermingling of race, gender, and faith in the creation of American nationalism. For much of the so-called mainstream in the 1920s and early 1930s, America was white, Protestant, and pure. Hyphenated Americans demonstrated to the order with clarity that various peoples did not fit the mold of the nation. Assimilation was not a virtue but a menace. Those so-called Americans were outsiders in larger culture, and the order hoped that they would remain that way. To explore the Ku Klux Klan's worldview provided a clear demarcation of Americanness in exclusionary terms. The order's strenuous dedication to white supremacy, faith, and strict notions of womanhood and manhood allowed one to examine how they constructed national culture. In the seams and fissures, the order's unflinching commitment to exclusion and dominance prevails alongside its pressing concern about the tenuous nature of white prowess.

To take seriously the Klan's claims of dominance and victimization presented a complex portrait of the order's relationship to the larger culture, real and imagined. Much scholarship purported "status anxiety" as the reason for the Klan's prominent rise in the 1920s, but the reality reflected anxiety and overinflated confidence simultaneously. Members lamented the changes in society in jeremiads ranging from the decline of religious culture to the public schools to new presentations of womanhood to miscegenation. Yet they also proclaimed that their dominance would revive a troubled nation to its original glory. Anxiety and desperation appear in the pages of the *Imperial Night-Hawk* and *Kourier,* but so do novel samplings of history and resounding praises of Protestantism and white masculinity. The order's positioning in the nation proved to be laced with ambiguity rather than forceful declarations of declension. The order configured members as victims, defenders, and winners in the course of American history. To examine the Klan, then, is to examine a group that proclaimed to be the "soul" of nation without much trepidation. Its vision of nation was not as fringe as it first appears. The focus on the hatred, violence, and racism of the 1920s Klan occluded its resonance with American cultural currents.

By placing the Klan in the mainstream, historiographical tides are forced to adapt. The order's imaginings of faith and nation point to currents in American religious history, including how nationalism was based on Protestantism, masculinity, anti-Catholicism, and whiteness. This study continues Edward Blum's assertions that nationalism after the Civil War forged whiteness and Protestantism to heal the divisive wounds of white Northerners and Southerners.[28] Nationalism unified whites who recently spilled the blood of one another by degrading newly enfranchised African Americans. A common enemy and a commitment to the same religious faith created a vision of a white republic that both North and South could embrace while ignoring the atrocities of the Civil War. For Blum, nationalism, whiteness, and Protestantism were bound together in such a way that a form of "ethnic nationalism" undercut attempts at a more racially inclusive nationalism by 1900.[29] The Klan's combination of faith, nation, race, and gender in its form of nationalism continued an exclusionary approach. The order adopted requirements for legitimate citizenship based on race and religion and thus excluded all who were not white or Protestant. The Klan proved more strident in its rendering of national character than the predecessors Blum documents. The order's white Protestant nationalism excluded not only African Americans but also Catholics and Jews. The narratives of leaders and members solidified the crafting of nation and citizens in the face of increasing diversity. America was a white Protestant nation, and all others became marginal characters in the stories of American progress and liberty.

That American nationalism contains this sordid and exclusive history helps to explain the prevalence of white Protestant narratives of American history, in which other religious and racial peoples enter and exit the narrative without much impact. The Klan's vision of history resonates with older narratives of white Protestant triumphalism, which chart familiar historical actors marching across the American wilderness while downplaying colonial encounters. The Klan's attempts at narratives of white Protestant dominance and progress, however, illuminate that those narratives were beginning to face opposition and fracture in the 1920s. The order had to bolster its nationalism with exaggerated stories and blindness to the racial and religious diversity of its historical moment. The Klan already had to respond to diversity while envisioning nationalism, but Klansmen and Klanswomen did not want to recognize the response. To recognize diversity would highlight the flaws of the order's vision of America. Instead, the Klan attempted to navigate a position as soul and savior of nation. Defense was needed, but the "soul" of the nation remained white, Protestant, and pure. The presence of religious and racial diversity meant that the Klan claimed a unified vision that no longer reflected reality. Members and leaders struggled to articulate a vision of nation that no longer existed. They constructed a white Protestant dominance despite the fact that such dominance was crumbling. The Klan's nationalism contained no room for diversity or inclusion. Exclusion was the foundation for nationalism.

Adding Klansmen and Klanswomen to our narratives implores a darker reading of religious nationalism. The Klan focused on the Puritans, Pilgrims, and other white Protestant pioneers ordained by God to find America and create a white Protestant nation. In the creation story of the ideal nation, Catholics, Jews, African Americans, and Native Americans were noticeably absent because the Klan did not recognize those peoples as legitimately American. The Klan's rendering of history provides an analysis of colonial power and influence that allows insight into a specific version of cultural colonialism from those who perpetuated and disseminated selective history to justify their ideals and their God-ordained place in the nation. The narratives provided members with the historical assurance that the Klan, and by extension white Protestants, were to remain the heirs of American culture and to maintain their favored position of dominance. The Klan's telling of American religious history resonated with narratives of white Protestant endeavor and influence on our culture. Violence, intolerance, and the impact of white Protestant dominance would rise to the forefront, as would the sometimes-selective grasp of historians who minimized conflict in their narratives. What would it mean if the Pilgrims, the Puritans, or Jonathan Edwards would have been "staunch Klansmen" if given the chance? Relying on the Klan's historical practice gives insight into how selective American religious history as a field tends to be. Amateur Klan historians were even better at hiding the intolerance and violence in our nation's past. The additional value of the study of the Klan is that this exploration gives historians insight into how the religiously intolerant imagine themselves.

The print culture of the order allowed for a window into the mind's eye of editors, leaders, and average Klansmen and Klanswomen. More important, print illuminated how they envisioned their exclusion of others in the language of tolerance and love. Through the study of the second order of the Klan, one can see the complexity of its vision as well as how members believed that they were doing what was best for the nation. In the order's attempts to restore the white Protestant nation, they strove to protect their beloved nation, their faith, and their families from what appeared to be pressing threats. Klan members judged what the nation and its people needed, and the order appointed its members as Knights to protect and defend exclusive values and principles. Protestantism proved foundational to defenses and presentations of nation. Where previous scholars have documented vituperative hate, the white Knights embraced the rhetoric of love to describe their Protestant heritage, Christian virtue, and motivation.

To see with the Klan is an arduous task, but it demonstrates the humanity of the members, no matter how reprehensible their actions and words. Faith in God and nation guided them, even if we would prefer not to see that. Through the pages of the *Night-Hawk* and *Kourier,* Klansmen and Klanswomen crafted their ideal nation, founded on faith and whiteness. The newspapers identified friend and foe, crafted ideal behaviors, lamented persecution and changing gender norms, uplifted paragons of masculinity and femininity, presented theologies, and warned of careless actions. On each page, members read the values and principles of their Klan, and at least attempted to embody those ideals. Through reading and practice, the *Night-Hawk* and its editors presented the Klan's envisage of the ideal world populated by white, native-born, Protestant Americans and sought to make it a viable reality. From white robes to fiery crosses and American flags, to expositions on motherhood and Christian Knighthood, to configurations of whiteness, the order's Protestantism proved foundational in each material and spiritual articulation of its world. The nation they inhabited was a religious one, and the threats to faith, nation, and race were one and the same. Christian patriots populated and led the Invisible Empire, which could not be separated from the Empire Invisible in their hearts and minds.

*"Passing the Torch"*:
The Klan's Brand in America

*Something that is beyond man is happening. America today begins to turn back to God. For too long, this country has wandered in darkness.*
—GLENN BECK (2010)

*We are going to take on the barbarism of war, the decadence of racism, and the scourge of poverty, that the Ku Klux—I meant to say the Tea Party. . . . You all forgive me, but I—you have to use them interchangeably.*
—REV. WALTER FAUNTROY (2010)

*So in America, now, let us—Christian, Jew, Muslim, agnostic, atheist, wiccan, whatever—fight nativism with the same strength and conviction that we fight terrorism. . . . The America that was attacked out of a bright blue sky nine Septembers ago was its best self—and we now are our best selves—not when we rage against differences but when we honor them.*
—JON MEACHAM (2010)

In 2008 *Mother Jones* published online Anthony Karen's photo-documentary of "Ms. Ruth," a contemporary seamstress and manufacturer of Ku Klux Klan robes and other miscellaneous hate regalia. Karen's photo essay for the leftist magazine documented Ms. Ruth's operation and her day-to-day routines: taking orders, sewing and constructing each and every robe by hand from her home, and frequently checking in on her bedridden daughter. Ms. Ruth cut, sewed, and blessed each robe for the newer generation of Klansmen and Klanswomen. *Mother Jones* aptly titled her an "Aryan outfitter," a play on the store Urban Outfitters that sells popular trends in clothing and home furnishings. The photo essay captures the mundane parts of Ms. Ruth's far-from-ordinary business, from her regular cigarette breaks to the image of Nathan Bedford Forrest, an officer in both the Reconstruction and the 1920s Klan, which graces her wall. Karen juxtaposes Ms. Ruth's ordinariness and kindness with her manufacturing of "hate couture." The audio clips of Karen and Ms. Ruth paired with the essay enhance the images, and readers/listeners learn that she is a fifth-generation Klan member and a long-standing supplier of white supremacist merchandise. She has cardboard patterns for each Klan hood and apron, and she sews not only the ordinary and iconic white Klan robes and an assortment of colored robes for a variety of Klan organizations, but also the more elaborate robes for contemporary Klan officers. This seamstress of "hate couture" produces one robe a day to pay for her infirm daughter's care while training her teenage granddaughter to take over "the tradition" of robe making.[1] In addition to the robes, Ms. Ruth markets flags, patches, and altar covers. Her husband sells her products at local flea markets alongside other white supremacist merchandise.

From the audio clips, it appears that Karen is a bit stumped by Ms. Ruth. While the Aryan outfitter might produce hate accoutrement, she fosters good relationships with her customers, whom she describes as "good people" and "Christian." She takes care of her daughter all day and all night, and, for Karen, she was a nice lady who welcomed him into her home. In between sewing and her daughter's care, Ms. Ruth explained to Karen the importance of the Klan historically as well as in the twenty-first century as a force of good and benevolence that protected, and still protects, the rights of white citizens. Her creation of white supremacist gear and her gracious invite to Karen seem at odds. Her customers pray for her daughter, and Ms. Ruth prays for them. Karen argued that in many ways Ms. Ruth is one of a kind. Her custom-made robes have a reputation above all others because each is hand sewn. In several of Karen's photos, Ms. Ruth blesses each robe by holding it close to her heart, closing her eyes, and praying for the person who purchased it. She wraps her thin arms tightly around the garment and recites, "God bless the person who wears this robe."[2] Yet Karen also notes the interesting ethical dilemmas of this assignment and affirms that he was not photographing Ms. Ruth to judge her but only to document her small business of crafting hate. Ms. Ruth signaled to readers of *Mother Jones* that hate was still present in our culture in merchandise, robes, and people long affiliated with the Ku Klux Klan. Ms. Ruth showcased that the Klan was still a part of America, even if the readers of the magazine no longer wanted it to be.

Nevertheless, the modern Ku Klux Klans, unlike their nineteenth- and early-twentieth-century predecessors, are no longer one large, centralized organization but rather many smaller, fragmented organizations.[3] Some have local and regional chapters, websites, and newsletters, but there are not necessarily any connections between the two disparate groups besides the popular use of the Klan moniker. Even so, the newer Klans still embrace the "look" of the previous Klans with robes, the cross, and the flag, and the main organizational goals still revolve around the protection and defense of white supremacy. Ms. Ruth demonstrates how artifacts are still essential to the Klan more than a century and a half after the Reconstruction Klan was founded. No longer does a special plant staffed with Klansmen and Klanswomen provide the regalia; instead, a single Klan member/supporter and her small staff produce robes and other products. The average robe is still white with a cross insignia, but the newer variations have color and flair that the older stark white robes lack. Ms. Ruth's ritual blessing highlights the important role that Christianity still has in the many manifestations of the Klan. By seeing and listening to Ms. Ruth, it becomes apparent that the Klan, albeit in a different form, still exists and consumes merchandise, regalia, and other miscellaneous objects while practicing some generalized form of Protestant Christianity. By engaging the ritual and product of Ms. Ruth, it becomes clear that Christianity remains an important component of contemporary Klan culture. The Klan movement might be much smaller and less accepted in the mainstream than its forebearer in the 1920s, but the Klan is still a part of American culture in the twenty-first century.

Examining modern and historical incarnations of the Klan indicates the long-standing presence and prevalence of Christian nationalism within the order and in the larger nation to promote exclusion as a valid expression of nationalism. For the 1920s Klan, Catholics, Jews, and African Americans were all lesser citizens than their white Protestant neighbors; today, Muslim Americans face a similar challenge to their status by contemporary neighbors locally and nationally. Through creation and maintenance of artifacts and print, the second Klan in the 1920s (and Ms. Ruth today) created a religious landscape in which white Christians needed to fight to save their nation from the imminent threat of immigrants. The order's vision of a religious and righteous nation became visible in hooded faces, robed bodies, burning crosses, and the American flag. Familiar symbols of patriotism and faith might seem somewhat unfamiliar in the Klan's use, but the Ku Klux Klan sought to dress members in religious virtue, patriotism, and tolerance, even if Klansmen and Klanswomen used these terms differently from the mainstream. Aryan outfitters of past and present continue to communicate a darker vision of nation, nationalism, and Protestant Christianity. The robes, the Klan's most identifiable object, still illustrate a feverish desire to return to America's fabled white Protestant origins, and this vision remains tinged with the Klan's hope of white Protestant redemption and recovery, as well as the echoing concern that the larger nation contests the Klan's version of America. In multicultural and pluralist visions of America, the 1920s order's vision is sidelined and downgraded in hopes of presenting a multitude of American experiences.

Ms. Ruth's artifacts and religious vision illuminate the Klan's persistence and tenacity to remain a part of the American nation, and the permutations of the Ku Klux Klan fall, rise, and reemerge again and again like the mythical hydra sprouting new heads as soon as one is removed. The Klan, it appears, is always with us, and the order's newest incarnations represent not only the legacy of the Klan but also the new imaginings of the Klan's purpose and function in the twenty-first century. The orders may no longer be unified, but their continued presence suggests the longevity of the Klan's "brand"—religious nationalism and political rhetoric formed by intolerance and white supremacy—still applies.

Ms. Ruth demonstrates the order's unique ability to reincarnate and reemerge in a variety of times and places in American history, as well as the audacity and permanence of the Klan's vision of white Protestant America. Klansmen are still Knights dressed in white robes, and the robes, the iconic image of Klan, have a continued presence and purpose. The robes still contain theological content and also showcase a certain theatricality that remains acceptable and expected for Klansmen and Klanswomen. The robe becomes a material connection to the order's sordid past. Moreover, the robe becomes the symbol for fear and terror in the American imagination. The haunting presence of white-robed Klansmen illustrates the order's long history of racism, anti-Semitism, anti-Catholicism, and intolerance. White-robed Klansmen still elicit much fear and disdain, despite comedian Dave Chapelle's best efforts to lampoon the order in his sketches about black white supremacists.

All the same, I often wonder about how the contemporary manifestations of the Ku Klux Klan compare to my study of the 1920s order. What binds them together? Is it only a shared name and visual identity? Are the goals of the 1920s order congruent with the newer incarnation of the Klan's brand? Is the legacy of the 1920s Klan a Klan seamstress like Ms. Ruth, a modern Klan website, or a sometime politician like David Duke? Or are we missing something important when we simply tie the 1920s order to the newer movements with the same moniker?

I posit that we need to expand our vision of the Klan as a brand or style of religious nationalism that appears not just in groups that label themselves "Klan" but also in other political actions and movements. The Klan's white Protestant America emerges in other places than Ms. Ruth's home, rallies, cross burnings, and David Duke speeches. The intolerance and exclusion of the 1920s order still haunts the American landscape, but it is not limited to those who wear robes and hoods.

*We now are our best selves—not when we rage against differences but when we honor them.*

Tolerance is held up as an American virtue, but our ideals often fall short of the historical reality. Much like the hooded order and robes, intolerance and exclusion remain with us. As I write this afterword, the ninth anniversary of the September 11, 2001, terrorist attacks has come and gone with much controversy, politicking, and intolerance. Florida pastor Terry Jones catapulted to national and global infamy by threatening to burn Qur'ans as a memorial to those (Christian) Americans who died in the September 11 attacks. In response to Jones and the media attention surrounding him, Jon Meacham of *Newsweek* and others called for Americans to discard our intolerance and become better, more tolerant people. For Meacham, Americans were better as a whole than those who would destroy any sacred scripture. He wrote: "So in America, now, let us—Christian, Jew, Muslim, agnostic, atheist, wiccan, whatever—fight nativism with the same strength and conviction that we fight terrorism. . . . the America that was attacked out of a bright blue sky nine Septembers ago was its best self—and we now are our best selves—not when we rage against differences but when we honor them."[4]

An editorial in the *New York Times,* reflecting not on the September 11 attacks but on the larger history of American "fear" of Others, documented many egregious cases of intolerance against Catholics, Jews, and Chinese and Japanese immigrants and citizens. The *Times* columnist concluded that Americans react badly to "new arrivals." The piece continued: "But we have a more glorious tradition intertwined in American history as well, one of tolerance, amity and religious freedom. Each time, this has ultimately prevailed over the Know Nothing impulse."[5]

For both authors, what was obscured in discussions of intolerance and violence was the triumph of American tolerance and religious freedom. The lasting legacy of America, then, is our ability to move past our prejudice and adapt to Others. For some, the election of our first African American president, Barack Hussein Obama, two years earlier signaled the new tolerant, "post-racial" America.[6] Yet in 2008, Ms. Ruth stitched Klan robes, and a Klan in Bogalusa, Louisiana, murdered a prospective member when she chose not to join their local chapter.[7] Simultaneously, white supremacist movements, previously on decline in the late 1990s and early 2000s, began growing steadily, and the Southern Poverty Law Center reported earlier this year that the number of active hate groups in the United States has grown to "record levels," to near 1,000 active hate groups. In the spring of 2010, 61 percent of Americans believed that the nation was in decline, and analysts of the "American radical right" feared the level of rage rising against the government generally and social programs specifically.[8]

For *Mother Jones* magazine, Ms. Ruth, the designer and creator of hate couture, showed that the artifacts of hatred are still in demand. If one is to believe the pundits, the rhetoric of American politics has reached a fevered pitch on both left and right, and division among Americans appears in the pages of newspapers. The nation appears divided, still, waging the fabled "culture wars" between progressive and traditional worldviews, in which surely the nation's soul is imperiled by the successes and failures of either side. For some, America is at a pivotal moment where unease at what lies ahead clouds optimism on both left and right, while pessimism and fear seem to run rampant for those on both sides of the political spectrum. Perhaps, we are not our "better selves."

Personally, I find myself in interesting physical and ideological spaces. After living almost three years in the Southwest, my new home in Knoxville, Tennessee, means that I have returned to the South, the region of my birth and upbringing. My native-born Florida was home to one of the most violent incarnations of the Klan, and my hometown, Marianna, is tainted by the legacy of the lynching of Claude Neal in 1934. Now I live in the state (in)famous for the birth of the Ku Klux Klan in Pulaski, the Scopes "Monkey" Trial of Dayton, a recent mosque controversy and subsequent arson in Murfreesboro, the arson of a local lesbian couple's home in nearby Vonore, and the defacement of a Qur'an at the doorsteps of a Knoxville mosque.[9]

While blogging on domestic terror at the Religion in American History blog, I received my first death threat for simply suggesting that Americans need to recognize the place of Christianity and religion more generally in domestic terrorism and the larger hate movement. This response to a mere blog post surprised me because I did not suggest anything particularly controversial or inflammatory. Instead, I posed a question as to why the media and other commentators were hesitant to examine the place of religiosity as motivation, or justification, of acts of domestic terror. My foray into contemporary events left me a bit stunned, and the stakes were certainly higher. Yet I still could not help but notice that the resonance of the 1920s Klan in today's political and public culture went beyond Ms. Ruth's robes and the rise of white supremacist movements.

Describing the 1920s Klan's lasting impact on American culture in the twenty-first century appeared to be a Herculean task. One could, as many historians have, trace the legacy of the 1920s Klan through the manifestations of the order in the 1960s, 1980s, and today. But the mere presence of the Klan today does not prove the longevity of the 1920s Klan's particular vision of white Protestant America. Would that vision be found in the newer, web-savvy versions of the order? Was this vision limited to the right-wing fringe monitored by the Southern Poverty Law Center? Or was this imagining of the American nation more diffuse and elusive? Where is the order's rightful legacy?

Before this incident, my former editor, Kalyani Fernado, at the University Press of Kansas, suggested that I write a contemporary afterword for my book to the show the relevance of my study of the 1920s Klan to our contemporary world. My historical study might have seemed pressing for this particular moment, but I was uncomfortable about making tenuous connections between the historical actors with whom I am familiar and my impressions of national politics, global affairs, or American culture. I feel qualified to judge the historical worlds of Klansmen and Klanswomen, but my neighbors and fellow citizens seem too close and too present for my own scholarly judgment. Or, as I often tell my students, I am much more comfortable studying the recent dead than the living and breathing. Reading and writing about pages upon pages of Klan newspapers informed my study of the men and women who took up robes and crosses, marched at home and in the nation's capital, hosted picnics, and perpetuated ugly stereotypes of Catholics, Jews, and African Americans as enemies of American culture. The *Night-Hawk* and the *Kourier* showcased the Klan's vision of white Protestant America and the centrality of intolerance and exclusion to the re-creation of this particular nostalgic vision of the nation. This religious history of the Klan allowed me to demonstrate the dominance of Protestant Christianity in the Klan's platform, political actions, and ritual to illuminate why millions of Americans became members and supporters of the hooded order.

The 1920s Klan has been a part of my scholarly life for several years as I have re-created its vision and its consequences. The white Protestant nationalism of the Klan, bolstered by exclusion and religious intolerance, is significant to the contemporary moment, but the question of how to transition my knowledge of the order into a coherent analysis of the contemporary moment with the same authority and precision is a good one. How do I comment not on the distant past but this very moment? This is a question that religious historians, particularly American religious historians, confront and wrangle when attempting to apply their knowledge of the stories of previous religious Americans to the present. Lived religious histories of the long departed bear their own complexity, but engaging my own vision of the American nation alongside the other competing visions that populate our media, television, film, and politics is difficult.

Applying ethnographic sensibilities to the Klan's textual community that oppose my own understanding of American history and American religious history allows a certain ease and distance. I could "read with" them somewhat comfortably. Reading with contemporary politicians, pundits, journalists, and even white supremacists is a trickier task. Yet, my editor was right. The 1920s Klan does showcase the complexity of the current moment and the place of the Klan's particular religious nationalism and political style. In many ways, the order's positions on race, gender, religion, and nation still resonate today. The Klan's vision of America still exists in our public and intellectual cultures, and this vision is still under assault from pluralism, diversity, and competing religious and ideological movements.

The decline of white (Protestant) America appears again in the early twenty-first century much like it did in the early twentieth century. There are still guardians of privilege, whiteness, and religious faith. Moreover, the contemporary "culture wars" might have emerged in the time of jazz, gin, and the second Ku Klux Klan.[10] The Klan I studied found its values, virtues, race, and religion under assault by those who obviously did not have the nation's best interest at heart. At first glance, the study of the 1920s Klan might seem very applicable to the current political and ideological battles over values, virtues, histories, ideas, and nation. Yet, I would caution those who want to take this case study as a straightforward guide to the twenty-first century. The similarities might resonate, but it is naive to apply the case study of the Klan to the twenty-first century without acknowledging the key differences in time and place. The campaigns and enemies have changed. The 1920s Klan feared Catholics, Jews, and African Americans. The threat of Islam has much more cultural currency today. Some right-leaning Catholics and Jews have sided with conservative Protestants on politics, values, and national culture rather than with their own religious brethren. Yet the 1920s Klan might apply as an object lesson in the American political and cultural battles of 2010.

From the beginning of this project, I have often wondered what the Klansmen and Klanswomen I study would think of the twenty-first century. Would they find this America to be substantially different from their own? How would they react to the new forms of media, multiculturalism, and our current president? Would their laments about the decline of America seem fulfilled? Is there any part of our contemporary moment that they would recognize? When I imagine what the world would look like to these historical actors, I can't help but wonder if maybe the differences would not be as jarring as the similar themes of declension, secular and religious enemies, and codified patriotism. For some Klan historians, the connections are obvious. For instance, Wyn Craig Wade explicitly links the 1920s Klan to religious fundamentalism to argue that the Christian Right has continued the Klan's legacy of hatred and intolerance through today.[11] He argues that the Klan, "in its corruption of American ideals, . . . has capitalized on some of the best-loved aspects of the American tradition.[12] The key to this analysis for Wade is the assumption that the Klan was somehow a "corruption" of valued American traditions like democracy, tolerance, and equality. Perhaps the better understanding is that the Klan is not just the seamier opposite of American virtues like freedom, liberty, and equality, but instead a reconfiguring of these terms. The order was not following a tainted vision of these ideals, but rather Klansmen and Klanswomen followed their own version of these values to support their vision of white Protestant nation. Tolerance, equality, and freedom only applied to certain American citizens, and this shallow application has a long historical legacy in the United States. For Wade, the Klan's corruption showcases the corruption of the Christian Right in their attempts to bring the nation back to a so-called moral foundation.

While I do not agree entirely with Wade's assessment, I do think we should examine how the Klan's brand of religious nationalism and rhetoric appears repeatedly by being bound to so-called American virtues. Understanding the 1920s Klan as indicative of the mainstream, conservative, and traditional values illuminates how the language of tolerance, freedom, and equality lacks common meaning. The Klan's attempts to describe and redescribe the American nation emphasize what is at stake in who claims dominance in narratives of American religious life and showcases how battles over the vision of nation are still ongoing. The Klan is part and parcel of the nation, and perhaps if we can appreciate the order's influence, then we can see how the Klan's legacy impacts our constructions of American culture and narrativity.

*"Passing the Torch."*

On September 19, 2010, the *Knoxville News Sentinel* ran a political cartoon entitled "Passing the Torch." The Rev. Terry Jones, pastor of the Dove World Outreach Program, stands in the visual foreground. His white hair and mustache blend in with his white long-sleeved T-shirt, which bears the slogan "Burn a Koran Day." He looks over his shoulder as he reaches to the figure behind him. Standing at the edge of the cartoon is a white-robed Klansman holding a burning torch toward Jones. The torch smolders as the Klansman looks on. The cartoon Klansman is in full regalia (robe, hood, and mask), and his eyes appear slightly dazed behind the hood of his robe. Is it possible that Terry Jones confuses the Klansman? Or is it just hard to represent facial expressions behind the order's infamous white hood? The cartoonist's agenda to bind Jones to the lasting legacy of the Klan and religious hatred becomes clear. Burning Korans equates to burning crosses. Jones, a pastor of a small congregation in Gainesville, Florida, became an international figure when he started a (now defunct) group on Facebook wed to his website, titled "Islam Is the Devil," and started using Twitter to promote his ideas and plans.[13] Through online social media, he claimed that he would burn 200 Korans on the ninth anniversary of the September 11 terrorist attacks. He had already written a book with the same title as the website. Yet Jones did not gain much attention, media or otherwise, until he requested that his Facebook fans and followers send in their own photos and ideas of how to destroy the sacred text of Islam.[14]

Jones quickly transitioned from an obscure pastor of a small congregation to an international representative of the supposed American hatred of Muslims. The association in the political cartoon, then, should be obvious: those like Jones who would burn the Koran are the same as the members of the Ku Klux Klan. The Klan represents a certain brand of intolerance and hatred, and Koran-burners obviously fall into the same lineage. In the cartoon, Jones's clothing, his outreached arm, and his T-shirt slogan all showcase his attachment to the Klan's long history of terror and racism. The white-T-shirt-wearing pastor does not wear robes; his face is not hidden. But his white clothing illustrates his sympathy and similarity to the hooded figure. The visual message of the cartoon is that Jones is fringe, much like the Klan, and he bears the order's legacy, which means he is representative of a small subset of Americans.

Yet the visual analogy does not hold up under much scrutiny. The Klan, at least the 1920s Klan, burned crosses not to protest Christianity or individual Christians but to show the light of Jesus in the flames of each fiery cross (and to terrorize those who found lit crosses on their lawns). Klansmen were not attacking larger Christian tradition. Instead, they employed the fiery cross to warn the enemies of white Protestant America and the Klan more generally. Moreover, the order imagined that each lit cross memorialized the importance of Jesus' sacrifice for humanity. On the other hand, Jones clearly wanted to destroy the artifact, the sacred text, of Islam. The potential destruction of the Koran was an attack on Islam that he associated with terrorism and the September 11 attacks. In his conflation of Islam and terror, Jones's symbolic protest denied that the majority of Muslims worldwide are not terrorists and sought to terrify and harm. The current of terror in the immolation of both cross and Koran cannot be denied. But the contexts of both fiery ends are significantly different. The 1920s Klan's fiery cross indicated the common prejudice of the Klan. Media, pundits, and politicians represented the Koran burning as an anomaly, a presentation of Jones's unique and uncommon hatred.

While Jones's anti-Muslim bigotry might have been more theatrical than other forms of intolerance directed at Muslims, this did not mean that Jones and his congregation were the only Americans who had animus toward Muslims. As William Saletan notes at *Slate,* Americans were resentful that Jones became indicative of our nation and our people. Yet Americans by and large make the same judgment about all Muslims based on the actions of the terrorists involved in the September 11 attacks. Saletan writes:

> This is how it feels to be judged by the sins of others who destroy in the name of your faith. You're no more responsible for 30 Christian extremists in Florida than Muslims are for the 19 hijackers of 9/11. Yet most of us, when polled, say that no Muslim house of worship should be built near the site of the 9/11 attacks. In saying this, we implicitly hold all Muslims

accountable for the crime of those 19 people. Now you know how it feels to be judged that way. It's inaccurate, and it's wrong.[15]

For Saletan, Jones and his congregation were not representative of all Americans, but their prejudice against Muslims was not unique to them. Many Americans equated Muslims and terrorism, even if they did not threaten to burn Korans. According to an *ABC News/Washington Post* poll, only 37 percent of Americans view Islam favorably, which is significantly less than the poll conducted in October of 2001 after the terrorist attacks. Moreover, 49 percent of Americans view Islam unfavorably, which demonstrates that Jones's intolerance might be more common than we might like to admit.[16] While Meacham can claim a larger trend of tolerance, Jones and public opinion about Muslims suggest otherwise.

*A dark vision of American life.*

Yet Jones was not the only figure branded with the iconic image of intolerance, bigotry, and racism. A constellation of new political movements, organized under the moniker of Tea Party and claiming the revolutionary spirit of the original Boston Tea Party, stirs populistic fervor, mobilizes voters, and seeks governmental reform. The Tea Party movements trace their origins back to CNBC pundit Rick Santelli's comments about the mortgage crisis and bailout. On February 19, 2009, Santelli called for voters to revolt against the plan while standing on the floor of the Chicago Mercantile Exchange. His rant, called the "Shout Heard Round the World," was a heated affair. The outburst was a couple minutes in length, and Santelli claimed what America needed was a new Tea Party, a revolution to give power back to voters. Voters, who like Santelli felt that the bailouts and stimulus packages were wrong, organized their own Tea Party events. The first Tea Party rally was held in Washington, D.C., on February 27, and the movement was born.[17] Santelli has become one face of the Tea Party, and Glenn Beck, a *Fox News* commentator, author, and radio host, has become another prominent persona of this burgeoning political movement, despite his attempts to suggest otherwise. Writing for the *Weekly Standard*, Matthew Continetti argues that Santelli and Beck represent two poles of the Tea Party movement. Both feel the country is "wildly off course," that the government "subsidizes bad behavior," and that by returning to the founders of the nation we can steer the country to the right course.[18] While Continetti is comfortable with Santelli's style and rhetoric, Beck makes him a bit nervous. He writes that Beck "provides his audiences with a dark vision of American life" in which "rich, highly educated, radical elites are using instruments of power to control the common man and indoctrinate his children." These "elitists" battle with "patriots by calling them racists and extremists." For Continetti, the danger is that Beck, unlike Santelli, finds the American nation utterly broken. The country made great by the founders' vision is crumbling, and Beck calls on his radio and television audiences to turn back the tides of dangerous "progressivism" and declare themselves the true patriots defending a declining nation.[19]

In his writing and in his television and radio shows, Beck urges Americans to take back their nation and bring the government back under the control of the people. His 9/12 Project urges voters to take back their country, their values, and their government. Beck is an amateur historian who looks to the Founding Fathers and particular conservative historians, including W. Cleon Skousen, not to "assault contemporary liberalism," but to deconstruct "the very foundations of the New Deal and the Progressive Era."[20] Beck's rendering of American history informs the audiences at his shows, his speeches, and his public events about what exactly the nation once was, the trouble that the nation now faces, and his belief about the rapid declension of America. Beck suggests that America was once unified and good, and he encourages his audiences to redeem their nation.

On August 28, 2010, Beck hosted a "Restoring Honor" rally to "celebrate America." The date coincided with the forty-seventh anniversary of Martin Luther King Jr.'s "I Have a Dream" speech, which occurred on the steps of the Lincoln Memorial. According to Beck, he did not realize the anniversary. He originally hoped the rally would be held on September 12 to echo his 9/12 Project, but the date was on Sunday, the Sabbath, which was not acceptable to Beck because of his religious faith. Later, Beck claimed that it must have been "divine providence" for the date to work out as such.[21] At the rally, Beck spoke fervently about the need to restore America to its previous greatness and to reinstate the role of the divine in this redemption. Beck stated, "Something that is beyond man is happening. America today begins to turn back to God. For too long, this country has wandered in darkness."[22] The rally was attended by at least 80,000 people, Tea Party supporters and otherwise, illustrating Beck's popularity and the desire of many citizens that America return to some fabled past.[23]

The rally proved to be highly controversial and generated much print, blog, and radio commentary. Civil rights activist Rev. Walter Fauntroy declared that the Tea Party movement was synonymous with the Ku Klux Klan. At a news conference of the National Press Club, two days before the rally, Fauntroy told reporters: "We are going to take on the barbarism of war, the decadence of racism, and the scourge of poverty, that the Ku Klux—I meant to say the Tea Party. . . . You all forgive me, but I—you have to use them interchangeably."[24] Fauntroy continued that he did not want to be painted as angry or reactionary, but "when this right-wing conservative exclusionary group comes to highjack our movement, we have got to respond."[25] Fauntroy equated Beck and his rally attendees to the same folks who tried to cut the cables of the sound system during King's famous speech. Stephen Colbert, the satirical host of Comedy Central's *The Colbert Report,* even noted wryly: "Finally someone is bringing Martin Luther King's movement back to its conservative white roots."[26] Colbert and Fauntroy pointed out one of the most common criticisms of the Tea Party movement: that it is a movement of white people attempting to restore white dominance in America. For some news outlets, *Salon* and *Newsweek,* to name just two, the umbrella term "Tea Party" pretty much describes movements of white people claiming victimized status and disenfranchisement in American culture.[27] *Newsweek* asks, "Are Tea Partiers Racist?" and their answer is a bit more complicated. Relying on a University of Washington Institute for the Study of Ethnicity survey, supporters of the Tea Party movement had "a higher probability [around 25 percent] . . . of being racially resentful than those who are not Tea Party supporters."[28] This preponderance for racial resentment quickly became a venue for Tea Party detractors to label the larger movement as racist. The NAACP even called for Tea Party organizations to dispel racists from their ranks.[29]

For *Salon*'s Christopher Hitchens, Beck's rally showcased the burgeoning white concern that "white America is within thinkable distance of a moment when it will no longer be the majority." Those attending Beck's Restoring Honor rally wanted to return to "the roots," or origins, of the nation with Pilgrims, Puritans, and founders.[30] What Hitchens argues is that the return to the roots and origins is loose code for the return to dominant whiteness. Using Beck's retelling of history, rally attendees and Beck's fans can imagine a nation in which American history starts with white colonists, continues to the founders, ignores slavery's role in the Civil War, and sees a dire threat in anything labeled progressive. The Tea Party, then, is a desperate move to restore something that white Christian Americans feel is almost lost. Beck is a lightning rod for both liberal and conservative criticism, and some Tea Party members disavow him because of his controversial style. The Tea Party emerged in the American news media as a movement with plenty of populist fervor but no substance.

Yet this rendering of Beck and the Tea Party is mostly unsatisfying. The goal, it seems, of much of the news coverage is to paint the movement as dangerous fringe—but fringe nonetheless. The desire to separate Tea Party supporters from mainstream politics and culture is an attempt to place their ideology and vision of history at the fringes of American life. To marginalize Tea Partiers is to marginalize the influence of their ideas on our larger nation as a whole. Fringe ideas equal fringe status. Yet the people who attended Beck's rally do not seem that different from other Americans. Alex McNeill attended the rally and wrote:

> Those with whom I spoke wanted to be sure that I understood the Tea Party is distinct from Glenn Beck or Sarah Palin, and that it is more than the sum of its spokespersons. Most wanted me to see that they were ordinary, hardworking, Christian Americans who were fed up, frustrated with a system that failed them again, angry over the country's direction, and interested in a return to (as the Restoring Honor website put it) "the values that founded this great nation."[31]

For McNeil, the people of the Tea Party found hope in Beck's rally and in the political movements, and their frustration was palpable. He continued, "Individually, most Tea Partiers are nice people, trying to do what's right, motivated by good intentions."[32] They seemed normal and caring, unlike their caricatures in other news stories and press. While McNeil generously assesses the motives of rally attendees, the lingering association of the Tea Party with extremism remained strong and unforgiving. Representative Sheila Jackson Lee, a Democrat from Texas, disagreed. In a workshop for the NAACP, Lee made a comparison similar to Fauntroy's, but a month earlier, saying:

> All those who wore sheets a long time ago have now lifted them off and started wearing . . . clothing . . . with a name . . . tea party. Don't you be fooled. Those who used to wear sheets are now being able to walk down the aisle and speak as a patriot because you will not speak loudly about the lack of integrity of this movement.[33]

While the members of the Tea Party might be ordinary and sincere, Lee was convinced that they were just a newer incarnation of the Ku Klux Klan.

*Who represents the Klan's legacy?*

Jones, Beck, and the Tea Party movement generate significant ire and journalistic ink, which cannot possibly be covered here. Yet the more important issue for me is the attempt to associate the Gainesville pastor and the larger Tea Party movement with the Klan. This is a bold and criticized move that demonstrates the legacy of the Ku Klux Klan in the American imagination. What is at stake in labeling both Jones and the Tea Party as inheritors of the Klan's legacy? Why brand Koran burning and a rally on Washington as indicative of the Klan? Who stands to gain with such representations? As a historian of religious intolerance and the Klan, I was waiting for the Klan to emerge in these public debates as the method to label persons and movements as nefarious and harmful as the white-robed vigilantes. The Klan's legacy, after all, revolves around violence, racism, misogyny, privilege, and white Protestantism. The men and women who burned crosses and donned robes become shorthand in our culture for anything nefarious, dangerous, or explicitly racist. The iconic Klansman carries both visual and ideological weight. Just the mention of the Klan in association with Jones or the Tea Party spurs media attention. Importantly, the image of the Ku Klux Klan, the white-robed Knights lighting crosses on fire, is a constant in the American imaginary. From John Grisham novels to television shows and film to music videos, the image of the Klan appears again and again in American popular culture to represent the seedy, backward, and dangerous. The long history of the order and its many manifestations is boiled down into the image of a Klan in regalia, an image of terror and intimidation. Binding people and movements to the Klan is an effective tool to showcase nefarious intentions and legacies.

White-robed Klansmen and the mention of the Ku Klux Klan appear as useful metaphors for intolerance, hatred, and violence. Images of Klansmen and Klanswomen still haunt our public spoken, written, and visual culture. This means that identifying a movement or person as being like the Klan carries heavy symbolic and ideological weight. To be labeled as a part of the lineage of the Klan signals one's participation in the corruption, prejudice, or outright hatred. This supposedly showcases a "corruption" of American ideals, a blatant acceptance of hatred and a danger to American society as a whole. To be labeled as "Klan" signifies detriment and destruction. The question that remains, then, is how this association bears fruit in our public discourse. Or to explain this more simply: what does one gain by labeling an adversary or competing movement as Klan? By describing the Tea Party or Jones as the same as the hooded order shows us that these political movements and this pastor are not a part of the American mainstream. Their ideas, then, do not hold cultural value, and other Americans are their opposites: tolerant, pluralist, and accepting. Yet I wonder who is the true inheritor of the Klan's legacy: the Klan seamstress, an inflammatory minister, or a broader populist movement? Who represents the vision of white Protestant America that the 1920s Klan fought hard to protect and redeem? In distinctly different ways, all three examples represent the Klan's brand of religious nationalism and vision of what America should be.

For Ms. Ruth, the legacy is the most identifiable because she manufactures Klan robes and artifacts. She most obviously claims the mantle of the Ku Klux Klan and inherits her membership from previous generations of her family. Her blessing ritual illuminates her Christian faith and the continued attachment between faith and intolerance. No one would deny that Ms. Ruth inherited the Klan's brand of Christian nationalism and white supremacy.

For Pastor Terry Jones, the legacy is not the burning of objects but his use of modern technology, intimidation, and exclusion to fight a so-called enemy of the American nation, Islam. In threatening Muslims and attempting to destroy sacred objects, he created a one-dimensional enemy of a white Christian nation that must be battled at all costs. The "torch" was not passed to him directly, but through a style of politics that highlights the dangers of pluralism and multiculturalism to the nation's fate. For Jones, the terrorist attacks made his views tangible and real. His threat to burn the Koran did not bind him to the Klan as much as his ideas about enemies and national safety. Moreover, Jones is representative of anti-Muslim fervor in the United States. While many Americans will not burn Korans, they will contest the ability of Muslims to build mosques and practice their religion freely.

Finally, the Tea Party's vision of American history and the destiny of the nation represents a crucial legacy of the Klan: the battle for who controls our national narratives. Long before Glenn Beck and his chalkboard, amateur Klan historians whitewashed national history to place white Protestants at the center of American life. Klansmen and Klanswomen feared the decline of white Protestant America, and they fought rhetorical battles to preserve their rightful place in nation. They were guardians of a certain vision of nation, much like the Tea Party hopes to be today. Of course, the preservation of nation benefits certain people at the cost of others. The Klan's brand is still present today. Yet the order's legacy is not merely contained by white-robed members of the modern Klan but also appears in the long-lasting legacy of America's religious intolerance and the fervent desire for the nation to return to its origins, but only if those origins are white and Protestant.

# Notes

INTRODUCTION. "LET'S GET BEHIND OLD GLORY
AND THE CHURCH OF JESUS CHRIST"

1. "Clendenin, W. Va., Klan Growing," *Imperial Night-Hawk* 1, no. 40 (January 30, 1924): 6.

2. Wyn Craig Wade, *Fiery Cross: The Ku Klux Klan in America* (New York: Simon & Schuster, 1987).

3. "The Mary Phagan Case," *Columbus Ledger,* May 9, 1913, 4.

4. "Mary Phagan—A Warning," *Macon Daily Telegraph,* May 7, 1913, 4.

5. See Leonard Dinnerstein, *The Leo Frank Case,* rev. ed. (1966; Athens: University of Georgia Press, 2008) and Steve Oney, *And the Dead Shall Rise: The Murder of Mary Phagan and the Lynching of Leo Frank* (New York: Vintage, 2003). For an excellent discussion of the long-standing fascination with the Leo Frank case in film, see Matthew Bernstein, *Screening a Lynching: The Leo Frank Case on Film and Television* (Athens: University of Georgia Press, 2009).

6. Franklyn Bliss Snyder, "The Ballad of Mary Phagan," *Journal of American Folklore* 31 (1918): 264–266; Douglas O. Linder, "Famous Trials: The Leo Frank Trial (1913)," accessed August 15, 2010, http://www.law.umkc.edu/faculty/projects/trials/frank/frankballad.html.

7. Snyder, "The Ballad of Mary Phagan."

8. "Mashed and Disfigured Body of Leo M. Frank, Pursued by a Clamoring Mob, Is Taken to Atlanta," *Columbus Enquirer-Sun,* August 17, 1915, 1.

9. Mary White Ovington, "Mary Phagan Speaks," *Lexington Herald,* September 12, 1915, 6.

10. "An Atrocious Horror," *Kansas City Times,* August 17, 1915, 1.

11. Nancy MacLean, "The Leo Frank Case Reconsidered: Gender and Sexual Politics in the Making of Reactionary Populism," *Journal of American History* 78 (December 1991): 920.

12. Wade, *Fiery Cross,* 123.

13. Ibid., 125.

14. Chester L. Quarles, *The Ku Klux Klan and Related American Racialist and Antisemitic Organizations: A History and Analysis* (Jefferson, N.C.: McFarland & Co., 1999), 53.

15. The Klan, then, received inspiration from other fraternal orders. For

commentary on the place of religion in fraternity, see Mark C. Carnes, *Secret Ritual and Manhood in Victorian America* (New Haven: Yale University Press, 1989), 54–65, 71–80. For a complication of Carnes's argument and description of a religious fraternity, see Amy Koehlinger, "'Let Us Live for Those Who Love Us': Faith, Family, and the Contours of Manhood among the Knights of Columbus in Late Nineteenth-Century Connecticut," *Journal of Social History* 38, no. 2 (Winter 2004): 455–468. For the relationship between the Klan and fraternities, see Glenn Zuber, "'Onward Christian Klansmen': War, Religious Conflict, and the Rise of the Second Ku Klux Klan, 1912–1928" (Ph.D. diss., Indiana University, 2004).

16. Wade, *The Fiery Cross,* 142.

17. For an account and analysis of the Leo Frank trial, see MacLean, "The Leo Frank Case Reconsidered," 917–948. Wyn Craig Wade argues that the death of Mary Phagan and the organization of the Knights of Mary Phagan are directly related to the birth of the Klan. See Wade, *Fiery Cross,* 144–145.

18. Quarles, *The Ku Klux Klan,* 55. "Burning crosses had never been a part of the Reconstruction Ku-Klux. They had come from the exotic imagination of Thomas Dixon, whose fictional Klansmen had felt so much tangible pride in their Scottish ancestry, they revived the use of burning crosses as signal fires from one clan to another." See Wade, *Fiery Cross,* 146.

19. See Leonard Dinnerstein, *Anti-Semitism in America* (New York: Oxford University Press, 1994), 58; Jay P. Dolan, *The American Catholic Experience: A History from Colonial Times to the Present* (Garden City, N.Y.: Doubleday, 1985), 127–157; Wade, *Fiery Cross,* 148–149.

20. Kathleen Blee, *Women of the Klan: Racism and Gender in the 1920s* (Berkeley: University of California Press, 1991), 17.

21. The 1920s Klan readily admitted that the organization was for white supremacy as well as American freedoms and Protestant Christianity. See Exalted Cyclops of Monroe Klan Number 4, Louisiana, "Klan a Patriotic, Benevolent, Fraternal Organization of Christian Americans," *Imperial Night-Hawk,* April 9, 1924, 2.

22. Wade, *Fiery Cross,* 33.

23. Ibid., 33–34.

24. Michael Newton, *The Invisible Empire: The Ku Klux Klan in Florida* (Gainesville: University Press of Florida, 2001), 1–2.

25. Ibid., 7.

26. The Invisible Empire included all the states that had Klan activity.

Dens were groups of Klansmen within a county, Province. The Province was overseen by a Grand Giant and his four assisting Goblins. The congressional district, Dominion, was headed by a Grand Titan and six Furies. A state, Realm, was governed by a Grand Dragon and his eight Hydras. In charge of all the states that composed the Invisible Empire was the commander, the Grand Wizard. Klansmen basically had their own terminology for anything imaginable, including days, months, seasons, and code words to communicate secretly with other Klansmen. Individual Klansmen were known as Ghouls. Wade, *Fiery Cross*, 38–39. See also Quarles, *The Ku Klux Klan*, 65–66, for a discussion of Klan terms and usage.

27. Wade, *Fiery Cross*, 72. Two African American men from Georgia were killed for voting Republican after the Klan had warned against voting. Wade's work, like most other works on the Klan, describes the violence of the Klan's actions in excruciating detail. The impact of Klan violence on victims encompasses the history, and the Klan becomes monstrous hate-filled Knights. Whether they are monstrous or not, there needs to be a more nuanced understanding of their actions and intents alongside the apparent violence.

28. Newton, *The Invisible Empire,* 7.

29. Wade, *Fiery Cross,* 65.

30. Quarles, *The Ku Klux Klan,* 58.

31. Wade, *Fiery Cross,* 253.

32. See Shawn Lay, ed., *The Invisible Empire in the West: Toward a New Historical Appraisal of the Ku Klux Klan of the 1920s* (Urbana: University of Illinois Press, 1992) and Leonard J. Moore, *Citizen Klansman: The Ku Klux Klan in Indiana, 1921–1928* (Chapel Hill: University of North Carolina Press, 1991) for the debunking of stereotypes of Klansmen and claims that Klansmen were ordinary citizens who embraced populism as a method of reform.

33. Nancy MacLean, *Behind the Mask of Chivalry: The Making of the Second Ku Klux Klan* (New York and Oxford: Oxford University Press, 1994), 8.

34. In "The Leo Frank Case Reconsidered: Gender and Sexual Politics in the Making of Reactionary Populism," Stanley Cohen argues that it is better to see the Klan as a populist movement rather than a nativist one because newer studies of the 1920s Klan deemphasize the place of race within the movement. See Stanley Cohen, "Ordinary White Protestants: The KKK of the 1920s," *Journal of Social History* 28, no. 1 (Autumn 1994): 155–165. According to David Horowitz, revisions in Klan scholarship "acknowledged Klan racism; hostility to immigrants, Catholics, and Jews; and the movement's obsession

with white Protestant cultural hegemony. But rather than viewing the 1920s KKK as an aberrant form of extremism, the revisionist histories described a mainstream social movement that drew support from a wide cross-section [*sic*] of the nation's white Protestants" (72). Again, populism motivated the order rather than nativism or extremism. See David A. Horowitz, "The Normality of Extremism: The Ku Klux Klan Revisited," *Society* 35, no. 6 (September/October 1998): 71–77.

35. Kenneth T. Jackson, *The Ku Klux Klan in the City, 1915–1930* (Chicago: Elephant Paperbacks, 1992), xv.

36. I mark the end of the second revival of the Klan at 1930 because membership had plummeted into the thousands. For some scholars the decline began in 1925, when Indiana Klan leader D. C. Stephenson was found guilty of the rape and second-degree murder of Madge Oberholtzer. The Klan played a fascinating role in the 1928 Democratic convention, in which members helped defeat the nomination of Al Smith. The *Kourier Magazine* continued to print Klan positions, opinions, and news until 1936. Please see the conclusion for a further discussion of the end of the 1920s Klan.

37. The historical lineage of the Klan is much more complicated after the 1920s. In the 1930s and 1940s, various Klans took a stand against "dreaded" Communism to protect America. By the 1950s there were a variety of different Klan organizations still attempting to defend the American way of life. In the 1960s multiple Klans emerged to counter the civil rights movement. These Klans were characterized by violence and racial hatred. Klansmen were ready to defend America again by taking a stand against the civil rights movement. In his *Invisible Empire,* Michael Newton noted that the 1960s marked a turning point for the Klan because the organization was no longer mainstream and would become increasingly more marginalized. In the late 1970s and early 1980s, the Klan emerged again under the skillful hands of David Duke, who "spun" the Klan's racist message into a racialist message: the Klan loved their white race rather than hated other races. This Klan accepted Catholics and established an explicit link between the Klan and Neo-Nazis. In recent years, it is hard to distinguish between the Klan and other hate groups because of the blending of their racialized ideologies and the popularity of Christian Identity, a racial faith which literally draws the world as good and evil, white and black. See Newton, *The Invisible Empire.*

38. Allan J. Lichtman, *White Protestant Nation: The Rise of the American Conservative Movement* (New York: Atlantic Monthly Press, 2008), 2.

39. Ibid., 10.

40. My work furthers the work of Leonard Moore and Shawn Lay, who sought to highlight the difference between the 1920s Klan and the other Klan movements with empathy, and suggests that religion is not only an essential component of the 1920s Klan but also the larger hate movement in the United States. See Lay, *The Invisible Empire in the West,* and Moore, *Citizen Klansman.*

41. The major exceptions being Kathleen Blee's *Women of the Klan* and Rory McVeigh, *The Rise of the Ku Klux Klan: Right-Wing Movements and National Politics,* Social Movements, Protest, and Contention (Minneapolis: University of Minnesota Press, 2009).

42. It is important to note that engagement with the 1920s Klan usually errs on the side of not believing what members say or write. This is highly problematic because this can lead to simplistic portraits of those involved in hate movements, especially the Klan, and means that we are in dire need of more complex and possibly more empathetic approaches.

43. For the beginnings of "status anxiety" approach, see John Moffatt Mecklin, *The Ku Klux Klan: The Study of an American Mind* (1924; reprint, New York: Russell and Russell, 1963). For a historiographical discussion of this approach, see Leonard J. Moore, "Historical Interpretations of the 1920s Klan: The Traditional View and Recent Revisions," in *The Invisible Empire in the West: Toward a New Historical Appraisal of the Ku Klux Klan of the 1920s,* ed. Shawn Lay (Urbana: University of Illinois Press, 1992), 17–38, especially 18–22.

44. Moore, "Historical Interpretations of the 1920s Klan," 22.

45. See MacLean, *Behind the Mask of Chivalry,* 114–124.

46. For discussions of the Klan's hatred and violence, see David Chalmers, *Hooded Americanism: The History of the Ku Klux Klan,* 3d ed. (1956; Durham: Duke University Press, 1987); William Loren Katz, *The Invisible Empire: The Ku Klux Klan Impact on History* (Washington, D.C.: Open Hand Publishing, 1986); Wade, *Fiery Cross;* Newton, *The Invisible Empire;* and Quarles, *The Ku Klux Klan.* In addition, Philip Jenkins tackles the Klan as a fascist organization in the 1930s. See Philip Jenkins, *Hoods and Shirts: The Extreme Right in Pennsylvania, 1925–1950* (Chapel Hill: University of North Carolina Press, 1997).

47. In a review of Newton's work, Glenn Zuber argues that Newton's attention to the Klan's violence is key, but he proposes to label the Klan as terrorists to bring their violence to the forefront. See Glenn Zuber, review of *Invis-*

*ible Empire, Journal of Southern Religion* 5 (2002), http://jsr.fsu.edu/2002/Reviews/Zuber.htm.

48. Moore, *Citizen Klansman*, 23.

49. See Lay, *The Invisible Empire in the West,* and Moore, *Citizen Klansman*. Of course, one might ask why Klansmen and Klanswomen decided to present their white supremacy blatantly in regalia, newspapers, and political actions when other American citizens did not.

50. Other studies of the Klan examine the nativism, nationalism, racism, and gender of the order. In many historical accounts, racism was the motivating factor for men and women to join the order. The foreign, including African American enfranchisement during Reconstruction and the "Catholic invasion" of the 1920s, menaced so-called American values. The Klan reacted to dangers lurking in the American landscape. To defend against those dangers, the order vigorously restated its social boundaries and articulated concern regarding the purity of the white race. The commitment to whiteness required strict racial boundaries.

Many accounts of the contemporary hate movement also center upon racism. James Ridgeway and Nick Ryan usually identified racism as the central facet of these organizations without reference to how racism came to predominate these groups. In their work, Betty A. Dobratz and Stephanie Shanks-Meile purported that race was the essential concern for the white separatist movement. This attachment to race can be understood in three ways: as racialist (love of one's race), racist (defense of one's race), and supremacist (race hatred). Dobratz and Shanks-Meile propose that this racism is economic: some whites feel that they are disadvantaged economically because of their skin color. This analysis, unfortunately, accepts race as a naturalized category rather than approaching race as a discourse. See the following journalistic accounts: James Ridgeway, *Blood in the Face: The Ku Klux Klan, Aryan Nations, Nazi Skinheads and the Rise of New White Culture* (New York: Thunder's Mouth Press, 1995), and Nick Ryan, *Into a World of Hate: A Journey among the Extreme Right* (New York: Routledge, 2004). For more on the white separatist movement, see Betty A. Dobratz and Stephanie Shanks-Meile, *"White Power, White Pride!": The White Separatist Movement in the United States* (Baltimore: Johns Hopkins University Press, 2000).

For a particular discussion of gender in the 1920s Klan, see Blee, *Women of the Klan,* and MacLean, *Behind the Mask of Chivalry*.

51. For denominations involved in the Klan, see Moore, *Citizen Klansman*.

For supposed ties to fundamentalism, see Wade, *Fiery Cross*. For the relationship of ministers and local congregations to Klan, see MacLean, *Behind the Mask of Chivalry,* and Robert Allen Goldberg, *Hooded Empire: The Ku Klux Klan in Colorado* (Urbana: University of Illinois Press, 1981). For the WKKK and Protestantism and women in the Klan in the 1920s, see Blee, *Women of the Klan.*

52. Several scholars have understood hate movements, and the Klan in particular, as proponents of so-called false religion. In her *New White Nationalism,* Carol Swain argued that these movements employed a false religion, which could not be affiliated with Christianity, and her solution for all hate groups was to introduce them to evangelical Christianity. In his *One Aryan Nation under God* (2001), Jerome Walters also noted that "real" Christianity could be the solution to Christian Identity's "twisting of scriptures." Moreover, religious historian Philip Jenkins noted in a review essay on new scholarship on hate groups that "it seems grossly unfair to stress the 'Christianity' of any hare-brained [*sic*] rightist militant who asserts he is fighting in the name of God or Jesus." These accounts of hate groups, especially Jenkins's assertion, demonstrate the utter lack of attention paid to how religion functions for these groups. Scholars like Swain, Walters, Hamm, and Jenkins assumed that the religious expressions of hate groups, including the Klan, were not legitimate because they were not representative of "true" Christianity. Robert Orsi has suggested that religion at best is ambiguous, and it can be employed in ways that are beneficial and detrimental, and thus arguments about good and bad religion miss the fluidity of religion as a system. See Carol Swain, *The New White Nationalism in America: Its Challenge to Integration* (Cambridge: Cambridge University Press, 2002); Jerome Walters, *One Aryan Nation under God: Exposing the New Racial Extremists* (Cleveland: Pilgrim Press, 2000); Robert Orsi, *Between Heaven and Earth: The Religious Worlds People Make and the Scholars Who Study Them* (Princeton: Princeton University Press, 2005), 187; Philip Jenkins, "The Other Terrorists," *Books and Culture* (November/December 2003): 8.

53. See, in particular, Walters, *One Aryan Nation under God.*

54. See Sydney Ahlstrom, *A Religious History of the American People* (New Haven: Yale University Press, 1973), 916–917.

55. Martin Marty, *Righteous Empire: The Protestant Experience in America,* Two Centuries of American Life (New York: Dial Press, 1970), 211.

56. Jackson, *The Ku Klux Klan in the City,* xv.

57. "Editorial Brevities," *Imperial Night-Hawk* 2, no. 34 (November 19, 1924): 7.

58. See James Aho, *This Thing of Darkness: A Sociology of the Enemy* (Seattle: University of Washington Press), 1994.

59. The *Imperial Night-Hawk* was a weekly published in Atlanta, Georgia.

60. See "Editorial Brevities," *Imperial Night-Hawk* 2, no. 34 (November 19, 1924): 7. The accuracy of this figure is hard to determine, but the specificity and modesty of the number make the circulation seem more plausible.

61. "Editorial Brevities," 7; emphasis added.

62. "Dawn Circulation Climbs to 50,000 as Fight for Americanism Stirs Nation Wide Interest," *Dawn* 1, no. 25 (April 7, 1923): 6.

63. Elaine Scarry, *The Body in Pain: The Making and Unmaking of the World* (New York: Oxford University Press, 1985), 125. Scarry writes that it is possible for *"the incontestable reality of the physical body to now become an attribute of an issue that at that moment has no independent reality of its own."* Scarry, of course, is talking about in the realm of torture. However, bodies become issues or beliefs in both her unmaking and making of sections of her text. The alteration of bodies, circumcision, flagellation, or dress present ideals and beliefs. Thus, we can examine how bodies "exhibit" beliefs to understand how those beliefs impact the believer. Moreover, Scarry presents the cultural and symbolic weight upon bodies, which only disappears in death. Our cultures mold us from facial expressions to accents to what is acceptable to believe. This happens through comportment as well as words.

64. See James W. Carey, *Communication as Culture: Essays on Media and Society* (Boston: Unwin Hyman, 1989), 13–36.

65. See David D. Hall, *Worlds of Wonder, Days of Judgment: Popular Religious Belief in Early New England* (Cambridge: Harvard University Press, 1989); *Cultures of Print: Essays in the History of the Book* (Amherst: University of Massachusetts Press, 1996); and Hugh Amory and David D. Hall, eds., *The Colonial Book in the Atlantic World* (Cambridge: Cambridge University Press, 2000).

66. See David Paul Nord, *Communities of Journalism: A History of American Newspapers and Their Readers* (Urbana: University of Illinois Press, 2001), 2–14, and *Faith in Reading: Religious Publishing and the Birth of Mass Media* (Oxford: Oxford University Press, 2004).

67. Candy Gunther Brown, *The Word in the World: Evangelical Writing,*

*Publishing, and Reading in America, 1789–1880* (Chapel Hill: University of North Carolina Press, 2004).

68. "Brand 'Searchlight' Statements False," *Imperial Night-Hawk* 1, no. 22 (August 29, 1923): 4.

69. "Klansmen Should Support Newspapers Which Battle for Klan Principles," *Imperial Night-Hawk* 1, no. 6 (May 9, 1923): 7.

70. "Wisconsin Pastor Proclaims Klan as Staunch Defender of Protestantism," *Imperial Night-Hawk* 1, no. 7 (May 16, 1923): 6.

71. Shawn Lay and Leonard Moore have both illuminated the importance of moving past demonization of subjects, and Jeffrey Kaplan has pointed out the importance of understanding far-right groups in their own contexts. See Lay, *The Invisible Empire in the West;* Moore, *Citizen Klansmen;* and Jeffrey Kaplan, *Radical Religion in America: Millenarian Movements from the Far Right to the Children of Noah* (Syracuse, N.Y.: Syracuse University Press, 1997). David Chidester's approach to convey humanity rather than moralizing about subjects is also useful. See Chidester, *Suicide and Salvation: An Interpretation of Jim Jones, the Peoples Temple, and Jonestown* (Bloomington: Indiana University Press, 1988), xi–xv, 1–46. Also, see Chidester's response to Stephen Prothero's "Bracketing Belief." Chidester, "Moralizing Noise," *Harvard Divinity Bulletin* 32, no. 3 (Summer 2004), http://www.hds.harvard.edu/news/bulletin/articles/orsi_et_al.html.

72. The question of empathy in ethnography is problematized by these groups, which society considers deplorable. Kathleen Blee is the foremost scholar on the ethics of studying deplorable people. See Blee's *Women of the Klan; Inside Organized Racism: Women in the Hate Movement* (Berkeley: University of California Press, 2002); "Studying the Enemy," in *Our Studies, Ourselves: Sociologists' Lives and Work,* ed. Barry Glassner and Rosanna Hertz (Oxford: Oxford University Press, 2003), 13–23; "Fieldworkers' Privilege? The Perils of Privilege," *Law and Social Inquiry* 24 (Fall 1999): 993–997; "White-Knuckle Research: Emotional Dynamics in Fieldwork with Racist Activists," *Qualitative Sociology* 21, no. 4 (1998): 381–399; and "Evidence, Empathy, and Ethics: Lessons from Oral Histories of the Klan," *Journal of American History* 80, no. 2 (September 1993): 596–606.

73. Lived religion is often applied to the religion of nonelites to show what is missing from the "official" story. However, lived religion should also be applied to elite sources as well, because the insights of how Klan leaders hoped

to practice religion and enforce it on members shows their ideal vision of how the world was supposed to be and their dedication to this preservation. See David Hall, ed., *Lived Religion in America toward a History of Practice* (Princeton: Princeton University Press, 1997), viii–ix.

74. See ibid.

75. See James Clifford, "Introduction: Partial Truths," in *Writing Culture: The Poetics and Politics of Ethnography,* ed. James Clifford and George E. Marcus (Berkeley: University of California Press, 1986), 1–26, and Orsi, *Between Heaven and Earth,* 2–3.

76. Blee, "White-Knuckle Research," 388.

77. Michael Barkun, *A Culture of Conspiracy: Apocalyptic Visions in Contemporary America* (Berkeley: University of California Press, 2003), x.

78. Ann Burlein, *Lift High the Cross: Where White Supremacy and the Christian Right Converge* (Durham, N.C.: Duke University Press, 2002), xvi–xvii.

79. See Karen McCarthy Brown, *Mama Lola: A Vodou Priestess in Brooklyn,* rev. ed. (1991; Berkeley: University of California Press, 2001).

80. See Michael Barkun, *Religion and the Racist Right: The Origins of the Christian Identity Movement* (Chapel Hill: University of North Carolina Press, 1996).

81. The discussion of past and present when discussing history and ethnography and the complicated relationship between the two comes directly from Amy Koehlinger. She deserves the credit for my use of such terminology and helping me think through how to do both.

CHAPTER ONE. "THANK GOD FOR THE KNIGHTS OF
THE KU KLUX KLAN": THE KLAN'S PROTESTANTISM

1. H. W. Evans, "A Message from the Imperial Wizard," *Kourier Magazine* 1, no. 3 (February 1925): 2.

2. "Altoona, Pa., Klans Help Santa," *Imperial Night-Hawk* 1, no. 41 (January 9, 1924): 6.

3. Henry P. Fry, *The Modern Ku Klux Klan* (Boston: Small, Maynard & Co., 1922; reprint, New York: Negro Universities Press, 1969), 90, found in Indiana Historical Society, Indianapolis.

4. Ibid., 91.

5. Ibid., 6.

6. Ibid., 8.

7. Ibid., 26–27.

8. W. C. Witcher, *The Unveiling of the Ku Klux Klan,* rev. ed. (Fort Worth, TX: W. C. Witcher, 1922), 32.

9. Ibid., 33.

10. Ibid., 34.

11. William Simmons, *Official Message of the Emperor of the Invisible Empire, Knights of the Ku Klux Klan, to the Initial Session of the Imperial Klonvokation* (Atlanta: Webb & Vary Print, 1922), 7–8, in the D. C. Stephenson Collection, M264, b.4, f.8, Indiana Historical Society, Indianapolis.

12. Ibid., 8.

13. For more on Colonel Simmons, see Wyn Craig Wade, *Fiery Cross: The Ku Klux Klan in America* (New York: Simon & Schuster, 1987), 140–147.

14. Simmons, *Official Message,* 8.

15. Evans, "A Message from the Imperial Wizard," 2.

16. Robert Moats Miller, "A Note on the Relationship between the Protestant Churches and the Revived Ku Klux Klan," *Journal of Southern History* 22, no. 3 (August 1956): 355–368. Robert Allen Goldberg demonstrates in his study of Colorado Klans that despite the attempt of national Protestant conventions to legislate relationships with the Klan, local churches were still affiliated with the order. See Goldberg, *Hooded Empire,* 187–188.

17. H. W. Evans, "The Klan Spiritual," *Imperial Night-Hawk* 2, no. 30 (October 22, 1924): 3. This speech was originally given at the Second Imperial Klonvokation, Kansas City, Missouri, September 23–26, 1924. It is unclear as to when the speech was exactly given.

18. Evans, "The Klan Spiritual," 2.

19. Ibid.

20. It should be noted that the term "Protestantism" used in this text is not meant to suggest a monolithic Protestantism. I am attempting to describe the Klan's own version of Protestantism that countered other forms of Protestantism during the 1920s rather than Protestantism writ large. For more analysis of other white Protestants in the 1920s, see Lichtman, *White Protestant Nation,* especially 26–30; Lynn Dumenil, *The Modern Temper: American Culture and Society in the 1920s* (New York: Hill & Wang, 1995), 169–200; and Barry Hankins, *Jesus and Gin: Evangelicalism, The Roaring Twenties and Today's Culture Wars* (New York: Palgrave Macmillan, 2010).

21. "A Message from the Imperial Wizard," *Kourier Magazine* 1, no. 3 (February 1925): 2.

22. "Jesus the Protestant," *Kourier Magazine* 1, no. 3 (February 1925): 2.

23. Ibid., 4.

24. "Protestantism," *Kourier Magazine* 1, no. 7 (June 1925): 2.

25. Ibid., 3.

26. Ibid.

27. Ibid., 2.

28. "Jesus the Protestant," 4.

29. Ibid., 5.

30. Exalted Cyclops of the Order, "Principles and Purposes of the Knights of the Ku Klux Klan," *Papers Read at the Meeting of the Grand Dragons, Knights of the Ku Klux Klan, at Their First Meeting Held at Asheville, North Carolina, July 1923*, Anti-Movements in America, ed. Gerald N. Grob (New York: Arno Press, 1977), 125.

31. Peter R. D'Agostino, *Rome in America: Transnational Catholic Ideology from the Risorgimento to Fascism* (Chapel Hill: University of North Carolina Press, 2004), 314.

32. Ray Allen Billington, "The Burning of the Charlestown Convent," *New England Quarterly* 10, no. 1 (March 1937): 4.

33. David Brion Davis, "Some Themes of Counter-Subversion: An Analysis of Anti-Masonic, Anti-Catholic, and Anti-Mormon Literature," *Mississippi Valley Historical Review* 47, no. 2 (September 1960): 205–224.

34. Jay Dolan blames much of the discrimination against Catholics in this time period on immigration. See Jay P. Dolan, *The American Catholic Experience: A History from Colonial Times to the Present* (New York: Double Day, 1985), 201–203.

35. Dolan argued that this process of imagination was a way for nativists to express their forbidden desires of violence, sexual perversion, and possibly sadism, in that nativist literature presented these desires to combat them. See Dolan, *The American Catholic Experience,* 221.

36. Mark S. Massa, *Anti-Catholicism in America: The Last Acceptable Prejudice* (New York: Crossroad Publishing Co., 2003), 29–30.

37. Ibid., 33–34. For more on the end of the 1920s Klan, please see the conclusion.

38. Evans, "The Klan Spiritual," 2.

39. Ibid., 6.

40. "Constructive Christianity," *Imperial Night-Hawk,* 2, no. 31 (October 29, 1924): 3.

41. "Knowing the Catholic Method," *Kourier Magazine* 1, no. 3 (February 1925): 9.

42. Dolan writes, "While this opposition was fundamental to the processes of making meaning and creating conceptual order, it was so subtle and shifting that it had to be reasserted or recreated constantly. Indeed, the difference between the two categories existed largely in such reassertion" (23). Reassertion of their differences from both Protestants and Catholics presented a method to claim separate identities. See Frances E. Dolan, *Whores of Babylon: Catholicism, Gender, and Seventeenth-Century Print Culture* (Notre Dame: University of Notre Dame Press, 2005).

43. "Constructive Christianity," 6.

44. According to Jenny Franchot, "Anti-Catholicism operated as an imaginative category of discourse though which antebellum American writers of popular and elite fictional and historical texts indirectly voiced the tensions and limitations of mainstream Protestant culture" (xvii). Franchot's model for the nineteenth century can easily be applied to the attempts of the Klan to define themselves in opposition to Roman Catholicism. The Klan employed anti-Catholicism to craft a Protestant image for their order. Franchot further suggested that antebellum anti-Catholicism helped craft a Protestant national identity, which is useful in thinking about how the Klan saw Catholics both as a threat to faith and nation. See Jenny Franchot, *Roads to Rome: The Antebellum Protestant Encounter with Catholicism* (Berkeley: University of California Press, 1994).

45. W. C. Wright, "A Klansman's Criterion of Character," *Imperial Night-Hawk* 1, no. 45 (February 6, 1924): 2

46. Ibid.

47. Ibid.

48. Ibid.

49. "Klankraft" is basically the practice of Klan ideals in one's life.

50. "The True Spirit of American Klansmen," *Imperial Night-Hawk* 1, no. 7 (May 16, 1923): 7.

51. Wright, "A Klansman's Criterion," 2.

52. *Imperial Night-Hawk* 1, no. 7 (May 16, 1923): 4.

53. "Altoona, Pa., Klans Help Santa," *Imperial Night-Hawk* 1, no. 41 (January 9, 1924): 6.

54. "Sordid Story of Girls' Shame Causes Klan at Shreveport to Pan Protestant Refuge," *Imperial Night-Hawk* 1, no. 6 (May 9, 1923): 2.

55. "Dr. Evans, Imperial Wizard, Defines Klan Principles and Outlines Klan Activities," *Imperial Night-Hawk* 1, no. 43 (January 23, 1924): 2.

56. *Proceedings of the Second Imperial Klonvokation Held in Kansas City, Missouri* (N.p.: Knights of the Ku Klux Klan Inc., 1924), 166. A Klonvokation was an annual meeting.

57. For Lisbon Klan's donations, see "Klan Komment," *Imperial Night-Hawk* 1, no. 39 (December 26, 1923): 5. For other Klans' charity during Christmas, see also "Wichita, Kansas, Klan No. 6 Delivers Hundreds of Christmas Baskets," *Imperial Night-Hawk* 1, no. 43 (January 23, 1924): 8; "Little Rock Klan Plays Santa Klaus Breaking All Records of the City," *Imperial Night-Hawk* 1, no. 41 (January 9, 1924): 3; "Bozeman, Mont., Klan Hears Grand Dragon," *Imperial Night-Hawk* 1, no. 46 (February 14, 1924): 5. For Klan hospitals, see "Dallas Klan Dedicates $85,000 Home for the Benefit of Orphan Babies," *Imperial Night-Hawk* 1, no. 27 (October 3, 1923): 5, and "New Klan Hospital Will Be Memorial to Martyr Who Gave Life for the Cause," *Imperial Night-Hawk* 1, no. 18 (August 1, 1923): 6. For martyr's education fund, see "Klansmen Asked to Aid Widow and Babies of Man Who Died for the Cause," *Imperial Night-Hawk* 1, no. 24 (September 12, 1923): 2–3. For Klan's service for "Negro Church," see "Klan Helps to Build Church for Negroes," *Imperial Night-Hawk* 1, no. 30 (October 24, 1923): 5.

For Klan giving, see "Should Scrutinize Charity Allotments," *Imperial Night-Hawk* 1, no. 6 (May 9, 1923): 4.

58. "Klansmen, Stop and Take Stock: Build for the Year 1924," *Imperial Night-Hawk* 1, no. 20 (January 2, 1924): 5.

59. "Klannish Co-operation," *Imperial Night-Hawk* 1, no. 41 (January 9, 1924): 4.

60. Rev. W. H. Stephens, "The Fiery Cross," *Imperial Night-Hawk* 1, no. 21 (August 22, 1923): 3.

61. *Proceedings of the Second Imperial Klonvokation,* 45.

62. "Christian Citizenship: The Gospel according to the Klan," *Imperial Night-Hawk* 1, no. 37 (December 12, 1923): 3.

63. W. C. Wright, "The Twelfth Chapter of Romans As a Klansman's Law of Life," *Imperial Night-Hawk* 1, no. 49 (March 5, 1924): 2.

64. Wade, *Fiery Cross,* 33–34. Wyn Wade described the Reconstruction uniform in detail. Elaine Parsons has written that the Reconstruction robes need to be understood as spectacle. She looks at the theatrical roots of this Klan and the symbolic import of the robes. For more on the Reconstruction robes, see Elaine Frantz Parsons, "Midnight Rangers: Costume and Perfor-

mance in the Reconstruction-Era Ku Klux Klan," *Journal of American History* 92, no. 3 (December 2005): 811–836.

65. William Simmons, *The Klan Unmasked* (Atlanta: W. E. Thompson, 1924), 87.

66. Ibid., 88.

67. Ibid., 91.

68. See "New Robe Plant Speeds Up Production As Thousands Request Regalia," *Imperial Night-Hawk* 1, no. 24 (September 12, 1923): 8, and "Regalia Factory and Printing Plant Will Save Much Money for Klans of Nation," *Imperial Night-Hawk* 1, no. 16 (July 18, 1923): 5.

69. "Louisiana Klansman Outlines the Aims, Purposes and Principles of His Order," *Imperial Night-Hawk* 1, no. 9 (May 30, 1923): 6.

70. "Louisiana Klansman," 33.

71. Exalted Cyclops of Texas, "The Seven Symbols of the Klan," *Imperial Night-Hawk* 1, no. 39 (December 26, 1923): 7. "Empire Invisible" is a play off "Invisible Empire," their term of Klandom. "Empire Invisible" refers to the celestial realm.

72. "Who Are These in White Robes?" *Kourier Magazine* 1, no. 7 (June 1925): 18.

73. Ibid., 19. The passage from Revelation is 7:13–15, as quoted in the *Kourier:* "And one of the elders answered, saying unto me, 'What are these which are arrayed in white robes and whence came they?' And I said unto him, 'Sir, thou knowest.' And he said unto me: 'These are they which came out of great tribulation, and have washed their robes and made them white in the blood of the Lamb. Therefore are they before the throne of God, and serve him day and night in His temple, and He that sitteth on the throne shall dwell among them" (18–19).

74. James Hardin Smith, "What Would Jesus Say?" *Dawn* 1, no. 8 (December 16, 1922): 5.

75. Scarry, *The Body in Pain,* 125.

76. Exalted Cyclops, "The Seven Symbols of the Klan," 7.

77. "Mis-use of Regalia Is Reported," *Imperial Night-Hawk* 1, no. 39 (December 26, 1923): 5.

78. "The Law of Secrecy Must Be Obeyed; Klansmen, Keep Your Visors Down!" *Imperial Night-Hawk* 1, no. 9 (May 30, 1923): 3.

79. "Elwood, Ind., Klan Aids Revival," *Imperial Night-Hawk* 1, no. 46 (February 14, 1924): 5.

80. "Klansmen of Louisiana Stand Firm before Catholic Boycott," *Imperial Night-Hawk* 1, no. 3 (April 1, 1923): 5.

81. "Louisiana Klansman Outlines the Aims, Purposes and Principles of His Order," *Imperial Night-Hawk* 1, no. 9 (May 30, 1923): 6.

82. "Go to Church Sunday," *Imperial Night-Hawk* 1, no. 3 (April 1, 1923): 5.

83. *Imperial Night-Hawk* 1, no. 5 (May 2, 1923): 6.

84. "Louisiana Klansman," 6.

85. Great Titan of the Realm of Texas, "How the Klan Can Be Made a True Civic Asset in Every Progressive Community," *Imperial Night-Hawk* 1, no. 23 (September 5, 1923): 6.

86. *Imperial Night-Hawk* 1, no. 29 (October 17, 1923): 6.

87. "The 'Man on the Fence' Becomes Uncomfortable," *Dawn* 1, no. 50 (October 13, 1923), 11.

88. *Imperial Night-Hawk* 1, no. 27 (October 3, 1923): 4.

89. "The 'Man on the Fence,'" 11.

90. Mrs. J. W. Northrup, "The Little Red School House Is One of the Most Sacred of American Institutions," *Imperial Night-Hawk* 1, no. 23 (August 22, 1923), 3.

91. Rev. W. C. Wright, "The Twelfth Chapter of Romans as a Klansman's Law of Life," *Imperial Night-Hawk* 1, no. 49 (March 5, 1924): 2.

92. Ibid., 2–3.

93. Ibid., 7.

94. Ibid.

95. "The Gathering of the Klans," *Imperial Night-Hawk* 2, no. 28 (October 8, 1924): 2.

96. W. C. Wright, *Religious and Patriotic Ideals of the Ku Klux Klan* (Waco, TX: W. C. Wright, 1926), 17.

97. "Constructive Christianity," 3.

98. Miller, "A Note on the Relationship," 357–360.

99. *Northwestern Christian Advocate* 70 (May 24, 1922), 581, quoted in Miller, "A Note on the Relationship," 358.

100. "Klan Aids Churches," 4.

101. "History Shows Secret Societies Have Advanced Christianity and Liberty," *Imperial Night-Hawk* 1, no. 7 (May 16, 1923): 3.

102. "Elwood, Ind., Klan Aids Revival," *Imperial Night-Hawk* 1, no. 46 (February 14, 1924): 5.

103. "God in the Klan," *Kourier Magazine* 3, no. 3 (February 1927): 18.

CHAPTER TWO. "TAKE THE CHRIST OUT OF AMERICA,

AND AMERICA FAILS!": THE KLAN'S NATIONALISM

1. Daisy Douglas Barr, "The Soul of America," *Knights of the Ku Klux Klan: Papers Read at the Meeting of Grand Dragons at Their First Annual Meeting Held at Asheville, North Carolina, July 1923*, Anti-Movements in America (reprint, New York: Arno Press, 1977), 135.

2. "To the Citizens of Wayne County," Ku Klux Klan, Wayne County Collection, box 1, folder 5, Indiana Historical Society, Indianapolis.

3. For Carolyn Marvin and David W. Ingle, the flag is an important emblem of nationalism, and they argue that patriotism could be considered a religious system on its own. They argue that the soldier carries a flag, which shows his willingness to die, much like Jesus carried the cross to demonstrate the same willingness (770). What is striking about their analysis is how they use Christian symbology to show the "religious" nature of patriotism. I argue that American patriotism is actually indebted to Christianity for its development. The Klan's reliance on cross and flag as patriotic exemplifies this. See Carolyn Marvin and David W. Ingle, "Blood Sacrifice and the Nation: Revisiting Civil Religion," *Journal of the American Academy of Religion* 64, no. 4 (Winter 1996): 767–780.

4. W. C. Wright, *The Religious and Patriotic Ideals of the Ku Klux Klan* (Waco, TX: W. C. Wright, 1926), 33.

5. Ibid.

6. "Patriotism," *Kourier Magazine* 2, no. 8 (July 1926): 14–15.

7. Barr, "The Soul of America," 135.

8. John Higham, in his seminal *Strangers in a Strange Land*, noted that nativism should be defined as a particular form of nationalism. Nativism "translates them [cultural antipathies and judgments] into a zeal to destroy the enemies of a distinctively American way of life" (4). Nativists, then, show great loyalty to their ideal of the nation and feel the need to combat enemies of said nation. The Klan, in many ways, is a nativist movement. However, I am more concerned with how Klansmen voiced their loyalties and render their enemies rather than exploring their nativism, which has been documented by several Klan scholars without understanding how they employ it. For more on nativism, see John Higham, *Strangers in a Strange Land: Patterns of American Nativism, 1860–1925*, rev. ed. (New Brunswick: Rutgers University Press, 2004).

9. My understandings of nationalism are indebted to both the work of

Benedict Anderson and Anthony Marx. In *Imagined Communities*, Anderson emphasizes the relationship between nationalism and print culture to foster a sense of imagined community. In *Faith in Nation*, Marx contradicts previous renderings of nationalism wed to Enlightenment principles and argues that European nationalism might instead be bound to tactics of religious exclusion to define who belongs to nation. See Benedict Anderson, *Imagined Communities: Reflections on the Origin and Spread of Nationalism*, rev. ed. (London: Verso, 1991) and Anthony Marx, *Faith in Nation: Exclusionary Origins of Nationalism* (Oxford: Oxford University Press, 2003).

10. "Texas Klansman Outlines Principles upon Which the Knights of the Ku Klux Klan Is Founded," *Imperial Night-Hawk* 1, no. 2 (April 4, 1923): 5.

11. "The Seven Symbols of the Klan," *Imperial Night-Hawk* 1, no. 39 (December 26, 1923): 6.

12. "The Symbol of the Fiery Cross," *Imperial Night-Hawk* 1, no. 45 (February 6, 1924): 8.

13. "The Seven Symbols of the Klan," 6.

14. Simmons, *The Klan Unmasked*, 33.

15. "The Fable of the Eagle and the Buzzards," *Imperial Night-Hawk* 1, no. 4 (April 25, 1923): 3.

16. "Dr. Evans, Imperial Wizard, Defines Klan Principles," *Imperial Night-Hawk* 1, no. 43 (January 23, 1924): 2.

17. H. W. Evans, "The Klan of Tomorrow," in *The Proceeding of the Second Imperial Klonvokation Held in Kansas City, Missouri* (N.p.: Knights of the Ku Klux Klan Inc., 1924), 141.

18. "The Practice of Klanishness" (Atlanta: William J. Simmons, 1918), 4.

19. Evans, "The Klan of Tomorrow," 141.

20. Ibid., 144–145.

21. For more recent commentary on Cosmopolitanism and its relationship to patriotism, see Martha Nussbaum, "Patriotism and Cosmopolitanism," *Boston Review* (1994), http://www.soci.niu.edu/~phildept/Kapitan/nussbaum1.html (accessed January 15, 2006).

22. Evans, "The Klan of Tomorrow," 145.

23. Ibid., 148–149.

24. "The Klan a Nation Builder," *Kourier Magazine* 1, no. 4 (March 1925): 8.

25. H. W. Evans, "The Destiny of the Klan: Our Mission of Militant Patriotism," *Kourier Magazine* 2, no. 9 (August 1926): 6.

26. Evans, "The Klan of Tomorrow," 150.

27. Ibid., 141.

28. In her recent work, Tracy Fessenden argues that the Puritans "bequeathed to subsequent generations the desire to record America's origins not as religiously or racially plural but instead as white and Protestant" (32). I would argue that the Klan is just one manifestation of this desire, and Klansmen erase the presence of Native Americans and Catholics in their renderings of American history to show the centrality of white Protestants for the development of nation. See Tracy Fessenden, *Culture and Redemption: Religion, the Secular, and American Literature* (Princeton: Princeton University Press, 2007), especially 16–33.

29. "The Menace of Modern Immigration," n.d., 30–31, Ku Klux Klan, Wayne County, M0407, Indiana Historical Society, Indianapolis.

30. "The Meaning of 100% Americanism," *Imperial Night-Hawk* 2, no. 5 (April 30, 1924): 2.

31. Ibid., 3.

32. "Grapes and Wild Grapes," *Kourier Magazine* 1, no. 4 (March 1925): 28–29. Interestingly, Anthony Marx also reflected on the importance of the Saint Bartholomew's Massacre in 1572, which was a significant event in the French religious wars. Marx, however, argues that Bartholomew should be the patron saint of nationalism because he was martyred, and this reflects the violence and intolerance in the formation of nationalism. I am not sure the author was alluding to a similar understanding of nationalism but rather suggesting that religious wars might occur in America. See Marx, *Faith in Nation*, 204–206.

33. "The Spirit of the Fathers," *Kourier Magazine* 3, no. 3 (February 1927): 12–13.

34. "Abraham Lincoln—Hiram Wesley Evans: A Character Analogy," *Kourier Magazine* 2, no. 11 (October 1926): 6.

35. "A Famous One Hundred Percent American of Colonial Days," *Imperial Night-Hawk* 2, no. 27 (October 1, 1924): 3.

36. "America for Americans," in Knights of the Ku Klux Klan, *Bramble Bush Government*, n.d., 1, Ku Klux Klan, Wayne County, M0407, Indiana Historical Society, Indianapolis.

37. "The Need of the Ku Klux Klan," *Kourier Magazine* 2, no. 5 (April 1926): 11.

38. "The American Public School," *Kourier Magazine* 2, no. 6 (May 1926): 11.

39. "The Little Red School House Is One of the Most Sacred American Institutions," *Imperial Night-Hawk* 1, no. 21 (August 22, 1923): 3.

40. For information on the Klan and legal battles on public education, see Glenn Zuber, "Onward Christian Klansmen! War, Religious Conflict, and the Rise of the Second Ku Klux Klan, 1912–1928" (Ph.D. diss., Indiana University, 2004), especially 316–359.

41. "The American Public School," 11.

42. Ibid., 12–13.

43. "Has the State the Right to Educate Her Children?" *Kourier Magazine* 2, no. 7 (June 1926): 25–26.

44. "American Citizens Must Awake to Needs of Public School," *Imperial Night-Hawk* 1, no. 6 (May 9, 1923): 5.

45. "A Great Need," *Kourier Magazine* 3, no. 3 (February 1927): 8.

46. Robert Orsi, *Between Heaven and Earth: The Religious Worlds People Make and the Scholars Who Study Them* (Princeton: Princeton University Press, 2004), 77. While Orsi is pointing out in particular how Catholics envisioned their children as bearers of the faith, I believe that his understanding of children also highlights the importance of children for the Klan to pass on not only Protestantism but also patriotism in their version of America. Orsi continued, "Children signal the vulnerability and contingency of a particular religious world and religion itself. . . . This is why discussions of children's lives are fraught with such great fear, sometimes sorrow, and sometimes ferocity among adults." Children become the objects by which religion (and I would argue nationalism) is made real for adults, and thus perceived threats to children are manifested as threats to a fragile worldview.

47. "Program Concerning Public School Problem Outlined by Imperial Wizard," *Imperial Night-Hawk* 1, no. 46 (February 14, 1924): 3.

48. "Seeking Aid for Public Schools," *Imperial Night-Hawk* 2, no. 14 (July 2, 1924): 2.

49. Ibid., 2–3.

50. "Reading the Bible in Our Schools," *Kourier Magazine* 3, no. 4 (March 1927): 31.

51. Tracy Fessenden writes about the so-called "Bible wars" in the mid-nineteenth century and the defense of the Bible in public schools. For Fessenden, Catholic objections to the "Protestant character of public schooling" allowed for "Protestant detractors . . . to show that Catholicism was the enemy

of the gospel and that the destruction of popery was therefore a sacred duty of all, implicitly Protestant, Americans" (68). What is interesting is that the Klan appeals for protection of the Bible in public schools mimics this early historical incident. See Tracy Fessenden, *Culture and Redemption: Religion, the Secular, and American Literature* (Princeton: Princeton University Press, 2007).

52. "Patriotism," 15.

53. "Reading the Bible in Our Schools," 31.

54. "Program Concerning Public School Problem," 2.

55. J. S. Fleming, *What Is Ku Kluxism? Let Americans Answer—Aliens Only Muddy the Waters* (Goodwater, Ala.: J. S. Fleming, 1923).

56. "Parochial Schools versus the American Public Schools," *Kourier Magazine* 2, no. 8 (July 1926): 16.

57. Ibid., 18–20.

58. Ibid., 20.

59. T. L. Bouscaren, "Talks of Americanism, Talk 4: Complete Education," *Our Sunday Visitor* 7, no. 46 (March 2, 1924): 1.

60. See David A. Horowitz, "The Normality of Extremism: The Ku Klux Klan Revisited," *Society* 35, no. 6 (September–October 1998): 71–78.

61. Anonymous, *Fifty Reasons Why I Am a Klansman*, n.d., Ku Klux Klan, Wayne County, M0407, Indiana Historical Society, Indianapolis.

62. Simmons, *Official Message of Imperial Wizard*, 12.

63. "Principles and Purposes of the Knights of the Ku Klux Klan," 133; emphasis added.

64. "Eyes of the Nation Are on Knights of the Ku Klux Klan," *Imperial Night-Hawk* 1, no. 39 (December 26, 1923): 4.

CHAPTER THREE. "GOD GIVE US MEN":
THE KLAN'S CHRISTIAN KNIGHTHOOD

1. "Louisiana Klansman Outlines the Aims, Purposes and Principles of His Order," *Imperial Night-Hawk* 1, no. 9 (May 30, 1923): 8.

2. Mrs. P. B. Whaley, "An American Mother's Prayer," *Imperial Night-Hawk* 1, no. 5 (May 2, 1923): 7.

3. "The 'Man on the Fence' Becomes Uncomfortable," *Dawn* 1, no. 50 (October 13, 1923): 11.

4. Ibid. According to the April 7, 1923, issue of the *Dawn*, the circulation had grown to 50,000. The editors noted that "such growth is unprecedented

in the class publication field." See "Dawn Circulation Climbs to 50,000 as Fight for Americanism Stirs Nation Wide Interest" 1, no. 24 (April 7, 1923): 6.

5. "Louisiana Klansman," 7.

6. The Klan, then, received inspiration from other fraternal orders. For commentary on the place of religion in fraternity, see Mark C. Carnes, *Secret Ritual and Manhood in Victorian America* (New Haven: Yale University Press, 1989), 54–65, 71–80. For a complication of Carnes's argument and description of a religious fraternity, see Amy Koehlinger, "'Let Us Live for Those Who Love Us': Faith, Family, and the Contours of Manhood among the Knights of Columbus in Late Nineteenth-Century Connecticut," *Journal of Social History* 38, no. 2 (Winter 2004): 455–468. For the relationship between the Klan and fraternities, see Glenn Zuber, "'Onward Christian Klansmen': War, Religious Conflict, and The Rise of the Second Ku Klux Klan, 1912–1928," (Ph.D. diss., Indiana University, 2004).

7. Wyn Wade, *The Fiery Cross: The Ku Klux Klan in America* (New York: Simon & Schuster, 1987), 142.

8. For denominations involved in the Klan, see Leonard J. Moore, *Citizen Klansman: The Ku Klux Klan in Indiana, 1921–1928* (Chapel Hill: University of North Carolina Press, 1991). For supposed ties to fundamentalism, see Craig, *Fiery Cross*. For the relationship of ministers and local congregations to Klan, see Nancy MacLean, *Behind the Mask of Chivalry: The Making of the Ku Klux Klan* (New York: Oxford University Press, 1994), and Robert Allen Goldberg, *Hooded Empire: The Ku Klux Klan in Colorado* (Urbana: University of Illinois Press, 1981). For the Women of the KKK and Protestantism or women in the Klan in the 1920s, see Kathleen Blee, *Women of the Klan: Racism and Gender in the 1920s* (Berkeley: University of California Press, 1991).

9. "Louisiana Klansman," 6.

10. "Go to Church Sunday," *Imperial Night-Hawk* 1, no. 3 (April 1, 1923): 5.

11. *Imperial Night-Hawk* 1, no. 5 (May 2, 1923): 6.

12. "Louisiana Klansman," 6.

13. Great Titan of the Realm of Texas, "How the Klan Can Be Made a True Civic Asset in Every Progressive Community," *Imperial Night-Hawk* 1, no. 23 (September 5, 1923): 6.

14. *Imperial Night-Hawk* 1, no. 29 (October 17, 1923): 6.

15. "What Is Tolerance?" *Kourier Magazine* 1, no. 2 (January 1925): 32.

16. Mark C. Carnes, *Secret Ritual and Manhood in Victorian America* (New Haven: Yale University Press, 1989), especially 2–14.

17. Ibid., 2.

18. Interestingly, the Knights of Columbus used the example of Christian knighthood to proclaim their place in "an unbroken lineage of valiant Christian knights" (461). For analysis of the Knights of Columbus and their rendering of knighthood, see Amy Koehlinger, "'Let Us Live for Those Who Love Us': Faith, Family, and the Contours of Manhood among the Knights of Columbus in Late Nineteenth-Century Connecticut," *Journal of Social History* 38, no. 2 (Winter 2004): 455–468.

19. Robert J. Higgs, *God in the Stadium: Sports and Religion in America* (Lexington: University Press of Kentucky, 1995), 4.

20. Ann Braude deftly contradicts this dominant portrayal of feminization by demonstrating that women have always been "numerically dominant" in America's religious spaces (87). Ann Braude, "Women's History Is American Religious History," in *Retelling U.S. Religious History,* ed. Thomas A. Tweed (Berkeley: University of California Press, 1997), 87–107.

21. For more on the Men and Religion Forward movement, see Gail Bederman, "The Women Have Had Charge of the Church Work Long Enough": The Men and Religion Forward Movement of 1911–1912 and the Masculinization of Middle-Class Protestantism," *American Quarterly* 41, no. 3 (September 1989): 432–465.

22. Stephen Prothero, *American Jesus: How the Son of God Became a National Icon* (New York: Farrar, Strauss & Giroux, 2003), 94.

23. Ibid., 95.

24. W. C. Wright, "A Klansman's Criterion of Character," *Imperial Night-Hawk* 1, no. 45 (February 6, 1924): 2.

25. G.W.W., "God Wants Men," *Kourier Magazine* 1, no. 10 (October 1925): 4.

26. Ibid., 5.

27. Ibid., 4–5.

28. Wright, "A Klansman's Criterion of Character," 6.

29. H. W. Evans, "The Klan Spiritual," *Imperial Night-Hawk* 2, no. 30 (October 22, 1924): 6.

30. Janet Moore Lindman, "Acting the Manly Christian: White Evangelical Masculinity in Revolutionary Virginia," *William and Mary Quarterly,* 3rd ser., 57, no. 2 (April 2000): 393–416.

31. Evans, "The Klan Spiritual," 7.

32. Sherwood Eddy, "The Ku Klux Klan, II," *Christian Century* 39, no. 33 (August 17, 1922): 1023.

33. For examples of Klan condemnations by the *Christian Century,* see Alva W. Taylor, "The Ku Klux Klan," *Christian Century* 39, no. 27 (July 6, 1922): 850–851; Sherwood Eddy, "The Ku Klux Klan," *Christian Century* 39, no. 32 (August 10, 1922): 993–995; Eddy, "The Ku Klux Klan, II," 1021–1023; Richard A. Schermerhorn, "Ku Klux Klan," letter to the editor, *Christian Century* 39, no. 38 (September 21, 1922): 1165; "Condemnation of the Ku Klux Movement," *Christian Century* 39, no. 40 (October 5, 1922): 1213; "Churches and the Ku Klux Klan," *Christian Century* 40, no. 3 (January 18, 1923): 69; "Ku Klux Klan and Theological Conservatism," *Christian Century* 40, no. 19 (May 10, 1923): 579–580; Frederick A. Dunning, "Ku Klux Fulfills the Scripture," *Christian Century* 41, no. 38 (September 18, 1924): 1205–1207.

34. In the mid-nineteenth century, there were attempts to masculinize Christianity, and by the early twentieth century, movements like the Men and Religion Forward movement (1911–1912) sought to bring more men into the churches. What motivated these men was a concern over the effeminacy of the church and their understanding of the masculinity of Christ. Similar to the Men and Religion Forward movement and remasculinization attempts of Bruce Barton, the Klan sought to banish the feminine image of Jesus and present the rugged carpenter that Jesus "really" was. Both the Klan and the *Christian Century* represent this desire for the masculine Christ to provide a model for men and boys alike. Stephen Prothero analyzes these attempts to remasculinize Jesus and shows how Jesus became the battleground for competing religious ideologies. See Stephen Prothero, *American Jesus: How the Son of God Became a National Icon* (New York: Farrar, Strauss & Giroux, 2003), especially 87–123.

35. James I. Vance, "The Old Rugged Cross," *Christian Century* 42, no. 8 (January 19, 1925): 249.

36. Ibid., 250.

37. For understandings of the wisdom and courage of Jesus, see "The Inevitable Cross," *Christian Century* 42, no. 14 (April 2, 1925): 434–436, and Fred Eastman, "Courage—Five Minutes Longer," *Christian Century* 44, no. 12 (March 21, 1927): 364–366. For concerns over masculinity and softness, see Hubert C. Herring, "The Blood Is the Thing," *Christian Century* 42, no. 21 (May 31, 1925): 668–669. Herring proposed the need for a bullfight in America to train men.

38. "Jesus as Efficiency Expert," *Christian Century* 42, no. 27 (July 2, 1925): 851. This editorial is a critique of Bruce Barton's *The Man Nobody*

*Knows* (1925). For more on the many faces of Jesus in American culture in particular, see Prothero, *American Jesus,* 3–16. Prothero notes that Klansmen molded Jesus into their own rendering, but he does not explore what the Klan's Jesus "looked like."

39. "Jesus as Efficiency Expert," 851.

40. Kirby Page, "Was Jesus a Patriot?" *Christian Century* 42, no. 26 (June 25, 1925): 827.

41. "Many Thousands Pay Silent Tribute to Klansman Murdered at Carnegie," *Imperial Night-Hawk* 1, no. 23 (September 5, 1923): 2.

42. "Preface," in *Papers Read at the Meeting of Grand Dragons, Knights of the Ku Klux Klan, at Their First Annual Meeting Held at Asheville, North Carolina, July 1923,* Anti-Movements in America, ed. Gerald N. Grob (New York: Arno Press, 1977), 2.

43. Ibid., 1.

44. Brown Harwood, introduction to Grob, *Papers Read at the Meeting of Grand Dragons,* 4.

45. Historian David Goldberg discovered that anti-Klan forces committed more violence against Klansmen than Klansmen committed against others. See "Unmasking the Ku Klux Klan: The Northern Movement against the K.K.K., 1920–1925," *Journal of American Ethnic History,* 15, no. 4 (Summer 1996): 32–48.

46. "Here's a Typical Example of How Some Newspapers Will Falsify About the Klan," *Imperial Night-Hawk* 1, no. 6 (May 9, 1923): 6.

47. "Klan Speaker Stoned and Shot At," *Imperial Night-Hawk* 1, no. 40 (January 2, 1924): 7.

48. "Maine Minister Declares That Klan Is Greatest American Secret Order," *Imperial Night-Hawk* 1, no. 10 (June 6, 1923): 6.

49. "New Klan Hospital Will Be Memorial to Martyr Who Gave Life for the Cause," *Imperial Night-Hawk* 1, no. 18 (August 1, 1923): 6.

50. "Texas Klan to Erect Memorial Hospital in Memory of Dead Klansman," *Imperial Night-Hawk* 2, no. 22 (August 27, 1924): 8. The plans for the memorial hospital occurred a year after Roberts's death.

51. "Carnegie, Pa., Mob Martyrs Klan Hero and Violates All Rights of Americanism," *Imperial Night-Hawk* 1, no. 22 (August 29, 1923): 5.

52. Ibid.

53. "Many Thousands Pay Silent Tribute to Klansman Murdered at Carnegie," *Imperial Night-Hawk* 1, no. 23 (September 5, 1923): 2.

54. Ibid.

55. "Klansmen Asked to Aid Widow and Babies of Man Who Died for the Cause," *Imperial Night-Hawk* 1, no. 24 (September 12, 1923): 2.

56. "Carnegie, Pa., Mob Martyrs," 5.

57. There was reported Klan growth after the martyrs. "Growth of Klans in South Is Steady," *Imperial Night-Hawk* 1, no. 24 (September 12, 1923): 3. Pennsylvania was included in the South.

58. Knights of the Ku Klux Klan, *Klansman's Manual* (N.p.: Knights of the Ku Klux Klan Inc., 1924), 60, located in K.K.K. Ephemera Collection, Hargrett Rare Book and Manuscript Library, University of Georgia Libraries, Athens; "To All Exalted Cyclops," n.d., 7, Ku Klux Klan, Wayne County, Indiana Records, 1916–1933 (bulk 1922–1927), M0407, box 1, folder 5, Indiana Historical Society, Indianapolis.

59. KKK, *Klansman's Manual,* 11.

60. Ibid., 12.

61. Paul S. Etheridge, "Brief Interpretation of By Laws and Constitution of the Klan," *Imperial Night-Hawk* 2, no. 23 (September 3, 1924): 2–3.

62. Ibid., 3.

63. Alva W. Taylor, "The Ku Klux Klan," *Christian Century* 3, no. 27 (July 6, 1922): 850–851.

64. H. W. Evans, "Our Crusading Army," *Kourier Magazine* 2, no. 11 (October 1926): 2–3.

65. Ibid., 4.

66. Ibid., 5.

67. "Principles and Purposes of the Knights of the Ku Klux Klan," in Grob, *Papers Read at the Meeting of Grand Dragons,* 132.

68. H. W. Evans, "Message from the Imperial Wizard," *Kourier Magazine* 1, no. 7 (June 1925): 1.

69. Julia Grant noted that the concern over boyhood and how to raise boys was primarily a concern over "feminization." By the 1920s, a masculine upbringing for boys became the norm. Parents were afraid that effeminate sons would become delinquents, while "regular" or "real" boys would become men. "Real" boys, however, were adventurous and sometimes got into trouble. See Julia Grant, "A 'Real Boy' Not a Sissy: Gender, Childhood, and Masculinity, 1890–1940," *Journal of Social History* 37, no. 4 (Summer 2004): 829–851.

70. William L. Butcher, "What Is a Boy?" *Kourier Magazine* 1, no. 12 (November 1925): 18.

71. "Responsibility of Klankraft to the American Boy," in Grob, *Papers Read at the Meeting of Grand Dragons*, 84–86.

72. Ibid.

73. Blee, *Women of the Klan*, 158.

74. "Responsibility of Klankraft to the American Boy," 89.

75. *Kloran, Junior Order of Ku Klux Klan,* n.d., 9. Ku Klux Klan, Wayne County, Indiana Records, 1916–1933 (bulk 1922–1927), M0407, box 2, folder 2, Indiana Historical Society, Indianapolis.

76. Ibid., 10.

77. Ibid., 14.

78. Blee, *Women of the Klan*, 158.

79. "God Give Us Men," in Grob, *Papers Read at the Meeting of Grand Dragons*, 154.

80. Harwood, "Introduction," 3.

81. Ibid., 4.

CHAPTER FOUR. "THE SACREDNESS OF MOTHERHOOD": WHITE WOMANHOOD, MATERNITY, AND MARRIAGE IN THE 1920S KLAN

1. Robbie Gill Comer, "American Women," *Kourier Magazine* 1, no. 5 (April 1925): 13.

2. "Klanswomen Adopt a Creed at Meeting of National Officers," *Imperial Night-Hawk* 2, no. 7 (May 14, 1924): 7.

3. Thomas Dixon Jr., *The Clansman* (Lexington: University Press of Kentucky, 1970), 189.

4. Ibid., 21.

5. Ibid., 284.

6. Ibid., 325.

7. George Alfred Brown, *Harold the Klansman* (Kansas City, Mo.: Western Baptist Publishing Co., 1923).

8. Ibid., 7.

9. Ibid., 157.

10. Allan J. Lichtman, *White Protestant Nation: The Rise of the American Conservative Movement* (New York: Atlantic Monthly Press, 2008), 19. I am borrowing this terminology of conservative maternalism directly from Lichtman, who provides the clearest vision of how women deployed motherhood and womanhood to become agents of reform.

11. "A Tribute and Challenge to American Women," in *Papers Read at the*

*Meeting of Grand Dragons, Knights of the Ku Klux Klan, at Their First Annual Meeting Held at Asheville, North Carolina, July 1923,* Anti-Movements in America, ed. Gerald N. Grob (New York: Arno Press, 1977), 92.

12. W. C. Wright, *Religious and Patriotic Ideals of the Ku Klux Klan* (Waco, TX: W. C. Wright, 1926), 7.

13. Ibid., 11.

14. See Lynn Dumenil, *Modern Temper: American Culture and Society in the 1920s* (New York: Hill & Wang, 1995), 99–144.

15. Nancy MacLean, *Behind the Mask of Chivalry: The Making of the Second Ku Klux Klan* (New York: Oxford University Press, 1994), 114–115.

16. C.B., "For Our Women," *Kluxer* 1, no. 18 (November 24, 1923): 28, located in Archives and Special Collections, Ball State University Archives, Muncie, Ind.

17. Ibid.

18. "A Tribute and Challenge to American Women," in Grob, *Papers Read at the Meeting of Grand Dragons*, 89.

19. Ibid., 90.

20. Ibid., 91.

21. Ibid., 92.

22. Ibid., 93.

23. Official Document Issued from the Office of the Grand Dragon, Realm of Indiana, Indianapolis, Indiana, Number 40 (May 6, 1925), Ku Klux Klan, Wayne County, Indiana Records, 1916–1933 (bulk 1922–1927), M0407, box 1, folder 3, Indiana Historical Society, Indianapolis.

24. Ibid.

25. Ibid.

26. P.H., "The Klan Celebrates Mother's Day," *Christian Century* 42, no. 21 (May 21, 1925): 677.

27. Ibid., 681.

28. "Was He a Slacker—? And Mother Came Also," *Kluxer* 1, no. 14 (October 27, 1923): 25.

29. W. J. Simmons, *The Practice of Klannishness* (Atlanta: W. J. Simmons, 1918), 5.

30. H. W. Evans, "Preserving the American Home," *Kourier Magazine* 3, no. 4 (March 1927): 9.

31. "Eminent Jurist Outlines the Duty of Citizens toward the Courts," *Imperial Night-Hawk* 1, no. 5 (May 2, 1923): 8.

32. "Klanswomen Adopt a Creed," 7.

33. Ibid.

34. Ibid.

35. "Klanhaven," *Kourier Magazine* 2, no. 12 (November 1926): 27.

36. *The Truth about the Women of the Ku Klux Klan* (Little Rock, Ark.: Parke-Harper, n.d.), 2, located in George R. Dale Collection, 1922–1979, box 1, folder 1, Archives and Special Collections, Ball State University, Muncie, Ind.

37. Ibid., 4.

38. Kathleen Blee, *Women of the Klan: Racism and Gender in the 1920s* (Berkeley: University of California Press, 1991), 51.

39. Ibid., 52 (for more information on the conflicts between the KKK and the WKKK, see pp. 57–67).

40. Robbie Gill, "American Woman," in *Inspirational Addresses Delivered at the Second Imperial Klonvokation* (N.p.: Knights of the Ku Klux Klan Inc., 1924), 51, located in KKK Ephemera Collection, Hargrett Rare Book and Manuscript Library, University of Georgia Libraries, Athens.

41. Ibid.

42. Ibid., 52.

43. Ibid., 54.

44. Ibid., 57.

45. Ibid., 59–60.

46. "Woman's Relation to Government," *Kourier Magazine* 1, no. 5 (April 1925): 19.

47. Blee, *Women of the Klan,* 53.

48. "Address Delivered by Mrs. Robbie Gill Comer," *Kourier Magazine* 2, no. 12 (November 1926): 13.

49. Ibid., 16.

50. Ibid., 17.

51. Ibid., 20.

52. Ibid., 21.

53. "The Klan Celebrates Mother's Day," 677.

54. *Proceedings of the Fourth Imperial Klonvokation Held in Chicago, Illinois, July 17, 18 and 19, 1928* (N.p.: Knights of the Ku Klux Klan Inc., 1928), 102, located in Archives and Special Collections, Ball State University, Muncie, Ind.

55. Ibid., 104.

56. Ibid., 105.

57. Ibid., 108.

58. Ibid., 110.

59. L. J. King, *Secret Confession to a Roman Catholic Priest* (Toledo, Ohio: L. J. King, 1925), 48, located in Anti-Catholic Printed Material Collection, box 7, folder 6, University of Notre Dame Archives, Notre Dame, Ind.

60. Blee, *Women of the Klan,* 86, 92.

61. Ibid., 90.

62. Helen Jackson, *Convent Cruelties, or My Life in a Convent,* 7th ed. (Toledo, Ohio: Helen Jackson, 1924), 12, located in Anti-Catholic Printed Material Collection, box 7, folder 5, University of Notre Dame Archives, Notre Dame, Ind.

63. Ibid., 28.

64. Ibid., 29–30.

65. Ibid., 34–35.

66. Ibid., 39.

67. Ibid., 47.

68. Ibid., 78.

69. Ibid., 80.

70. Ibid., 82.

71. Blee, *Women of the Klan,* 89.

72. King, *Secret Confession to a Roman Catholic Priest,* 8.

73. Ibid., 9.

74. Ibid., 15.

75. *Chronology of the Life of "Pastor" Chiniquy* (Huntington, Ind.: National Catholic Bureau of Information), 9, located in Anti-Catholic Printed Material Collection, box 5, folder 8, University of Notre Dame Archives, Notre Dame, Ind.

76. King, *Secret Confession to a Roman Catholic Priest,* 28.

77. Ibid., 29.

78. Ibid., 101.

79. Marie Anne Pagliarini, "The Pure American Woman and the Wicked Catholic Priest: An Analysis of Anti-Catholic Literature in Antebellum America," *Religion and American Culture* 9, no. 1 (Winter 1999): 97–128.

80. Ibid., 98.

81. Tracy Fessenden, "The Convent, the Brothel, and the Protestant Woman's Sphere," *Signs* 25, no. 2 (Winter 2000): 451–478.

82. Ibid., 466–469.

83. *Record of Anti-Catholic Agitators* (n.d.), 8–9, located in Anti-Catholic Printed Material Collection, box 6, folder 7, University of Notre Dame Archives, Notre Dame, Ind. For more on Helen Jackson's misconduct, see *A Pseudo "Ex-Nun" Thwarted* (St. Louis, Mo.: Central Bureau, 1921), 7–12, located in Anti-Catholic Printed Material Collection, box 5, folder 6, University of Notre Dame Archives, Notre Dame, Ind.

84. H. W. Evans, "Preserving the American Home," *Kourier Magazine* 3, no. 4 (March 1927): 10.

85. Ibid., 9.

86. Ibid., 10.

87. Ibid.

88. "Another Grand Dragon Says," *Kourier Magazine* 3, no. 4 (March 1927): 11.

89. *Proceedings of the Fourth Imperial Klonvokation,* 108.

90. "When Is a Marriage Not a Marriage?" *Christian Century* 14, no. 49 (December 9, 1926), 1510.

91. Ibid., 1511.

92. *Official Document, Office of the Grand Dragon, Realm of Georgia, Knights of the Ku Klux Klan* 1, no. 3 (December 1926): 4, located in Manuscripts Collection, Hargrett Rare Book and Manuscript Library, University of Georgia Libraries, Athens.

93. H. C. Hengell, "Catholic Marriage Laws according to the New Code," *Our Sunday Visitor* 7, no. 5 (May 20, 1923): 1.

CHAPTER FIVE. "WHITE SKIN WILL NOT REDEEM A BLACK HEART":
THE KLAN'S WHITENESS, WHITE SUPREMACY, AND AMERICAN RACE

1. H. W. Evans, *The Attitude of the Knights of the Ku Klux Klan toward the Roman Hierarchy* (n.p., n.d.), Ku Klux Klan Collection, Wayne County, M0407, box 1, file 6, Indiana Historical Society, Indianapolis. The revised creed was printed on the back cover of the pamphlet. The title of this chapter is taken from a phrase in the "Address of Imperial Official," *Kourier Magazine* 1, no. 1 (December 1924): 25.

2. H. W. Evans, "The Klan of Tomorrow," in *Proceedings of the Second Imperial Klonvokation Held in Kansas City, Missouri* (N.p.: Knights of the Ku Klux Klan Inc., 1924), 148.

3. William Simmons, *Official Message of the Emperor of the Invisible Empire, Knights of the Ku Klux Klan, to the Initial Session of the Imperial Klon-*

*vokation* (Atlanta: Knights of the Ku Klux Klan Inc., 1922), 6, located in D. C. Stephenson Collection, M264, box 4, folder 8, Indiana Historical Society, Indianapolis.

4. Simmons, *Official Message,* 8.

5. "The Klansmen's Creed," *Imperial Night-Hawk* 1, no. 5 (May 2, 1923): 7.

6. The *Imperial Night-Hawk* proclaimed any Protestant minister interested in the Klan would receive their publication for free. Protestant ministers were also encouraged to send their names and addresses if they wanted to join. "Notice to Protestant Clergymen," *Imperial Night-Hawk* 1, no. 10 (June 6, 1923): 6.

7. In his *Rituals of Blood,* Orlando Patterson claims that lynching, a religious sacrifice, was spearheaded by the Ku Klux Klan in the early twentieth century (202). Further, he argues that "the people who eventually founded the KKK and who led the sacrificial lynch mobs" were one and the same (214). Additionally, he equates the Knights of Mary Phagan's lynching of Leo Frank with Klan lynching (217). While this is a compelling argument, Patterson lacks historical evidence to back up his claims about the Klan and lynching. The Klan was involved in violence, but Allan Lichtman argues that lynching actually decreased in the United States as the Klan grew in the 1920s (42). See both Orlando Patterson, *Rituals of the Blood: Consequences of Slavery in Two American Centuries* (Washington, D.C.: Civitas Counterpoint, 1998) and Allan J. Lichtman, *White Protestant Nation: The Rise of the American Conservative Movement* (New York: Atlantic Monthly Press, 2008), 42–46.

8. William Joseph Simmons, *The Klan Unmasked* (Atlanta: W. E. Thompson, 1924), 49.

9. Evans, *The Attitude of the Knights.*

10. "Louisiana Klansman Outlines the Aims, Purposes and Principles of His Order," *Imperial Night-Hawk* 1, no. 9 (May 30, 1923): 6.

11. Evans, "The Klan of Tomorrow," 146.

12. "Fifty Reasons Why I Am a Klansman," (n.d.), 7–8, located in Ku Klux Klan Collection, Wayne County, M0407, Indiana Historical Society, Indianapolis.

13. H. W. Evans, "Dr. Evans, Imperial Wizard, Defines Klan Principles and Outlines Klan Activities," *Imperial Night-Hawk* 1, no. 43 (January 23, 1924): 2.

14. Matthew Frye Jacobsen, *Whiteness of a Different Color: European Immigrants and the Alchemy of Race* (Cambridge: Harvard University Press, 1998), 69.

15. "The Menace of Modern Immigration," (n.d.), 4, located in Manuscripts, Indiana Historical Society, Indianapolis.

16. Ibid., 5.

17. Ibid., 6.

18. Grand Dragon of the Realm of South Carolina, "Poorly Restricted Immigration Is One of the Greatest Perils Confronting America," *Imperial Night-Hawk* 1, no. 22 (August 29, 1923): 2.

19. Ibid., 3.

20. H. W. Evans, "Imperial Wizard Outlines Attitude of the Klan toward Unrestricted Immigration," *Imperial Night-Hawk* 1, no. 4 (April 25, 1923): 5.

21. Ibid., 6.

22. Evans, "Dr. Evans, Imperial Wizard, Defines Klan Principles," 2.

23. "Much Pressure Being Used to Delay Passage of the Immigration Bill," *Imperial Night-Hawk* 1, no. 48 (February 27, 1924): 6.

24. "Johnson Selective Immigration Law Signed By President," *Imperial Night-Hawk* 2, no. 11 (June 11, 1924): 2.

25. "Bramble Bush Government," *Kourier Magazine* 1, no. 1 (December 1924): 13, 14.

26. "Address of Imperial Official," *Kourier Magazine* 1, no. 1 (December 1924): 25.

27. Interestingly, the Klan admitted that the organization was for white supremacy as well as American freedoms and Protestant Christianity. See Exalted Cyclops of Monroe Klan Number 4, Louisiana, "Klan a Patriotic, Benevolent, Fraternal Organization of Christian Americans," *Imperial Night-Hawk* 2, no. 2 (April 9, 1924): 2.

28. Evans, *The Attitude of the Knights*, 2.

29. Evans, "Dr. Evans, Imperial Wizard, Defines Klan Principles," 3.

30. H. W. Evans, "The Attitude of the Knights of the Ku Klux Klan toward the Roman Catholic Hierarchy," *Imperial Night-Hawk* 1, no. 1 (March 28, 1923): 2.

31. Evans, "Dr. Evans, Imperial Wizard, Defines Klan Principles," 3.

32. Wright, *Religious and Patriotic Ideals,* 44.

33. Evans, "Dr. Evans, Imperial Wizard, Defines Klan Principles," 3.

34. "The Menace of Modern Immigration," 24.

35. Ibid., 23.

36. Ibid., 22.

37. Simmons, *Official Message,* 10, 11.

38. F.L.L., "The Negro—His Relation to America," *Kourier Magazine* 2, no. 2 (January 1926): 17.

39. Ibid., 18.

40. Ibid., 19.

41. W. C. Wright, *The Religious and Patriotic Ideals of the Ku Klux Klan* (Waco, TX: W. C. Wright, 1926).

42. "Christianity and Racialism: Reply to Dr. Glenn Frank," *Kourier Magazine* 2, no. 3 (February 1926): 30, 31.

43. Ibid., 32.

44. George Alfred Brown, *Harold the Klansman* (Kansas City, Mo.: Western Baptist Publishing Co., 1923), 19.

45. Ibid., 194.

46. F.L.L., "The Negro—His Relation to America," 18.

47. Wright, *Religious and Patriotic Ideals,* 44.

48. Ibid., 43.

49. Ibid., 44.

50. "Fifty Reasons," 7–8.

51. "Questions Answered: Questions and Answers Given as a Basis for an Interview to a Certain National Magazine," (n.d.), 9, Indiana Historical Society, Indianapolis.

52. Evans, "The Klan of Tomorrow," 146.

53. Brown, *Harold the Klansman,* 191.

54. Ibid., 192–193.

55. Ibid., 193.

56. Ibid., 194.

57. Evans, "The Klan of Tomorrow," 146.

58. Ibid., 147.

59. "Wizard Tells About Assaults on Klan," *Imperial Night-Hawk* 1, no. 24 (September 12, 1923): 4.

60. "The Purpose of This Publication," *Imperial Night-Hawk* 1, no. 1 (March 28, 1923): 4.

61. "Bigotry," *Imperial Night-Hawk* 1, no. 5 (May 2, 1923): 7.

62. See "Ohio Klansmen in Act of 'Riotous Conduct' Which Caused Them to Be Jailed," *Imperial Night-Hawk* 1, no. 16 (July 18, 1923): 8. A Klansman's funeral was alleged to be broken up by the Roman Catholic chief of police in Springfield, Ohio. See "Jewish Rabbi Would Change Battle Hymn," *Imperial Night-Hawk* 1, no. 11 (June 13, 1923): 8. The rabbi did not want Jewish chil-

dren to be forced to sing "Onward Christian Soldiers" or "The Battle Hymn of the Republic" at public schools because the songs were against their religious beliefs. See also "Was This Tolerance?" *Dawn* 1, no. 25 (April 14, 1923): 5. The Klan accused its enemies of ransacking a building in which Klan members lived. This event confirmed their beliefs of being persecuted.

63. "Wizard Tells About Assaults on Klan," *Imperial Night-Hawk* 1, no. 24 (September 12, 1923): 4.

64. David J. Goldberg, "Unmasking the Ku Klux Klan: The Northern Movement against the K.K.K., 1920–1925," *Journal of American Ethnic History* 15, no. 4 (Summer 1996): 42.

65. "Bombers Wreak Vengeance Inspired by Papist Propaganda," *Dawn* 1, no. 25 (April 14, 1923): 9.

66. "Was This Tolerance?" 5.

67. Carol Mason notes that white people often claim that they are victimized despite the absence of "alienation, exploitation, or oppression" in their histories. See Carol Mason, "Miscegenation and Purity: Reproducing the Souls of White Folk," *Hypatia* 22, no. 2 (Spring 2007): 106. Robyn Wiegman also notes that in post–Civil War America whites refigured their place in American society, as having lost the dominant position, and took on an injured status. See Robyn Wiegman, "Whiteness Studies and the Paradox of Particularity," *boundary* 26, no. 3 (Autumn 1999): 117.

68. Goldberg, "Unmasking the Ku Klux Klan."

69. Simmons, *The Klan Unmasked*, 87.

70. Elaine Frantz Parsons, "Midnight Rangers: Costume and Performance in the Reconstruction Era Ku Klux Klan," *Journal of American History* 92, no. 3 (December 2005): 820.

71. According to Nicholas Mirzeoff, "Photography seeks to record with the highest degree of realism the individuality of a subject, but . . . this sense of an individual is exactly what cannot be photographed. . . . Photography becomes an outlet to see myself seeing myself" (*An Introduction to Visual Culture* [London: Routledge, 1999], 71–72, 236). Thus, when the Klan takes photographs, what is being represented? The traces of individuals are absent, which leads me to think that the Klan's photographs are taken to show the solidarity of community.

72. Chris Ruiz-Velasco relies on the works of Thomas Dixon to present a rendering of whiteness. According to Ruiz-Velasco, the Klan robes in Dixon's work provide "white racial unity" (155). He writes, "The elision of personal

difference also marks the elision of personal culpability, and the anonymity of the white robe furthers marks the unity of whiteness. This unity of whiteness configures into a hyper-whiteness, one that disallows any gradations and insists on the symbolic white purity and homogeneity of the robe" (156). Moreover, Dixon connects whiteness inherently to goodness. See Chris Ruiz-Velasco, "Order Out of Chaos: Whiteness, White Supremacy, and Thomas Dixon, Jr.," *College Literature* 34, no. 4 (Fall 2007): 155–156.

73. See Exalted Cyclops of Texas, "The Seven Symbols of the Klan," *Imperial Night-Hawk* 1, no. 39 (December 26, 1923): 7.

74. Evans, "Dr. Evans, Imperial Wizard, Defines Klan Principles," 3.

75. "Regalia Factory and Printing Plant Will Save Much Money for Klans of Nation," *Imperial Night-Hawk* 1, no. 16 (July 18, 1923): 5.

76. Edward J. Blum, *Reforging the White Republic: Race, Religion, and American Nationalism 1865–1898* (Baton Rouge: Louisiana State University Press, 2005), 9.

77. Evans, "The Klan of Tomorrow," 140.

78. Ibid., 141.

79. Ibid., 142.

80. Ibid., 143.

81. Ibid.

82. Ibid., 145.

83. Ibid., 146.

84. H. W. Evans, "The Klan's Next Duty: Send Home Every Unfit Alien," *Kourier Magazine* 2, no. 3 (February 1926): 1.

85. Simmons, *Official Message of the Emperor of the Invisible Empire,* 9.

86. Evans, "The Klan of Tomorrow," 150–151.

87. H. W. Evans, "The Klan's Mission—Americanism," *Kourier Magazine* 1, no. 12 (November 1925): 5.

88. Ibid., 6; emphasis added.

89. Matthew Frye Jacobson, *Whiteness of a Different Color: European Immigrants and the Alchemy of Race* (Cambridge: Harvard University Press, 1998), 71.

90. Mason, "Miscegenation and Purity," 102.

91. "Official Document, Office of the Grand Dragon, Realm of Georgia, Knights of the Ku Klux Klan," 2, no. 3 (March 1927): 4, located in Ku Klux Klan, Athens Klan #5 (Athens, Ga.) records, box 2, folder 8, Hargrett Rare Book and Manuscript Library, University of Georgia Libraries, Athens.

CHAPTER SIX. "ROME'S REPUTATION IS STAINED WITH
PROTESTANT BLOOD": THE KLAN–NOTRE DAME RIOT OF MAY 1924

1. *The Truth about the Notre Dame Riot on Saturday May 17th 1924* (Indianapolis: Fiery Cross Publishing Co., 1924), 9, located in Special Collections, Ball State University, Muncie, Ind.

2. "Klansmen Unalterably Opposed to Religious Intolerance," *Imperial Night-Hawk* 2, no. 18 (July 30, 1924): 4.

3. Charles Edward Jefferson, *Roman Catholicism and the Ku Klux Klan* (New York: Fleming H. Revell Co., 1924–1925), 141.

4. Ibid., 142–143.

5. Ibid., 147.

6. Ibid., 148.

7. Ibid., 173.

8. See Todd Tucker, *Notre Dame vs. the Ku Klux Klan: How the Fighting Irish Defeated the Klan* (Chicago: Loyola Press, 2004).

9. For more on Protestant attraction and repulsion to Catholics, see Jenny Franchot, *Roads to Rome: The Antebellum Protestant Encounter with Catholicism* (Berkeley: University of California Press, 1994).

10. "Klansmen Unalterably Opposed," 4.

11. Ibid.

12. "Texas Klansman Outlines Principles upon Which the Knights of Ku Klux Klan Is Founded," *Imperial Night-Hawk* 1, no. 2 (April 4, 1923): 7.

13. H. W. Evans, " The Attitude of the Knights of the Ku Klux Klan toward the Roman Catholic Hierarchy," *Imperial Night-Hawk* 1, no. 1 (March 28, 1923): 2.

14. Ibid.

15. Ibid., 7.

16. Ibid., 2.

17. "Catholic-Controlled New York Assembly Passes Bill Seeking to Destroy the Klan," *Imperial Night-Hawk* 1, no. 7 (May 16, 1923): 5.

18. "Attempt to Discredit Ku Klux Klan Proves to Be Boomerang," *Imperial Night-Hawk* 2, no. 17 (July 23, 1924): 3.

19. "Catholic Church Most Powerful Organization, Says Brisbane," *Imperial Night-Hawk* 2, no. 4 (April 23, 1924): 6.

20. *Knights of the Klan versus Knights of Columbus* (Oklahoma City: Reno Publishing Co., n.d), n.p., located in Special Collections, University of Georgia Libraries, Athens.

21. Ibid.

22. "The Real Oath of the K.K.K. vs. the Fake Oath of the K.C.," *Our Sunday Visitor* 11, no. 5 (May 21, 1922): 1.

23. "An Honest and Dignified Statement of the Facts for Fair-Minded People," *Our Sunday Visitor* 7, no. 28 (October 28, 1923): 3.

24. "Effects of Klan Propaganda on the Church," *Our Sunday Visitor* 7, no. 23 (September 23, 1923): 2.

25. "Indiana Protestants Outraged by Infuriated College Students," *Imperial Night-Hawk* 2, no. 10 (June 4, 1924): 2.

26. "Love vs. Hate," in *The Truth about the Notre Dame Riot on Saturday May 17th 1924* (Indianapolis: Fiery Cross Publishing Co., 1924), 20, located in Special Collections, Ball State University, Muncie, Ind.

27. "Indiana Protestants Outraged," 2.

28. "Klansmen and Opponents in Street Clash," *South Bend News-Times* 41, no. 141 (May 20, 1924): 1

29. Wingfoot, "The Story of the Riot," in *The Truth about the Notre Dame Riot on Saturday May 17th 1924* (Indianapolis: Fiery Cross Publishing Co., 1924), 5, located in Special Collections, Ball State University, Muncie, Ind.

30. Ibid., 6.

31. Ibid., 7.

32. "Story by Fiery Cross Staff Correspondent after Riot," in *The Truth about the Notre Dame Riot on Saturday May 17th 1924* (Indianapolis: Fiery Cross Publishing Co., 1924), 12, Special Collections, Ball State University, Muncie, Ind.

33. "Excerpts from Story Written by a Non-Klan Editor," in *The Truth about the Notre Dame Riot on Saturday May 17th 1924* (Indianapolis: Fiery Cross Publishing Co., 1924), 19, located in Special Collections, Ball State University, Muncie, Ind.

34. Wingfoot, "The Story of the Riot," 5.

35. "Excerpts from Story Written by a Non-Klan Editor," 18–19.

36. Wingfoot, "The Story of the Riot," 8.

37. Ibid., 8–9.

38. "Story by Fiery Cross Staff Correspondent after Riot," 13.

39. Ibid., 16–17.

40. "Klansmen and Opponents in Street Clash," 2.

41. "Heads, Not Fists," *Notre Dame Daily* 2, no. 118 (May 17, 1924): 2, lo-

cated in Notre Dame Printed and Reference Material Drop Files, PNDP 83-Nd-1, University of Notre Dame Archives, Notre Dame, Ind.

42. "Yesterday's Bulletin," *Notre Dame Daily* 2, no. 118 (May 17, 1924): 2, located in Notre Dame Printed and Reference Material Drop Files, PNDP 83-Nd-1, University of Notre Dame Archives, Notre Dame, Ind.

43. Tucker, *Notre Dame vs. The Klan,* 152–153.

44. Ibid., 154.

45. Ibid., 156.

46. "Bureau of Information Department," *Our Sunday Visitor* 8, no. 22 (September 12, 1924): 3.

47. "Klansmen and Opponents in Street Clash," 1.

48. Ibid., 1–2.

49. Ibid., 2.

50. For Todd Tucker, the riot primed the Notre Dame football team for its national championship. Catholic Notre Dame showed the national white, Protestant populace that they were a force to be reckoned with in football and as a part of American culture more largely. Historian Mark Massa notes that it is of special importance that Notre Dame football ascended in a period of vehement anti-Catholicism. Notre Dame football became a point of admiration for American Catholics, whether or not they attended the university. See Tucker, *Notre Dame vs. The Klan,* especially 184–191, and Mark S. Massa, *Catholics in American Culture: Fulton Sheen, Dorothy Day and the Notre Dame Football Team* (New York: Crossroad Publishing Co., 1999), 196.

51. Image of J. E. Hutchison Letter, May 26, 1924, Ku Klux Klan and Notre Dame Material, University of Notre Dame Archives, Notre Dame, Ind.

52. Image of Kluxer Letter, n.d., Ku Klux Klan and Notre Dame Material, University of Notre Dame Archives, Notre Dame, Ind.

53. "Bureau of Information Department," *Our Sunday Visitor* 8, no. 22 (September 12, 1924): 3

54. "Love vs. Hate," 20.

55. Ibid., 20–21.

CONCLUSION. "GUARDIANS OF PRIVILEGE:" WHAT THE KLAN
TELLS US ABOUT AMERICAN (RELIGIOUS) HISTORY

1. Stanley Cohen, "Ordinary White Protestants: The KKK of the 1920s," *Journal of Social History* 28, no. 1 (Autumn 1994): 164.

2. "Wisconsin Pastor Proclaims Klan as Staunch Defender of Protestantism," *Imperial Night-Hawk*, 1, no. 7 (May 16, 1923): 6.

3. M. William Lutholtz, *Grand Dragon: D.C. Stephenson and the Ku Klux Klan in Indiana* (West Lafayette, Ind.: Purdue University, 1991), 55.

4. Ibid., 152–153.

5. Ibid., 154.

6. Richard K. Tucker, *The Dragon and the Cross: The Rise and Fall of the Ku Klux Klan in Middle America* (Hamden, Conn.: Archon Books, 1991), 134.

7. Lutholtz, *Grand Dragon,* 159.

8. "The Klan's Invisible Empire Is Fading," *New York Times,* February 21, 1926.

9. See Kelly J. Baker, "Religion and the Rise of the Second Ku Klux Klan, 1915–1922," *Readex Report* 4, no. 3 (September 2009), http://www.readex .com/readex/newsletter.cfm?newsletter=244.

10. Mark S. Massa, *Anti-Catholicism in America: The Last Acceptable Prejudice* (New York: Crossroad Publishing Co., 2003), 33.

11. Wyn Craig Wade, *Fiery Cross: The Ku Klux Klan in America* (New York: Simon & Schuster, 1987), 254.

12. Allan J. Lichtman, *White Protestant Nation: The Rise of the American Conservative Movement* (New York: Atlantic Monthly Press, 2008), 44.

13. Ibid., 2; emphasis added.

14. Michael Kazin, "The Grass-Roots Right: New Histories of U.S. Conservatism in the Twentieth Century," *American Historical Review* 97, no. 1 (February 1992): 145.

15. Leonard J. Moore, "Good Old-Fashioned New Social History and the Twentieth-Century American Right," *Reviews in American History* 24, no. 4 (December 1996): 560.

16. Nancy MacLean, "Guardians of Privilege," in *Debating the American Conservative Movement 1945 to the Present,* ed. Donald T. Critchlow and Nancy MacLean (Lanham, Md.: Rowman & Littlefield, 2009), 139.

17. Wade, *The Fiery Cross,* ix.

18. David H. Bennett, *The Party of Fear: The American Far Right from Nativism to the Militia Movement,* rev. ed. (New York: Vintage Books, 1995), especially 2–13.

19. See John Corrigan and Lynn S. Neal, eds., *Religious Intolerance in America: A Documentary History* (Chapel Hill: University of North Carolina Press, 2010).

20. Kenneth T. Jackson, *The Ku Klux Klan in the City, 1915–1930* (Chicago: Elephant Paperbacks, 1992), xv.

21. Leo P. Ribuffo, *The Old Christian Right: The Protestant Far Right from the Great Depression to the Cold War* (Philadelphia: Temple University Press, 1983), xviii.

22. "The Kind of Man Who Joins the Klan," *Evening News* 76, no. 80 (October 1, 1921): 6.

23. Kathleen Blee, *Women of the Klan: Racism and Gender in the 1920s* (Berkeley: University of California Press, 1991), 2.

24. In his *Ordinary Men,* Christopher Browning presents the history of Reserve Police Battalion 101 to show how the men were complicit in the Holocaust and to document their history. He argues for understanding perpetrators in human terms to move beyond caricature. Christopher Browning, *Ordinary Men: Reserve Police Battalion 101 and the Final Solution in Poland* (reprint, New York: HarperPerennial, 1998), xix–xxi.

25. Bennett, *The Party of Fear,* 217.

26. The place of moral judgment in history is a contentious topic fraught with steep dichotomies between those who argue that historians should embrace their critical powers of judgment and those who find danger in crafting our narratives in terms of morality. In "Beyond Consensus: The Historian as Moral Critic," John Higham derides the detachment of historical studies that could lead to the absence of morality. Historians must recognize the chasm between their own moral systems and those of their historical actors, but they also have an obligation to reflect on the complexity of the human experience. Historians must also focus on what the actors "ought" to have done. Adrian Oldfield continues this line of thinking and suggests historians should show how actors could have done things differently. This way historians can begin to see the "heroes" and "villains" of the narratives. For Oldfield, part of the responsibility to one's field is to be a "moral educator." James Axtell notes that abstaining from judgment makes the past indecipherable, so historians need to make judgments as end products of their writing and research. According to Axtell, historians judge, so we should be explicit about our decisions and how they mold our narratives. The *Journal of the History of Ideas* hosted a roundtable on the so-called moral turn in history, during which George Cotkin argued that the moral turn should not be explicitly about judgment but rather a reflection on the complexity of human intention and action. Instead of focusing on "ought," historians should pass

judgment with care and be aware of their own limitations. In response, Neil Jumonville warned of the problem of discerning the moral. Michael O'Brien suggested that historians are bad moral philosophers, so the moral turn might prove unwise. See George Cotkin, "History's Moral Turn," *Journal of the History of Ideas* 69, no. 2 (April 2008): 293–315; Neil Jumonville, "The Complexity of Moral History: Response to Cotkin," *Journal of the History of Ideas* 69, no. 2 (April 2008): 317–322; Michael O'Brien, "Anomalies Not for Turning: Response to Cotkin," *Journal of the History of Ideas* 69, no. 2 (April 2008): 323–326; Lewis Perry, "Turn, Turn, Turn: Response to Cotkin," *Journal of the History of Ideas* 69, no. 2 (April 2008): 333–337.

27. Harry Stout, *Upon the Altar of Nation: A Moral History of the Civil War* (New York: Viking, 2006), xii.

28. Edward J. Blum, *Reforging the White Republic: Race, Religion, and American Nationalism 1865–1898* (Baton Rouge: Louisiana State University Press, 2005), 3.

29. Ibid., 7.

AFTERWORD. "PASSING THE TORCH": THE KLAN'S BRAND IN AMERICA

1. Anthony Karen, "Aryan Outfitters: Meet the KKK's Seamstress of Hate Couture," *Mother Jones,* March 2008, http://motherjones.com/photoessays/2008/03/aryan-outfitters (accessed April 2, 2008). A special thank-you to Amy Koehlinger for sending me this photo essay, which has proved helpful and pivotal in my analysis of the modern Klan. She deserves special credit for passing along the documentary.

2. Ibid.

3. Historian David Bennett notes that the Klan fragmented into many divisive and different organizations after the 1980s. See David H. Bennett, *The Party of Fear: The American Far Right from Nativism to the Militia Movement,* 2nd ed. (New York: Vintage Books, 1995), 431–433. Moreover, the Southern Poverty Law Center tracks current movements that claim the Klan label. As of 2009, there were over one hundred chapters of the Klan from dozens of competing organizations. See "Ku Klux Klan," *Intelligence Files,* Southern Poverty Law Center, http://www.splcenter.org/get-informed/intelligence-files/ideology/ku-klux-klan (accessed November 15, 2010).

4. Jon Meacham, "In Perspective: Religion in America," *PBS,* September 10, 2010, http://www.pbs.org/wnet/need-to-know/culture/in-perspective-religion-in-america/3488/ (accessed September 13, 2010).

5. Nicholas D. Kristoff, "America's History of Fear," *New York Times,* September 4, 2010, http://www.nytimes.com/2010/09/05/opinion/05kristof.html ?_r=1 (accessed September 10, 2010).

6. Many commentators hoped that Obama's presidency might usher in a new and better postracial America. Here's only one example of many. See Daniel Schorr, "A New, 'Post-Racial' Political Era in America," National Public Radio, January 28, 2008, http://www.npr.org/templates/story/story.php ?storyId=18489466 (accessed October 15, 2010).

7. Larry Keller, "Klan Murder Shines Light on Bogalusa, La.," *Intelligence Report* 134 (Summer 2009), http://www.splcenter.org/get-informed/ intelligence-report/browse-all-issues/2009/summer/into-the-wild (accessed September 13, 2010).

8. Mark Potok, "Rage on the Right: The Year in Hate and Extremism," *Intelligence Report* 137 (Spring 2010), http://www.splcenter.org/get-informed/ intelligence-report/browse-all-issues/2010/spring/rage-on-the-right (accessed September 15, 2010).

9. See "Arson Reported at Tennessee Mosque Site," *USA Today,* August 29, 2010, http://www.usatoday.com/news/religion/2010-08-29-arson28_ST_N .htm (accessed September 13, 2010); Josh Ault, "Lesbian Couple in Vonore Says House Fire Is a Hate Crime," *WATE.com*, September 10, 2010, http:// www.wate.com/global/story.asp?s=13134384 (accessed September 13, 2010); Anthony Welsch, "Mosque Leaders Downplay Shot, Burned Koran Left at Mosque Entrance," *WBIR*, September 13, 2010, http://www.wbir.com/news/ local/story.aspx?storyid=134130&catid=2 (accessed September 13, 2010).

10. For both Lichtman and Hankins, the 1920s mark the beginning of the culture wars between Left and Right and the increasing polarization of political discourse. While their arguments are persuasive, I wonder if perhaps the polarization narrative assumes too much about how the "middle" is persuaded by left and right. See Allan J. Lichtman, *White Protestant Nation: The Rise of the American Conservative Movement* (New York: Atlantic Monthly Press, 2008), especially 2–7, and Barry Hankins, *Jesus and Gin: Evangelicalism, the Roaring Twenties, and Today's Culture Wars* (New York: Palgrave Macmillan, 2010), especially 1–4.

11. See Wyn Craig Wade, *The Fiery Cross: The Ku Klux Klan in America* (New York: Simon & Schuster, 1987). For Wade, this incarnation of the Klan would not have been as popular without attaching itself to fundamentalism. However, Wade has an ulterior motive in which he seeks to link the violent

Klan to the Christian Coalition in the 1980s to show the violence of both movements and their danger to American society. However, this historical link seems tenuous at best.

12. Ibid., 402.

13. Matthew Weaver, "Qur'an Burning: From Facebook to the World's Media, How the Story Grew," *Guardian,* September 10, 2010, http://www.guardian.co.uk/world/2010/sep/10/quran-burning-how-the-story-grew (accessed October 1, 2010).

14. Ibid.

15. William Saletan, "We Didn't Start the Fire," *Slate*, September 8, 2010, http://www.slate.com/id/2266535/ (accessed September 8, 2010).

16. "ABC News/Washington Post Poll: Views of Islam," *ABC News,* September 8, 2010, http://a.abcnews.go.com/images/US/ht_cordoba_house_100908.pdf (accessed October 12, 2010).

17. Ed Pilkington, "How the Tea Party Movement Began," *Guardian,* October 5, 2010, http://www.guardian.co.uk/world/2010/oct/05/us-midterm-elections-2010-tea-party-movement (accessed October 6, 2010).

18. Matthew Continetti, "The Two Faces of the Tea Party: Rick Santelli, Glenn Beck, and the Future of Popular Insurgency," *Weekly Standard* 15, no. 39 (June 28, 2010), http://www.weeklystandard.com/articles/two-faces-tea-party (accessed August 20, 2010).

19. Ibid.

20. Ibid.

21. Huma Khan, "Glenn Beck's Rally Panned By Civil Rights Leaders," *ABC News,* August, 20, 2010, http://abcnews.go.com/Politics/glenn-becks-planned-rally-runs-trouble-civil-rights/story?id=11440553 (accessed August 20, 2010).

22. Huma Khan and Kevin Dolak, "Glenn Beck's 'Restoring Honor' Rally Draws Thousands," *ABC News*, August 28, 2010, http://abcnews.go.com/Poltics/thousands-gather-dc-becks-restoring-honor-rally/story?id=1150433 (accessed October 6, 2010).

23. Ibid.

24. John R. Parkison, "Tea Party Spells K.K.K., Rights Leader Says," *ABC News*, August 26, 2010, http://abcnews.go.com/Politics/tea-party-compared-kkk-rev-walter-fauntroy/story?id=11489233 (accessed August 26, 2010).

25. Ibid.

26. Stephen Colbert, "Yahweh or No Way: Blues Brothers and Glenn

Beck," *Colbert Report*, June 23, 2010, http://www.colbertnation.com/the-colbert-report-videos/313496/june-23–2010/yahweh-or-no-way—the-blues-brothers—glenn-beck (accessed June 25, 2010).

27. See Joan Walsh, "The Tea Partiers's Racial Paranoia," *Salon*, April 15, 2010, http://www.salon.com/news/opinion/joan_walsh/politics/2010/04/15/tea_party_racial_paranoia (accessed April 15, 2010), and Arian Campo-Flores, "Are Tea Partiers Racist?" *Newsweek*, April 26, 2010, http://www.newsweek.com/2010/04/25/are-tea-partiers-racist.html (accessed April 27, 2010).

28. Campo-Flores, "Are Tea Partiers Racist?"

29. See Brian Montopoli, "NAACP Issues Report on Link between Tea Party Factions and 'Racist Hate Groups,'" *CBS News,* October 20, 2010, http://www.cbsnews.com/8301–50344_162–20020160–503544.html (accessed October 26, 2010).

30. Christopher Hitchens, "White Fright," *Slate,* August 30, 2010, http://www.slate.com/id/2265515/ (accessed August 31, 2010).

31. Alex McNeill, "'Me' the People: A Day with the Tea Party," *Religion Dispatches,* August 30, 2010, http://www.religiondispatches.org/archive/atheologies/3236/me_the_people%3A_a_day_with_the_tea_party/ (accessed September 2, 2010).

32. Ibid.

33. Michael Bersin, "NAACP in Kansas City: Representative Sheila Jackson Lee on the Tea Party and Human Rights," *Show Me Progress: Missouri's Progressive Politics Community,* July 12, 2010, http://showmeprogress.com/diary/4773/naacp-in-kansas-city-representative-sheila-jackson-lee-on-the-tea-party-and-human-rights (accessed August 20, 2010).

# Bibliography

ARCHIVAL SOURCES

Anti-Catholic Printed Material Collection (ANT). University of Notre Dame Archives (UNDA), Notre Dame.

Dale, George R., Collection, 1922–1979. Archives and Special Collections. University Libraries, Ball State University, Muncie, Ind.

Jett, John Quincy. Papers. Hargrett Rare Book and Manuscript Library. University of Georgia Libraries, Athens.

Ku Klux Klan, Athens. Klan #5 (Athens, Ga.) Records. Hargrett Rare Book and Manuscript Library, University of Georgia Libraries, Athens.

Ku Klux Klan Charter, LaPorte, Indiana. Indiana Historical Society, Indianapolis.

Ku Klux Klan Collection, ca. 1865–1921. Hargrett Rare Book and Manuscript Library, University of Georgia Libraries, Athens.

Ku Klux Klan Collection, 1913–1970. Archives and Special Collections. University Libraries, Ball State University, Muncie, Ind.

Ku Klux Klan, Crown Point (Lake County). Records, 1913–1932. Indiana Historical Society, Indianapolis.

Ku Klux Klan, Local Officers. Indiana Records. Indiana Historical Society, Indianapolis.

Ku Klux Klan, Logansport. Indiana Records. Indiana Historical Society, Indianapolis.

Ku Klux Klan, Odon Unit. Klan 90 Records. Indiana Historical Society, Indianapolis.

Ku Klux Klan, Wayne County. Indiana Records, 1916–1933 (bulk 1922–1927). Indiana Historical Society, Indianapolis.

Ku Klux Klan and Notre Dame Material (UKKK). University of Notre Dame Archives (UNDA), Notre Dame, Ind.

Stephenson, D. C., Collection, 1922–1978. Indiana Historical Society, Indianapolis.

Walsh, Matthew J., Papers (MWA). University of Notre Dame Archives (UNDA), Notre Dame, Ind.

NEWSPAPERS AND PERIODICALS
*Atlanta Imperial Night-Hawk*
*Atlanta Kourier Magazine*
*Chicago Christian Century*
*Chicago Dawn*
*Dayton (Ohio) Kluxer*
*Huntington (Ind.) Our Sunday Visitor*
*Notre Dame Daily*

BOOKS, ARTICLES, AND ONLINE SOURCES
*ABC News.* "ABC News/Washington Post Poll: Views of Islam."
http://a.abcnews.go.com/images/US/ht_cordoba_house_100908.pdf
(accessed September 8, 2010).
Ahlstrom, Sydney. *A Religious History of the American People.* New Haven,
Conn.: Yale University Press, 1973.
Aho, James. *This Thing of Darkness: A Sociology of the Enemy.* Seattle:
University of Washington Press, 1994.
Amory, Hugh, and David D. Hall, eds. *The Colonial Book in the Atlantic
World.* Cambridge, UK: Cambridge University Press, 2000.
Anderson, Benedict. *Imagined Communities: Reflections on the Origin and
Spread of Nationalism.* Rev. ed. London: Verso, 1991.
Ault, Josh. "Lesbian Couple in Vonore Says House Fire Is a Hate Crime."
*WATE.com.* http://www.wate.com/global/story.asp?s=13134384 (accessed
September 10, 2010).
Baker, Kelly J. "Religion and the Rise of the Second Ku Klux Klan, 1915–
1922." *Readex Report* 4, no. 3 (September 2009). http://www.readex.com/
readex/newsletter.cfm?newsletter=244.
Barkun, Michael. *A Culture of Conspiracy: Apocalyptic Visions in
Contemporary America.* Berkeley: University of California Press, 2003.
———. *Religion and the Racist Right: The Origins of the Christian Identity
Movement.* Chapel Hill: University of North Carolina Press, 1997.
Bederman, Gail. *Manliness and Civilization: A Cultural History of Race and
Gender in the United States, 1880–1917.* Chicago: University of Chicago
Press, 1995.
———. "'The Women Have Had Charge of the Church Work Long Enough':
The Men and Religion Forward Movement of 1911–1912 and the

Masculinization of Middle-Class Protestantism." *American Quarterly* 41, no. 3 (September 1989): 432–465.

Bennett, David H. *The Party of Fear: The American Far Right from Nativism to the Militia Movement.* 2nd ed. New York: Vintage Books, 1995.

Berlet, Chip. *Right-Wing Populism in America: Too Close for Comfort.* New York: Guilford Press, 2000.

Bernstein, Matthew. *Screening a Lynching: The Leo Frank Case on Film and Television.* Athens: University of Georgia Press, 2009.

Bersin, Michael. "NAACP in Kansas City: Representative Sheila Jackson Lee on the Tea Party and Human Rights." Show Me Progress: Missouri's Progressive Politics Community. http://showmeprogress.com/diary/4773/naacp-in-kansas-city-representative-sheila-jackson-lee-on-the-tea-party-and-human-rights (accessed July 12, 2010).

Billington, Ray Allen. "The Burning of the Charlestown Convent." *New England Quarterly* 10, no. 1 (March 1937): 4–25.

Blake, Aldrich. *The Ku Klux Kraze: A Lecture.* Oklahoma City: A. Blake, 1924.

Blee, Kathleen. "Evidence, Empathy, and Ethics: Lessons from Oral Histories of the Klan." *Journal of American History* 80, no. 2 (September 1993): 596–606.

———. "Fieldworkers' Privilege? The Perils of Privilege." *Law and Social Inquiry* 24 (Fall 1999): 993–997.

———. *Inside Organized Racism: Women in the Hate Movement.* Berkeley: University of California Press, 2002.

———. "Studying the Enemy." In *Our Studies, Ourselves: Sociologists' Lives and Work,* ed. Barry Glassner and Rosanna Hertz, 13–23. Oxford, UK: Oxford University Press, 2003.

———. "White-Knuckle Research: Emotional Dynamics in Fieldwork with Racist Activists." *Qualitative Sociology* 21, no. 4 (1998): 381–399.

———. *Women of the Klan: Racism and Gender in the 1920s.* Berkeley: University of California Press, 1991.

Blum, Edward J. *Reforging the White Republic: Race, Religion, and American Nationalism 1865–1898.* Baton Rouge: Louisiana State University Press, 2005.

Brown, Candy Gunther. *The Word in the World: Evangelical Writing, Publishing, and Reading in America, 1789–1880.* Chapel Hill: University of North Carolina Press, 2004.

Brown, George Alfred. *Harold the Klansman.* Kansas City, Mo.: Western Baptist Publishing, 1923.

Brown, Karen McCarthy. *Mama Lola: A Vodou Priestess in Brooklyn.* Berkeley: University of California Press, 2001.

Browning, Christopher. *Ordinary Men: Reserve Police Battalion 101 and the Final Solution in Poland.* New York: HarperPerennial, 1998.

Burlein, Ann. *Lift High the Cross: Where White Supremacy and the Christian Right Converge.* Durham, N.C.: Duke University Press, 2002.

Campo-Flores, Arian. "Are Tea Partiers Racist?" *Newsweek.* http://www.newsweek.com/2010/04/25/are-tea-partiers-racist.html (accessed April 26, 2010).

Carnes, Mark C. *Secret Ritual and Manhood in Victorian America.* New Haven, Conn.: Yale University Press, 1989.

Chalmers, David. *Hooded Americanism: The History of the Ku Klux Klan.* Durham, N.C.: Duke University Press, 1987.

Chidester, David. "Moralizing Noise." *Harvard Divinity Bulletin* 32, no. 3 (Summer 2004). http://www.hds.harvard.edu/news/bulletin/articles/orsi_et_al.html (accessed March 4, 2006).

———. *Suicide and Salvation: An Interpretation of Jim Jones, the Peoples Temple, and Jonestown.* Bloomington: Indiana University Press, 1988.

Clifford, James, and George E. Marcus, eds. *Writing Culture: The Poetics and Politics of Ethnography.* Berkeley: University of California Press, 1986.

Cohen, Stanley. "Ordinary White Protestants: The KKK of the 1920s." *Journal of Social History* 28, no. 1 (Autumn 1994): 155–165.

Colbert, Stephen. "Yahweh or No Way: Blues Brothers and Glenn Beck." *Colbert Report.* http://www.colbertnation.com/the-colbert-report-videos/313496/june-23-2010/yahweh-or-no-way---the-blues-brothers---glenn-beck (accessed June 23, 2010).

*Columbus Enquirer-Sun.* "Mashed and Disfigured Body of Leo M. Frank, Pursued by a Clamoring Mob, Is Taken to Atlanta." August 17, 1915, 1.

*Columbus Ledger.* "The Mary Phagan Case." May 9, 1913, 4.

Continetti, Matthew. "The Two Faces of the Tea Party: Rick Santelli, Glenn Beck, and the Future of Popular Insurgency." *Weekly Standard* 15, no. 39. http://www.weeklystandard.com/articles/two-faces-tea-party (June 28, 2010).

Corrigan, John, and Lynn S. Neal, eds. *Religious Intolerance in America: A Documentary History.* Chapel Hill: University of North Carolina Press, 2010.

Cotkin, George. "History's Moral Turn." *Journal of the History of Ideas* 69, no. 2 (April 2008): 293–315.

Crew, Danny O. *Ku Klux Klan Sheet Music: An Illustrated Catalogue of Published Music, 1867–2000*. Jefferson, N.C.: MacFarland, 2003.

Critchlow, Donald T., and Nancy MacLean. *Debating the American Conservative Movement 1945 to the Present*. Lanham, Md.: Rowman & Littlefield, 2009.

D'Agostino, Peter R. *Rome in America: Transnational Catholic Ideology from the Risorgimento to Fascism*. Chapel Hill: University of North Carolina Press, 2004.

Davis, David Brion. "Some Themes of Counter-Subversion: An Analysis of Anti-Masonic, Anti-Catholic, and Anti-Mormon Literature." *Mississippi Valley Historical Review* 47, no. 2 (September 1960): 205–224.

Davis, Lenwood G. *The Ku Klux Klan: A Bibliography*. Westport, Conn.: Greenwood Press, 1984.

Dinnerstein, Leonard. *Anti-Semitism in America*. New York: Oxford, 1994.

———. *The Leo Frank Case*. Rev. ed. Athens: University of Georgia Press, 2008.

Dixon, Thomas, Jr. *The Clansman*. Lexington: University Press of Kentucky, 1970.

Dobratz, Betty A., and Stephanie Shanks-Meile. *"White Power, White Pride!" The White Separatist Movement in the United States*. Baltimore: Johns Hopkins University Press, 2000.

Dolan, Frances E. *Whores of Babylon: Catholicism, Gender, and Seventeenth-Century Print Culture*. Notre Dame: University of Notre Dame Press, 2005.

Dolan, Jay P. *The American Catholic Experience: A History from Colonial Times to the Present*. Garden City, N.Y.: Doubleday, 1985.

Dumenil, Lynn. *Modern Temper: American Culture and Society in the 1920s*. New York: Hill & Wang, 1995.

Evans, Hiram Wesley. *Is The Ku Klux Klan Constructive or Destructive? A Debate between Imperial Wizard Evans, Israel Zangwill and Others*. Girard, Kans.: Haldeman-Julius Co., 1924.

*Evening News*. "The Kind of Man Who Joins the Klan." October 1, 1921, 6.

Ezekiel, Raphael S. *The Racist Mind: Portraits of Neo-Nazis and Klansmen*. New York: Viking, 1995.

Feldman, Glenn. *Politics, Society, and the Klan in Alabama, 1915–1949*. Tuscaloosa: University of Alabama Press, 1999.

Ferber, Abby L., ed. *Home-Grown Hate: Gender and Organized Racism*. New York: Routledge, 2004.

Fessenden, Tracy. "The Convent, the Brothel, and the Protestant Woman's Sphere." *Signs* 25, no. 2 (Winter 2000): 451–478.

———. *Culture and Redemption: Religion, the Secular, and American Literature.* Princeton, N.J.: Princeton University Press, 2007.

Fossett, Judith Jackson. "(K)night Riders in (K)night Gowns: The Ku Klux Klan, Race, and Constructions of Masculinity." In *Race Consciousness: African-American Studies for the New Century,* ed. Judith Jackson Fossett and Jeffrey A. Tucker, 35–49. New York: New York University Press, 1997.

Franchot, Jenny. *Roads to Rome: The Antebellum Protestant Encounter with Catholicism.* Berkeley: University of California Press, 1994.

Frost, Stanley. *The Challenge of the Klan.* New York: AMS Press, 1969.

Fry, Henry Peck. *The Modern Ku Klux Klan.* New York: Negro Universities Press, 1969.

Gardell, Mattias. *Gods of the Blood: The Pagan Renewal and White Separatism.* Durham, N.C.: Duke University Press, 2003.

Gerlach, Larry R. *Blazing Crosses in Zion: The Ku Klux Klan in Utah.* Logan: Utah State University Press, 1982.

Girard, René. *Violence and the Sacred.* Trans. Patrick Gregory. Baltimore: Johns Hopkins University Press, 1979.

Goffman, Erving. *Presentation of Self in Everyday Life.* New York: Anchor Books, 1959.

Goldberg, David. "Unmasking the Ku Klux Klan: The Northern Movement Against the K.K.K., 1920–1925." *Journal of American Ethnic History* 15, no. 4 (Summer 1996): 32–49.

Goldberg, R. A. *Hooded Empire: The Ku Klux Klan in Colorado.* Urbana: University of Illinois Press, 1981.

Grant, Julia. "A 'Real Boy' Not a Sissy: Gender, Childhood, and Masculinity, 1890–1940." *Journal of Social History* 37, no. 4 (Summer 2004): 829–851.

Grob, Gerald N., ed. *Papers Read at the Meeting of the Grand Dragons, Knights of the Ku Klux Klan, at Their First Meeting Held at Asheville, North Carolina, July 1923.* Anti-Movements in America. New York: Arno Press, 1977.

Hall, David D. *Cultures of Print: Essays in the History of the Book.* Amherst: University of Massachusetts Press, 1996.

———. *Lived Religion in America: Toward a History of Practice.* Princeton, N.J.: Princeton University Press, 1997.

————. *Worlds of Wonder, Days of Judgment: Popular Religious Belief in Early New England*. Cambridge, Mass.: Harvard University Press, 1989.

Hankins, Barry. *Jesus and Gin: Evangelicalism, The Roaring Twenties and Today's Culture Wars*. New York: Palgrave Macmillan, 2010.

Higgins, Robert. *God in the Stadium: Sports and Religion in America*. Lexington: University Press of Kentucky, 1995.

Higham, John. *Strangers in a Strange Land: Patterns of American Nativism, 1860–1925*. Rev. ed. New Brunswick, N.J.: Rutgers University Press, 2004.

Hitchens, Christopher. "White Fright." *Slate*. http://www.slate.com/id/2265515/ (accessed August 30, 2010).

Horowitz, David, ed. *Inside the Klavern: The Secret History of the Ku Klux Klan in the 1920s*. Carbondale: Southern Illinois University Press, 1999.

————. "The Normality of Extremism: The Ku Klux Klan Revisited." *Society* 35, no. 6 (September–October 1998): 71–77.

Jackson, Kenneth T. *The Ku Klux Klan in the City, 1915–1930*. Chicago: I. R. Dee, 1992.

Jacobsen, Matthew Frye. *Whiteness of a Different Color: European Immigrants and the Alchemy of Race*. Cambridge, Mass.: Harvard University Press, 1998.

Jefferson, Charles. *Roman Catholicism and the Ku Klux Klan*. New York: Fleming H. Revell Co., 1924–1925.

Jenkins, Philip. *Hoods and Shirts: The Extreme Right in Pennsylvania, 1925–1950*. Chapel Hill: University of North Carolina Press, 1997.

Jumonville, Neil. "The Complexity of Moral History: Response to Cotkin." *Journal of the History of Ideas* 69, no. 2 (April 2008): 317–322.

*Kansas City Times*. "An Atrocious Horror." August 17, 1915, 1.

Kaplan, Jeffrey, and Tore Bjorgo, eds. *Nation and Race: The Developing Euro-American Racist Subculture*. Boston: Northeastern University Press, 1998.

————. *Radical Religion in America: Millenarian Movements from the Far Right to the Children of Noah*. Syracuse, N.Y.: Syracuse University Press, 1997.

Karen, Anthony. "Aryan Outfitters: Meet the KKK's Seamstress of Hate Couture." *Mother Jones,* March 2008. http://motherjones.com/photoessays/2008/03/aryan-outfitters (accessed April 2, 2008).

Katz, William Loren. *The Invisible Empire: The Ku Klux Klan Impact on History*. Washington, D.C.: Open Hand Publishing, 1986.

Kazin, Michael. "The Grass-Roots Right: New Histories of U.S. Conservatism

in the Twentieth Century." *American Historical Review* 97, no. 1
(February 1992): 136–155.

Keller, Larry. "Klan Murder Shines Light on Bogalusa, La." *Intelligence
Report* 134 (Summer 2009). http://www.splcenter.org/get-informed/
intelligence-report/browse-all-issues/2009/summer/into-the-wild
(accessed September 13, 2010).

Khan, Huma. "Glenn Beck's Rally Panned by Civil Rights Leaders." *ABC
News.* http://abcnews.go.com/Politics/glenn-becks-planned-rally-runs-
trouble-civil-rights/story?id=11440553 (accessed August, 20, 2010).

Khan, Huma, and Kevin Dolak. "Glenn Beck's 'Restoring Honor' Rally Draws
Thousands." *ABC News.* http://abcnews.go.com/Poltics/thousands-gather-
dc-becks-restoring-honor-rally/story?id=1150433 (accessed August 28,
2010).

Knights of the Ku Klux Klan. *Proceedings of the Second Imperial Klonvokation.*
N.p.: Knights of the Ku Klux Klan, 1924.

Koehlinger, Amy. "'Let Us Live for Those Who Love Us': Faith, Family, and
the Contours of Manhood among the Knights of Columbus in Late
Nineteenth-Century Connecticut." *Journal of Social History* 38, no. 2
(Winter 2004): 455–468.

Kristoff, Nicholas D. "America's History of Fear." *New York Times*, September
4, 2010. http://www.nytimes.com/2010/09/05/opinion/05kristof.html?_
r=1 (accessed September 10, 2010).

Lay, Shawn. *The Invisible Empire in the West: Toward a New Historical
Appraisal of the Ku Klux Klan of the 1920s.* Urbana: University of Illinois
Press, 1992.

Lester, John C. *Ku Klux Klan: Its Origin, Growth and Disbandment.* New York:
Neale, 1905.

Lichtman, Allan J. *White Protestant Nation: The Rise of the American
Conservative Movement.* New York: Atlantic Monthly Press, 2008.

Linder, Douglas O. "Famous Trials: The Leo Frank Trial" (1913).
http://www.law.umkc.edu/faculty/projects/trials/frank/frankballad.html
(accessed August 15, 2010).

Lindman, Janet Moore. "Acting the Manly Christian: White Evangelical
Masculinity in Revolutionary Virginia." *William and Mary Quarterly* 57,
no. 2 (April 2000): 393–416.

Lutholtz, M. William. *Grand Dragon: D. C. Stephenson and the Ku Klux Klan
in Indiana.* West Lafayette, Ind.: Purdue University, 1991.

MacLean, Nancy. *Behind the Mask of Chivalry: The Making of the Ku Klux Klan*. New York: Oxford University Press, 1994.

———. "The Leo Frank Case Reconsidered: Gender and Sexual Politics in the Making of Reactionary Populism." *Journal of American History* 78 (December 1991): 917–948.

*Macon Daily Telegraph*. "Mary Phagan—A Warning." May 7, 1913, 4.

Marty, Martin. *Righteous Empire: The Protestant Experience in America*. Two Centuries of American Life. New York: Dial Press, 1970.

Marvin, Carolyn, and David W. Ingle. "Blood Sacrifice and the Nation: Revisiting Civil Religion." *Journal of the American Academy of Religion* 64, no. 4 (Winter 1996): 767–780.

Marx, Anthony. *Faith in Nation: Exclusionary Origins of Nationalism*. Oxford, UK: Oxford University Press, 2003.

Mason, Carol. "Miscegenation and Purity: Reproducing the Souls of White Folk." *Hypatia* 22, no. 2 (Spring 2007): 98–121.

Massa, Mark S. *Anti-Catholicism in America: The Last Acceptable Prejudice*. New York: Crossroad Publishing Co., 2003.

———. *Catholics in American Culture: Fulton Sheen, Dorothy Day and the Notre Dame Football Team*. New York: Crossroad Publishing Co., 1999.

McNeill, Alex. "'Me' the People: A Day with the Tea Party." *Religion Dispatches*. http://www.religiondispatches.org/archive/atheologies/3236/me_the_people%3A_a_day_with_the_tea_party/ (accessed August 30, 2010).

McNichol Stock, Catherine. *Rural Radicals: Righteous Rage in the American Grain*. Ithaca, N.Y.: Cornell University Press, 1996.

McVeigh, Rory. *The Rise of the Ku Klux Klan: Right-Wing Movements and National Politics*. Social Movements, Protest, and Contention. Minneapolis: University of Minnesota Press, 2009.

Meacham, Jon. "In Perspective: Religion in America." *PBS,* September 10, 2010. http://www.pbs.org/wnet/need-to-know/culture/in-perspective-religion-in-america/3488/ (accessed September 13, 2010).

Mecklin, John. *The Ku Klux Klan: The Study of an American Mind*. New York: Russell & Russell, 1963.

Metcalf, Peter. *They Lie, We Lie: Getting on with Anthropology*. London: Routledge, 2002.

Miller, Robert Moats. "A Note on the Relationship between the Protestant Churches and the Revived Ku Klux Klan." *Journal of Southern History* 22, no. 3 (August 1956): 355–368.

Mirzeoff, Nicholas. *An Introduction to Visual Culture*. London: Routledge, 1999.

Montopoli, Brian. "NAACP Issues Report on Link between Tea Party Factions and 'Racist Hate Groups.'" *CBS News*. http://www.cbsnews.com/8301-50344_162-20020160-503544.html (accessed October 20, 2010).

Moore, Leonard J. *Citizen Klansman: The Ku Klux Klan in Indiana, 1921–1928*. Chapel Hill: University of North Carolina Press, 1991.

———."Good Old-Fashioned New Social History and the Twentieth-Century American Right." *Reviews in American History* 24, no. 4 (December 1996): 555–573.

Newton, Michael. *The Invisible Empire: The Ku Klux Klan in Florida*. Gainesville: University Press of Florida, 1997.

———. *The Ku Klux Klan: An Encyclopedia*. New York: Garland Publishing, 1991.

*New York Times*. "The Klan's Invisible Empire Is Fading." February 21, 1926, 1.

Nord, David Paul. *Communities of Journalism: A History of American Newspapers and Their Readers*. Urbana: University of Illinois Press, 2001.

———. *Faith in Reading: Religious Publishing and the Birth of Mass Media*. Oxford, UK: Oxford University Press, 2004.

O'Brien, Michael. "Anomalies Not for Turning: Response to Cotkin." *Journal of the History of Ideas* 69, no. 2 (April 2008): 323–326.

Oney, Steve. *And The Dead Shall Rise: The Murder of Mary Phagan and the Lynching of Leo Frank*. New York: Vintage, 2003.

Orsi, Robert. *Between Heaven and Earth: The Religious Worlds People Make and the Scholars Who Study Them*. Princeton, N.J.: Princeton University Press, 2005.

Ovington, Mary White. "Mary Phagan Speaks." *Lexington Herald*, September 12, 1915.

Pagliarini, Marie Anne. "The Pure American Woman and the Wicked Catholic Priest: An Analysis of Anti-Catholic Literature in Antebellum America." *Religion and American Culture* 9, no. 1 (Winter 1999): 97–128.

Parkison, John R. "Tea Party Spells K.K.K., Rights Leader Says." *ABC News*. http://abcnews.go.com/Politics/tea-party-compared-kkk-rev-walter-fauntroy/story?id=11489233 (accessed August 26, 2010).

Parsons, Elaine Frantz. "Midnight Rangers: Costume and Performance in the Reconstruction-Era Ku Klux Klan." *Journal of American History* 92, no. 3 (December 2005): 811–836.

Patterson, Orlando. *Rituals of the Blood: Consequences of Slavery in Two American Centuries.* Washington, D.C.: Civitas Counterpoint, 1998.

Perry, Lewis. "Turn, Turn, Turn: Response to Cotkin." *Journal of the History of Ideas* 69, no. 2 (April 2008): 333–337.

Pilkington, Ed. "How the Tea Party Movement Began." *Guardian*, October 5, 2010. http://www.guardian.co.uk/world/2010/oct/05/us-midterm-elections-2010-tea-party-movement.

Potok, Mark. "Rage on the Right: The Year in Hate and Extremism." *Intelligence Report* 137 (Spring 2010). http://www.splcenter.org/get-informed/intelligence-report/browse-all-issues/2010/spring/rage-on-the-right.

Prothero, Stephen. *American Jesus: How the Son of God Became a National Icon.* New York: Farrar, Strauss & Giroux, 2003.

Quarles, Chester L. *The Ku Klux Klan and Related American Racialist and Antisemitic Organizations: A History and Analysis.* Jefferson, N.C.: McFarland & Co., 1999.

Ribuffo, Leo P. *The Old Christian Right: The Protestant Far Right from the Great Depression to the Cold War.* Philadelphia: Temple University Press, 1983.

Ridgeway, James. *Blood in the Face: The Ku Klux Klan, Aryan Nations, Nazi Skinheads, and the Rise of New White Culture.* New York: Thunder's Mouth Press, 1995.

Ruiz-Velasco, Chris. "Order Out of Chaos: Whiteness, White Supremacy, and Thomas Dixon, Jr." *College Literature* 34, no. 4 (Fall 2007): 148–165.

Ryan, Nick. *Into a World of Hate: A Journey among the Extreme Right.* New York: Routledge, 2004.

Saletan, William. "We Didn't Start the Fire." *Slate*, September 8, 2010. http://www.slate.com/id/2266535/.

Scarry, Elaine. *The Body in Pain: The Making and Unmaking of the World.* New York: Oxford University Press, 1985.

Simmons, William Joseph. *The Klan Unmasked.* Atlanta: W. E. Thompson Publishing Co., 1924.

———. *The Practice of Klannishness.* Atlanta: W. J. Simmons, 1918.

Sims, Patsy. *The Klan.* 2nd ed. Lexington: University Press of Kentucky, 1996.

Snyder, Franklin Bliss. "The Ballad of Mary Phagan." *Journal of American Folklore* 31 (1918): 264–266.

Southern Poverty Law Center. "Ku Klux Klan." *Intelligence Files.*

http://www.splcenter.org/get-informed/intelligence-files/ideology/ku-klux-klan (accessed 2010).

Stout, Harry. *Upon the Altar of Nation: A Moral History of the Civil War.* New York: Viking, 2006.

Swain, Carol M. *The New White Nationalism in America: Its Challenge to Integration.* Cambridge, UK: Cambridge University Press, 2002.

Tucker, Richard K. *The Dragon and the Cross: The Rise and Fall of the Ku Klux Klan in Middle America.* North Haven, Conn.: Archon Books, 1991.

Tucker, Todd. *Notre Dame vs. The Ku Klux Klan: How the Fighting Irish Defeated the Klan.* Chicago: Loyola Press, 2004.

Tweed, Thomas. *Retelling U.S. Religious History.* Berkeley: University of California Press, 1997.

*USA Today.* "Arson Reported at Tennessee Mosque Site." http://www.usatoday.com/news/religion/2010-08-29-arson28_ST_N.htm (accessed August 29, 2010).

Wade, Wyn Craig. *The Fiery Cross: The Ku Klux Klan in America.* New York: Simon & Schuster, 1987.

Walsh, Joan. "The Tea Partiers's Racial Paranoia." *Salon,* April 15, 2010. http://www.salon.com/news/opinion/joan_walsh/politics/2010/04/15/tea_party_racial_paranoia.

Walters, Jerome. *One Aryan Nation under God: Exposing the New Racial Extremists.* Cleveland: Pilgrim Press, 2000.

Weaver, Matthew. "Qur'an Burning: From Facebook to the World's Media, How the Story Grew." *Guardian,* September 10, 2010. http://www.guardian.co.uk/world/2010/sep/10/quran-burning-how-the-story-grew.

Welsch, Anthony. "Mosque Leaders Downplay Shot, Burned Koran Left at Mosque Entrance." *WBIR,* September 13, 2010. http://www.wbir.com/news/local/story.aspx?storyid=134130&catid=2.

Wiegman, Robyn. "Whiteness Studies and the Paradox of Particularity." *boundary* 26, no. 3 (Autumn 1999): 115–150.

Wright, W. C. *Religious and Patriotic Ideals of the Ku Klux Klan.* Waco, TX: W. C. Wright, 1926.

Zuber, Glenn. "Onward Christian Klansmen: War, Religious Conflict, and the Rise of the Second Ku Klux Klan, 1912–1928." Ph.D. diss., Indiana University, 2004.

———. Review of *Invisible Empire. Journal of Southern Religion* 5 (2002). http://jsr.fsu.edu/2002/Reviews/Zuber.htm.

# Index

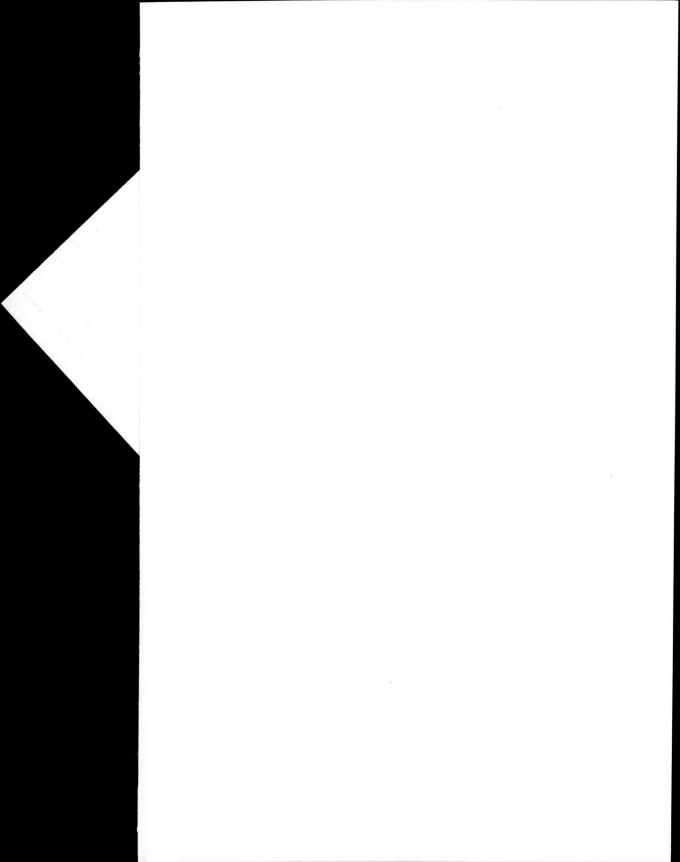

**DATE DUE**

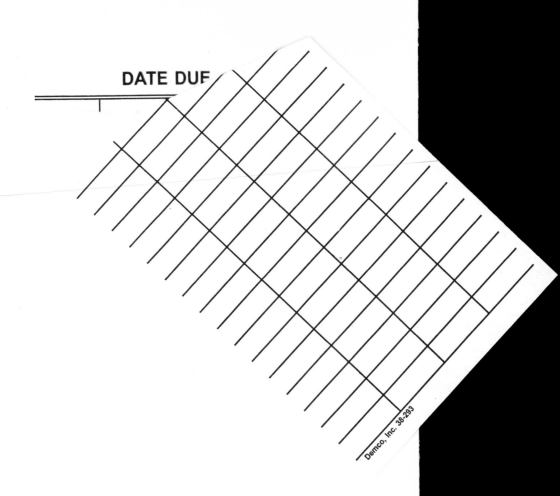

Demco, Inc. 38-293